GÜNTHER-DIETZ SONTHEIMER

Essays on Religion, Literature and Law

GÜNTHER-DIETZ SONTHEIMER

Essays on Religion, Literature and Law

Edited by

HEIDRUN BRÜCKNER
ANNE FELDHAUS
ADITYA MALIK

INDIRA GANDHI NATIONAL CENTRE FOR THE ARTS
NEW DELHI

MANOHAR
2004

First published 2004

ISBN 81-7304-521-6

Published by
Indira Gandhi National Centre for the Arts
Janpath, New Delhi 110001
in association with
Ajay Kumar Jain for
Manohar Publishers & Distributors
4753/23 Ansari Road, Daryaganj
New Delhi 110002

Typeset by
A J Software Publishing Co. Pvt. Ltd.
New Delhi 110005

Printed at
Lordson Publishers
Delhi 110007

Contents

Acknowledgements

The editors gratefully acknowledge the permission of the following copyright holders to reprint the articles in this volume:

Ferdinand Enke Verlag, Stuttgart, for *Religious Endowments in India: The Juristic Personality of Hindu Deities*, c 1965;

I. Müller-Sontheimer, Stuttgart, for *Some Notes on Biroba, the Dhangar God of Maharashtra*, c 1974;

Popular Prakashan, Bombay, for *Field Reserch in Maharashtra and Karnatak, The History of Some Pastoral Communities and Their Cults*, c 1974;

Harrassowitz Verlag, Wiesbaden, for *The Dhangars: A Nomadic Pastoral Community in a Developing Agricultural Environment*, c 1975, and *The Rāmāyaṇa in Contemporary Folk Traditions of Maharashtra*, c 1991;

The Cultural Department of the Embassy of the Federal Republic of Germany, New Delhi, for *Some Memorial Monuments of Western India*, c 1976;

Franz Steiner Verlag, Wiesbaden, for *God, Dharma and Society in the Yādava Kingdom of Devagirī according to the Līḷācaritra of Cakradhar*, c 1982; Steiner Verlag Wiesbaden GmbH, Stuttgart, for *Folk Deities in the Vijayanagara Empire: Narasiṃha and Mallaṇṇa/Mailār*, c 1985;

Anthropos-Institut, St. Augustin, for *The Prehistoric Background to Pastoralism in the Southern Deccan in the Light of the Oral Traditions and the Cults of Some Pastoral Communities*, c 1980;

The South Asia Institute, University of Heidelberg, for *King Vikram and Kamaḷū Śinde, the Shepherd. Bhakti Episodes from an Oral Epic of the Dhangars of Maharashtra*, c 1977, *On the Memorials of the Dead in the Tribal Area of Central India*, and *The Hero- and Satī-Stones of Maharashtra*, both c 1982;

G.C. Tripathi, Allahabad & H. Kulke, Kiel, for *The Vana and the Kṣetra: The Tribal Background of Some Famous Cults*, c 1987, 1994;

I. Müller-Sontheimer, Stuttgart & H. Kulke, Kiel, for *Hinduism: The Five Components and their Interaction*, c 1989, 1997.

Introduction

The present volume continues the publication of selected English papers by G.-D. Sontheimer begun in 1997 with a volume of *Essays on Khaṇḍobā* [EK].[1] Whereas the ten articles of the earlier volume had a thematic focus on the 'folk god' Khaṇḍobā, the fourteen articles chosen for publication in this volume span a wider thematic and temporal range. Five of these predate the earliest one in EK. They have been arranged in chronological order, starting with a lengthy and learned paper on the juristic personality of Hindu deities, first published in 1965 in a German journal of comparative law. This article provides an important link between Sontheimer's study of law and of Indology.

Sontheimer (b. 1934) was enrolled for both subjects—law and Indology—at the University of Tübingen from 1953-8. At the department of Indology and Comparative Religion he studied Sanskrit, Indian Philosophy and Religion (with H. von Glasenapp, 1891-1963, who retired in 1959), and Hindi. He graduated in law in 1958. In the same year, he gained a scholarship to study Hindu Law and Dharmaśāstra at the Law College and the Bhandarkar Oriental Research Institute of the University of Poona, where he stayed up to 1961. It was during this period that he met D.D. Kosambi, who first took him out for field research in archaeology, prehistory, and folk religion. This probably laid the foundation for his characteristic later approach to Indian studies. In 1961, he joined the School of Oriental and African Studies of the University of London, where he acquired a postgraduate diploma in English Law in 1962 and a Ph.D. in Hindu Law and Dharmaśāstra in 1964. The thesis for the Ph.D. was on *The Joint Hindu Family* (published in 1977, see LP).

In his 1965 article on the Juristic Personality of Hindu Deities (*Religious Endowments in India*), Sontheimer bases his discussion on a large number of Sanskrit sources, ranging from the Dharmaśāstras to Mīmāṃsā and Vedānta texts (Brahmasūtras with various commentaries), as well as on religious practice, popular belief and case-law. He observes that popular practice and the theories developed in the courts hardly agree and that 'neither the ancient discussions of the *Mīmāṃsakas*, nor the modern doctrines based in part on Western models, are apt for the situations we have been discussing' (1965, pp. 99-100).

The next major area of Sontheimer's research and publications was the history and religion of pastoral groups in the Deccan (Dhangars, Gollas, Kurubas) and the interdependence of folk religion and scriptural religion. After joining the South Asia Institute of the University of Heidelberg as a research assistant (German: 'Assistent') in 1965, Sontheimer stayed in Maharashtra for several months every year (1966-72). While heading the New Delhi branch of the South Asia Institute (1973-5), he conducted field-work not only in Maharashtra, but also in Rajasthan, Madhya Pradesh and Andhra Pradesh, and got involved deeply in the documentation and study of hero- and *satī*-stones. During the same period, he underwent 'habilitation' (approx. D. Lit.) with a thesis on the origin, history and environment of pastoral deities in Maharashtra and a lecture on hero- and *satī*-stones. In May 1974 he presented his inaugural lecture (on the *bhakti* saints of Maharashtra) and became a member of the faculty.[2]

The thesis was published in German in 1976 (see LP) and a revised English version of it (tr. Anne Feldhaus) was published in 1989. A book (with L. Leshnik) on pastoralists and nomads in South Asia came out in 1975, another one (with S. Settar) on hero-stones in 1982 (based on a 1975 seminar). Several articles contributing to these two areas are included in the present volume: 'Some Notes on Birobā, the Dhangar God of Maharashtra' (1974) and 'Field Research in Maharashtra and Karnatak: the History of Some Pastoral Communities and Their Cults' (1974). For these two studies Sontheimer was especially indebted to D.D. Kosambi, with whom he had first encountered a group of Dhangars in 1958. In 'Field Research . . .' Sontheimer stresses the need to combine the study of various types of sources such as written and oral ones and the methodologies of various disciplines such as anthropology, history, archaeology, iconography and epigraphy in order to gain information on the history of cults and on the communities associated with them. 'The Dhangars: A Nomadic Pastoral Community in a Developing Agricultural Environment' (1975) provides an ethnography of the Haṭkar Dhangars. 'The Prehistoric Background to Pastoralism in the Southern Deccan in the Light of the Oral Traditions and the Cults of Some Pastoral Communities' (1980, with M.L.K. Murty) is a learned attempt to make use of the contemporary study of a community for the interpretation of prehistoric data and vice versa. Historical, iconographic and epigraphic analyses are combined for an understanding of hero- and *satī*-stones so widespread all over the Deccan and other parts of India. Sontheimer documented thousands of these memorials, many of which he was the first to discover. About a hundred such photographs are reprinted in the present volume as part of three articles: 'Some Memorial Monuments of Western India' (1976); If 'Hero- and *Satī*-Stones of Maharashtra' (1982); and 'On the Memorials to the Dead in the Tribal Area of Central India' (1982). These articles provide useful descriptions and classifications of hero- and *satī*-stones and—as far as possible—analyse them in the context of other extraneous historical, social and religious references, physical ecology and literary sources. Sontheimer identified the worship of heroes and *satīs* as an important element of folk religion.[3]

Three articles focus more exclusively on textual studies, two of which deal with aspects of oral literature. Thus, in 'King Vikram and Kamaḷū Śinde, the Shepherd: *Bhakti* Episodes from an Oral Epic of the Dhangars of Maharashtra' (1981) Sontheimer gives an example of the folk variety of *bhakti* and comments, inter alia, on the difference between an orally presented text studied in its context and the version of a printed pamphlet. In 'The *Rāmāyaṇa* in Contemporary Folk Traditions of Maharashtra' (1991) he studies oral varieties of the classical epic, trying to show 'how folk traditions in Maharashtra borrowed elements from the classical *Rāmāyaṇa* and subordinated them to their own local beliefs, needs and conditions. By doing so the folk tradition retained its own identity in the past . . .'. 'God, Dharma and Society in the Yādava Kingdom of Devagirī according to the *Līḷācaritra* of Cakradhar' (1982) is part of Sontheimer's larger, unaccomplished project to prepare a complete translation of this medieval Marāṭhī text.[4]

Besides these three textual studies and translations, Sontheimer's literary interest and gift resulted in a number of translations he contributed to the *South Asian Digest of Regional Writing* from 1972 onwards, but these are not included in the present volume. Among the unpublished manuscripts he left behind are a collection of Indian oral folktales in German translation as well as a translation of the short Marāṭhī novel *Jaṭāyū* by Keshav Meshram. It was, among other things, his translations that gained Sontheimer the Tagore Literature Prize of the Indo-German Society in Germany in 1987.

In 1971, the Heidelberg indological trio—Hermann Berger ('Classical Indology'), Lothar Lutze ('Modern Indian Languages and Literatures') and G.-D. Sontheimer ('History of Indian Religion and Philosophy') that was to give shape to Heidelberg Indology for the next twenty years—had initiated the institution of 'Interregional Seminars', which were conducted annually during the summer term. The contributions were published in the newly founded *South Asian Digest of Regional Writing*, of which Sontheimer became the editor-in-chief (1972-92).[5] Even before the *Digest*, a publication series *Neuindische Studien* (Modern Indian Studies) had been founded and edited jointly by Berger, Lutze and Sontheimer. Most of the volumes consist of linguistic descriptions of oral languages, some of them studied for the first time (see LP).

Of the three remaining articles included in this volume two may be considered as building blocks for a model of Hinduism finally worked out in 'Hinduism: The Five Components and Their Interaction' (1989). In 'Folk Deities in the Vijayanagara Empire: Narasiṃha and Mallaṇṇa/ Mailār' (1985) Sontheimer tests his own notion of the typical folk deity and its rise under particular historical circumstances by extending his study to Narasiṃha as a popular god of the Vijayanagara empire and subsequent Nāyaka kingdoms. He concludes: 'What seems important in our context is the far-reaching cohesion and similarity between the folk Murukaṉ, Narasiṃha, Mallaṇṇa, Mailār, and Khaṇḍobā as far as mythology and ritual are concerned. What emerges from this are the contours of a parallel, cohesive folk culture which was no doubt interlinked with the Purāṇas. But, on this level, purāṇic and sectarian Śaivism and Viṣṇuism was not in focus.'

'The *Vana* and the *Kṣetra*: The Tribal Background of Some Famous Cults' (1987) is an attempt to identify indigenous terms 'used to express a basic religious, economic and spatial separatedness' and to use the respective concepts as tools for the analysis of processes of integration, assimilation and transformation.[6] *Hinduism: The Five Components and their Interaction* (1989) is Sontheimer's most comprehensive statement of his view of Hinduism and has therefore been placed at the end of the book.[7] In contradistinction to simple oppositions such as great tradition versus little tradition, etc., Sontheimer tries to do justice to the multiplicity of (oral and written) textual traditions and perspectives and of actual Hindu religious practices by distinguishing five components (1 The work and teachings of the Brahmans; 2 Asceticism and renunciation; 3 Tribal religion; 4 Folk religion; 5 *Bhakti*). He does not view them as separate strands or 'water-tight compartments' but as continually interacting constituents. This concept was the result of more than thirty years of exposure to and interaction with Hinduism.

From the early sixties onwards, Sontheimer had documented his fieldwork not only by (about 40,000) slides and photographs but also by hundreds of three-minute super 8 films, adding up to more than thirty hours. Since the mid-1980s he started producing a number of documentary films and a half-documentary on the folk religion of Maharashtra (see LP). Films like *Vārī—An Indian Pilgrimage* (1990) and especially *King*

Khaṇḍobā's Hunting Expedition (1992)—both in collaboration with the film-maker Henning Stegmüller—add an aesthetic and poetic dimension to his work expressing a very special perceptivity. It is here that we catch a glimpse of the scholar's inner world.

By the time of his premature death (1992) Sontheimer had become one of the most popular academic teachers and research guides among German Indologists.[8] With his great dedication and gentle persistence he had gained acceptance and appreciation for his approach and area of study by his Sanskrit philologist colleagues. His research was regularly sponsored by the German Research Association (DFG), and this is acknowledged in many of his publications. None of his grant proposals was ever rejected.

Sontheimer would certainly have hesitated to re-publish the papers included in the present volume without major reworking and updating. Some he might not have included at all. The editors felt, nevertheless, that these papers—some of which are hardly accessible any more—should be made available to scholars in India and elsewhere. Editing has been limited to the correction of printing mistakes and other kinds of small errors and to the updating of bibliographical references. Since, unlike in the EK volume, overlappings in the reference literature listed for each article are not many, we have not prepared a unified bibliography for this volume.[9]

NOTES

1. It also contains a list of Sontheimer's publications [LP] and of unpublished materials such as slides, films (Super 8), tape recordings of oral Marāṭhī literature and transcriptions in Marāṭhī script (attached to LP).
2. Sontheimer was made head of the department of History of Indian Religion and Philosophy at the South Asia Institute in 1975; he obtained an extraordinary professorship in 1977, and a regular one in 1979.
3. Cp. also his volume on *The Concept of Hero(-ine) in Indian Culture*, edited by Heidrun Brückner, Hugh van Skyhawk and Claus Peter Zoller, Delhi, 2003.
4. An audio-recording of the recitation and interpretation of the entire text was found in Sontheimer's estate.
5. The first volume, *Features of Localisation in Contemporary Indian Fiction*, was published in 1972. It opened with an essay by S.H. Vatsyayan on 'The role of the writer in contemporary Indian society' which emphasized the importance of oral literature in traditional India, thereby providing one of the keynotes of future seminars. It also contained translations from Hindī, Bengālī, Marāṭhī, Tamil and Kannaḍa literature (see LP for further titles).
6. For a detailed appreciation of this article see Hermann Kulke 'The Vana in the

Kṣetra? Some Remarks on Günther Sontheimer's Concept of the Vana and Kṣetra'. In: A. Malik, A. Faldhaus and H. Brückner (eds.), *In the Company of Gods: Günther-Dietz Sontheimer Memorial Volume*, Delhi, 2003.

7. Cp. also EK, Intr. pp. 13-14 and H. Brückner, 'Some Reflexions on Günther Sontheimer's Understanding of "Folk Religion" and His Model of the Five Components of Hinduism'. In: A. Malik, A. Feldhaus, Ḥ. Brückner (eds.), *In the Company of Gods: Günther-Dietz Sontheimer Memorial Volume*, Delhi, 2003.
8. A list of published Ph.D. theses supervised by him is attached to the LP.
9. Acknowledgments: The editors would like to thank Ms. Edeltraud Bienek, formerly of Heidelberg, for locating and identifying the more than a hundred original slides and photographs, reprinted with four of the articles in the present volume, in the Sontheimer estate; Matthias Ahlborn, formerly of Tübingen, for checking and comparing the reference literature of all the articles; Edeltraud Bienek, Heike Moser and Thomas Vogel, Würzburg, for help with the proof-reading. E. Bienek, Th. Vogel and M. Ahlborn, former students of Sontheimer, considered their help as an act of *gurusevā*.

Religious Endowments in India: The Juristic Personality of Hindu Deities

I. INTRODUCTION: THE PROBLEM

The dispute on the question whether a deity as symbolized or personified by an idol can be a sentient being and as such an owner of property arises very early in Indian history. However, even today the exact legal consequences of a gift to a Hindu deity and the legal nature of a Hindu deity as personified or symbolized by an idol cannot be said to be settled beyond doubt. The Supreme Court of India has dealt with this question in the case of *Deoki Nandan* v. *Murlidhar*.[1] But in this case the exact point for decision was whether a particular deity consecrated according to provisions in a will was open to public worship. T.L. Venkatarama Ayyar, J., held that the idol, though a juristic person capable of holding property, is not the beneficial owner of the endowed property, and that it is only in an 'ideal sense' that the deity is owner of the endowed property. Further, it was stated that the true beneficiaries are the worshippers and that the purpose of the endowment is the maintenance of that worship for the benefit of the worshippers. The decision refers to Privy Council judgments which in fact say that a deity is owner only in an ideal sense, but do not specifically deal with the question of ownership of the deity. The proposition in *Deoki Nandan's* case derives further support from Sanskrit legal texts backed by *pūrvamīmāṃsaka* doctrines which have been discussed by Sir Asutosh Mookerjee in the well-known case of *Bhupati Nath Smrititirtha* v. *Ram Lal Maitra*.[2] But we should keep in mind that the actual point for decision in this case was whether a bequest to *trustees* for the establishment of an image and its worship after the testator's death was valid. This question was answered in the positive, but as the order of reference to the F.B. assumed (in question (i)) that it is a principle of Hindu law that a gift, other than to a sentient being capable of accepting it, is invalid, the answer of the F.B. was extended to this problem as well. It was held *obiter* that a gift to a deity would be invalid as it is not a sentient being and is incapable of accepting property. Though the judgement demands respect, based on the Sanskrit learning of Sir Asutosh Mookerjee, it does not disclose the full picture and leaves us in doubt as to in whom the property vests which is dedicated to a deity.[3] The uneasiness with which *Bhupati's* case was received by some jurists may be recorded in the words of J.C. Ghose: '. . . The Mimamsa may deny the efficacy of the worship of Gods and their capacity to accept gifts and even deny their existence. But the great mass of Hindus believe in the existence of Gods and the efficacy and necessity of gifts to them. Making gifts to the Gods is practised every day by all Hindus. They believe that their Gods accept them graciously and are pleased. . . .'[4]

Deoki Nandan's case may not have taken into account popular attitudes in respect of deities and may not be the last pronouncement on this problem, especially because the decision turned on the question whether a particular temple was open to public worship, for which the *ratio decidendi* turned strictly upon the intention of the testator who caused the consecration of an idol and endowed it with property.

Another writer on this problem, S.C. Bagchi, follows Sir A. Mookerjee's course and skilfully combines Western legal theories on the Juristic Person with *pūrvamīmāṃsaka* doctrines in order to show that a deity is 'not a complete juristic person' and that religious endowments 'can be assimilated to purpose trusts'.[5] But before we introduce any theories on the juristic personality as evolved in the West we should re-examine the Indian position and primarily base the answer on Indian sources. Though the negation of the deity as personified or symbolized by an idol is supported by *pūrvamīmāṃsaka* authors, this theory is not endorsed by popular opinion or practice.

The problem is not merely theoretical because we ought to know what happens if property is donated to a deity. Does it become a *res nullius*, to be protected by the State which may regulate the use of the property, deflect the property or may perhaps allocate some of the excess property of rich temples to the use of poor temples? Or does the property vest in the *purpose* recognized as a juridical person, the purpose being symbolized by the idol?[6] But this is not the intention of the donor, who makes a gift to the deity and not to an abstract purpose. The only intentions accompanying the gift may be that the deity should be owner and that the deity should be pleased. Even if we assume that the property vests in the purpose, what happens to the excess of the property, if the purpose, the maintenance of the worship, is already secured by donations?

II. POPULAR THEORIES, DOUBTS RAISED BY THE *PURVAMĪMĀṂSĀ* AND THE ANSWER TO THESE DOUBTS IN THE *VEDĀNTA* (*UTTARAMĪMĀṂSĀ*)

(1) POPULAR VIEWS ON DEITIES TODAY

Religious reality in India beyond the fringe of even a minority of the literate people, leaves no doubt that deities are regarded by most Hindus as symbolized or personified by an idol and that deities are considered in many ways as corporeal and sentient. Though the modern trend amongst westernized upper classes is to disregard idol worship or to stress faith in God without elaboration of ceremonial worship, and Hinduism knew that the Supreme Being need not be worshipped with idols, the majority of Hindus firmly believe in deities personified by idols, or their presence symbolized by the idol. We find that deities are treated like human beings and a deity is awakened in the morning, is dressed and fed to be worshipped by visitors, receiving gifts of cash, flowers and coconuts, and is put to sleep at early midnight.[7] To ignore in this context the fact that gifts are made to the deity and for its needs would amount to overlooking the real intentions of the donors.

(2) THE ORIGIN OF WORSHIP OF DEITIES IN THE FORM OF IDOLS

How far the practice of worshipping deities in the form of idols dates back in Indian history is a matter of conjecture. Probably autochthonous deities were worshipped before the Aryan invaders had settled in India. It is not clear, however, to what extent idol worship was known in Ancient India amongst the Aryan population, and the *Ṛgveda* reveals scant evidence on this problem. The religion of the Aryans was dominated by the worship of abstract nature deities[8] and the elaborate ceremonies of the five great sacrifices. Eventually the importance of the Vedic gods receded and a new pantheon evolved, recognized by the Brāhman priest, and, if not, new idols were installed, forming a useful instrument in absorbing and civilizing all over India pre-existing primitive cults. The changes involved by the 'intrusion of purāṇic deities into strict Vedic doctrines', as N.C. Sen-Gupta calls it,[9] is incidentally revealed in the *Manusmṛti* (II, 152) where the fact that the *devalaka-brāhmaṇa* is not invited at a *śrāddha* seems to indicate that some Brāhmans had turned to a new source of subsistence and were looked down upon by Brāhmans who followed the more orthodox occupation of teaching the Vedas and sacrificing according to Vedic rites. But probably the Vedic sacrifices had become too complex and expensive and they were eventually replaced by symbolic offerings.[10] *Devapūjā*, the worship of deities, the erection of temples, became more favoured by the Brāhman who maintained himself by attending images either for a salary or by appropriating what was placed before them. That a deity was considered as a sentient being and was actually believed to 'reside' in the image is evident from the way Mahāpuruṣa, i.e. Viṣṇu, is to be worshipped according to the *Baudhāyanagṛhyasūtra*,[11] where it is said that the deity has to be invoked for worship and has to be bidden good-bye, unless the image is fixed on a pedestal.

In the *purāṇas* we frequently come across rules laid down for the proper construction of temples and the consecration and vivification of deities. The ceremony of vivifying the idol, *prāṇa-pratiṣṭhā*, can hardly be said to have only symbolic character, but at the root of this ceremony there must have been the belief that a sentient deity begins to 'reside' in the idol for the purpose of a personal relationship between the worshipper and the deity.[12]

(3) THE CONFLICT IN THE *PŪRVAMĪMĀṂSĀSŪTRA* AND THE REJECTION OF THE POPULAR VIEW

Jaimini and his commentator Śabara are very much alive to conflict.[13] Though Śabara aims at the exposition of the meaning of Dharma, his primary object is to expound a system of interpretation of the Vedic sacrificial ritual. The amount of space Śabara devotes in the *devatādhikaraṇa*[14] to explain the function of a deity at a sacrifice is inordinate and shows the strength of the popular view. Śabara states the popular theory in the propositions of the *pūrvapakṣin* (*sū*. 6-8): the deity is described as having a material body,[15] as eating food in the form of offerings,[16] a deity owns wealth,[17] the deity is actually pleased (*prasīdati devatā*) and rewards the worshipper with the desired fruit (*prītā satī phalaṃ prayacchati*).

The *siddhāntin* on the other hand undertakes to demolish these notions[18]: the object of the sacrifice is the *apūrva*, the transcendental result, which is produced by the sacrifice. That which prompts the act and yields the fruit can only be learnt from the Vedic text and not by means of sense-perception or any other means of cognition. The Vedic word clearly states that the fruit proceeds from that which is spoken of in connection with 'desire for heaven' because in texts like *jyotiṣṭomena svargakāmo yajeta* the sacrifice and not the deity is spoken of in connection with the 'desire for heaven'. The deity is only a subordinate factor and the substance to be offered and the deity are both accomplished entities; while that which is denoted by the root 'to sacrifice' (*yaj*) is something that has to be accomplished, and whenever an accomplished thing and a thing to be accomplished are spoken of together, the former is mentioned only for the purpose of the latter. The deity, i.e. the worshipped entity, is not the principal factor as in ordinary practice; in this case it need not be as in ordinary practice; as a matter of fact, it is in this case the worshipping of the worshipped that forms the principal factor: *na lokavat iha bhavitavyam, iha pūjyamānapūjā pradhānaṃ.*[19] The details of the sacrifice are prompted by the objective of the sacrifice, which is the transcendental result.

The *pūrvapakṣin* had based his views on the evidence of *smṛti*-texts (*smṛtinā*), custom (*upacārāt*) and Indicative Texts (*anyārthadarśanāt*).

The *siddhāntin* directs his arguments primarily against the evidence adduced from the *mantra*- and *arthavāda*-texts from which *smṛti*-texts and custom must derive their authority. Thus the indicative texts cited by the *pūrvapakṣin* do not prove that deities possess physical form and the texts can be interpreted otherwise. Only if we look at the surface of the texts, do we arrive at the notion regarded by some people as the basis of the *smṛtis*. For instance, the Vedic text 'O Indra, I take hold of your right hand', cited by the *pūrvapakṣin*, does not prove the notion that Indra has hands; this is not a perceptible fact and would be thus either an absurd statement or a eulogistic declaration. If one holds that 'Indra has a material body' the addressing of that deity by the term 'Indra' can only be for the purpose of invoking him, and the invoking can be only for speaking to him, but there are no recognized means whereby the deity is related to the speaker and thus the invoking must be useless. It follows that the words of invocation are not for the purpose of being addressed, but only for the purpose of indicating the deity. And under the view held by the *siddhāntin*, namely that deities have no material body, the words should be regarded as serving the same purpose of indicating the deity. In the circumstances the vocative ending used in the vocation would be taken as serving the purpose of eulogizing.

The sense of the eulogy is that the deity is such an instrument of accomplishing the desired result that it accomplished it on being invoked in the same manner as if being endowed with intelligence (body, etc.). Thus it is by being treated as an intelligent being that the deity Indra is invoked by means of a word. The deity is told 'we have taken hold of Your hand'. But this only means that we are dependent on the deity. This serves the purpose of reminding us that 'we should proceed to perform the rites in honour of the particular deity Indra'.

The conclusion is that there is no Indicative Text which points to the fact of deities being like human beings.

Is there any 'feeding' or 'eating', i.e. does the deity eat the *havis* (offering) in the case of sacrifices? The 'proofs' adduced from *smṛtis*, custom and Indicative Texts are refuted by the fact that deities have no material body.

At the end of his discussion Śabara reverts to the question whether the deity owns anything, in order to show that the deity cannot *give* anything: the customary use of 'village of the deity' and 'the field of the deity' is purely figurative. One can only speak of property in a thing (*svatva*) when one has the power to make use of it as one likes.[20] Deities have no such power.

From the offerings by worshippers accrues prosperity to the worshippers. From the fact that temple-priests make use of various things the opponent concludes that such use is according to the wish of the temple-priests themselves. In fact even those who speak of the deities as possessing the thing do not deny the will of the priests (as determining the actual using of the thing); in fact they themselves say that 'the deity does as the attendant priests wish'; and that a person who follows the will of another and who cannot makes use of things according to his own wish, cannot be the owner of those things.

It is evident that Śabara wants to stress the importance of the Vedic sacrificial ritual and he therefore goes to the extent of holding that deities are not regarded as objects of worship and exist only in the words of the Vedic texts. His reference to the question of the ownership of deities is especially intended to show that the reward for the sacrificial act cannot come from the deity, because in order 'to give anything' the deity must be an owner and *possess* property. Though later legal writers have made use of Jaimini's and Śabara's work in legal contexts it should be noted that his reference to legal points is subservient to the purpose of the *Mīmāṃsāsūtra*.

Śabara's statement that deities cannot make use of the property and that it is at the wish of the temple-priests that the property is to be utilized, does not solve the question in whom the property actually vests. The *pūrvapakṣin* is of the opinion that the property vests in the deity, though the *pūrvapakṣin* has to admit that the intention of the attendant priests plays a role. This shows us that priests were managers of the property, deriving probably substantial advantages from dedications to deities, and later legal authors may have had an interest in utilizing Śabara's proposition that deities could not really be owners—a proposition which would tend to confirm the advantages priests derived from determining the use of the dedicated property.

The problem for Śabara was to show that Vedic texts which speak of deities having corporality etc. are mere allegories and that 'a careful study of these texts will prevent misinterpretation'. Accordingly *smṛti*-texts and custom which speak of the corporality of the deities have their basis in the *mantra*- and *arthavāda*-texts only for those who look at the mere surface of the texts. But this *prima facie* meaning of the Vedic texts was held to be acceptable by Bādarāyaṇa and Śaṅkara.

(4) BĀDARĀYAṆA'S *BRAHMASŪTRA* AND SAṄKARA'S *BHĀṢYA*: SANCTION OF THE POPULAR VIEW AND ANSWERS TO THE DOUBTS OF THE MĪMĀṂSAKAS

(a) *Object of the Discussions in the Devatādhikaraṇa*

In Śaṅkara's *Bhāṣya* on Bādarāyaṇa's *Brahmasūtra*[21] we find that the popular view on the corporality of deities is confirmed. The intention of Bādarāyaṇa and Śaṅkara was to show that deities are entitled to Brahma-knowledge and thus it becomes necessary to ascertain whether the *devatā* does exist, especially in view of the conclusions arrived at by Śabara, to whom Śaṅkara refers by name and whose opinion on the nature of the deity is evidently known to Śaṅkara.[22] Śabara's *pūrvapakṣin* had based his views on three sources, (a) *smṛti*, (b) *upacāra*, (c) *anyārthadarśanam*. Śaṅkara similarly bases his views on three sources, (a) *itihāsa* and *purāṇa*, (b) *lokāḥ*, and (c) *mantrārthavādau*. The five attributes of a *devatā* suggested by the *pūrvapakṣin* of the *Mīmāṃsāsūtra-bhāṣya* are not dealt with in detail and Śaṅkara concentrates on the question of the corporality and later, in the *phalādhikaraṇa*, on the question as to who yields the fruit of the sacrifice, the deity or the *apūrva*. Yet when he speaks of corporality he significantly adds 'etc.' implying that all other attributes may be comprehended in his treatment, though it was not necessary for his purposes to elaborate.[23]

A detailed account of the discussion in the *devatādhikaraṇa* would go beyond our purpose and in the following we give only an abstract.

(b) *Corporality of Deities according to Vedic Injunctions*[24]

The Vedic injunctions which direct offerings to be offered to Indra and other gods necessarily imply certain characteristic shapes, because the sacrificer cannot implant on his mind or think of deities such as Indra, etc., as having no form of their own (*svarūpa*), nor can oblations be offered to particular individual deities if they are not firmly established in the mind. Accordingly we read in the Veda: 'When an oblation is taken up in hand for being offered to a particular deity, (the sacrificer) should meditate on that deity while pronouncing "*vaṣaṭ*".'[25]

(c) *Is the deity a Part of a Mantra?*

Śaṅkara turns against the interpretation by Śabara when he maintains that it is not possible to consider the essential form or character of a thing to consist in the word only and thereby to suppose that a divinity is nothing but a word forming a part of a *mantra*.[26]

(d) *Corporality of Deities according to Itihāsas and Purāṇas*

Similarly, *itihāsas* and *purāṇas*, in as much as they have *mantras* and *arthavādas* as their source, are able to establish the corporality etc. of deities in the way explained above. *Itihāsas* and *purāṇas* may possibly also have a source such as direct perception, etc. It is quite possible that what is not directly perceptible to us may have been perceptible to the ancients. The *smṛtis* mention how Vyāsa and others held direct converse with gods etc. But a person who would say that even the ancients, like the moderns, did not possess the power to hold converse with gods etc. may just as well deny the variety of this transitory world. He would also similarly say that just as in modern times there was no Kṣatriya ruling the entire world, even so there was no Kṣatriya ruling the entire world at other times also, and would thereby even deny the injunction to perform the *rājasūya* sacrifice. He would also think that even as in modern times so in the past also, the duties of castes, *āśramas* and religion were in the same almost disordered condition (as they happen to be now) which would render the Scriptures, which prescribe such arrangements, meaningless. Therefore it would be proper to understand that, because of their eminent religiosity, the ancients could have direct converse with gods etc.[27]

(e) *Corporality according to Popular Opinion*

Not only *purāṇas* and *itihāsas* constitute sources of knowledge, but also worldly experience which must not be declared to be unfounded if it is possible to accept it.[28]

(f) *Devas are Intelligent Beings and Animate Material Elements*

Devas are not qualified for Brahma-knowledge according to the *pūrvapakṣin* in the *Brahmasūtra* (I, iii, 32), as words denoting the *devas*, e.g. 'sun', are used in the sense of 'sphere of light'. Bādarāyaṇa defends the competency of the *devas* on account of passages indicative of it (I, iii, 33) and Śaṅkara comments that words denoting *devas*, like, e.g. *āditya* etc., which refer to light etc., nevertheless convey the idea of certain divine selves (persons) endowed with intelligence and pre-eminent power; for they are used in that sense in the *mantras* and *arthavāda* passages; or the *devas* possess, in consequence of their pre-eminent power, the capability of residing within the light and so on and of assuming any form they like. The non-intelligence of light and the like insofar as they are material elements is admitted in the case of the sun etc. But from the words in the *mantras* and *brāhmaṇas* it appears that the *devatās* are intelligent beings of divine nature which animate material elements.

(g) *The Parabrahman*

The *parabrahman* has different names, forms, attributes and powers owing to difference of function.

(5) INTERPRETATION OF SOURCES OF AUTHORITY

We may revert to the differences which distinguish Śaṅkara's approach from that of the *pūrvapakṣin*, whose views resemble the arguments of the *pūrvamīmāṃsā-siddhāntin*.[29] The *pūrvapakṣin* objects to the sources from which the personality of deities is supposed to be known, thus *loka*[30] cannot constitute an independent means of knowledge, as a thing from ordinary life is known only if it is recognized by the acknowledged means of knowledge such as perception, but none of them applies in the present case. *Itihāsas* and *purāṇas* are of human origin and thus in need of other means of knowledge. The *arthavāda* passages cannot be considered to constitute by themselves reasons for the existence of the personality of the *devatās*. They form syntactical wholes with the injunctive passages and have merely the purpose of glorifying what is enjoined in the latter. *Mantras* being employed at different stages of the sacrifice, have merely the purpose of denoting things connected with the sacrificial performance, and do not constitute an independent means of knowledge for the existence of the deities: *asmād abhāvo devādināṃ vigrahasya*. 'For these reasons the *devas* and similar beings have no shape or body.'

Śaṅkara, on the other hand, takes the view that in the case of the Injunction and the *arthavāda* in question connected with the *vidhi*, the words constituting the *arthavāda* form a separate group of their own which refers to some accomplished thing (as opposed to an action to be accomplished); and only subsequent to that, when it comes to be considered what purpose they subserve, do they enter on the function of glorifying the injunction.

We may examine as an example the injunctive passage, 'He who is desirous of prosperity is to offer Vāyu a white animal.' All the words contained in this passage are directly connected with injunction. This however is not the case with the words constituting the corresponding *arthavāda* passage, which is 'Vāyu is the swiftest deity. Vāyu approaches with his own share. Vāyu lends him with prosperity.' The words of the *arthavāda* are not grammatically connected with words of the injunction but form a subordinate unity of their own, which contains the praise of Vāyu, and glorify the injunction, insofar as they give us to understand that the action enjoined is connected with a distinguished divinity.

Śaṅkara concludes: 'He who admits therefore the authoritativeness of the scriptural word has no right to deny that the shape of Indra and other gods is such as we understand it to be from the *mantras* and *arthavādas*'.

Moreover Śaṅkara lays down the rules that (i) when a matter conveyed by the subordinate *arthavāda* passage can be known by some other means of knowledge, the *arthavāda* acts as a mere *anuvāda*, i.e. a statement referring to something already known, or recalling a fact. (ii) When its content is contradicted by other means of knowledge it acts as a *guṇavāda*, i.e. a statement of a quality, suggested by the *arthavāda* sentence. (iii) Where again neither of the two above-mentioned conditions is found, as in the case of the text in question, i.e. 'Indra having hands', a doubt may arise whether the *arthavāda* is to be taken as a *guṇavāda*, on account of the absence of other means of knowledge, or as an *arthavāda* referring to something known (as indicated by the meaning of the text), i.e. an *anuvāda* on account of the absence of contradiction by other means of proof. Śaṅkara lays down the rule that those who actually perceive and believe in the ideas implied should consider it an *anuvāda* and not a *guṇavāda*.[31]

In the case of *mantras*, as well as in the case of *itihāsas* and *purāṇas*, the same rules apply. But *itihāsas* and *purāṇas* are moreover considered to be based on direct perception, for what is not accessible to our perception may have been within the experience of people in ancient times, as with Vyāsa mentioned above.

Lastly, Śaṅkara states that conceptions of ordinary life also must not be declared to be unfounded, if it is possible to accept them.

(6) THE DEITY AS GIVER OF THE 'FRUIT' OR 'REWARD'

In the *phalādhikaraṇa* (III, ii, 38-41), the question is discussed whether God is the giver of the fruit (*phala*) or whether it is the result of *apūrva* as maintained in the *Mīmāṃsāsūtra*. Jaimini's and Śabara's view is that the result is yielded on account of *dharma* as enjoined in the text: *svargakāmo yajeta*. 'He who is desirous of the heavenly world should sacrifice.' In any case fruits are yielded from the God, according to Śaṅkara, having in view the deeds done by the soul or, if it is preferred, having in view *apūrva* springing from the deeds. The Vedānta embodies the view that all creation is brought about by the God. That the God is the giver of the fruits of action, is known from the fact that he creates all creatures according to their own actions.

(7) RĀMĀNUJA ON THE BRAHMASŪTRA

It is to be expected that Rāmānuja as a prominent representative of theism would approve of Śaṅkara's view on the corporality of the *devatā*. He confirms that 'the *dharmaśāstras*, *itihāsas* and *purāṇas* also, which are founded on the different *brāhmanas*, *mantras* and *arthavādas*, clearly teach that Brahmā and the other gods as well as *asuras* and other superhuman beings have bodies and sense-organs, constitutions of different kinds, different abodes, enjoyment, and function. Owing to their having bodies, the gods are also qualified for meditation on the *brahman*.'[32]

(8) NIMBĀRKA, ŚRĪNIVĀSA AND ANNAMBHAṬṬA

In Nimbārka's commentary on the *Brahmasūtra*, the *Vedānta-Pārijāta-Śaurabha*, and in the work of his disciple Śrīnivāsa, the *Vedānta-Kaustubha*,[33] we find that the corporality of gods is similarly asserted (vol. I, pp. 179 ff). Nimbārka and Śrīnivāsa even go beyond Śaṅkara, and maintain that the gods are entitled not only to the knowledge of *brahman* in general but also to those *vidyās* in which they themselves are implicated, e.g. they are entitled to the *madhuvidyā*, the 'honey-meditation', in order to worship *brahman* in its causal state, the gods themselves being *brahman* in its effected state (p. 193). In the *Brahmasūtravṛtti-Mitākṣara* of Annambhaṭṭa[34] the opinion of Śaṅkara that the *devas* may assume any form finds the following expression: *asti hy aiśvaryayogād devānāṃ jyotīrūpeṇāvasthātuṃ, taṃ taṃ vigrahaṃ gṛhītvā ca vyavahartuṃ sāmarthyam.*[35] 'The deities being endowed with great powers have the capacity to exist in the form of light, but when they assume any form (*vigraha* can also mean idol or image) they are capable to act, or to converse.'

Annambhaṭṭa also deals with the objection that gods cannot really be seen to eat and cannot be pleased, consequently coming to a compromise with the *Mīmāṃsaka* on this point: 'the gods do not eat the relinquished oblation, as can be seen from direct perception; how can it be said that they are satiated, though they do not eat? And how can it be said that they are pleased, if they are not satiated? Though they have not eaten, yet it is possible that they have satisfaction because of the mere relinquishment in favour of, or with a view to, their satisfaction.'[36]

Annambhaṭṭa maintains that the deities have corporality and the power of sense-perception and concludes: *tasmāc cetanāvattvāt vigrahavattvāc ca devānāṃ brahmavidyādhikāro'stīti siddham.*[37]

From the instances in the Vedānta literature we may draw the conclusion that the popular belief, that deities could be perceived as corporeal and sentient beings, had gained full scholarly recognition. It may be objected that the discussion in the Vedānta literature is not relevant in legal contexts, but this argument would not destroy the popular theory, because just as legal authors have used the non-legal arguments of the *Pūrvamīmāṃsā* system to support their views, e.g. that the gods have no right to conduct or perform a sacrifice because in a sacrifice you must use your own property, so the popular theory may derive its sanction from the Vedānta authority. The establishment of the personality of the deities and the acceptance of the figurative meaning of the Vedic texts as a basis for the popular view seem to be relevant, especially as in practice the popular theory proved stronger than the legal theory of the *Pūrvamīmāṃsakas*.

III INFLUENCE OF PŪRVAMĪMĀṂSĀ THEORIES IN MEDIEVAL LEGAL TEXTS

(1) POSSIBLE MOTIVES BEHIND THE EMPLOYMENT OF *PŪRVAMĪMĀṂSĀ* NOTIONS

Śabara's aim was the preservation and interpretation of the Vedic ritual. The rising practice of *pūjā* (= worship) and gifts to a deity could be visualized and accepted by him only in terms of the Vedic sacrifice. From the Veda as the authority on which *dharma* and the social and religious order was based, the brahmanical class derived its spiritual and religious superiority and power. The main occupations of the Brāhman were in theory to teach the Veda and to perform sacrifices.[38] The Brāhman had this privilege and was supposed to know how to employ the property according to the intricate Vedic ritual. The success of the sacrifice was dependent on its proper performance. The Veda being the basis of authority, the new forms of worship could be accepted in terms of the Vedic ritual and not *vice versa*. The popular form of worship presupposed a direct relationship between the worshipper and the deity, confining the Brāhman priest to a subservient role. If spiritual merit could be gained by donating property to a deity and by pleasing it thereby, the priest would have the mere role of a servant, or 'shebait' according to modern parlance, of the deity, performing relatively simple daily offerings and temple service—activities which would moreover open priestly occupations to persons who might not be learned in the Veda or qualified as priests.

The approach of the *Pūrvamīmāṃsaka* on the other hand was an intelligible and plausible method of preventing the assimilation of all priestly functions to the mere service of an 'idol', to which property had been donated by a donor, who intended to please it and to gain the fruit of his action from the deity without intricate ritual, thus confining the activity of the priest to the fulfilment of the donor's intentions. Śabara showed that the property was to be employed by the priest in a sacrifice where the deity played a subservient part and where the sacrifice as such yielded the fruit, or the *apūrva*.

The possibility that a deity might become the owner of sacrificial offerings or donations, deemed to be equivalent to sacrificial offerings, might moreover be detrimental to a social order where the sources of acquisition of property were prescribed for different castes. The main income of the Brāhman was acceptance of gifts, and already Gautama had laid down on what sources of ownership the different classes should rely. After stating the sources of acquisition common to all castes, like inheritance etc., he says: 'For the Brāhman acquisition (medieval commentators gloss it as "Acceptance") is an additional mode; for the Kṣatriya conquest; for the Vaiśya and the Śudra wages. For the Vaiśya additional modes are agriculture, trading, tending cattle, and money lending.'[39] Gifts of land and gold to Brāhmans constituted a substantial source of maintenance, as we know from inscriptional evidence, and a widespread, favourite mode of gaining spiritual merit. On the other hand, when the possibility of a direct relationship between a devotee and a deity became both popular and respectable, and gifts directly given to a deity were consequently another mode of acquiring merit, the danger of a distraction from the purpose of the institution of *dāna* (gift) to Brāhmans arose. The danger would be more, if the purpose of the gift was solely the satisfaction of the deity, limiting the control of the Brāhman priest over the property, especially if the property was deemed to vest in the deity. Eventually gifts to deities were recognized by legal writers, but interpreted in terms similar to the terms of the Vedic sacrificial act as understood by Jaimini and Śabara: the property vests in the deity only in a figurative sense, so that property donated to a deity would be still under the control of the priest, so that, similarly with the Vedic ritual, it might be employed by the priest according to his discretion, the latter not infrequently amounting to a substantial proprietary claim upon the dedicated property.

(2) BHĀRUCI

This author in his commentary on the *Manusmṛti*[40] refers to the problem in his comment on book XI, *śloka* 26, where it is said:

devasvaṃ brāhmaṇasvaṃ ca lobhenopahinasti yaḥ
sa pāpātmā pare loke gṛdhrocchiṣṭena jīvati.

Bühler translates this as follows[41]: 'That sinful man, who through covetousness, seizes the property of the gods, or the property of the Brāhmaṇas, feeds in another world on the leavings of vultures.'

Bhāruci comments:

What is set apart with determination that it is for the purpose of the deity that is 'god's property'. In the context of the subject it is that which has been obtained for sacrificial purposes, and nothing else. In the same way the term 'property of the Brāhmans' is also to be understood. For that property which is obtained for the feeding of Brāhmans in *śrāddha* ceremonies and in connection with similar statements (in the *smṛti*), the term 'god's property' is also employed. Though the same be called 'god's property' according to popular usage it is not under discussion here, because it is inconsistent with the topic. The gods have no sense of 'mineness', because they have no right (in respect to property). Whatever 'god's property' is mentioned in the *śāstra* that can be said to be 'god's property' with reference to the time of the act of donation (for sacrificial purposes). And that time during which the deity enjoys it, is momentary, and after (the property) has ceased to be enjoyed by the deity, it cannot be considered as 'god's property'. And consequently what has been obtained for the sacrifice is to be used completely for the sacrifice. Nothing is to be deflected for oneself. But he who through folly does not employ everything for this purpose if he transgresses the regulation, this statement of censure is made. And it is also to be understood as an exemplification of the case of the notorious Brāhman (i.e. of the *śloka* 25 where a Brāhmaṇ who does not use the whole property which he has begged for the sacrifice is censured).[42]

Devasvam according to Bhāruci is property given to a Brāhman for sacrificial purposes. It cannot become the god's property, because gods can have no 'right' (*adhikāra*) over property. The *śāstra* uses the expression *devasvam* in connection with an act of making the donation to a Brāhman for sacrificial purposes. When the deity 'enjoys' the property after the donation it is 'god's property' until the property has been used for the sacrifice and afterwards the property can hardly be called *devasvam*: it means the donated object after donation and prior to the sacrifice. The Brāhman priest is admonished to utilize the property for sacrificial purposes, otherwise he would be guilty of the appropriation of 'god's property'. The provision indicates thus that the right of the priest in the donated property is limited.

(3) MEDHĀTITHI

One of the most influential authors was Medhātithi, who is said to have lived in the North of India,[43] where the *pūrvamīmāṃsaka* views seem to have been stronger than in the South. In his commentary on the *Manusmṛti*[44] the problem is noticed and interpreted according to the views of the *pūrvamīmāṃsaka* followers. In his comment on XI, *śl.* 26 Medhātithi examines the term *devasvam* and directs his criticism against the popular notions on the term. Property (*svatva*) in the time of Medhātithi[45] was indicated when one said or thought '*mamedam iti*'—'this is mine', which implied a *sambandha*, an invisible relationship between owner and object.[46] And the earliest legal as well as popular characterization of property was that 'one can do as one likes' with the object in question: *yatheṣṭha-viniyoga-bhāva*. 'The presence of an application at pleasure'.[47]

Medhātithi comments:

Property that is relinquished in the name of gods for the purpose of performance of sacrifices and the like is 'god-property' (i.e. not god's property, see below), because in the case of the gods there is an absence of the primary relation of property and proprietor.[48] For the gods do not use wealth according to pleasure, nor can they be seen exerting themselves for the protection (of the wealth). And property in everyday life is considered to conform with this. Therefore whatever is surrendered in the name of a god, saying 'this is not mine, this is the god's', is god-property, and such property is enjoined for Agni in the *darśapūrṇamāsa* and other (Vedic) sacrifices and is also enjoined by the well-known practice of the learned (for the gods worshipped) in the Durgā-sacrifice and other secondary devices.[49]

We notice that Medhātithi discredits the worship of non-Vedic gods as secondary means of gaining merit, indicating his strong *pūrvamīmāṃsā* bias towards a strict interpretation of the Vedas in preference to the popular worship. His argument on the concept of property seems destructive of the popular view, but it would eventually be not as effective, because it depends on the definition of what is Property; one may point to the example of minors and lunatics who may be owners though not possessing the capacity to use the property at pleasure.

In the following Medhātithi tackles the question of property donated to 'images' and he first refers to the opinion of his opponent:

It may be argued that by popular usage (a thing) pertaining to the four-armed or other images of gods is called 'god-property' and that it is proper to apply the popular meaning of words (employed) in the *śāstra*.

It would be so, if the term 'god-property' would become well-known as a whole (and not separately as 'god' and 'property'); but because the term 'god-property' is notorious by its component parts as 'god-property', the meaning not as of the whole (but as consisting of the meanings of the component parts) is preferable.[50]

Nor is the assumption possible even by means of adducing another passage, that the four-armed and the like have the status of gods in a primary sense, for that is removed by the very use of (the term) 'image'.[51]

Nor can it be argued that, although there is no god in the primary sense, still let such property be 'god-property' by usage. Well, be it so. But there cannot be the relation of property and proprietor and the use of the term 'property' must be reconciled in the manner stated above (i.e. property relinquished in the name of gods for the purpose of performance of sacrifices and the like is god-property).[52]

Medhātithi refers us to the 2nd chapter of the *Manusmṛti*, where he comments on *śloka* 186 as follows:

It should be noticed that such expressions as 'property of the gods', 'cattle of the gods', 'thing of the gods', etc. mean cattle etc. supposed to be intended for the gods. In the section dealing with Punishment (or: in the administration of justice) the term 'gods' is desired to be used in the sense of image only; otherwise the regulations bearing upon the subject would become liable to be infringed (or: otherwise there would be a breakdown of the established order). (The term) 'things of the gods' in texts relating to them such as 'things of the gods, Brāhmaṇas, and kings are, however, to be regarded as belonging to the highest (class) etc.', (is) only (possible) through an imaginary relation of property in the images, themselves imagined to have the form of gods. For the gods have no relation to property and proprietor, and, as the primary sense is inadmissible (here), the secondary sense alone should be accepted.[53]

We understand that Medhātithi recognizes for the protection of the image and the property connected therewith the application of the popular usage of the term *devatā* to the image. He expands the admonition which Bhāruci directed to the Brāhman to the general public, indicating that by now substantial wealth was being donated to deities. His acceptance of the popular meaning of god-property only as far as the protection of the property is concerned increases the impression that donations to deities tended to be to the advantage of the priest as well.

(4) MEDIEVAL LEGAL WRITERS AFTER MEDHĀTITHI: ŚULAPĀṆI, ŚRĪKṚṢṆA, GOSVĀMI, JAGANNĀTHA

The view of the *Mīmāṃsakas* was perpetuated by legal writers after Medhātithi. Śulapāṇi in his *Śrāddha-viveka*[54] raises the question who is competent to sacrifice. Śrīkṛṣṇa commenting on the work of Śulapāṇi maintains that gods are incompetent to sacrifice because they do not own property, which is prerequisite for the competence to sacrifice: *yāge tu svaṃ viniyuñjita*. 'One should use one's own property in a sacrifice.'

This again follows Śabara's commentary[55] where it is said that the *adhikāra* to the sacrificial act is not possessed by animals, cripples, the blind, deaf and dumb as well as the deities. Śrīkṛṣṇa thinks that gods cannot declare their acceptance by saying 'this is mine' (*mamedaṃ svīkārābhāvād dravya-svāmy-abhāvaḥ*), as gods are made of *mantras*: *devatā mantramayī, prajeśaṃ mantra-vigrahaṃ*.

Śrīkṛṣṇa refers to the *Uttaramīmāṃsā* (Vedānta) where it is advocated that deities have consciousness and can reward the votaries who offer sacrifices. Still a gift to the god is not a gift in the primary sense: *devāya dānaṃ gauṇam tasya mukhyasampradānatvābhāvāt kintv anirākarttṛkaṃ sampradānatvaṃ. tat tu tyājya-dravya-svāmitvāropa-viṣayatvaṃ*. 'A gift to the god is secondary because the state of being primary recipient in respect of it, is absent. Nevertheless there is the state of being a recipient characterized by one who has no power to act. But this places restriction on the ownership in the object to be offered.' The recipient in the primary sense is one who can himself have ownership of the offerings: *sampradānaṃ tad eva syāt pūjānugrāhakaṃ mayā, dīyamānasya dravyasya svāmitvaṃ labhate yadi*.

'That alone can be the principal recipient, capable of furthering the worship, which can acquire ownership in the thing offered by me. Hence by abdication in favour of a deity the abdicator's rights shall go, but no right shall accrue in the primary sense to the deity according to the *smṛtis*. So the uses of '*devagrāma*', etc., are secondary.'

Śulapāṇi[56] continues: *devatātvañ ca vedameya-tyāgoddeśyatvaṃ. uddeśyatvañ ca tasyedam-ity-āropajñāna-viṣayatvaṃ*. 'The status of being a deity means one, in reference to which there can be an offering according to the Vedas. And *uddeśyatva* means the status of the supposititious knowledge that the thing offered belongs to the offeree.'

Raghunandana explains '*devadravya*' thus: *deva-niṣṭhālīka-svāmitva-nirūpita-svatvavad-dravyaṃ*. 'A thing possessed of Property described by an *imaginary* ownership inhering in the *deva*.'[57] Raghunandana further says in connection with the tooth-stick offered to a deity: *devasya svatvānutpādanād dāna-padaṃ gauṇam*. 'The word *dāna* is, in this context, used in a secondary sense, because Property is not produced in the deity.'

In his *Śuddhi-tattva* Raghunandana cites from the *Matsyasūkta*: *deve dattvā dānāni deve dadyāc ca dakṣiṇāṃ. tat sarvaṃ brāhmaṇe dadyād-anyathā niṣphalaṃ bhavet*.[58] He arrives at the conclusion that as the deity cannot in any real sense accept the gift, the ownership of all offerings to the deity really inheres in the Brāhman ministrant, who seizes it first. This seizure is called by Vācaspati '*uttarāpratipatti*', i.e. acceptance just after the offering as a 'secondary or immediately subsequent appropriation'.[59]

Gosvāmin commenting on the *Ekādaśi-tattva* by Raghunandana (*jalāśayotsarga*) says: *deva-pūjādau devatā-prītim-uddiśya dravyatyāgān na devānāṃ tatra svatvaṃ.*[60] 'In as much as articles are only offered in the worship of the deity, etc., with the object of the satisfaction of the deity, the deity has no Property.' Gosvāmin follows Raghunandana, drawing the conclusion that a deity cannot have any right, because of the absence of consciousness. He refers to a middle course that out of deference to the texts, deities have satisfaction through the offerings of votaries and can reward them, but this has not led to their recognition as having such consciousness as to be recipients in the sense the institution of *dāna* postulates.

Raghunandana makes an exception in the case of the land on which the idol stands. Here the deity is a primary recipient: *deva-sampradānaka-dānāni.*[61] It may be suggested that in this case the endowment was of a complete kind so that even the priest could not claim any right in the property, let alone dispose of it. In the eyes of the worshipper it must have been difficult to see in the land on which the temple was situated anything else than the deity's property in a 'primary' sense, and here the jurist compromises with popular reasoning. The anomaly of allowing the deity to be a true recipient of land (if only that particular plot), whilst not such in respect of money, does not alarm so great a jurist as Raghunandana.

We see from the texts referred to above that the concept of the corporality of the *devatās* was not accepted or not accepted in its full consequence so as to lead to the recognition of the god's having beneficial rights. The difficulty was the insistence on the *pūrvamīmāṃsā* interpretation and the desire to exclude the possibility that the institution of *dāna* was applied to gifts to deities. The consequence was that the popular belief that gods own property did not gain ground amongst legal authors and it was held that they own only in a secondary or figurative sense, implying that the Brāhman priest was the true recipient of the gift. Gods cannot accept a gift, and even if it is admitted that they are sentient beings, there is nowhere a recognition that they are recipients in a secular-legal sense.

These views as to gift to deities have been summarised by Jagannātha:

> The text of Dhaumya [on gift to an absent person] ordains, that the gift shall be delivered to the son or other heir, in like manner as donations or the like given in honour of deities must be delivered to the priest and the rest. Consequently, in the case of gift acceptance alone generates property. (1) Accordingly an inanimate being can have no property, through the want of the requisite acts from the effect with which acquisition originates, until final acceptance. (2) But, according to the opinion of those

who maintain property to be vested by acceptance[62] a thing which is given to a deity, whose essence is a text of the Scriptures [i.e. *mantra*], becomes the property of that deity. Let it now be asked by way of objection, what is (3) the conclusion of those who maintain the animation of the deities? The apparent difficulty is reconciled, although deities, according to this opinion, be animated, by not admitting their acceptance of gifts. In the like manner, insects and the rest have no property in water and other things consecrated for the benefit of all beings'[63].

We can see from the texts which we have cited above that the main argument against the corporality of a *devatā* and its capacity to hold property is derived from the *pūrvamīmāṃsā* doctrines according to which deities are purely hypothetical entities, posited to assist in the performance of a sacrifice and subordinate to it. For the *Uttaramīmāṃsaka*, however, the deities can be real sentient corporeal beings capable of holding property (*vigrahatvādi* . . .) in accordance with the popular theory. The motive of a gift bestowed on an idol is not always to benefit the Brāhman or to promote the purpose of worship, but that the deity may be pleased or prompted to respond. To benefit the Brāhman or to contribute to the worship are secondary motives, when a gift is placed before the deity, the primary intention being to benefit the deity. The intention or the expectation of the donor that the property is to inhere in the *devatā*, ought to be given consideration in law, as there is nothing according to popular usage as sanctioned in the Vedānta to prevent a deity from holding property. If the normal institution of gift or *dāna* does not suit the case of donations to deities, as acceptance is a necessary prerequisite for the vesting of the property, does this mean that the deity *cannot* become owner and that the popular theory has therefore to be discarded? It appears that in practice there existed no difficulty in the donor's dedicating property to the deity, whose servants appropriated the property on behalf of the deity and used the property for the benefit of the deity. The property in the eyes of the public belonged to the deity and the concept of a juridical person as developed in Anglo-Hindu law offered a juristic construct which supplemented the legal incapacities of the deity or idol.[64]

IV. HISTORICAL EVIDENCE OF USAGES IN PRE-BRITISH TIMES

From the mass of inscriptions we may at random select a few illustrations which throw light on the actual practice concerning dedications to deities and on the attitudes of the donor, worshipper, temple-servant, and the king as the protector or administrator of the property, towards the deity.

(1) TWO TYPES OF GIFTS

Gifts of lands, etc., were either made to Brāhmans (*brahmadeya*) or to deities (*devadānam*). Sometimes a scheme provides for a clear division between the property intended for individual learned Brāhmans or a community of Brāhmans, and the deity. Thus in the grant of Sadāśiva-Rāya[65] the village is granted and divided equally between the god Cennakeśava and the Brāhmans: *śrī cennakeśavāyārddham arddhaṃ viprebhya ityapi*. A half is thus left for the god, while the other half is split up into 30 *vṛttis* to be divided among the Brāhmans (who are not temple-servants), two *vṛttis* being set apart for the daily worship of the god. However inscriptions occur where the gift is made jointly to the Brāhmans and the deity, the property not being expressly divided, as e.g. in the 2nd Candrāvatī Plate of Candra Deva, where villages were donated to Brāhmans and the god Candra Deva for purposes of worship: . . . *tathā vaṅkaṇipatta-lāyāṃ majuadagrāma*[ḥ] *sarvvādāyasahitaḥ candrāvatyāṃ devaśrī-candramādhavāya pūjādyarthaṃ śāsano kṛtya pradatta iti.*[66]

(2) RECIPIENT OF THE GIFT

(a) The God

If property is dedicated to a god, he is invariably mentioned in the dative case; thus we read in the Piṭhāpuram Pillar Inscription of Pṛithvīśvara[67] which refers to a grant by queen Jāyāmbikā, widow of king Goṅka (III), mother of Pṛithvīśvara, during whose reign the grant was recorded: . . . *śrīpirāpuravāsine* [read: *piṭhāpura*] *bhagavate śrīkuntīmādhavadevāya* [1. 152]. The Tamil version is as follows: *śrīpiṭhāpuramuna śrīkun*[*ti*] *mādhavadevarakuṃ* . . . [1. 139f.]. In the second Piṭhāpuram Inscr.[68] we read: . . . *śrīkunttīmādhavadevaraku* . . . [1. 111]). In the third Piṭhāpuram Pillar Inscr.[69] it is engraved: . . . *kunttīmanorañjanamādhavāya* [1. 82] And: . . . *śrī*[*pī*]-[*ṭha*]*purani*[*va*]*asine śrīkunttīmādhavadevāya* . . . [1. 84f.]. A Tamil inscription from Kāñcīpuram[70] records a gift to the god Allāḷanātha: . . . *Allāḷanāthaṇukku* . . . [1.7]. often we read *devargge* in Kanarese inscriptions: to the god.[71]

Whereas the preceding examples are all taken from southern India, illustrations from north India are not missing. A village grant by Lalitaśūradeva (*E.I.* XXXI, No. 38) in the years AD 853/54 near Śrīnagar was directed 'to the holy Lord Nārāyaṇa, installed at Garuḍagrāma by Bhaṭṭa Śrīpuruṣa' . . . *Garuḍa-grāme bhaṭṭa-Śrīpuru-ṣeṇa pratiṣṭhāpita-bhagava*[*te*]. *Śrī-Nārāyaṇa-bhaṭṭārakāya* . . . [1.20f.].

It is significant that gifts to a deity are never made to the image of the deity X or to the temple of the deity, but that the gift is always directed to the god indicating his name, and sometimes the place in which he is supposed to reside.[72] This points to the attitude not to consider the image as a mere idol or *pratimā* as Medhātithi would hold. We do not find, of course, any justification for the concept that the deity is merely a matter of only a word from a *mantra*.

(b) The Brāhman Priest as Trustee and the Deity as Beneficiary

Very often the god is mentioned alone as the recipient of a gift, often the priest and the deity are mentioned jointly, and frequently we find examples of the priest acting as a 'trustee', the deity being the 'beneficial owner', as for example in an inscription from Karnatak in which we read . . . *Rāmeśvara-devargge* . . . [1.10] . . . *Baṇṇekallaṃ sarva-namasyamāgi Amṛtarāsi(śi)jiyargge dhārā-purvakaṃ-mādi koṭṭar*[.]— '. . . gave (the village of) Baṇṇekal . . . , as a *sarvanamasya-grant*, with libations of water to Amṛtarāśijī, for the god Rāmeśvara . . .' Here we have a typical example where, while the gift is made to the god, the priest is to utilize the property for the god.[73]

(3) MOTIVES AND UTILIZATION OF GRANTS

The inscriptions which record donations to deities do not negate the impression that the donation is made in order to 'please' the deity, and that the reward for the act is expected to come from the deity and is not considered to be a result of the act as such and *apūrva*. However, the motives in donations for the purpose of gaining spiritual merit (*sukṛtim*) for oneself, relatives, superiors etc., are ambiguous insofar as both motives may have acted as incentives, namely the *apūrva* gained on account of the act, an idea connected with the *karma* theory, as well as the idea that the desired result may be gained by pleasing the deity. Temporal results were certainly not infrequently considered as being caused by the deity and at least the typical example of a father's gratitude to a deity for the birth of a son points to this: an illustration is the gift of 32 cows by a Brāhman 'who prayed for a son and was blessed with one'.[74]

A very frequent cause for dedicating property is to expiate a crime. Whereas Manu and other legal authors merely lay down that *prāyaścitta* should be practised by liberality, which must primarily have included gifts to Brāhmans, we come across inscriptions of the Cōḷa time which show us that murders were expiated by a penalty which consisted of a donation to a deity. Thus a certain Kōpperuñjiṅgadeva of Kūḍal in Kīḷ-āmūr-nāḍu donated a golden forehead plate for a deity in expiation (*prāyaccittam*) of the killing of certain officials of the Hoysaḷa king.[75] Whether there is at the root of this practice the lingering idea that the deity is to be reconciled after the crime has been committed does not appear unequivocally from these illustrations, though the possibility exists. An inscription which reads '. . . the penance-practising Rāmanātha finished (repairing) the temple of holy Rāmanāyakar, the god at Rāmeśvaram, who bears the fault of his devotees', points to the conclusion that it is not the *act* alone which expiates, but that the expiation is prompted by the deity.[76]

In many inscriptions there is no further specification by the donor as to how the property is to be used, especially in the case of such simple gifts as lamps, where at the most it is said that the sheep or the land donated are to be used for the maintenance of the lamp, which is 'to continue as long as the moon'. Other inscriptions record donations of lands and lay down that the lands or villages are to be used 'for providing perfumes, flowers, incense, lights, ointments, offerings, oblations of rice etc., (and) dancing, singing, music, sacrifices etc., for the repair of what may be broken or cracked and for the maintenance of servants and attendants as well as the execution of new work . . .'.[77]

In other inscriptions the property is divided into shares for which the proportionate land-revenue was allotted to Brāhmans, the requirements of the god and the temple, and to persons connected with the upkeep of the endowment.[78]

Though, due to the obvious incapacity of the deity to make use of the property itself, the donation is utilized by persons serving the deity, the property is supposed to be used primarily for the benefit of the deity according to the intentions of the donor or according to the expert knowledge of the priest who is responsible for the execution of the grant. Whatever motives the donor may have had when he donated the property, we get no indication that the ownership is to vest in the priest or that property is 'relinquished in the name of the god for the purpose of performance of sacrifices and the like'; rather the intention of the donor is to make the god the beneficial owner and as the deity would not act itself, utilization for its needs is carried out by its servants. To say that the deity owned only in a figurative sense and the donation was only relinquished for purposes of sacrifice etc., is a deduction which is not confirmed by the spirit or the contents of the inscriptions. Whenever the details of the utilization of the property are laid down, the provisions tend to secure the requirements of the deity and do not indicate that the real purpose is an intention to confer a benefit on the worshippers, an intention which is at the most subsidiary.

(4) MANAGEMENT

(a) *Receiving of Gift*

We have noted cases where the property was handed over to the priests so that they might utilize the property for the deity.[79] In other cases money is deposited in the 'treasury of the god' for the expenses of festivals etc., the details of the expenses laid down and fixed.[80]

(b) *Economic Activities*

In a Setupati Copper Plate Grant[81] we are told that certain villages are granted (with the words: 'that the god may enjoy them', a frequent formula in inscriptions), the donation being entrusted to certain trustees, and these persons are ordered to conduct this act of *dharma* and to *keep it always on the increase*. Perpetual income was secured in many ways, as we learn e.g. from an inscription which records the grant of a bazaar shop so that out of the rent the expense of an annual festival may be defrayed.[82] The Ahar stone inscription records[83] that with money belonging to the goddess Kanakaśrīdevī a shop was purchased containing three rooms. Out of the rent of this property, funds were to be provided for saffron, flowers, incense, lamps, flags, and for perpetual cleaning and plastering, white-washing and repair work in the temple.[84]

In the Maṇṇārkōyil Inscription of Jaṭāvarman Sundara-Cōḷa-Pāṇḍyadēva the sale of land to Viṣṇu, or Rājēndra-Cōḷa-Viṇṇagar, by a corporation of Brāhmans is recorded: 'We, the members of the assembly of Śrī-Rājarāja-caturvedimaṅgalam, gave the land (a *brahmadeya*) with libations of water to the Supreme Lord of Rājēndra-Cōḷa-Viṇṇagar, having sold it completely and obtained the entire price and having executed the sale deed.'[85]

Whatever the motive of the sale might have been, the inscription shows that property might be conveyed to a deity without mentioning any further recipients. The mention of the deity as the recipient is enough (one might suppose) to vest the property, and whatever derivative powers and rights the servants of the deity may claim, the deity has the legal ownership. Thus when the temple lands were redistributed amongst the servants of the temple Tiruvārūr (Tanjore District), the authority for the new arrangement purported to be based on an order of the god itself, dated in the 24th year of his 'friend', Tribhuvanavīradēva.[86] To assign temple property to two persons in recognition of the benefits they conferred on the temple during a famine[87] may have been just another way of saying that the deity rewarded a devotee out of its property, though according to Śabara the deity does not own anything and consequently cannot give anything. An inscription of the year 1223 records a gift of a house to a person who had improved the temple, from the properties of the temple after the residents had petitioned the deity and had received its sanction.[88]

(5) PROTECTION OF THE PROPERTY BY THE KING AND THE DEITY AS TUTELARY POWER AND OWNER OF THE COUNTRY

(a) No doubt the property of a deity was protected against interference by theft, robbery and encroachment of enemies, as long as the position of the ruling king was safe, whose duty it was to protect the temple and the property.[89] A rule in the *Mitākṣarā*, laid down in the same manner by *Aparārka* and in the *Vīramitrodaya*, enjoins the duty of the king to protect the temple (*devagṛha*).[90]

At times the whole empire was dedicated to the deity, as in the case of the Vijayanagara empire, which was administered by Harihara, whereas the legal owner or the *de jure* sovereign of the empire was supposed to be the god Virūpākṣa of Hampi. It seems that Harihara, who ruled jointly with his brother Bukka, handed over or purported to hand over the territory to the sage Vidyāraṇya, as the head of the local Advaita *maṭha* and the agent of the god Virūpākṣa. Vidyāraṇya readmitted the two brothers to Hinduism, returning the empire to Harihara and commissioning him to administer the country on behalf of the god Virūpākṣa.[91]

(b) *Supervision and Management of the Interior Affairs of the Temple*

Usually a grant was made in the presence of witnesses, and at the donation of a village by a king the residents of a whole district might be called together to witness the procedure.[92] This may primarily have had the purpose of publicizing the grant, but may also simultaneously have assured that the property would be utilized for the deity. The priests among themselves, the residents of the village, like the merchants who contributed a considerable amount of wealth, and the king, in fact 'all' have to protect the dedicated property.[93] In the year 14 of Parakesari Rājarāja II, the Mahāsabhā of Tirukkaḍavūr (Tanjore) decided to confiscate for the temple the property of those *māheśvaras* who, contrary to their obligations as custodians of the Śiva-temple and its observances, intermingled freely with the Vaiṣṇavas, and themselves wore or sold the flowers grown for the deity.[94] This decision may have been caused mainly by the enmity existing between Vaiṣṇavas and Śaivas, though it also shows that the different bodies of priests watched the proper utilization of the property. Misdeeds by a member of the managing body of the temple were brought to the notice of the king by the assembly of Brāhmans of Tirrupputtūr. The irregularities committed by the Brāhman did not only consist of 'bringing a Brāhmaṇa widow from a foreign country and using her as his wife', but the Brāhman also took away the cooked offerings made in the temple and appropriated to himself the articles given for offerings to the god, received bribes from the tenants of the temple lands and gave credit for their dues in the books of the temple treasury, cut the trees in the *devadāna* lands of the temple using them for building his own house, etc. The decision of the king is unfortunately not known because the inscription is partly destroyed.[95]

We do not know the motives which made some temple servants sacrifice their lives by entering fire in order to attest the ownership of certain *devadāna* lands against the claim set up by four persons who had ultimately to make them over to the temple. Was it just to save the property as such or was it a way of showing one's devotion to the deity by preserving the right of the deity?[96] Perhaps both.

Property belonging to some temple was misappropriated by some persons during a famine and they were required by the *madhyasthas* and residents of the village to make reparation for their acts.[97] The committee of enquiry into the affairs of the Tirumāṇikka-Malaiyuḍaiya-nāyanār temple included officials of the king Somīśvaradēva, the *māhēśvaras*, *sthānikas*, and merchants of Śivapādaśekhara-puram.[98] These inscriptions prove that after the dedication of the property the deity's interests were not entirely at the mercy of the priest, but that other persons also had a say in the protection of the property of the deity.

Normally the administration and management of the temples were in the hands of several bodies of priests.[99] The *Kōyiloḷugu*[100] describes the change in the administration at the advent of the Mohammedan invaders:

> Originally there was one ruler over all the lands of the Cēra, Cōḷa and Pāṇḍya maṇḍalas, and then there were three kings ruling over the three *maṇḍalas*, in fact, till the Śaka year 1249, Akṣaya, the kings did not control the *devadāya* and *brahmadāya* lands, but left them under the control of the Brāhmans and only enquired into

complaints received regarding their administration and meted out justice duly. Then the Muhammadans came, laid waste the *devadāya* and the deity had to seek refuge in gardens and other places till he came back to Śrīraṅgam in Śaka 1293, Paritāpi, then all these *maṇḍalas* came under the Rāya, who was the Narapati; and the Rāya and his servants, viz., the many commanders of forts, made gifts of many villages with libations of water and began to administer the *tiruviḍaiyāṭṭam* lands which were *devadānas* in the same way as they administered the palace lands (*araṇmanaicaīrmai*) by appointing in Śrīraṅgam as their own servants a *maṇiyam* and a *samprati*.

Here official administration of religious endowments was necessitated as an emergency measure by reason of the collapse of the endowments due to foreign invasions and peculation.

V. CASE LAW

(1) EARLY PRIVY COUNCIL CASES CONCERNING THE LEGAL NATURE OF THE IDOL

(a) The early British administration of justice tended to stress the concept of the ownership of the deity who was considered to be the entity in which the property vested for its worship. No doubt one of the reasons was that it was held desirable to scrutinize grants to deities which tended sometimes to be devices for fraud upon the revenue system, as in the case of the *Collector of Moorshedabad* v. *Bishenath Rai*.[101] Another reason was to prevent temple property from becoming practically the personal property of the priest.

(b) *Maharanee Shibessouree* v. *Mothooranath Acharjo* (*13 Moo. I. A. 270*)

This case concerned a sale of rights to rents of lands which were dedicated 'for the religious services of an Idol'. The vendors and respondents were entitled to the rents of these lands on account of a grant by the *shebait*[102] and the suit was dismissed without prejudice to the plaintiffs' bringing a fresh suit to establish the title of the vendors, as holding by a hereditary title entitling them to transfer without the *shebait's* consent.

After stating that the land itself and the rents connected by tenure were dedicated to the religious service of the idol, Lord Chelmsford, who delivered the judgement of the Judicial Committee, continued: 'The rents constituted, therefore, in legal contemplation its [the idol's] property. The shebait had not the legal property, but only the title of the manager of a religious endowment. In the exercise of that office she could not alienate the property, though she might create proper derivative tenures and estates conformable to usage.'

Here we find a clear statement that the property dedicated to an idol vests in it in legal terms. Primarily the property is vested in the deity, though the *shebait* may create derivative tenures and estates conformable to usage.

(c) *Prosunno Kumari Debya* v. *Gulab Chand Baboo*[103]

In this case the respondent had obtained two decrees against the *shebait* of an idol upon his bonds for the repayment of moneys alleged therein to have been borrowed for the service of the idol and the expenses of the temple. Both decrees directed that the debt should be paid by the *shebait* personally, or else be realized from the profits of the *dewuttur lands*.[104] The appellants sued as *shebait* in succession to the judgment debtor to set aside the decree and to have the *dewuttur* property released from attachment and execution thereof.

The main point for decision was whether the profits of the *dewuttur* lands can be attached and appropriated during the incumbency of succeeding *shebait* by virtue of judgments obtained against a former *shebait* in respect of *debts* properly and necessarily incurred by him for the service and benefit of the idol. After stating that the question was not raised whether the lands themselves could be sold under decrees, and that there is doubt that land dedicated for the maintenance of religious worship and charities connected with it is alienable and referring to *Maharanee Shibesouree's* Case,[105] the judgment proceeded:

But, notwithstanding that property devoted to religious purposes is, as a rule, inalienable, it is in their Lordships' opinion competent for the shebait of property dedicated to the worship of an idol, in the capacity as shebait to incur debts and borrow money for the proper expenses of keeping up the religious worship, repairing the temple or other possession of the idol, defending hostile litigation, and other like objects. The power, however, to incur such debts must be measured by the existing necessity for incurring them. The authority of the shebait of an idol's estate would appear to be in this respect analogous to that of the manager of an infant heir, which was thus defined in a judgment of this Committee.[106]

It is only in an ideal sense that property can be said to belong to an idol; and the possession and management of it must in the nature of things be entrusted to some person as shebait, or manager. It would seem to follow that the person so entrusted must of necessity be empowered to do whatever may be required for the service of the idol, and for the benefit and preservation of its property, at least to as great a degree as the manager of an infant heir. If this were not so the estate of the idol might be destroyed or wasted, and its worship discontinued for want of the necessary funds to preserve and maintain them.

Assuming, then, that a shebait may incur debts, or borrow money for necessary purposes, in the sense above explained, it appears to be right and reasonable that judgments obtained against a former shebait in respect of debts so incurred should be binding upon succeeding shebaits, who, in fact, form a continuing representation of the idol's property.

If such debts, and the judgment founded upon them, were not held to be thus binding on successors, the consequence would be that no shebait would be able to obtain assistance in times of need; for, on an opposite state of law, he might defeat the creditors, who had afforded it, by at once transferring the property to other shebaits, as was actually done in the present case by Rajah Baboo, who, after the decrees were obtained against him, appointed the appellants, his wife and nephew, shebaits in his place.[107]

It is obvious that the object in this quotation is to establish the possibility of alienation of property dedicated to a deity. Such alienation had to be justified against a belief that such property is *res extra commercium* for all purposes. It is in the course of the justification of the alien ability of property dedicated to a deity that the statement is made that such property belongs to an idol 'only in an ideal sense'.

(2) INFLUENCE OF WESTERN AND MUSLIM CONCEPTS IN CONJUNCTION WITH THE *PŪRVAMĪMĀṂSAKA'S* VIEW

(a) *The Dakor Temple Case*

The question in whom donations of immoveables and moveables vest was dealt with in the case of *Manohar Ganesh Tambekar* v. *Lakshmiram Govindram.*[108] The case was instituted by the hereditary manager and some priests whose duty was to conduct pilgrims and perform worship for them, against the *sevaks* serving the idol and succeeding to their offices by hereditary descent, being paid Rs. 150 a year out of the income of the temple. The issue was whether the *sevaks* can take the immoveable property held by them and especially the accumulated offerings of articles of value laid at the feet of the idol and the revenue arising from this source 'absolutely as their own without any trust or annexed duty, and whether, if they enjoy by a kind of agency or representation of the idol conceived as a personality, they fulfil the duty they owe to this ideal person in enjoying the growing revenues, or are bound to widen the range of the deity's beneficence in proportion to the expansion of his mundane means'.

The judgment in the following suggests that the devotees are interested in the proper application of offerings. This is no doubt true but the primary intention is to make a gift to the deity, the priest being entrusted with the proper application of it.

In the following the position of the idol is compared with the Roman *foundation*, and it is said:

The Hindu law, like the Roman law and those derived from it, recognizes not only corporate bodies with rights of property vested in the corporation apart from its individual members, but also the judicial persons called Foundations. A Hindu, who wishes to establish a religious or charitable institution, may, according to his law, express his purpose and endow it, and the rules will give effect to the bounty. . . . A trust is not required for this purpose; the necessity of a trust in such a case is indeed a peculiarity and a modern peculiarity of the English law. In early times a gift placed, as it was expressed, 'on the altar of God' sufficed to convey to the Church the lands thus dedicated. Under the Roman law of pre-Christian ages such dedications were allowed only to specified national deities. After Christianity had become the religion of the empire, dedications for particular churches or for the foundations of churches and of religious and charitable institutions were much encouraged.[109] The officials of the Church were empowered specially to watch over the administration of the funds and estates thus dedicated to pious uses, but the immediate beneficiary was conceived as a personified realization of the Church, hospital, or fund for ransoming prisoners from captivity.

The nature of the dedicated property is described:

Property dedicated to a pious purpose is, by the Hindu as by the Roman law, placed *extra commercium*, with similar practical savings as to sales of superfluous articles for the repayment of debts and plainly necessary purposes.

It was admitted by the defendants that the land bestowed on the idol could not be sold, and this restriction was held to be consistent with the grants having been made to the juridical person symbolized or personified in the idol at Dakor. The judgment continued:

It is not consistent with the juridical person's being conceived as a mere slave or property of the *sevaks* whose very title implies not ownership, but service of the god. It is indeed a strange, if not wilful confusion of thought, by which the defendants set up the Shri Ranchod Raiji as a deity for the purpose of inviting gifts and vouchsafing blessings, but, as a mere block of stone, for the purpose of their appropriating every gift laid at its feet. But if there is a juridical person, the ideal embodiment of a pious or benevolent idea as the centre of the foundation, this artificial subject of rights is as capable of taking offerings of cash and jewels as of lands.

The defendants were held answerable as trustees for maladministration analogous to the Indian Trust Act (II of 1882, ss. 88, 95). The conclusions were summed up in the following remarks:

The law which protects the foundation against external violence guards it also internally against maladministration, and regulates, conformably to the central principle of the institution, the use of its augmented funds. It is only as subject to this control in the general interest of the community that the State through the Law Courts recognizes a merely artificial person.[110] It guards property and rights as devoted, and thus belonging, so to speak, to a particular purpose only on a condition of basing the application when either the purpose has become impractical, useless or pernicious, or the funds have augmented in an extraordinary measure. This principle is recognized in the law of England as it was in the Roman law, whence indeed it was derived by the modern Codes of Europe. It is equally consistent with Hindu law, which, as we have seen, undoubtedly recognizes artificial persons, such as the institution at Dakor, and could not, any more than any other law, support a foundation merely as a means of squandering in waste or profligacy the funds dedicated by the devout to pious uses.

We notice that the judgment relies heavily on Western notions of dedication to pious uses and considers the essence of the gift to the deity to be rather the facilitation of worship. It does not contemplate the deity as the actual object of the gift. We have indicated that the popular attitude is to 'impress' the deity with the gift and the object of the gift is not the general purpose of worship as such. It consequently appears that the decision is based on the notion that the deity symbolizes or personifies a 'pious or benevolent idea' recognized as a 'merely artificial person'. The 'pious idea' symbolized by the idol is subject to control by the State through the Law Courts.

(b) *The Judgment of Mr. Ameer Ali in the case of Vidya Varuthi Thirtha* v. *Balusami Ayyar*[111]

The influence of extraneous legal views is also visible in this case, which examines the legal position of a head of a *maṭh* and his right in the property for purposes of limitation. Ameer Ali declines to recognize any parallels in the Hindu system of law with the English institution of trust: 'It is also to be remebered that a "trust" in the sense in which the expression is used in English law is unknown in the Hindu system pure and simple.'

According to Ameer Ali only gifts were possible:

Hindu piety found expression in gifts to idols and images consecrated and installed in temples, to religious institutions . . . and for all purposes considered meritorious in the Hindu social and religious system, to brahmans, goswamis, sanyasis, etc. When the gift was to a holy person, it carried with it in terms or by usage and custom certain obligations. Under the Hindu law the image of a deity of the Hindu pantheon is, as has been aptly called a 'juristic entity', vested with all the capacity of receiving gifts and holding property. . . . When the gift is directly to an idol or a temple, the seizin to complete is necessarily effected by human agency. . . . In almost every case he [manager] is given the right to a part of the usufruct the mode of enjoyment and the amount of the usufruct, depending again on usage and custom. In no case was the property conveyed to or vested in him, nor is he a 'trustee', in the English sense of the term, although, in view of the obligations and duties resting on him, he is answerable as a trustee, in the general sense, for maladministation.

The judgment in the following suggests that the introduction of the concept of trust was due to the establishment of the Mohammedan rule which introduced the institution of *waqf*. But the idea of trust existed from early times in India, and the legal owner may be a priest who was entrusted with the use of the property for the beneficiary, the deity, or the legal owner may be a guild with which the capital was permanently deposited and which had to contribute part of the income for the worship of the deity.[112] Side by side there existed in practice the possibility of making a gift to the deity directly. The belief that the concept of trust is unknown to the Hindu system of law and is of Muslim origin may have added to the belief that property can vest in the deity only in an ideal sense, if we consider Mr. Ameer Ali's remarks on this:

But the Mahommedan law relating to trusts differs fundamentally from the English law. It owes its origin to a rule laid down by the prophet of Islam; and means 'the tying up of property in the ownership of God the Almighty and the devotion of the profits for the benefits of human beings'. When once it is declared that a particular property is *waqf* or any such expression is used as implies *waqf*, or the tenor of the documents shows that a dedication to pious or charitable purposes is meant, the right of the *wakif* is extinguished and the ownership is transferred to the Almighty. The donor may name any meritorious object as the recipient of the benefit.

(c) *Bhupatinath Smrititirtha* v. *Ram Lal Maitra*[113]

In this important case, to which we have referred already in the beginning, the theories of the *Pūrvamīmāṃsaka* and concepts prevalent in the West merged in order to refute the popular view. Two questions of law had been referred to the Full Bench:

(i) Does the principle of Hindu law, which invalidates a gift other than to a sentient being capable of accepting it, apply to bequests to trustees for the establishment of an image and the worship of a Hindu deity after the testator's death, and make such a bequest void?
(ii) Whether the cases of *Upendra Lal Boral* v. *Hem Chundra Boral*,[114] *Rojomoyee Dassee* v. *Troylukho Mohiney Dassee*,[115] and *Nogendra*

> *Nandini Dassi* v. *Benoy Krishna Deb*[116] have been correctly decided, so far as they lay down the proposition that a gift to a Hindu deity, whose image is to be established and consecrated in future, is void?

Sir Asutosh Mookerjee proceeds to prove that the deity is not a juridical person for all purposes, is not capable of the same rights and subject to the same liabilities as an ordinary sentient being and that, as a gift requires acceptance of the donee, a dedication to a Hindu deity has not the same characteristics as a gift to a human being. He discusses the passage of Jīmūtavāhana on gift[117] and concludes that the creation of ownership in the donee presupposes the acceptance of a gift as a necessary condition for its validity and that the institution of *dāna* thus does not apply to the case of a gift to a deity, as an abandonment in favour of the deity is not comprehended within the term 'gift'.

He continues:

> It is obvious from this that in the case of donations, after the owner has parted with the rights and before the subject-matter has been accepted, the property is in a peculiar position so that when the term 'property' is used in relation to what has been dedicated to the deity, it has a secondary sense from what it bears when used in relation to persons.[118]

The passages cited by Śūlapāṇi in his *Śrāddhaviveka* are referred to, which explain the use of the dative case when a donation is made to a god as secondary, just as the expression *devagrāma* etc. is to be used figuratively. References to Śabara's *Bhāṣya* as well as the comment of Medhātithi on Manu XI, 26 complete the picture, and result in the conclusion that 'according to strict Hindu juridical notions there can be no gift in favour of the Gods'.

Against the formidable array of Sanskrit passages we can only make the reservation that popular practice did not impress Sir Asutosh Mookerjee sufficiently.

A reference to a passage from Kātyāyana in which dedications of property for religious purposes is encouraged, though, we may say, in general terms,[119] is considered to prove that property is rather dedicated to *religious purposes* than to a *deity*, so that in the particular case the bequest that an image of a deity should be established and that the property should be applied for the maintenance of the worship is operative.

The conclusion that the object of the gift is not the deity, but that property is dedicated to a religious purpose as such is illustrated—not as support but to show the consonance of Western and Hindu legal theories—with the help of decisions from English law[120] which tend to suggest the proposition that strictly speaking there need not be an idol in existence as legatee, similarly as in English law 'a gift to be employed "in the service of My Lord and Master" and "for the worship of God" are valid'.

Jenkins, C.J., similarly considers directions in wills to use the property 'for purposes of worship' in general terms are valid and comes to the conclusion that in that case the direction in the will for 'spending the surplus income in the *sheba* and worship of Kalee after establishing the image after the name of my mother' is valid. His Lordship says: 'The pious purpose is still the legatee; the establishment of the image is merely the mode in which the pious purpose is to be effected.' He suggests that the expression 'in an ideal sense' does not mean more than 'that the dedication to a deity is a compendious expression of the pious purpose for which the dedication is designed'.[121]

Sir Asutosh Mookerjee gives the following summary of his judgment:

(i) The view that no valid dedication of property can be made by a will to a deity, the image of which is not in existence at the time of the death of the testator, is based upon a double fiction, namely, first, that a Hindu deity has the same characteristics and is subject to the same restrictions as a gift to a human being. The first of these propositions is too broadly stated, and the second is inconsistent with the first principles of Hindu jurisprudence.

(ii) The Hindu law recognizes dedications for the establishment of the image of a deity and for the maintenance and worship thereof. The property so dedicated to a pious purpose is placed *extra commercium* and is entitled to special protection at the hands of the Sovereign whose duty it is to prevent fraud and waste in dealing with religious endowments: *Manohar Ganesh Tambekar* v. *Lakshmiram Govindram*[122] affirmed, on appeal by the Judicial Committee in *Chotalal Lakshmiram* v. *Manohar Ganesh Tambekar*.[123] It is immaterial that the image of the deity has not been established before the death of the testator or is periodically set up and destroyed in the course of the year.[124]

Strictly speaking this case is an authority for the proposition that a bequest to trustees for the establishment of an image and worship of a Hindu deity after the testator's death cannot be subsumed under the ordinary institution of a gift. No doubt Hindu law recognizes gifts to a trustee for religious purposes such as the establishment of the image of a deity and for the maintenance and worship thereof, and we admit that the institution of gift does not apply directly in the case of a gift to a deity, because of the incapacity to act; but if the deity is recognized as a juridical person, the device can be viewed as making the act of acceptance superfluous in the case of private endowments and in the case of public endowments the acceptance of the priest on behalf of the deity may complete the transfer.

(3) THE DEITY AS JURISTIC ENTITY

(a) *Jagadindra Nath Roy* v. *Hemanta Kumari Debi*[125]

In this case the Judicial Committee voice further doubts whether a deity can be more than an ideal owner. The case concerned the question whether the son of a *shebait*, posthumously adopted by the widow of the *shebait*, could sue as *shebait* inheriting the right of management and the right to sue in respect of the property vested in the idol.

In the course of the judgment their Lordships say, 'there is no doubt that an idol may be regarded as a juridical person capable as such of holding property though it is only in an ideal sense that property is so held. And probably this is the true legal view when the dedication is of the completest kind known to law. But there may be religious dedications of a less complete character. The case of *Sonatun Bysack* v. *Sreemutty Juggutsoondree Dossee*[126] and *Asutosh Dutt* v. *Doorga Churn Chatterjee*[127] are instances of less complete dedications in which, notwithstanding a religious dedication, property descends (and descends beneficially) to heirs subject to a trust or charge for the purpose of religion. Their Lordships desire to speak with caution, but it seems possible that there may be other cases of partial or qualified dedications not quite so simple as those to which reference has been made. But assuming the religious dedications to have been of the strictest character, it still remains that the possession and management of the dedicated property belongs to the *shebait*. And this carries with it the right to bring whatever suits are necessary for the protection of the property. Every such right is vested in the *shebait*, not in the idol.'

We gather from the excerpt of the judgment that their Lordships of the Privy Council suspected generally a beneficial interest for the shebaits or trustees rather than for the deity. It is implied that even if there is no beneficial interest in the property whatsoever for the *shebait*, the beneficiary is not the deity and accordingly the property vests in the deity only in an ideal sense.

(b) *The Right of Suit*[128]

The case of *Jagadindra Nath Roy* v. *Hemanta Kumari Debi*,[129] to which we have referred above, is an important authority for the right of the *shebait* to sue in his *own* name. Normally the interest of the deity of the idol and the interest of the *shebait* coincide, but if there are several *shebaits* the possibility of dispute between them arises. In the case of *Pramatha Nath Mullick* v. *Pradyumna Kumar Mullick*[130] the Privy Council—apart from the decisive rejection of the argument that an idol is a mere chattel—held that the will of the idol as to its location must be respected and that accordingly the suit should be remitted in order that the idol might appear by a disinterested friend to be appointed by the Court.[131] As far as the property of the deity is concerned, the interests are ordinarily also represented by the *shebait*, because in most cases the *shebait* by protecting his interest in the shebaitship protects the interests of the deity as well.[132]

(c) *The Proprietary Right of the Shebait in the Estate of the deity*

Incidents of shebaitship are the possession and management of the dedicated property, the right of suit for the protection of the property and the power of alienation on grounds of necessity or benefit to the idol's estate. But is shebaitship a mere office, or is a proprietary *right* attached to it? The case of *Manohar Mukherji* v. *Bhupendranath Mukherji*[133] is one of the leading authorities on this question. The problem in this case was to decide whether shebaitship devolved like any other species of heritable property, with the consequence that the *shebait* is prevented from disposing of his property in such a way as to create any interest in favour of an unborn person and that it is not permissible to create a line of succession unknown to Hindu law.[134]

Though it is admitted in the case that property vests in the deity the discussions evidently follow the course taken by the *Mīmāṃsaka* and the case of *Bhupatinath Smrititirtha*[135] with the result that the deity is not recognized as a *beneficial owner*. On account of the refusal to view the problem from the position of the worshipper and donor, *Manohar's* case, as well as other cases, suffers from a certain vagueness as to who the beneficiaries are. The case of *Manohar* clearly states (p. 478) that 'the deity is the recipient of the gift only in an ideal sense; the dedicated property belongs to the deity only in an ideal sense; in reality the property dedicated is in the nature of *an ownerless thing*. . . . When a Hindu creates an endowment, its management is primarily in him and his heirs, and unless he appoints a *shebait*, he himself fills that office and in him rests that limited ownership—notwithstanding that he is the donor and, on the other hand, the recipient on behalf of the deity, the juridical person,—which has to be exercised until the property offered to the deity has been suitably disposed of. The true principle of Hindu law is what is mentioned in the *Chāndogya-Upaniṣad*, namely that the offerings to gods are offerings for the benefit of all beings' (5, 24, 2-5). The text of the *Matsyasūkta* (as cited by Raghunandana) is added: 'Having made offerings to a God, the sacrificial fee also should be given to the god. The whole of that should be given to a Brahmin, otherwise it is fruitless.' (p. 478). The text from the *Chāndogya-Upaniṣad* does not tell us anything specifically on the beneficial interest of the *shebait* nor on his power over the property and seems to refer merely to the spiritual benefit a sacrifice or donation to the deity may yield. The text of the *Matsyasūkta* does not as such imply that the Brāhman has a beneficial interest in the donation apart from the sacrificial fee, but rather indicates that the Brāhman has a right to use the property 'for purposes of worship' according to the *Mīmāṃsā* or to use it for the benefit of the deity in sacrifices or worship etc.

Before we continue the discussions on the nature of shebaitship in *Manohar's* case it would be useful to state the position reflected in popular practice and according to popular notions.

According to common practice the worship is primarily concentrated on the deity, as personified or symbolized by an idol. In the simplest case offerings (*prasād*) are first given to the deity and if there are eatables a portion of it at least is kept for the deity and the rest of it may be distributed as *prasād* (gift from the deity) by the priest among the worshippers or may be consumed by himself. The more wealth the deity possesses and the more prestige is attached to a deity, the more elaborate the forms of worship become. The priest or *shebait* has to apply the property according to the prestige and respectability the deity enjoys which corresponds with the amount of property donated to the deity. After the demands of the deity—in forms of daily worship, foods, festivals, repair of the temple, and not the least facilities for worshippers, because the deity expects worship—are fulfilled, the excess of the property may be used by the *shebait* for his own purposes, unless there is a specific and complete dedication with directions as to how the excess of the property should be deposited or invested, and that the income of such excess property must be used for the benefit of the deity. Thus the *shebait's* discretionary power extends firstly to the amount of property to be spent for the benefit of the deity and secondly to how to use the excess property or the income, which in most cases gives him a right, though the utilization should conform with the dignity of his office. It is from this excess of property or its income, which is still the deity's property, that the *shebait* may derive his maintenance as a kind of remuneration for his services, the amount depending on custom or on the provisions in the dedication deed. Sometimes the income of the temple may be used for charitable purposes, the gods' doing some charity with the superfluous wealth being a possibility conceivable in Hindu eyes. Whatever interests or benefits are attached to the property of the deity they are secondary and derivative, the property primarily vesting in the deity and intended to benefit it.

In the context of our discussions it is essential to know how the proposition that shebaitship is a proprietary right has been supported. *Manohar's* case follows the case of *Vidya Varuthi* v. *Balusami*,[136] where it had been said that 'normally the manager of an idol or its endowed property has a right to a part of its usufruct'. Dedications are subdivided into three kinds:

(i) where the whole property and its income are dedicated to the idol,
(ii) where properties are dedicated to the idol but a portion of the usufruct is given to the beneficiaries, including the *shebait*, and
(iii) where secular property is charged with the expenses of the worship of the idol.[137]

In all these cases the extent of the right was said to differ, though, it was suggested, the nature of the rights was fundamentally the same. 'In some cases the *shebait* has a larger discretion than in others, and in some cases, again, he has also a proprietary right to the usufruct or a part of it upon the very terms of the endowment which he has not got in others, but in all such cases he has, such as *shebait*, certain rights of a limited character in the endowed property.'[138]

On p. 491 the position of the *shebait* is summed up:

> Of course, if there are specific trusts, the shebait will have to carry them out to the letter, or if any specified amounts are to be spent for some particular items of worship they too have to be spent in the manner directed, but if the only provision is that the worship is to be carried on, the shebait, so long as he does carry them on, in accordance with usage of the particular debuttar or such custom as may have attached thereto, and has not committed an act which may amount to maladministration or mismanagement, must naturally have a very large discretion as to what to spend and in what way. The expenses to be incurred must, of course, be consistent with the dignity of the

endowment. The deity would not take or consume anything; and to take an extreme case, if, offering the worship of the deity, the shebait distributes it amongst the beneficiaries there is hardly any reason to say that he has not discharged his duty. . . .

The shebaitship is considered to involve a proprietary interest even though no emoluments are attached to it, because the *shebait* deals with the property in his management 'as if he has some property, though not the full rights of property, in it, the legal property vesting in the idol'. Though he cannot alienate the property of the deity except for legal necessity he may create derivative tenures and estates conformable to usage and an alienation without necessity will endure only for the period of the tenure of his office,[139] as if he were a limited owner. It is in him and not in the idol that the right of suit is vested and it is his minority that counts for the purpose of limitation.[140]

Shebaitship then, according to Mukherji, J., in *Manohar's* case (p. 494) 'in its true legal conception involves two ideas: the ministrant of the deity and its manager; it is not a bare office but an office together with certain rights attached to it'.

One may argue that the intentions of a testator and founder of an idol, to create a line of succession which he deems best for the preservation of the property of the idol, should be given effect to as far as possible. The interest of the deity as owner should determine the selection of the *shebaits* which might not correspond to the ordinary law of succession.

In fact the *dictum* of the P.C. in *Gossami Sri Gridhariji* v. *Romanlalji Gossami*[141] includes this possibility when it is said:

> According to Hindu law, when the ownership of a Thakur has been founded, the shebaitship is held to be vested in the heirs of the founder, in default of evidence that he has disposed of it otherwise, or there has been some usage, course of dealing or some circumstance to show a different mode of devolution.

The rule that shebaitship devolves in the ordinary line of descent must be subject to the condition that this line of descent is not inconsistent with or opposed to the purpose the founder had in view, as was emphasized by the Judicial Committee in the case of *Mohan Lalji* v. *Gordhan Lalji Maharaj*.[142] The case of *Shri Kishen* v. *Jagannathji*[143] deals with the situation where the founder managed the property having employed a *pujārī* for the worship and admittedly having no beneficial interest in the property whatsoever. Could the line of succession to the office which was inconsistent with the ordinary Hindu law be given effect to? This case distinguished between *shebait* and bare manager.

Whether on creation of an endowment the office of a shebait in the legal sense of the term comes into existence or not would depend upon the circumstances in each case; and it cannot be said that in each case on creation of an endowment 'shebaitship' automatically comes into existence. The law recognizes the founder's right to management of and control over the endowed property, because by dedication he divests himself of his proprietary right absolutely, but so long as there is no appropriation of the property for the purposes for which it is dedicated, there is an obligation on him to see to its preservation, and accordingly a corresponding right of control so long as the property itself exists. This does not mean that he holds the property as shebait even though he has assigned to himself the position of a bare manager and also appointed another person to look after the service and worship of the deity in whose favour the endowment has been created.

The Courts followed the concept of shebaitship as developed in *Manohar's* case. Thus in the case of *Bhabatarini Debi* v. *Ashalata Devi*[144] the appointment of a *shebait* in a deed of dedication was followed by provisions purporting to lay down who should succeed in the *shebaiti.* But these provisions were found to be ineffective. The judgment refers approvingly to *Manohar's* case and it was observed:

. . . that the effects of that case and of the Board's decision which affirmed it[145] was however to emphasize the proprietary element in the shebait right, and to show, though in some respects anomalous, it was an anomaly to be accepted as having been admitted in Hindu law from an early date. Taking their stand upon the proposition that the entire office is vested in the person who holds it at any given time they arrive at the conclusion that it is impossible to give recognition to any interest as vested in another . . . it must be recognized that the shebait must completely represent the idol or the endowment of the deity, the religious purposes, the debutter property, but the idol is the owner of the property and the limit set to the shebait's power of disposition is set not to preserve the interest of the next shebait but to maintain and preserve by proper management the endowment or religious institution.

And we may quote the following excerpt which gives the conclusion in a nutshell:[146]

It must now be taken that shebaiti is property, that it is not a catena of successive life-estates, but it is heritable—heritable property which in the first instance is vested in the founder. . . . It is only with some difficulty that any theory can successfully hold together the two elements of 'office' and 'property', but the shebaiti right involves both and neither element is to be discarded.

In *Raikishori Dassi* v. *Official Trustee*[147] the cases cited above were followed with approval and it was added that even if there are no emoluments attached to the office the *shebait* has 'some kind of property'.[148]

Thus the right of management and possession, and the right of suit as such are held to be a proprietary right vesting in the *shebait*. Besides this there may be an interest in the income according to usage or if the deed specifically provides for it, after the requirements of the deity are fulfilled. This trend in the decisions would not militate against the concept that property vests primarily in the deity not only as a legal owner but also as a beneficiary, whereas the position of the *shebait* consists of a subsidiary beneficial interest with legal powers as a kind of agent.

(d) *Deoki Nandan* v. *Murlidhar*[149]

This case is based on the *Pūrvamīmāṃsaka* view as presented in *Bhupati Nath Smrititirtha* v. *Ram Lal Maitra* and negatives the popular theory. To decide the question whether an endowment is public or private it was held to be convenient to find out the true beneficiaries of religious endowments. And it was stated that[150]

> . . . under Hindu law an idol is a juristic person capable of holding property and the properties endowed for the institution vest in it. But does it follow from this that it is to be regarded as the beneficial owner of the endowment? Though such a notion had a vogue at one time, and there is an echo of it in these proceedings (vide para. 15. of the plaint) it is now established beyond all controversy that it is not the true position. It has been repeatedly held that it is only in an ideal sense that the idol is the owner of the endowed property [reference to the respective P.C. cases]. It cannot itself make use of them or dispose of them, or even protect them [Medhātithi and Śabara are referred to]. In short, the idol can have no beneficial interest in the endowment. . . .
>
> Thus according to the texts, the gods have no beneficial enjoyment of the properties and they can be described as their owners only in a figurative sense (gaunartha), and the true purpose of a gift of properties to the idol is not to confer any benefit on God, but to acquire spiritual benefit by providing opportunities and facilities for those who desire to worship. . . . When once it is understood that the true beneficiaries of religious endowments are not the idols but the worshippers, and the purpose of the endowments is the maintenance of that worship for the benefit of the worshippers, the question whether an endowment is private or public presents no difficulty. . . .

The judgment disregards popular theories as it seems to suggest that the idol cannot be a complete juristic person and that the endowment is a kind of institution for the purpose of the maintenance of the worship.[151] The deity thus becomes a mere figure-head or 'trustee' for some purpose, or a depository of the rights of the beneficiaries. The true intentions are interpreted by the judges in terms of the position taken by Śabara and Medhātithi and not Śaṅkara; the donor ordinarily does not intend to confer a benefit on the worshippers primarily, but he wants to provide primarily for the needs and requirements of the deity, whom he regards as a sentient and corporeal being. The average Hindu does not hope to gain spiritual benefit by providing opportunities for worshippers if he donates to a deity, but the spiritual benefit according to the donor's belief derives from the deity who can yield the reward of the donations. The fact that provisions for needs of the deity may correspond with the requirements of the worshippers does not make them primary beneficiaries. Nevertheless it is possible to see in the decision a recognition of *phala* as the spiritual benefit, though the method of gaining *phala* is said to be the providing of opportunities and facilities for those who desire worship—a notion which seems to be based on western precepts. The conclusion that 'the question whether an endowment is private or public presents no difficulty' because a donor only wants to benefit worshippers, and one has consequently only to find out the intention of the donor as to whether he wanted to benefit individuals or the general public, seems to be a fictitious interpretation of the intentions of the endower.

VI. CONCLUSIONS

The question remains whether the intentions of the donor according to popular theory can be expressed in legal terms. If the problem is viewed from the angle of the average donor the deity as symbolized or personified by the idol is real and is not only the depository of the right, but also the beneficiary. Does then the deity have full juristic personality? The P.C. seem to have come to the conclusion that a deity is only in an ideal sense owner, mainly on account of the fact that the deity has no legal capacity to act and has to stand behind the manager or *shebait*. A.S. Nataraja Ayyar[152] suggests that the concept of the juristic personality of the deity as developed in India is a step further than the law of trusteeship. The legal ownership is vested in the deity as the beneficiary, though the duties of a trustee are in the *shebait* and to this extent the idea of trust for the preservation, management, and improvement of the endowment of the idol is necessary. Nevertheless, this theory advanced by A.S. Nataraja Ayyar still remains a fiction and does not take into account the proprietary interest of the *shebait*.

On the other hand the doctrine that the deity cannot be a beneficial owner, because it cannot act or enjoy property, and consequently cannot be owner of property or owner only in an ideal sense is in practice a negation of the actual intentions of the worshippers.

Nor does the suggestion satisfy, that the donor does not make a gift to the deity, but to the abstract purpose of worship, the deity being a mere adjunct to this purpose, so that the property vests in the purpose symbolized by the idol. This tends to be the attitude of persons who believe the idol to be nothing more than a symbol of the 'Supreme Being', of the philosophical Brahma. A donor who makes a gift 'for the purpose of worship' may still transfer the property to the *shebait* and create a purpose trust. However, at present Hindus still make gifts to deities, and to impose the institution of purpose trust on such donations and to assume that the deity cannot benefit and is owner only in an ideal sense would tend to disregard the real intentions of the donors.

It is possible to take another view of the problem. In view of the recurrence in various parts of the world of property 'belonging' to temples, shrines, or deities, the Indian learning may teach a useful lesson. As we have seen, the popular practice of Hindus and the theories developed in the courts in India hardly agree. It remains to be seen whether a closer concord can be reached between them. On the other hand, we may step back, look once again at our materials, and isolate from them what is essential.

Dedications have been made through the centuries as an act of worship of the deities concerned: whether *phala* ('reward', 'fruit') accrues from the deity or not from the deity is open to debate, but that the act is meritorious is not questioned. What is intended is that the deity shall obtain such benefit from the donation or bequest as a deity (which, by reason of its divine nature, owns the world in any case) may derive from such a gift. Proof that the deity is deriving benefit is obtained from the acts of worship facilitated with the money or other valuables in question. Thus it is impossible to think of a gift or bequest to a deity without at the same time visualizing the preservation of the corpus of the property and as far as possible its income, in order that worship shall be supported out of it. Since the donor or testator himself cannot invariably supervise the worship, whether because of absence or lack of qualification, and since his family and descendants are not invariably able to supervise the endowment on his behalf, it follows that in all ages society through either judicial or executive officials must have exercised the function of supervision, so long as the institution of dedications to deities was recognized by that society. In order to effect that supervision there must lie in some hands the right to require the property to be managed properly, and there is bound to be some tension between the persons actually handling assets and those (if they are, as they must ultimately be, different people) who have the right to detect and suppress abuses. From the commencement, we have seen, the worship must by its very nature be capable of exhausting capital and income, or on the other hand of failing to exhaust it. Consequently, there must be a possibility of accumulating income, of determining not to spend all the income on worship, and thus of disposing of the income in ways which might appear inconsistent with the original intention of the donor or testator. The two ideas, namely that the deity 'owns' the assets, and that the persons responsible for the worship, such as our *shebaits*, have a proprietorial interest in the assets or the income, are inevitable; but neither is necessary, and neither is capable of being utilized for all and every purpose. One may usefully quote the words of that great Hindu law scholar, Golap Chandra Sarkar Sastri.[153] At that time, prior to *Bhupati Nath*'s case, it had been held in several cases (of which the author disapproved) that the idol itself, the actual image, was the object of dedications—a view we now know was only a temporary aberration, though one of great interest.

> It is doubtful whether it [the theory that gifts can be made to deities] is a legitimate and proper use of what is a mere fiction for explaining certain legal incidents. The dedicated property may as well be deemed vested in the Sebayet [*sic*] as trustee; the donor never declares the person in whom the property is to be vested; all that he intends is, that the rents and profits of the dedicated property must be appropriated to the worship. The fiction is introduced by lawyers and judges for convenience, but it is not absolutely necessary that the property must be deemed as vested in the deity or in a fictional person.

From this, historically accurate, viewpoint we can submit (i) that it is quite unnecessary to investigate whether property may vest in a deity; (ii) the notion that the *shebait* has a right of property in the actual capital and income of the endowment is likewise plausible but unnecessary; (iii) just as it is superfluous to posit property in the idol or in the *shebait* it is equally unnecessary to assume that the endowment is 'an ownerless thing';[154] and (iv) all that is required is machinery to enable endowed properties to be managed so as to effect the intention of the donor or testator. Such legal action as is required, therefore, for the protection of the endowment may as well be brought in the name of the endowment (which actually happens in India in regard to endowments other than *maṭhs* or those to or for a deity's worship), or in the name of the deity (it is unimportant), and to search for a *legal personality* merely in order to enable suits to be brought or defended in the interests of the endowment, is quite superfluous.[155] It is submitted that neither the ancient discussions of the *Mīmāṃsakas* nor the modern doctrines based in part on Western models are apt for the situations we have been discussing.[156]

NOTES

1. A.I.R. [*All India Reporter*] 1957 S.C. 155: [1956] S.C.R. 756.
2. I.L.R. [*Indian Law Reports*] 37 Cal. 128 (F.B.).
3. The other approach to the question has been excellently advocated by A.S. Nataraja Ayyar in the relatively new and little-known journal *Vyavahara Nirnaya, A Journal of the Law Faculty and Its Law Union*, University of Delhi, 1954, vol. III, No. 1, pp. 106-77. The author takes the view that a deity can be a beneficiary and owner and has full juristic personality.
4. *Principles of Hindu Law*, 3rd ed., Calcutta, 1917, vol. I, p. 933.
5. *Juristic Personality of Hindu Deities*, Calcutta, 1933.
6. This is the suggestion by Bijan Kumar Mukherjea, *The Hindu Law of Religious and Charitable Trust*, 2nd ed., by T.L. Venkatarama Ayyar, Calcutta, 1962, pp. 38f. On p. 40 he concludes: 'The idol as representing and embodying the spiritual purpose of the donor is the juristic person recognised by law and in this juristic person the dedicated property vests.' The same viewpoint was explained in his 'Juristic personality of the Hindu "idol"', *Indian Law Review*, 1 (1947), 277-89. See S.R. Baj, 'Personality of an Idol in Hindu Legal Philosophy', *Jaipur Law Journal*, 3 (1963), 229-36, and the *Report of the Hindu Religious Endowment Commission* (*1960-2*), publ. by the Govt. of India, e.g. at p. 36, for further opinions. For a critical appraisal of trends to reform Hindu temples, see D.E. Smith, *India as a Secular State*, Princeton, 1963, Ch. 9.
7. As in the case of the goddess Yogeśvarī, the senior goddess of Poona in Maharashtra, to cite one instance amongst thousands. See D.D. Kosambi, *Introduction to the Study of Indian History*, Bombay, 1957, p. 41. See also the description of the typical worship common to ancient India and not unfamiliar to modern India in A.L. Basham's *The Wonder That Was India*, London, 1954, pp. 335f. In the case of *Rambrahma Chatterjee* v. *Kedar Nath Banerjee* (1922) 36 Cal. L.J. 478, 483, cit. in the Privy Council case of *Pramatha Natha Mullick* v. *Pradyumna Kumar Mullick* (1925) 52 I.A. [Law Reports: Indian Appeals series] 245 (250f.) we find a vivid description of the daily routine of worship and the relationship between worshipper and deity.
8. In *Ṛgveda* IV, 24, 10 (Poona ed., 2 (1963), 609), which refers to an idol of Indra, we find the conception of an idol as such belonging to the worshipper and capable of being hired out for a price for magical purposes:

   ka imam daśabhir mamendraṃ krīṇāti dhenubhiḥ?
   yadā vṛtrāṇi jaṅghanad athainaṃ me punar dadat.

   A.B. Keith, who refers to this in an article entitled '*The Personality of an Idol*', (1926) 30 Cal. W.N. xlviii-xliv (repr. in *Journ. of Comp. Legislation and Int. Law* (1925) 255-7) translates: 'Who will pay ten cows for my Indra? When he has slain with his aid his foe, let him restore him to me.' Keith points out that the concept of the idol as a chattel in this passage was not followed in later religious practice as reflected in the epics, *purāṇas and tantras*, etc. Keith welcomes in his article the decision of the P.C. in *Pramatha Nath Mullick* v. *Pradyumna Kumar* 52 I.

A. 245, which (at pp. 256f.) emphatically asserts that the idol was not a chattel. The idol may not be destroyed or injured, as this would be in violation of the sanctity attached to the idol, whose legal entity and rights as such the law of India has long recognized (p. 257).

9. *Evolution of Ancient Indian Law*, Calcutta, 1953, pp. 247f.
10. Manu III, 67-71.
11. II, 14; cit. by P.V. Kane, *History of Dharmaśāstra*, vol. II, pt. 2, pp. 272f.
12. On the 'consecration' or 'vivification' of images, see Pandit Prannath Saraswati, *The Hindu Law of Endowments*, Tagore Law Lectures, 1892, Ch. IV. The ceremony is important as the deity resides permanently in the *vivified* image, whereas the deity is only temporarily associated with images of clay for festivals.
13. *The Mīmāṃsā Darśana, with the commentary of Śavara Svāmin*, ed. by Maheśchandra Nyāyaratna (Bibliotheca Indica ser.), 2 vols, 1873-87; tr. Gaṅganātha Jhā, *Shabara-Bhāsya*, 3 vols. with index vol., Baroda, 1933-6. The 2nd vol. of the B.I. ed., pp. 139-46, and the 3rd vol. of Jha's tr., pp. 1429-37 have been used here.
14. IX, 1, 6-9 (text pp. 139-46, tr. pp. 1429-37).
15. *vigrahatva devatā*; for instance, people speak of and paint Yama with a mace in his hand, there are *smṛti*-texts describing material bodies of deities and there is a Vedic text, 'O Indra, I take hold of your right hand' (*Ṛg*-V. 10, 47, 1).
16. *devatā bhuṅkte*; *smṛti*-texts actually speak of deities, people treat them as eating—giving them different kinds of food, and there is a Vedic text, e.g., 'O Indra, please eat and drink of what has been offered.'
17. *arthapati devatā*; because *smṛti*-texts declare that deities own wealth and there is the customary use of such expressions as 'God's village' and 'God's field'.
18. On *sū*. 9.
19. Text p. 141; tr. p. 1433.
20. On this definition of Property see below, p. 27.
21. I, iii, 26-33: *devatādhikaraṇa*; ed. M.M. Anantkṛṣṇa Śāstrī, with commentaries *Bhāmatī*, *Kalpataru*, and *Parimala*, Bombay, 1938; transl. V.M. Apte, Bombay, 1960.
22. See e.g. III, ii, 53: . . . *ācāryeṇa Śabarasvāminā*.
23. P. 317: *mantrārthavādetihāsa-purāṇa-lokebhyoḥ vigrahattvādyavagamāt*.
24. I, iii, 34; text p. 346.
25. The passage is from the *Aitareya Brāhmaṇa* (III, 8, 1), p. 346: *api ca vidhibhir-evendrādi-daivatyāni havīṃṣi codayadbhir-apekṣitam-indrādināṃ svarūpaṃ. na hi svarūparahitā indrādayaś-cetasy āropayituṃ śakyante, na ca cetasy anārūḍhāyai tasyai tasyai devatāyai haviḥ pradātuṃ śakyate. śrāvayati ca 'yasyai devatāyai havir-gṛhītaṃ syāt-tāṃ dhyāyed-vaṣaṭ-kariṣyan' iti*.
26. P. 346: *na ca śabda-mātram-artha-svarūpaṃ sambhavati, śabdārthayor bhedāt. tatra yādṛiśaṃ mantrārthavādayor-indrādīnāṃ svarūpam-avagataṃ na tattādṛśaṃ śabda-pramāṇakena pratyākhyātuṃ yuktaṃ*.
27. Text p. 346: *itihāsa-purāṇam api vyākhyātena mārgeṇa sambhavan mantrā-*

rthavāda-mūlatvāt prabhavati devatā-vigrahādi sādhayitum. pratyakṣādi-mūlam api sambhavati. bhavati hy asmākam apratyakṣam api cirantanānāṃ pratyakṣaṃ. tathā ca vyāsādayo devādibhiḥ pratyakṣaṃ vyavaharantīti smaryate. yas tu bruyād idānīntanānāṃ iva pūrveṣāṃ api nāsti devādibhir-vyavahartuṃ sāmarthyam iti, sa jagad-vaicitryaṃ pratiṣedhet. idānīm iva ca nānyadāpi sārvabhaumaḥ kṣatriyo 'stīti bruyāt. tataś ca rājasūyādi-codanoparundhyāt. idānīm iva ca kālāntare 'py avyavasthita-prāyan-varṇāśrama-dharmān-pratijānīta. tataś ca vyavasthā-vidhāyi śāstram anarthakaṃ syāt. tasmād-dharmotkarṣa-vaśāc cirantanā devādibhiḥ pratyakṣaṃ vyavajahnur iti śliṣyate. api ca smaranti- 'svādhyāyād iṣṭadevatā-samprayogaḥ' (*Yoga-sūtra 2, 44*) *ityādi.*

28. P. 348: . . . *lokaprasiddhir api na sati sambhave nirālambanā'dhyavasātuṃ yuktā.*
29. I, iii, 32-3.
30. The world of factual experience.
31. P. 346: *yatra tu tad-ubhayaṃ nāsti tatra kiṃ pramāṇāntarābhavādguṇavādaḥ syād āhosvit-pramāṇāntarāvirodhād vidyamāna-vāda iti pratītiśaraṇair-vidyamāna-vāda aśrayaṇīyo na guṇavādaḥ.*
32. See III, i, 25-32; tr. by George Thibaut, *Sacred Books of the East*, 48, p. 330.
33. Tr. and annotated by Rama Bose, 3 vols., Calcutta, 1940.
34. Pp. 58ff; ed. by Sri P.S. Rama Sastri, Madras, 1950.
35. P. 58.
36. P. 59: *na ca tyaktaṃ havir-devatā na bhuṅkte pratyakṣavirodhāt, abhuñjānā ca kathaṃ tṛptā? atṛptā ca kathaṃ prasīded iti vācyaṃ, abhuñjānāyā api tad-uddeśena tyāga-mātreṇa prīti-sambhavāt.*
37. P. 60.
38. E.g. Jaimini says that Kṣatriyas and Vaiśyas cannot be priests (*ṛtviks*), the *sattra* (a sacrifice extending over many days or years) could be only performed by Brāhmans: VI, 6, 18. Kane, op. cit., vol. II, pt. 1, p. 109.
39. X, 38-41; cf. Jhā, *Hindu Law in Its Sources*, Allahabad, 1933, vol. 2, pp. 1-4. Manu censures Brāhmans who earn their living in ways other than by accepting gifts from virtuous people (*sat-pratigraha*), teaching the Vedas, performing sacrifices for people, and, by implication, strictly connected activities. I, 88; X, 76; cp. with III, 64-5, 150-68. See also J.D.M. Derrett, 'The Right to Earn in Ancient India: A Conflict between Expediency and Authority', *JESHO*, 1 (1957), pp. 66-87.
40. *Manu-śāstra-vivaraṇa*, or *Ṛjuvimalā*. I owe the reference to Dr. J.D.M. Derrett from a manuscript in his possession.
41. *Sacred Books of the East*, 25, 435.
42. The text is as follows: *devārthaṃ yat prakalpya sthāpyate tad devasvaṃ. prakaraṇa-sāmarthyād yajñārthaṃ bhikṣitaṃ nānyat. brāhmaṇasvam apy evam eva vijñeyaṃ. yad brāhmaṇa bhojanārthaṃ pratigṛhītaṃ śrāddhādiṣu samānavādārthaṃ ca devasvenāsya grahaṇam. evaṃ ca sati yad idaṃ loke prasiddhaṃ devasvaṃ tan-nehābhidhīyate prakaraṇa-virodhāt. devatānāṃ ca mamatā nāsti anadhikārāt. śāsta-[=śāstra]dṛṣṭaṃ ca yayad devatsaṃ [=yasya*

yadeva tat-svaṃ] tat sampradānakāla evopadeśa-sāmarthyād devasvam iti śakyate vaktuṃ. kṣaṇikaś cāsau(,) devatopabhogakāla[ḥ](-)nivṛtte ca(,) tasmin devatopabhoge devasvaṃ tad ity aśakyaṃ vyapadeṣṭum. evaṃ ca sati yajñārthaṃ bhikṣitaṃ sarvaṃ yajña evopabhojyaṃ. na kiñcid ātmopabhogāya sthāpanīyaṃ. yas tu mohān na sarvam upayuṅkte tasya niyama-vyatikrama 'yaṃ nindārthavādaḥ. dṛṣṭāntārthaṃ vā prasiddhasya brāhmaṇasya grahaṇam.

43. See Kane, op. cit., vol. 1, p. 269; he is an author of *c*. AD 800.
44. *Manusmṛti with Manubhāṣya of Medhātithi*, ed. G. Jhā, Calcutta, 2 vols., 1932-9 and tr. G. Jhā, 5 vols. in 9 parts, Cal., 1921-6, are used in the following.
45. See 'The Development of the Concept of Property in India *c*. AD 800-1800', by J.D.M. Derrett, *ZVR*, 64 (1962) 15-130 at pp. 101f.
46. *Sva-svāmi-sambandha*; the expression occurs already in Kauṭalya's *Arthaśāstra* I, 1; 3, 16. See Derrett, ubi cit.
47. Derrett, ubi cit., pp. 113ff. for the earliest attempts of a definition of Property and the difficulties experienced thereby.
48. Jhā, vol. II, p. 375; *devān uddiśya yāgādi-kriyārthaṃ dhanaṃ yad-utsṛṣṭaṃ tad-devasvaṃ. mukhyasya sva-svāmi-sambhandasya devānām-asambhavāt.*
49. *na hi devatā icchayā dhanaṃ niyuñjate. na ca paripālana-vyāpārās-tāsāṃ dṛśyate. svaṃ ca loke tādṛśam ucyate. tasmād-devoddeśena yad-uktaṃ nedam mama devatāyā idam iti tad-devasvaṃ. tac ca darśapūrṇamāsādi-yāgeṣv-agnyādidevatābhyaś-coditaṃ. śiṣṭa-samācāra-prasiddhyaiva gauṇopāya-durgā-yāgādiṣu.*
50. Pp. 375f.: *nanu caturbhujādi-pratimā sambandhi loke devasvam ucyate. loka-prasiddhaś ca śabdārthaḥ śāstre grahituṃ nyāyyaḥ.*
    syād evaṃ yadi devaśabdo nirbhāgaḥ prasiddham-upeyāt. devānāṃ svaṃ devasvam ity avayava-prasiddhyā 'samudāyārthaḥ prakṛṣṭaḥ.
51. *na ca vākyāntara-prakalpanā-pramāṇenāpy asti mukhyaṃ catur-bhujādīnāṃ devatvaṃ. pratimā-vyavahāreṇaivāpahṛtaṃ.*
52. *na ca yad-yukta-lakṣaṇam asty atha samācārato devasvaṃ bhavatu. sva-svāmibhāvas tāvan nāsti yathoktena ca prakāreṇa sva vyavahāropa-pattir iti śiṣṭaṃ dvitīye.*
53. Jhā, vol. I, p. 177: *evaṃ 'devasvaṃ', 'devapaśavo', 'devadravyam' ityādayo vyavahārās tādarthyenopakalpiteṣu paśvādiṣu draṣṭavyāḥ. daṇḍādhikāre tu pratikṛti-viṣayam eva devatā-vyavahāram icchanti. anyathā vyavasthā-bhaṅgaḥ syāt. kalpita-devatā-rūpaṇām pratikṛtīnāṃ kalpitenaiva sva-svāmi-bhāvena yat-sambandhi tad eva 'deva-brāhmaṇa-rājñāṃ tu dravyaṃ vijñeyam uttmam' ityādiṣu 'devadravyaṃ'. na hi devatānāṃ sva-svāmi-bhāvo 'sti mukhyārthā-sambhavād gauṇa evārtho grāhyaḥ.*
54. *Śrāddha-viveka-saṃgraha, vivṛitti* by Śrīkṛiṣṇa Tarkālaṃkāra, ed. Śrīyukta Mathurānātha Tarkaratna, Calcutta, 1881, p. 23.
55. Śab. on Jaimini VI, i, 5; tr. p. 974.
56. *Śrāddha-viveka*, p. 25.
57. *Ekādaśī-tattva*, as cited by S.C. Bagchi, *Juristic Personality of Hindu Deities*, Calcutta, 1933, p. 56.
58. *Śuddhi-tattva*, with comm. by Kāśirāma Vācaspati, ed. with a Bengalī translation

by Hṛṣikeśa Śāstri, Calcutta, 1908, p. 557. The text is also cited in the *Maṭha-pratiṣṭhā-tattva* of Raghunandana; see *Institutes of the Hindoo Religion by Rughoo Nundun*, vol. II, Calcutta (?), 1835, p. 358. The text is judicially discussed in *Girijanund* v. *Sailajanund* (1896) 23 Cal. 645, 654-6; in *Bhupati Smrititirtha* v. *Ram Lal Maitra* (1909) I.L.R. 37 Cal. 128, 168-9; and in *Manohar Mukherji* v. *Bhupendranath Mukherji* (1932) I.L.R. 60 Cal. 432, 478; see below pp. 47ff.

59. *Śuddhi-tattva*, p. 557.
60. Bagchi, op. cit., ibid.
61. *Maṭha-pratiṣṭhā-tattva*, p. 358.
62. E.g. Jīmūtavāhana, *Dāyabhāga*, Colebrooke's tr. Ch. I, para. 22.
63. *Vivāda-bhaṅgārṇava*, Colebrooke's tr., Madras ed., vol. 2, p. 190. MS Ind. Off. 1768, fo. 8 (b).
64. An early case cit. in vol. 2. of W.H. Macnaghten's *Principles and Precedents of Hindu Law* (pp. 703f.), follows strictly the *pūrvamīmāṃsaka* theories as developed by Bengal legal authors: if property is *relinquished* to a deity and the priest is not *given* that property, it 'belongs' to the deity, but the right of use remains in the heirs of the founder, not in the heirs of the priest. Another case of the early British times, *Collector of Moorshedabad* v. *Bishenath Rai* [1807] 1 Macn. Sel. Rep. 174: 6 Ind. Dec (Old Ser.) 170, which deals with the question whether certain lands are exempt from revenue as *dewuttur* [lit. belonging to a god], speaks of land as 'assigned to the idol Gopaul Thakoor'.
65. *E.I.* [*Epigraphia Indica*] XIV, No. 25. 2nd Vijayanagara dynasty. AD 1584.
66. *E.I.* XIV, No. 15; AD 1098-9; cp. also *E.I.* IV, No. 34; Khālimpur Plate of Dharmapaladeva, ninth cent. Bengal, which records a grant of four villages 'to the holy lord N[u]nna-Nārāyaṇa who has been installed there (by us), and to the Lāṭā Brāhmaṇas, priests and other attendants who wait upon him, may it please your Majesty to grant four villages . . .' [1.50f.] *tatra pratiṣṭhāpita-bhagavan-N[u]nna-Nārāyaṇa-bhaṭṭārakāya tatpratipālaka-Lāṭadvija-dēvārccakādi-pāda-mūla sametāya pūjōpasthānādi karmmaṇē*. . .
67. *E.I.* IV, No. 4; Śake 1108.
68. *E.I.* IV, No. 10.
69. *E.I.* IV, No. 33.
70. *E.I.* XXXI, No. 16, Inscr. 1; *c.* AD 1230.
71. E.g. *E.I.* IV, No. 50: Dharwar Distr. AD 975. Cp. Gai, *Historical Grammar of Old Kannada*, Poona, 1952, pp. 50ff. for the termination *-gge*.
72. The artist of the idol is mentioned in the Candrāvatī Plate cited above thus: . . . who made (the translator inserts: image of) the illustrious Candramādhava. *E.I.* XIV, No. 15.
73. *E.I.* IV, No. 30. We may here refer to an inscription which entrusts the property connected with the office of head priest to a person of special confidence. The dedication assigns substantial rights in the income of the property to this person. This office of superintending is called *mirāśu*, a term especially in use in south India in pre-British times and the early British time, signifying a village

being held by absolute hereditary proprietorship. H.H. Wilson, *A Glossary of Juridical and Revenue Terms*, s.v. In our case the property was charged with the duty of conducting ceremonies. *Arch. Sur. of S. India*, IV, *Tamil and Sanskrit Inscriptions*, No. 8, p.79 (from Rāmeśvaram). See also *E.I.* VII, p. 201 (Karnāṭak, AD 865): the property belonging to the God Mahādeva was entrusted to a certain person, *because he was able to protect and increase it*.

74. *Annual Rep. of Govt. Epigr. Collection* (Madras), 371 of 1909, hereinafter cited only by no. and year. K.A. Nilakanta Sastri, *The Cōḷas*, Madras, 1937, vol. II, pt. II, p. 605.
75. 73 of 1918, from Vriddhācalam, South Acrot. An inscription similarly aiming at expiation of a crime is, e.g., 110 of 1919: a buffalo spoiled some crops in the fields; the owner of the crops beat the buffalo, and it died as a result; the Bhaṭṭas [Brāhmans] who were consulted decided that in expiation of the offence 48 sheep were to be given for half a lamp before Agnīśvaramahādeva. See also 92 of 1906: lamp for manslaughter. 554 of 1921: a quarrel between two watchmen of the temple ends in the death of one of them at the hands of the other. Expiation: 72 sheep for 3/4 lamp. See further instances in Nilakanta Sastri, op. cit. See also 2nd ed., Madras, 1955, p. 541: Inscription of the year 1199 which states that the land had been originally held by a Brāhman who, having stolen the jewels of the goddess, was compelled to give it up along with his house and his slaves as *devadāna*: 490 of 1912.
76. *Arch. Sur. of S. India*, vol. IV, *Tamil and Sanskrit Inscriptions*, p. 59.
77. *E.I.* XXXI, No. 38, Plate 1, see above, p. 32.
78. E.g. *E.I.* IV, No. 50; see also J.D.M. Derrett, *BSOAS*, 19 (1957), pp. 162ff. for similar schemes and an example of tax evasion by this method.
79. Cp. also 371 of 1908, Nilakanta Sastri, op. cit., p. 602: five *kāśu* to the *seva-brāhmaṇas* who took charge of the land.
80. *E.I.* XI, No. 4, xx.
81. *Arch. Sur. of S.I.*, IV, *Tamil and Sanskrit Inscriptions*, No. 7, p. 78.
82. *E.I.* XI, No. 4, xv.
83. *E.I.* XIX, pp. 52ff.
84. Temples sometimes served as banks, the interest being invested in purchase of land. See Puspi Niyogi, *Contributions to the Economic History of Northern India (from the tenth to the twelfth c.* AD), Calcutta, 1962, p. 299.
85. According to *E.I.* XI, No. 30, the date is *c.* AD 1033-4 (?). [4] . . . *vilaikk = aṟa viṟṟu = p* [*poru*] *ḷ-ara = kkoṇḍu viṟṟu vilai-olai-ceydu nīrōḍu aṭṭi = kkuḍutōm Rājendra-Viṇṇagar paramasvāmigaḷukku śrī-Rāja-rāja-ccaruppēdimaṅgalattu mahāsabhaiyōm* [.]
86. 554 of 1904.
87. 560 of 1302. *South Ind. Inscr.*, VIII, p. 151.
88. 91 of 1920. K.A. Nilakanta Sastri, op. cit., 2nd ed., p. 514.
89. But see the iconoclastic exploits of Harṣa as depicted in the *Rājataraṅginī* VII, 1080-98.
90. On Yājñavalkya II, 186.

91. See *Kelandinṛpa Vijaya*, cit. by K.A. Nilakanta Sastri and N. Venkataramanayya, in *Further Sources of Vijayanagara*, 3 vols., Madras, 1946, vol. III, pp. 6f.; vol. I, pp. 44f. Harihara adopted the sign-manual 'Virūpākṣa'. See e.g. *Ep. Carn.* XII, Tumkur, Nos. 1 and 2, signed: *Śri Virūpākṣa*. The case of Vijayanagara was not solitary, the Gajapati rulers of Orissa were similarly placed, and in about AD 1750 the Maharaja of Travancore surrendered his kingdom to the god Śrī Padmanābhasvāmī. The king's being an agent of the god proved to be a very effective assurance of the loyalty of the subjects and prevented any further disturbances from the side of the people, which shows that the deity can be a very potent force. V. Nayam Aiya, *The Travancore State Manual*, Trivandrum, 1906, vol. I, p. 362. The act of the king created considerable difficulty when India was consolidated after 1947 and the Maharaja declared himself unable to take the oath as the head of the integrated States of Travancore-Cochin, because he had ruled Travancore not as the head but on behalf of and as a servant to the tutelary deity. The Indian Govt. on the other hand wanted some assurance of his allegiance. See V.P. Menon, *The Story of the Integration of the Indian States*, Bombay, etc., 1956, pp. 278, 280 ff.
92. *E.I.* IV, No. 4; Śake 1108; *E.I.* XI, No. 4 xv: joint gift of barley corn measuring one *hāraka* in the presence of the village *pañca* (*pañca-kula*) for celebrating the festival of the god Śāntinātha.
93. *E.I.* IV, No. 4: ... [1. 166 f.] *tasmād ayaṃ dharma(ḥ)ssarvveḥ paripālaīyaḥ.* Śake 1108. Cp. *S. Ind. Inscr.*, VII, pt. 2, No. 436: it was the duty of the public to point out misappropriations and the person who did so was to be given a part of the gifted property (from Hampi, AD 1412).
94. 257 of 1925.
95. *Ann. Rep. of Govt. Epigr. Coll.* (Madras) of the year 1909, p. 83, para. 28. The inscription is from about the end of the thirteenth century.
96. 188 of 1925.
97. 255 of 1927.
98. From Śivāyam (Trivandrum), 49 of 1913.
99. *S. Ind. Inscr.*, III, pt. 3, No. 128: a complaint concerning non-payment of contributions to the temple was preferred to the king by the *dēvakarmis* (those in charge of temple service), *uṇṇaligai uḍaiyār* (those in charge of the sanctum of the temple), and the *panmāhēśvaras* (the Śaiva Brāhmans of the locality).
100. History of the temple of Śrīraṅgam, pp. 147-8, cit. in K.A. Nilakanta Sastri and N. Venkataramanayya, *Further Sources of Vijayanagara History*, vol. II, text, p. 56; transl., vol. III, p. 42.
101. (1807) I Macn. Sel. Rep. 174: 6 Ind. Dec. (Old. Ser.) 170; see supra, fn. 64.
102. H.H. Wilson, *A Glossary* . . . , s.v.: 'a person, who has the management and superintendence of an endowed temple, persons attached to and officiating in a temple.' The term is derived from *sevā*, which implies *service*. 'Shebait' appears as early as 1296: *JASB*, 55 (1896), pp. 229-71.
103. (1875) 2 I. A. 145, 23 Weekly Rep. 253.
104. Land granted rent-free to a deity. See H.H. Wilson, *A Glossary* . . . , s.v.,

dewuttur or *debuttar* is a corrupt form of Sanskrit *deva* and *tra* = what preserves the deity, or *deva* and *uttara* = what belongs to the deity. The derivation from *devottaram* seems preferable, a term which in itself signifies that the deity has a superior interest (but hardly property) in the object.

105. 13 Moo. I. A. 270; see supra, (b).
106. *Hunooman Persaud Panday* v. *Mussumut Babooee* 6 Moo. I. A. 243.
107. The Hindu law permits gifts of their *shebaities* by *shebaits* to members of the family who stand immediately in the order of succession to them.
108. (1887) I.L.R. 12. Bom. 247.
109. Savigny, *System of Modern Roman Law*, vol. II, book II, ch. II, sec. 88 [Jural Relations], transl. by W.H. Rattigan, London, 1884, from: *System des heutigen Römischen Rechts*, 2. Bd., Berlin, 1840. The discussions in the case are based on para. III of this chapter dealing with *Stiftungen oder unsichtbaren juristischen Personen*.
110. Savigny, *System* . . . , sec. 88.
111. (1922) 48 I. A. 302, at pp. 311f.
112. On *nīvi*-trust, see J.D.M. Derrett, at 64 *ZVR*, 68ff.
113. (1909) I.L.R. 37 Cal. 128 (F. B.).
114. (1897) I.L.R. 25 Cal. 405.
115. (1901) I.L.R. 29 Cal. 260.
116. (1902) I.L.R. 30 Cal. 521.
117. See above, fn. 62. The comments of Rāmabhadra, Śrīnātha and Śrīkṛṣṇa on these passages of Jīmūtavāhana (cit. at p. 145 of the decision) lays down in effect that acceptance of a gift is a necessary condition for its validity.
118. At p. 146.
119. See P.V. Kane's ed. and transl., Bombay, 1933, p. 71, *śloka* 566: *svasthenārtena vā deyaṃ bhāvitaṃ dharmakāraṇāt. adattvā tu mṛte dāpyas tatsuto nātra saṃśayaḥ*. P. 234: If a gift was promised by a man for a religious purpose whether when in good health or when afflicted with disease, the son should be made to pay it, if the father (the promisor) dies without (actually) giving it over; there is no doubt on this.
120. In *re Darling* [1896] 1. Ch. 50; *Attorney General* v. *Pearson* (1817) 3 Mer. 353, 409; 17 R.R. 100, *Powerscourt* v. *Powerscourt* (1824) 1 Molloy 616; *Felan* v. *Russel* (1842) 4 Ir. Eq. Rep. 701; *Mills* v. *Farmer* (1815) 19 Ves. 482; I Mer. 55.
121. P. 140. A passage from the *Mahānirvāṇa-tantra* referred to (sec. 12, vv. 92-4) is worth citing in this connection: 'Property thus given by a man or appropriated (by him) to religious uses cannot be set aside by his son and the rest. The giver is competent to take care of the wealth, or property endowed for religious purposes. He can no longer resume it, because Dharma is then master or owner of such property, endowed for religious purposes. Let the owner himself or his representative, O Goddess, appropriate to pious uses the corpus of a property or its income according as it may have been resolved." The *M. n. t.* is a late eighteenth century work and its *vyavahāra* part may not be out

of touch with English legal conceptions (as suggested by Dr. J.D.M. Derrett in connection with the rules of succession). Thus 'property given for religious uses' sounds like a gift under English law given in general terms for the advancement of religion 'in the service of My Lord and Master'. The suggestion that *dharma*, or, we may say, the pious purpose, becomes the owner comes close to the Roman *institution* or the German *Stiftung*, where the purpose as such becomes the legal owner. But cp. § § 80 BGB, esp. § 88: *Umwandlung oder Aufhebung der Stiftung*—which may be the consequences if the property vests in the purpose.

122. (1887) I.L.R. 12 Bom. 247.
123. (1899) I.L.R. 24 Bom. 50: L.R. 26 I.A. 199.
124. In the case of temporary images which are destroyed at the end of the festival a provision for the deity will have to be in the form of a trust as the deity is 'residing' only temporarily in the image.
125. (1904) L.R. 31 I.A. 203.
126. (1859) 8 Moo. I.A. 66.
127. (1879) L.R. 6 I.A. 182.
128. This involved subject, rendered unduly complex by discordant Calcutta cases, is exhaustively discussed by T.L. Venkatarama Aiyar in the 2nd ed. of B.K. Mukherjea's *Hindu Law of Religious and Charitable Trust* (1962) at pp. 237-53. The propositions are in many cases beyond the scope of this paper, but they illustrate the uncertainties of modern Hindu law.
129. L.R. 31 I.A. 203.
130. L.R. 52 I.A. 245: see supra fn. 7.
131. In his discussion of this case A.B. Keith takes it as an authority that the idol, when consecrated, has not only symbolic significance, but is a real being, and capable of ownership of property. See above fn. 8. This tendency is confirmed in some decisions from Bengal where the idol *as such* is mentioned as a party in suits: see e.g. *Radha Charan Saha* v. *Sree Sree Iswar Jaykali Bigraha* (1941) 46 C.W.N. 94. The word *bigraha* (*vigraha*) means 'image'.
132. For cases in which the *shebait* had precluded himself from protecting the interests of the deity, see e.g. *Sushama Roy* v. *Atul Krishna Roy* A.I.R. 1955 Cal. 624; *Behari Lal* v. *Thakur Radha Balabh Ji* A.I.R. 1961 All. 73: suit by a worshipper who was also helping the manager in managing the temple to recover possession of property alienated by the manager the transfer 'not being beneficial to the interest of the deity'; *Śaṅkaranarayana Iyer* v. *Shri Poovanathaswami Temple* A.I.R. 1949 Mad. 271 (F.B.); suit by a '*de-facto*' manager. See also *Vikrama Das* v. *Daulat Ram* A.I.R. 1956 S.C. 382.
133. (1932) I.L.R. 60 Cal. 452.
134. These principles were laid down in the *Tagore case*, (1872) 9 Ben. L.R. 377.
135. (1910) I.L.R. 37 Cal. 128 (F.B.).
136. L.R. 48 I.A. 302, 311; see above p. 42.
137. P. 488: for the construction of a deed according to which a village was dedicated

and entrusted to a person, see the recent case of *Ramkishorelal* v. *Kamalnarayan* A.I.R. 1963 S.C. 890.

138. P. 488. See also Mitter, J., at p. 504, who refers to *Vidya Varuthi Tirtha* v. *Balusami Ayyar* L.R. 48 I.A. 302, and concludes: '... it would seem to follow that a shebait has some sort of beneficial interest *in the endowment or the debattar estate.*' In *Gobinda Das Nath* v. *Shyama Charan Nath* (1940) 44 C.W.N. 1004, at pp. 1007f., *Manohar's* case is referred to and the above passage is discussed. It was held that this does not mean that the shebait has any right of ownership in the *debutter* estate. The judges were said to have merely discussed whether the *shebait* was a bare trustee or whether he was not a bare trustee to find out whether the shebaiti right was property. 'They nowhere held that the shebait of an absolute debuttur had any right of ownership in the property dedicated. That right is completely in the deity.'
139. *Abhiram Goswami* v. *Shyama Charan Nandi* (1909) I.L.R. 36 Cal 1003: L.R. 36 I.A. 148.
140. *Jagadindra Nath Roy* v. *Hemanta Kumari Debi* (1904) I.L.R. 32 Cal. 129: L.R. 31 I.A. 203.
141. (1889) I.L.R. 17 Cal. 3 (20): L.R. 16 I.A. 137 (144).
142. (1913) I.L.R. 35 All. 283.
143. A.I.R. 1953 All. 289.
144. 70. I.A. 57: A.I.R. 1943 P.C.: (1943) I.L.R. 2 Cal. 137. In the case of *Ganesh Chandra* v. *Lal Behary* L.R. 60 I.A. 448, the P.C. had already relied on *Manohar's* case.
145. L.R. 63 I.A. 448: A.I.R. 1936 P.C. 318.
146. At p. 66 of I.A.; p. 83 of A.I.R.
147. A.I.R. 1960 Cal. 235.
148. The Report of the *Hindu Religious Endowment Commission* (1960-2) turns against rights in offerings unless they were made to the shebait *personally* and recommends not to regard the office of shebaitship and emoluments thereof as private property (pp. 36, 42, 58, 62).
149. A.I.R. 1957 S.C. 133: [1958] S.C.R. 756.
150. At p. 136 of A.I.R.
151. The case refers approvingly to the observations by Sir Lawrence Jenkins C.J., in *Bhupati Nath Smrititirtha* v. *Ram Lal Maitra* I.L.R. 37 Cal. 128 (138) (see above pp. 43ff). The idea 'that the pious purpose is the legatee' and 'that the dedication to a deity may be a compendious expression of the pious purposes for which the dedication is designed' was also adopted in *Upendra Nath Poddar* v. *Anath Chandra Lodh* I.L.R. [1951] 1 Cal. 665, where a contention was raised that the dedication was not to the *service* of the deity, but to the *deity* as such. At p. 672 Bachawat, J., answers the contention: 'A gift to a deity is *ex necessitate rei* a gift for a religious purpose. The deity is the symbol of the religious purpose. It exists only for the religious purpose. In fact, it is the religious purpose itself. Dedication to and for the religious purpose. Treated

as a foundation or corporation, the deity exists for no other purpose except for the purpose of religion and a dedication to the deity must, in my judgment, be held to be a disposition of property for a religious purpose.' Though this sounds persuasive, it is nevertheless difficult to imagine the deity as merely representing a purpose, having in mind the average Hindu worshipper.

152. Op. cit., pp. 174f.; see fn. 3 above.
153. Golapchandra Sarkar, *A Treatise on Hindu Law*, 3rd edn., Calcutta, 1907, pp. 443-4.
154. As per Mukerji, J., in *Manohar* v. *Bhupendranath* (1932) 60 Cal. 452, 478 (FB); see above, p. 47.
155. In *Masjid Shahid Ganj* v. *Shiromani Gurdwara Prabandhak Committee* (1940) 44 C.W.N. 957 (967) P.C. Sir George Rankin expresses doubts as to the propriety of creating juristic persons for purposes of suits and says: 'From these considerations special to Hindu law no general licence can be derived for the invention of fictitious persons. It is as true in law as in other spheres "*entia non sunt multiplicanda praeter necessitatem*".'
156. I am obliged to Dr. J.D.M. Derrett for comments on this article while in draft.

Some Notes on Birobā, the Dhangar God of Maharashtra

In Chapter III and IV of his *Myth and Reality* (Bombay, 1952) Professor Kosambi discussed the evidence of prehistorical and historical survivals gathered during his intensive field research, especially in the Poona District. These fascinating chapters demonstrate the author's grasp over what he called 'Combined Methods in Indology',[1] enlisting the assistance of archaeology, history, ethnography, sociology, and philosophy. In support of his views, Professor Kosambi incidentally dealt with the semi-nomadic shepherd sections of the Dhangars in Maharashtra, telling us in a very concise manner more about their past than anybody before him. Perhaps this is the occasion to add a few notes on his remarks about Birobā, one of the most widespread and favourite gods of the Dhangars.[2] 'Birobā worship', Kosambi said, 'centres somewhere in Sātārā District'.[3] Actually, a centre of Birobā worship is found at Ārevāḍī near Ḍhalgāon in the Sāṅglī District, where an annual pilgrimage on the fifth till seventh day of the light half of the month Caitra (March-April) attracts 20,000 Dhangars. From Ārevāḍī Birobā has spread to many places in the Sātārā District, as, for instance, to Kurolī Siddheśvar near Dahīvāḍī, Pāṅgrī, and Ṭākevāḍī, where Birobā has assumed the name Sātobā. The Ārevāḍī-Birobā has also wandered into the Poona District and has settled at Bhāde, near the Vīr Dam, and at Kāṭecīvāḍī, near Bāramati, and numerous other places where Dhangars have their *vāḍī-s*, which are seasonal camps or, more and more—with the spread of agriculture—permanent settlements. Often the important Birobā temples are situated on migratory tracks, as for instance Ārevāḍī itself, which serves as a camping site on the route of the Dhangars from the Kolhapur area. With the beginnings of the rains these groups take their sheep from the drier east and north-east via Panḍharpūr up to *Kurḍūvāḍī* in the Usmānābād District and return after three months. Before Birobā came to Ārevāḍī he spent his youth in Cinclī, a town 30 miles from Sāṅglī in Karnatak, in the company of his foster-sisters Ekā and Māyevā. Though Māyevā/Māyākkā/Mhākubāī—Skt. Mahākālī—figures prominently in the traditions of the Dhangars and in the traditions of the corresponding community in Karnatak, the Kurubas, there is nothing about the Dhangars in the locally published *caritra* of this goddess.[4]

According to one set of oral traditions, Birobā—after a meandering migration towards the west—arrived at Paṭṭaṇ Kuḍolī, a big village ten miles from Kolhapur, which has developed into a major place of pilgrimage, the biggest *yātrā* (*jatrā*) being celebrated between Dasarā and Divāḷī on the third day of the dark half of the month Aśvin (September/October). A huge body of oral traditions has accumulated around the Paṭṭaṇ Kuḍolī cult. In Ārevāḍī, and more emphatically in Paṭṭaṇ Kuḍolī, Birobā is the younger brother of Iṭṭhal/Viṭhobā of Paṇḍharpūr, and Birobā's *mūrti*, an aniconic stone, is on the left of Iṭṭhal/Viṭhobā's aniconic *mūrti* when facing the devotee.

But we must be careful in making such statements, because there is rarely a singularity of views on the part of the *bhaktas*. Even an individual *bhakta* may offer different explanations at different times. His conception of the deities comprises many beliefs which derive from various social and psychological levels. One *bhakta* would maintain that Viṭhobā is greater from the point of status, because his *bhakti* is more tenacious, but in age Viṭhobā is younger than Birobā. The aniconic stone (*piṇḍ*) of Viṭhobā is smaller in size as compared with Birobā's, because the smaller size reflects the modesty of Viṭhobā, who becomes great by making others great and does not show off his greatness. Another view of a *bhakta* who comes from far away to the annual *yātrā* is that Viṭhobā is indeed elder than Birobā and he is referred to as *dādā* (elder brother). However, the *piṇḍ* in the temple is smaller in size, because Birobā is a greater *bhakta* and there is no dark spot on his character. For the simple Dhangar in his *ovīs* Viṭhu and Biru are often identical.

Many features of the pastoral Gavḷī Viṭhobā have crept into the traditions of the Dhangars. One such incident is the dispute between Rukmiṇī/Padmāvatī and Viṭhobā which is told in the *Pāṇḍuraṅga-māhātmya* of the *Padma-purāṇa*.[5] Rukmiṇī had taken offence that Viṭhobā/Kṛṣṇa should still be attached to Rādhā/Rāhī and withdrew to the Diṇḍīra-Forest. There, on the site of the present Paṇḍharpūr, Kṛṣṇa found her. The Dhangar/Gavḷī version is told by Durga Bhagwat[6] and reoccurs in versions from Paṭṭaṇ Kuḍolī, though in a different and less purāṇified guise. Here, like the temple of Rukmiṇī in Paṇḍharpūr; the temple of Kāmabāī, the wife of Birobā, in Ārevāḍī; and the temple of Bhāgulek, the daughter of Iṭṭhal/Birobā and his wife Padubāi, in Paṭṭaṇ Kuḍolī are separate.

Birobā or Birāppā is one of the major gods of the Kurubas in Mysore and he is known beyond Bijapur up to Telengana. Considering the wide dissemination of this god, it is surprising how little this cult has been thought worthy of study outside the Dhangar community. This may partly stem from the fact that Birobā is often erroneously identified with one of the *bāvan* (fifty-two) *vīr-s*.[7] As Kosambi correctly states in his *Myth and Reality*: 'He [Birobā] should be distinguished from the Māṅg-Vīr cults set up by people of the low Māṅg caste to placate the spirit of some dead adult, just as their Ceḍā is a boy's ghost that refuses to be laid unless given a cult.'[8] These spirits of deceased adults and the *ceḍā* belong to the fifty-two *vīr-s*, who are all kinds of spirits as, for instance, malevolent and benevolent *bhūt-s*, *asura-s*, or minor godlings inhering in idols. The *bāvan vīr-s* are part of the *mantraśāstra* and their study lends the adept the power over them. Gods can have *vīr-s* as their servants and Khaṇḍobā is sometimes said to have fifty-two *vīr-s* under his power.[9] The priest of a deity may even be able to lend the services of a servant spirit of the deity for some time.[10] It is quite possible that Birobā may have been a *yakṣa* at a time when the Dhangars were a community constantly on the move and not a semi-nomadic group, just an annex to agriculture or even themselves settled farmers. The *Mahāmāyūrī-mantra* mentions Vīr as the patron *yakṣa* of the Karhāḍ region.[11] But Birobā has long since developed into a full-fledged god with a mythology of his own, temples and important *yātrā-s*. One of the fifty-two *vīr-s* is Bhairava/Bahirobā and this fact and the superficial phonetic similarity of Birobā/Bahirobā presumably adds to the identification with Bhairava. Here the matter ends for the *mantraśāstrī*. Ask any educated Maharashtrian with a knowledge of Sanskrit mythology and he will have no objection to equating Birobā and Bhairava on grounds of external phonetic similarity. And ever since Molesworth compiled his Marathi dictionary we come across the identification with Bhairava: 'Birobā', Molesworth says, '... A peasant-appellation of the god Bhairav.'[12] Bhairava, indeed, is the guardian deity *par excellence* of the Maharashtrian peasant, but is just not a pastoral god. Thus, if one asks a Maratha farmer instead of a Dhangar to show the Birobā temple, one will surely be misdirected to a village Aṣṭa-Bhairav temple which has nothing to do with Birobā. A superficial glance, for instance, at the little village of Bhāde near the Vīr Dam in the Purandar Taluka of the Poona District, where, like in many other places, we find the temple of the Dhangar Birobā at the fringe of the village on a hillock, away from the usual ubiquitous peasant Aṣṭa-Bhairava temple, may not suffice to convince that the cults are distinct. Those Dhangars, however, who are still alive to their history and traditions are emphatic that Birobā has nothing to do with Bhairava. And justly so, because their traditions are quite different.

To illustrate this point one of the versions collected by me in different parts of Maharashtra may be briefly told.[13] This short excerpt cannot indicate the wealth of detail, singular beauty and forceful style of the original told by a Dhangar who is a *pujārī* of Birobā and a factory worker at the same time. Recently he has begun to forget details about the history of Birobā, partly because of an attack of typhoid, but much more so, because he is turning his interest to the texts of the great Sanskrit traditions. He has bought popular Marāṭhī editions of the Mahābhārata and Rāmāyaṇa and has them read to him. He memorizes these texts by heart, turning them eventually into *ovī-s* which are sung at festivals in his village. In other words, we have a patent instance of how the great traditions slowly erase local traditions. According to this version of the myth, Birobā was born by Sūravantī (Sūryavantī) or Gaṅgā, whom Śiva had forgotten in a golden casket on the earth and who on Śiva's command had been afterwards sheltered by the Earth in her womb or rather in an anthill. Eventually the field, including the anthill, was ploughed and the casket was unearthed, followed by flocks and flocks of sheep.[14] The casket was handed over to the king, who was without child and who adopted the child. The girl, however, wanted to perform *tapas* in a seven-storeyed *vāḍā* amidst the jungle. Her *tapas* was so immense that even Śiva was worried and granted her a boon. She desired a child by immaculate conception. Śiva gave her certain tasks to accomplish, for instance, to swallow the sun. On her objection that Sūrya was a man, Śiva said that she should wait till the sun had just risen half above the horizon in which case the sun would be neuter. In her *thālī* Śiva put the god Vīr in the form of an atom to be incarnated in her. He had been the only one of the 33 crores of gods who was able to complete the study of the *bāvan vīr-s*. The conception was discovered and reported to the king. He ordered Sūravantī to be killed and when this proved to be impossible and the child was born from the left side of the mother, the king ordered the child to be killed. But the servants of the king only exposed it in the deepest jungle, where even birds could not fly and the sun was so hot that even the stones were parched by the heat. It was the month of Caitra. The crying of the child was heard by Pārvatī and Śaṅkar, who descended to provide for the child's needs. Two sisters were created from Śaṅkar's ash and Pārvatī's *kuṅkum* in the *hom* altar. The two sisters were to bring up the child. After a long migration the three reached Cinclī in Karnatak.

We need not proceed. At this point of the myth the stage is set for Birobā's numerous adventures, the legends about the spread of his cult, his marriage and his settlement in Ārevāḍī. The episodes have a peculiar semi-pastoral background and show the efforts to come to terms with other deities and settled communities. From the first part of the legend it is already evident that we cannot assign Birobā to the Bhairava mythology of the Purāṇas. Rather, we may see some affinity with Kārttikeya/Ṣaṇmukha/ Skanda of the *Skanda-purāṇa*. Birobā—born of Sūravantī or Gaṅgā—was found in the thicket, just like Skanda—according to one version of the myth of his birth—was 'born-in-thicket' (*śara-bhū*). There is a close association of Birobā with the mothers or sisters as in Skanda's case. Birobā was brought up by two foster-sisters who—the Dhangars say—are two of the seven mothers. One episode of the myth of Birobā tells us that an old woman, while migrating with her cows, used to carry Birobā on her head in a box. Subsequently her son was killed by Birobā in the form of a snake and merged into Birobā. Full of anger the woman threw the box into an unfathomable pool where Birobā was worshipped by the seven *āsarā-s* (*apsara-s*) for twelve years. The close association with the sisters/mothers is also reflected in the quarrels between Birobā and his wife Kāmabāī, mentioned above; a quarrel originated when Birobā, having won his wife after prolonged adventures, preferred to visit the bāzār at Ḍhalgāon with his sister Māyevā against the entreaties of his wife to stay with her.

There is another contact with the *Skanda-purāṇa*, that is, the *Kāśīkhaṇḍa* of the *Skanda-purāṇa*. In chapter 64 of the Marāṭhī version of the *Kāśīkhaṇḍa*[15] which deals with the establishing of the Vīreśvara-liṅga, the story is told how King Mitrajit's wife, who was without child, was advised to venerate Śiva with sincere *bhakti* on the third day of the light half of the month Mārgaśīrṣa (November/December) in order to bear a child. The child was born, but when the astrologer was consulted about the child's destiny, it was found that the child was destined to kill its parents. The *mantrī* advised throwing the child into the sea. The queen however wanted the child to be returned to Vikaṭāgaurī (Śiva's wife) and wanted her to take charge of the child. The child was returned to Vikaṭāgaurī. She summoned eight *yoginīs* (attendants), who went to Kailāsa and handed over the child to the eight mothers (*mātṛkā-s*). The mothers looked after the child for eight years and then returned the child to Gaurī at Kāśī. Gaurī fondled it and called it 'Vīr'. One day while it was playing in the temple it was recognized by Bindumādhava (a form of Viṣṇu) as Gaurī's *varaputra* (son granted as a boon). He told Vīr to worship Śiva. Vīr established a *liṅgam* and worshipped it for 100 years. Finally Śiva appeared in the *liṅgam* and, pleased by the *bhakti* of Vīr, named the *liṅgam* Vīreśvaraliṅgam.

This does not mean that the Dhangars have directly borrowed their 'Vīr' from the *Kāśīkhaṇḍa*, but the text is popular in Maharashtra and its diffusion may have helped to contribute towards the formation of the myth of Sūravantī and Birobā. It may be added that in Hunnūr, Taluka

Maṅgaḷveḍhā, District Śoḷāpūr, the present writer saw a print of the type available in bāzārs near temples, showing Mhāliṅgrāyā Mhāḷāppā, a famous *bhakta* of Birobā, worshipping Birobā under the name Bireśvarliṅg.

If Birobā is not Bhairava, is there any connection between Birobā and Vīrabhadra? Kosambi said: 'However, the Vīrabhadra of some Purāṇas, supposedly a general of Śiva's army in battle, may reflect the Vīr cult.'[16] Indeed wherever any Dhangars or especially Kurubars are settled we find that the identification with Vīrabhadra has made some progress. For instance in Dhotre, Taluka Puntāmbe, in the Ahmednagar District we find Birobā identical with Vīrabhadra. Perhaps the identification of Birobā with Vīrabhadra emanates from Liṅgāyat quarters which had considerable influence in Maharashtra. According to a strong tradition, Khaṇḍobā, the famous Maharashtrian deity worshipped especially by the Dhangars, was, like his wife, a Liṅgāyat *vāṇī*; that his second wife Bāṇāī is Dhangar nobody doubts. In many places where Dhangars are settled, e.g. in Huljantī (Maṅgaḷveḍhā Taluka), where Mhāḷiṅgrāyā Mhāḷāppā is chiefly worshipped, and Hunnūr, which has a famous Birobā temple and is connected with Huljantī by many oral traditions, Birobā is considered to be a Liṅgāyat. One of the most important gods of the Liṅgāyats, besides Śiva and Nandī, is Vīrabhadra. I obtained one version of a Birobā Vīrabhadra legend from a Kannaḍa booklet entitled *Hālumatada Caritra* which deals with the religion and history of the Kurubars.[17] Here the demon called Hiraṇyakaśipu received a boon from Brahmā and he won the three worlds. His over-bearing attitude caused the gods to approach Viṣṇu, and he in the form of Narasiṃha killed him. However, Narasiṃha's appearance was so dreadful that the people in the world could not bear it. The gods headed by Brahmā came to Śaṅkar and sought Śaṅkar's advice. Śaṅkar sent Vīrabhadra and his *gaṇa* in order to pacify Narasiṃha, or, if necessary, to kill him. Ultimately Narasiṃha was killed and his head was brought to Śaṅkar, who tied it to his neck. As a consequence Mahāviṣṇu was enraged with Vīrabhadra. When Pārvatī and Śaṅkar were sitting on Kailāsa, Vīrabhadra approached them and told them that he had the desire to visit the earth. They granted him his wish. Vīrabhadra took birth in the womb of Sarasvatī, the wife of Brahmā. But Mahāviṣṇu took the form of an old Brahman and appeared before Sarasvatī telling her that the child would have a very bad character and that she should not look at his face. When the child was born Sarasvatī took the child and left it in a burial ground (*smaśān*). There the birds and animals forgot their animosity and looked after it supplying water and shelter. The deities of the forest pitied the child. Even Agni, Jala, Vāyu, Bhūmi, Ākāś, and Candra felt pity. A woman named

Māyammā came to the *smaśān*, rescued the child and called it Vīrliṅg. Afterwards, a demon of the Kaśyapa-Gotra, by name Koṇāsūr, molested the 700 Kurubars. They approached Vīrliṅg and asked him to save them. He killed Koṇāsūr at Koṇṇūr. The Kurubars became his worshippers and he became their *ādidev* or *kula-devatā*. He is called Vīreśvar and he is Vīrabhadra's incarnation.

Here again we come across Māyammā/Māyevā who finds Vīrliṅg in a *smaśān* (instead of in a thicket). Māyevā or Skt. Mahākālī, the foster-sister of Birobā, can also be considered to be a kind of sister of Vīrabhadra, if we follow the *Śivapurāṇa*, where she is said to be born like Vīrabhadra from Śaṅkar's matted hair.[18]

The picture which emerges leaves little scope for assuming that Birobā is identical with Bhairava at the present stage of the history of Birobā. Even though the Dhangars, while singing their *ovī-s*, occasionally refer to Biroba as 'Kāśīliṅga Birāppā' and Kāśīliṅga may refer to Bhairava, and though the Dhangars in their *ovī-s* occasionally refer to Birobā as having the form of Bhairī (Bhairava) they have no explanation for this and there are no legends connected with Bhairava. Eventually the identification of Birobā and Bhairava will make some progress because of the phonetic contamination of Birobā with Bahirobā/Bhairava and because the Dhangars will eventually accept and assimilate what *kīrtankār-s*, *ovīkar-s*, *gurav-s* and other people more in touch with the great tradition will tell them about their gods. The texts of the great tradition, the Purāṇas, tend to subsume Vīrabhadra and Bhairava under the terrific aspect of Śiva and in their efforts to abstract and standardize tend to equate Bhairava and Vīrabhadra, though even in the Purāṇas the cause of the emanations of Vīrabhadra and Bhairava and their specific tasks are distinct.

NOTES

1. *Indō-Iranian Journal* (*IIJ*), VI (1963) 177-202.
2. The present writer is compiling an account of the history and religion of some semi-nomadic pastoral and settled agricultural sections of the Dhangars of Maharashtra. The intention to work on the Dhangars originated when I had the opportunity to accompany Professor Kosambi on his field research in the years 1959-60. My own field research was carried out for about 15 months in the years 1967-9. I am grateful to the German Research Association for having granted me financial aid.
3. *Myth and Reality*, p. 121.
4. Anant Śaṅkar Jośī, *Śrī Mahākālī Caritra vā Śrī Cinclī Kṣetra Varṇan*, Cinclī vā Morab, 1961.

5. Chapter I of the *Pāṃḍuraṃga-māhātmyam* [in Marāṭhī], Mumbaīt Gaṇpatkṛṣṇajī yāṃce chapkhānyāce mālaka Ātmarām Kānhobā yāṇīm chāpilā, āvṛtti 5 vī, Śake 1811. Not found in the Veṅkaṭeśvara Press edn.
6. 'Paṇḍharīcā Viṭhobā', in *Satyakathā*, July 1969, 27-31.
7. For a list of the fifty-two *vīr-s* see the *Mahārāṣṭra Vākyasampradāy Koś*, vol. II, Poona, 1947, p. 286. The knowledge about what *bāvan vīr* means is faint amongst the Dhangars. The term is often confused with *bāvan birudeṃ*, which means the 52 paraphernalia of a Dhangar, e.g. *tambākhu*, *batvā* (a little bag for keeping tobacco and lime), *kāṭhī* (stick), *ghoṅgaḍī* (blanket), but also the objects connected with cult, e.g. the musical instruments, *ḍhol* (drum), *kaitāḷ* (cymbals or a kind of castanet), *pavā* (flute), and so on.
8. Op. cit., p. 121.
9. See R.E. Enthoven, *The Folklore of Bombay*, Oxford, 1924, pp. 193ff., 206. Molesworth, *A Dictionary, Marāṭhī and English*, Bombay, 1857, s. Birobā.
10. Enthoven, op. cit.
11. Kosambi, op. cit.
12. Molesworth, op. cit. See also, e.g. S.R. Devle, in *Svarājya*, 1 Nov. 1968, p. 13: '. . . Bhairav, Kālbhairav, Bahirobā, Birobā, Ḍolsobā, Poṭobā, Bhairavanāth hī sarva Kāl Bhairavācī rūpe hot. . . .'
13. A version of the myth in the *ovī*-form is given in *Ek hotā rājā*, ed. Sarojinī Bābar, Mahārāṣṭra Rājya Lokasāhitya Mālā, Puṣpa 10, Mumbaī(?), 1964. The myth is also briefly told in Durgā Bhāgwat, *Lokasāhityācī Rūparekhā*, Mumbaī, 1956, pp. 405f.
14. The legends centring around anthills are legion, the anthill invariably being connected with the origin of sheep. Sheep forming a line while being driven from or to the *vāḍā* strikingly resemble and are actually compared with ants. In connection with the legend told here a legend about the birth of the nephew of Basava, Cennabasava, is of interest: Basava, with his elder sister Nāyalambikā, proceeded to Kalyāṇa to enter the service of the Kalacuri king Bijjala (1156) as a prime minister. When Basava was praying for some gift, he saw an ant emerge from the ground with a small seed in its mouth. Basava took this seed home, and his sister without his knowledge swallowed it and became pregnant. By the interference of Śiva a son was born, who was the incarnation of Śiva in the form of ẓaṇmukha. See Edgar Thurston, *Castes and Tribes of Southern India*, Madras, 1909, vol. IV, article on Lingayat.
15. Śivadās Gomā, *Kāśīkhaṇḍa* [pothī], Nirṇayasāgara Press, Mumbaī, 1960; Sanskrit version: Veṅkaṭeśvara Press ed., ch. 83.
16. *Myth and Reality*, p. 121.
17. Yallangavḍa Ph. Āṭṭikoḷḷa, *Hālumata caritra* [in Kannaḍa], Dhārvāḍ, 1949, pp. 53-5.
18. *Śivapuraṇa, Rudrasaṃhitā* 2, 32, 22 (25), Veṅkaṭeśvara Press ed.: tajjaṭāyas-samudbhūto vīrabhadro mahābalaḥ//pūrva-bhāgena devarṣe mahā-bhīmo gaṇāgraṇīḥ//22//. . . mahākālī samutpannā taj-jaṭā-para-bhāgataḥ//25//

Field Research in Maharashtra and Karnatak: The History of Some Pastoral Communities and Their Cults

Professor G.H. Khare has shown us that the study of the history of Maharashtra, and for that matter the history of India in general, should not only relate to political history, but should also include the history of cults. Such research supplements the political history of Maharashtra which has understandably fascinated historians to a greater degree than the study of the history of cults and the history of groups associated with these cults.

For five years—about four months each year, and once eight months—the present writer has been collecting material bearing upon the theme of this note: the history of the Dhangars, the Gavaḷīs, the Kurubas and other pastoral communities especially in Maharashtra and Karnatak.[1] Some remarks as regards the sources and methods adopted and some illustrations of what sort of results are to be expected from the source material are offered here.

The subject actually requires the combination of various disciplines and methods and the tapping of various sources. Ideally a full-time team would have been necessary, as one person cannot do full justice to all these fields. Emphasis was placed on the oral tradition collected in the area of field research. The area included the districts of Poona, Satara, Kolhapur, Belgaum, Sangli, Sholapur, Osmanabad, Aurangabad and Ahmednagar. As far as possible ethnography, history, archaeology, iconography and epigraphy were used as a corrective while studying these oral traditions. And, of course, we have had the important works of Professor Khare himself, of Professor D.D. Kosambi (with whom I first visited the Dhangars in the years 1958-61), Irawati Karve, R.C. Dhere, G.A. Deleury, Durga Bhagwat, M.S. Mate, Sarojini Babar, and many others. The confidence placed in Gazetteers or Enthoven's work inter al. can sometimes be misleading and disappointing.

Before discussing the oral traditions the written sources should not be forgotten: the Purāṇas (e.g. the Kāśīkhaṇḍa), the Māhātmyas (in Sanskrit, Marāṭhī, and Kannaḍa), published and unpublished, local *pothīs* and the numerous, obscure temple leaflets and brochures, which are helpful initially and are by no means to be despised. But caution is necessary, because such texts may reflect a certain developed and consolidated stage of the cult while ignoring the aspect that the cult was or is closely associated with a pastoral group. Or the author may express the particular predilections of the community to which he belongs. In one case a Brahman author had composed an eulogy of a Dhangar cult in *ovī*-form (unpolished *pothī*). The work contained some hints on the history of the cult. Most of the work, however, was interesting insofar as it showed how a local (local at least in the view of the composer) Dhangar cult was interpreted in an idiom and with a mentality to suit a more sophisticated supralocal audience with a taste for Sanskrit. E.g. the name of the village was, on account of a superficial phonological similarity, associated with the Ṛṣi Kauṇḍinya. In general one can experience, as one would expect, that putting down in writing by *mānkarīs*, *pujārīs* and enthusiastic *bhaktas* erases the local or regional historical niceties and—if one can use the expression—'universalizes'[2] the local or regional history of cult.

The *Śrīnāth M(h)askobā devāce Caritra* of Vīr in the Purandar Taluka of the Poona District is rather an exception to this situation.[3] The text seems to have been agreed upon by all communities involved in the cult and, in fact, has achieved a kind of scriptural authority in the village. The little book, of which the first edition appeared in 1889, vividly depicts how a pastoral cult brought by immigrant Dhangars becomes a cult of all castes and is identified with Kālabhairava, how religious rights (*mān*) are required and enjoyed, what festivals and rites are performed as well as the connection of village and cult to king Shāhū of Sātārā, etc. As the book is a local authority the inquirer will be referred to its contents by members of all castes; 'It is all in the book'—was the persistent answer initially. After repeated visits and stays different details, aspects and prior stages of the cult were revealed. Additional oral texts could be collected, especially from illiterate devotees of the cult, e.g. Gosāvīs and Dhangars, who came from Ahmednagar and Satara Districts. Besides, the history of the cult could only be explained by tracing the route of the god backwards; this leads us to Mhasvad, where the god is called Śīd (Skt. *siddha*) and Śidobā or towards Atpadi (Sonārī Śīd) to Kharsuṇḍī (Kharsuṇḍī Śīd), to Bilur near Jath, and, finally, north towards Sonārī near Parenda in the Osmanabad District, from where the god was brought by the Dhangars. The booklet says 'Sonārī in the Belgaum district'[4] but this slip may have been made owing to a misunderstanding by the author of his source of information by bringing together two areas that lie at the two opposite ends of a pastoral region. Because between Sonārī in the northern Osmanabad District with its important Bhairava cult centre and the southern Belgaum with Cinclī (a cattle-market for Khilārī bulls and the eventual home of Mayevvā, the foster-sister of the god Birobā) was rather an area of pastoralism and of movements of pastoralists than an area of settled agriculturists before the great extension of regular plough cultivation in post-British times. Even if one goes to Sonārī, or rather to the older village Kandārī, a few miles to the north of Sonārī, one finds that the village has grown out of four *vastīs*. The inhabitants of one of the *vastīs* were Gavaḷīs, of another Gosāvīs. The predecessors, who were 'thieves' (*bhamṭyā*), disappeared. Such 'thieves' or 'robbers' are frequent concomitants of early settlement (cf. Corācī Alandi, Corācī Undavḍī, etc.).

Thus, in comparison the Mhaskobā of Vīr is a young cult; it has come from the East and it marks a final stage and settling of a group of Dhangars who moved not so much between north and south, but between east and west. Even today many of the Haṭkar (Khilārī) Dhangars move with their sheep towards the West to the Māvaḷ up the Nirā Valley after the rainy season, and return to the Desh with the beginning of the rainy season. That their routes are at times prehistoric is shown by microliths in many places of their habitation and areas of movement.[5] Kamaḷājī Śīd, the Dhangar who brought Mhaskobā, had his *vāḍā* on the bank of the Nirā river, where the god first appeared. At that time there was there forest and scrub jungle. Today there is the first temple of Mhaskobā and not far from the temple towards the east (near the leper colony) a good assemblage of microliths was found, though the soil of the upper bank has been disturbed by the left-hand canal.

The canals of the Vīr Dam effected a lot of change, e.g. agriculture with irrigation drove an important Dhangar group from the left bank (Limbut) to the foothills of Śingnapūr (Jāvāli). And yet it is still acknowledged that the god of Limbut, Bhairava, was 'brought by a Dhangar from Kāśī' and the temple record shows the names of the Dhangars involved in the cult and their present dispersion.

The *Māhātmya* of the popular Someśvar of Karanje[6] shows us who were there before the area developed into a part of the sugar-cane belt: probably a Gosāvī (*sādhu*) pointed out the god who could give a child to the Gavaḷī woman Malubāī. The *Māhātmya* studied in context teaches us two things: how and by whom the knowledge of gods was spread and the existence of Gavaḷīs at the origin of the cult. Even today one can see the deserted ruins of Gavaḷī-vāḍās, e.g. near Guḷunce near the town of Nirā on a foothill of a larger hill. Today there are few Gavaḷīs; they have disappeared because the spreading of agriculture has deteriorated and diminished pastures, and jungles have vanished. Their successors, the Dhangars, can at the most keep sheep, though they are known to have kept herds of cows and bullocks (*khilārī*) in the same area, and especially outside the famine tract. Some cults, like the Bābīr of Rūī near Nhāvī (Indapur Taluka, with a large number of microliths to the South of the present temple), which deserves a study by itself, and the Masan-Vīr of Vālhā, have been Gavaḷī cults. The *pujārīs* of the Bābīr are even now Gavaḷīs but the *bhaktas* are mainly Dhangars.

Even more important (and grossly underestimated) than the *written literature* are the innumerable *oral traditions*. A large number of them were collected in some sixty places including villages, Dhangarvāḍīs and temples in the area of field research. The oral traditions are essentially of three types:

(1) Myths and legends of gods, saints (*śīds*) and temples from the Dhangars and Gavaḷīs contained in *ovīs*.
(2) Traditions relating to the local history, especially village and temple traditions, told by members of all castes.
(3) Personal recollections and experiences of Dhangar elders, but also of other generations.

Personal observations of the present social conditions and the customs of the Dhangars served to elucidate the texts, written as well as oral. We shall mainly refer here to (1) which consists of a collection of *ovīs* of such deities and saints as Suravantī, Birobā, Satobā, Iṭṭhal-Birobā, Khaṇḍobā (Mailār, Mallaṇṇa), Yellammā, Yeḷu Gāvlan, Bābir, Mhaskobā, Kālabhairava, Śidobā, Birobā-Nāgobā, Dhuḷobā-Bhivāī-Kamaḷā Śīd (Śindhe)-Dariappā Malingrayā Mālappā, Arkeri Amokśiddh, Khilubā Bhakta, Kanhobā, etc. It proved not to be sufficient to collect one version of an *ovī* of a god from one place. A single version may be of interest to the folklorist, who has other objects in mind and for whom epic, legends, tales, fables, and riddles are equally important as far as literary value and linguistic analysis are concerned. But even the folklorist may do well not only to collect, e.g. one *ovī* of Suravantī and Birobā from one particular place. If this is collected from many places he may not only be able to detach local accretions, but may thus even be able to isolate the skeleton of the *ovī* and may even find how, from where and from which source the myth has originated.[7] Not only the contents, but also the style of singing the *ovī* has regional variations, e.g. in Kolhapur, Sangli, the Maṅgaḷveḍhā Taluka of Sholapur, Karnatak, and in the Nīrā-Bhīmā-Valley. The oldest generation in Kolhapur in the village of Paṭṭan Kuḍoḷī still retains an antiquated style of singing, less ornate than the new style, which is imported from Sangli and is much more melodious and rhythmical. The semi-nomadic Dhangars of the hills bordering the Bhīmā-Karhā and Nīrā-Valleys sing in a style which gives one the impression of being much more antiquated and original. Contents of *ovīs* can differ substantially from region to region. Take, e.g. some features of a version from Kuṇḍal (Sangli District) of an episode from Birobā's life. The little god was borne by Suravantī through immaculate conception. He is an incarnation of the god *Bāvan Vīr*, who had been placed by Śaṅkar in the form of an atom in Suravantī's *thāli*. After the son was born he was—after an abortive attempt to kill him—exposed by the king's servants in a dry and lonely forest. There he was found by two sisters, huntresses, by name Ekavvā and Māyevvā. The two became the foster-sisters of Birobā. [We never hear in this version what was happened to Suravantī after Birobā was exposed.] Eventually the two foster-sisters and Birobā came after a long migration to Cinclī in Belgaum District. Cinclī's Māyevvā (Skt. Mahākalī) is Birobā's sister and Birobā spent his youth in Cinclī. In this version the two sisters were created by Śaṅkar from his ash and from Parbatī's *kukū* in the *hom*-altar.

In the second version—which is part of an *ovī* from a little Dhangarvāḍī called Algujdarā near Rākh in the Purandar Taluka—the origin of Ekavvā, and Māyevvā is given. After the child has been exposed in the forest we hear:

बालूबयाचा वाडां का। लेकी हाकाया म्हाकाया।
नितं पारदी जावाचा। नितं शिकारी जायाच्या।
नाही पोटी ना काइ फळ। नाही दिरव्याला काइ तॉटा।
नऊ लाखाची तान्ही का। नऊ लाखाची जाणी का।
भाकडा गणतं लागना। गाया म्हशीचं खिलार।
गडी तिनी ओ ठेवल। गन गावडं ठेवल।

[There was] the *vāḍā* of Bālubāī. [Her] daughters [were] Hākāyā and Mhākāyā
[They] always went hunting. Always went for *śikār*.
There was no fruit in their womb at all. There was no lack of wealth.
Nine *lākhs* of lambs. Nine *lākhs* of sheep.[8]
[One] could not count the milkless [barren] animals. A herd of cows and buffaloes.
She kept servants. A host of Gāvaḍās [herdsmen] she kept.

In the light of other evidence a single passage like this may lead to further information. Bālūbāī or Bānubāī (Bānāī-Bālāī) is, according to another version, from Jāvaḷī near Śikhar-Śingnapūr, the *mirdhīn*, i.e. the head of twelve Dhangarvāḍās who protected Birobā's sheep.[9] Bānubāī is also said to be from a Gāvaḍā family and especially those Dhangars who kept cattle were called Gāvaḍās.[10] The phrases *nine lākh* and *twelve vāḍās* are constantly recurring and widespread expressions among the Dhangars and may reflect something of their former importance.

The reference to the *twelve vāḍās* of the Dhangars recurs in the name of the Haṭkar Dhangars of the Parbhani District, who are called the *bārā haṭṭikars*—the 'twelve *haṭṭikars*'—and *bārā haṭṭi*, meaning the twelve settlements or 'countries' of the Haṭkar Dhangars.[11] In Hunner, a Birobā centre in the Maṅgaḷveḍhā Taluka of the Sholapur District, the term occurred in a prose version of an *ovī* about Birobā [the text is left 'unimproved']: [Birobā asks Śiva]

तर बाराहट्टी म्हनून्शानी गाव हाय म्हनला येक।
बारा हट्टी म्हन्जे धारा वाड्या येक गाव हाय म्हन्ला।
तित एक डोंगर हाय म्हनला त्या डोंगरावर जाऊन बस।
आन् त्या बाराहट्टी म्हन्ला धनगराचा वाडा हाय म्हन्ला।
तत त्या वाड्याव (र) म्हन्ला मायावा नावाची मुलगी हाय।

'Then what should I do?' [Birobā asks Śiva and Śiva answers:] 'There is a village called *bārāhaṭṭi*, which means a twelve-vade village. There is a mountain. Go and sit on the mountain and in this *bārāhaṭṭi* Dhangar-vāḍā there is a girl called Māyavvā. . . .'

Thus S.B. Joshi is right when he derives from the term *haṭṭi/hāṭa*, etc., *vāḍī/vāḍā*, *pāḍi/pāḍā*, etc., the terms *haṭṭikara* (which, as he shows, is a synonym of *govāḷi* in old Kannaḍa lexica) and Haṭkar rather than leaving the matter rest at the secondary popular etymology of Haṭkar *haṭa* ('stubborn').[12]

Bānubāī or Bālubāī is, of course, well known as the second wife or keep of Khaṇḍobā, and Professor Khare has shown how widespread is the association of Khaṇḍobā with the Dhangar or Kuruba wife.[13] The stay of Khaṇḍobā/Mailār with the shepherds, his marriage being a kind of *rākṣasa* or *gandharva* marriage, and many other features indicate the king's contact with groups outside settled agricultural life and his association with these groups, e.g. through Hegaḍe, the Dhangar minister. One beautiful *ovī* from Chitalenagar near Māḷśiras depicts in detail the life of Khaṇḍobā and his service as a herdsman amongst the Dhangars. One story[14] is that Bāṇāī was one of the daughters of Indra who because of her presumptuousness was reduced by Indra to the size of a little child, kept in a box, and left in the jungle of Candanpur. Some Dhangars who were grazing their sheep found her. . . .

Eventually, Khaṇḍobā accepted service and looked after the sheep. One day he went to the river, skinned the sheep and goats, severing the meat from the bones. Bāṇāī accepted the offer of marriage reluctantly in return of the revival of the sheep and goats. He took her along on his horse and she recognized Khaṇḍobā. After the marriage festivity which was arranged by the Dhangars he went with her to Jejuri. . . .

In another *ovī* from Kolvihire near Jejuri we learn at the beginning that Khaṇḍobā went hunting. When he was thirsty, he found a Dhangar who refused to give him water. . . . [the story of Bāṇāī follows] . . .

Hunting, skinning of sheep (like game), the association with the Dhangars, the river (where the sheep should have been washed by Khaṇḍobā as a servant)—all these pieces taken together remind us of the annual Somvatī Festival when Khaṇḍobā is carried to the Karhā River near Jejuri for his ritual bath. The Dhangars consider this procession a hunting excursion. Formerly, the hunting party used to go up to the *māl* at the Bhuleśvara Temple on the opposite ridge of the Karhā Valley, and deer and tigers were hunted. Today, of course, at the most a rabbit can be caught and the lucky hunter is supposed to sprinkle some blood on the *pālkhī*. I have never seen during my observations of the festival anything being caught during the procession, and the large crowd certainly would drive away a rabbit if there is any left in the area. But anybody who sees the numerous Dhangars trooping with their spears [*jhendā*, *barsi*] in quick speed in front of the *pālkhī* to be on time to participate in the ritual bath would agree to this interpretation of the ceremony whatever other aspects it may have picked up in the course of time.

That the Dhangars were leaning towards hunting and were warriors (like the Rāmośīs) is not difficult to show. Here we shall only point out that in one pictorial representation of Khaṇḍobā with four arms he has in his left front arm a lance or spear exactly of the type many of the Haṭkar Dhangars carry and worship today.[15] The Haṭkar Dhangars carry a spear which has below its blade—now mostly blunted by a knot—a small woollen wreath (*goṇḍā*) symbolizing Lakṣmī, the wealth of the Dhangars consisting of sheep and wool. This leads to another digression: The lance (*veḷ*) of Murukaṉ. There is more and more evidence accumulating about the basic identity of Murukaṉ, Malhārī, Mailār, Mallaṇṇa, Khaṇḍobā, Kārttikeya, and Skanda.[16] At the root of all these deities is a prototype of a god of the hills, a warrior and hunter being associated with pastoral groups who are not necessarily nomadic and often cultivate millets. The integration of these groups into the fold of regular plough cultivation and 'Sanskritic' culture is the next step and is still going on. Regional variations may sometimes blur this basic identity.

There is much similarity between Birobā and Khaṇḍobā. One common aspect is that both of them are warriors having a horse and a sword, and that they fight against demons. Like Khaṇḍobā, Birobā is not actually a shepherd. Often we find that a *meṇḍhaka*, a shepherd, is created by Birobā to look after the sheep. His name is Māyājī. There are temples of Birobā and Māyājī or Māyabā, e.g. in Odhane near Supe. In one *ovī* from Jeūr near Nirā we hear that after the birth of Birobā his name has to be established by the Brahman: After some search he found that his *khatri* (*kṣatriya*) name was Birobā and his ordinary name was Tāyajī. Tāyajī and Māyajī [T(S)āyaba and Māyabā] reoccur as names of two Gavaḷī brothers who migrated to Corācī Ālandī bringing with them a god who is called Mhātobā.[17] Their names also occur in connection with Bābīr. It is tempting to see a relationship[18] between *Cēyōn̲* (Murukan̲), the god of the hills and the god of war, and *Māyōn̲* (the shepherd god Kṛṣṇa) on the one hand and Khaṇḍobā/Birobā/Sāyabā and Māyā (Kṛṣṇa), or rather Viṭhobā, the Gavaḷī.[19]

What then about Aiyanār? R.C. Dhere takes up the suggestion of his identity with Khaṇḍobā.[20] I think there is more similarity between Aiyanār and our Mhaskobā/Bhairava. Like Aiyanār he is essentially a village *kṣetrapāl* for all his pastoral seminomadic past and not so much a territorial god like Murukan̲ and Khaṇḍobā. But Aiyanār has two wives, one may object, and Mhaskobā apparently only one: Jogeśvarī/Jogāī. But there are traditions told by Gosāvīs about Bālubāī being the second wife of Mhaskobā, though she is not installed in the temple at Vīr. This becomes clearer if one goes to Kharsuṇḍī or Biḷur near Jath in the Sangli District, where Jogubāī is said to have come with Kālabhairava from Kāśī whereas Bālubāī, his dearest wife, has come from Sūrdī with her brother. There is much homogeneity between this cult at Biḷur and Mhaskobā's cult at Vīr, again showing their common pastoral past. These cults are historically and structurally related in many respects.

Only a few hints could be given here as to how field research or the 'study of texts in context' (to use an expression by Milton Singer) may yield further information on the history of cults and the communities associated with them.

NOTES

1. The author acknowledges with gratitude the many-sided help of Dr. S.N. Bhavasar and Mr. R.P. Nene. Mr. R.B. Zagade helped (and still helps) transcribing tape-recorded texts. Mr. R.S. Atkar was an indispensable assistant by way of driving me in a jeep under all conditions. The research was partly financed by the German Research Association and the South Asia Institute of the University of Heidelberg. I am most grateful to these institutions.

2. See McKim Marriott, 'Little Communities in an Indigenous Civilization', in: McKim Marriott (ed.), *Village India, Studies in the Little Community*, Chicago, Phoenix edn., 1969, p. 197.
3. Hari Bālakṛṣṇa Āroḷe, *Śrīnāth Maskobā devāce Caritra*, Vīr, 4th edn. [1971]. I have not seen the first edition of 1889; there is no change in the two following editions. A translation of the booklet, together with additional texts and an analysis of the cult, has been completed.
4. P. 4.
5. See D.D. Kosambi, *Myth and Reality*, Bombay, 1952, Chs. III and IV. In general Kosambi's theory of the coincidence of microlithic routes, area of Dhangar habitation, cult spots and the pastoral Dhangars was confirmed by further finds.
6. *Śrī Somnātha Māhātmya* (in Marāṭhī) Ambavade, 15th ed., Śake 1888 (AD 1966), Ch. I. See also S.G. Bokil, 'Śri Someśvar-Karanje', in *Puruṣārtha*, June-July 1963, pp. 328f.
7. Such a critical edition of the *ovīs* is under preparation.
8. Local explanations of *tanhi* and *jani*.
9. *Mirdha* means, according to Molesworth, *A Marathi-English Dictionary*, a village-overseer, the captain of spearmen that precede *rajas* and grandees. The term is quite common around Jejuri and means a leader of a Dhangarvāḍā.
10. Sakhārām Bābu Lakaḍe (Dhangar) from Jāvalī. Cp. Molesworth, s.v. the *adhikārī* among the Dhangar people?; *gāvaḍī*—a cow (in Khandesh). In Kannaḍa the term occurs as *gauḍa*. The surname *gauḍā* occurs among the Dhangars in Kolhapur and Karnatak.
11. See Syed Siraj ul Hassan, *The Castes and Tribes of H.E.H. The Nizam's Dominions*, Bombay, 1920, pp. 248f.
12. S.B. Joshi, 'Etymology of Place-names Paṭṭi-Haṭṭi', in vol. 13 (1952) *ABORI*, pp. 50ff. Id., *Marhāṭi Sanskṛti*, Mumbai, 1952, pp. 37ff.
13. *Mahārāṣṭrācīm cār daivatem*, B.I.S.M., Puṇem, 1958, pp. 87ff.
14. Told in R.C. Dhere's *Khaṇḍobā*, Puṇem 2, 1961, pp. 52f.
15. Śrī-māṇika-prabhu-kṛta *sacitra Malhārī Māhātmya* [in Marāṭhī], āvṛtti 1 li, Belagāṃva, 1917. In his right front he holds the usual sword.
16. See now, e.g., Asim Kumar Chatterjee, *The Cult of Skanda-Kārttikeya in Ancient India*, Calcutta, 1970. H. Bechert shows that the old Tamil god Sēyōṉ/Murukaṉ lives on in Ceylon as Kataragama deviyo, adding that the essential features of the old south Indian religion have been better preserved by the Singhalese than by the Dravidians of South India and that, accordingly, the comparison between the two cultures of South India and Ceylon would yield interesting results. But we suggest that the study of 'popular' cults in Western and South India can equally well yield information of the earlier stages of religion in South India. See H. Bechert, 'Eine alte Gottheit in Ceylon und Südindien', in *Beiträge zur Geistesgeschichte in Indien, Festschrift für Erich Frauwallner*, Wien 1968, pp. 33-42.
17. See D.D. Kosambi, op. cit., p. 147.

18. This was suggested to me by Professor Hermann Berger.
19. See Durga Bhagwat, 'Paṇḍhāricā Viṭhobā', in *Satyakathā*, July 1969, p. 27. In this story Viṭhobā is said to have been a *maṇḍalik* ('princeling') of Malhārīdev-Khaṇḍobā. Viṭhobā lived in Māḷśiras. The story of Viṭhobā, M(a)hāliṅgrāyā, Viṭhal, Pādubāī-Rukmiṇi, and the Viṭhal-Birobā cult has been told on the basis of a version from Paṭṭan Kuḍolī in a forthcoming article.
20. Dhere, op. cit., p. 29. See also on Aiyanār Louis Dumont, 'Definition Structurale d'un dieu populaire Tamoul, Aiyanar, le maitre', *Journal Asiatique*, 1953, pp. 255-70.

The Dhangars: A Nomadic Pastoral Community in a Developing Agricultural Environment

gelāmelā pāūs paḍelac koṅkaṇāṃt
'At all events it will rain in the Konkan'
(MOLESWORTH, *A Dictionary, Marāṭhī and English*, s.v. *gelā*)

THE HAṬKAR DHANGARS

The community with which we propose to deal are Dhangars who call themselves Haṭkar-Dhangars or Khilārī-Dhangars to distinguish themselves from other Dhangar communities in the same area. Some of these communities or endogamous divisions which the Dhangars of our area mention, if asked, are the Saṇgars, who weave *ghoṅgaḍīs* (coarse woollen blankets), Mhaskars (or Mhaskes), who rear buffaloes, and Khuṭekars, who also weave blankets. We have come across Saṇgars in the Man Taluka of the Satara District and in the Khanapur Taluka of the Sangli District. Khuṭekars seem to be spread over a very large region in central, western and southern Maharashtra.[1] The Haṭkars claim to be socially higher than the Khuṭekars, and a caste legend, ubiquitous in our area, tells how the Khuṭekars had to abandon their occupation as shepherds:

Formerly the god Birobā had entrusted the Khuṭekars with the tending of sheep. Many years passed, but one day a Khuṭekar Dhangar wanted to attend a marriage. He did not find anybody who was able to keep the sheep properly. Thus he put them into the holes of an anthill and covered the anthill with branches of a thorny, dry bush. The anthill was situated in a field and the farmer came to plough it. The anthill was hit by the plough and the sheep came out like ants [i.e. one after the other in a row]. The farmer wondered what they could be and he set fire to the branches. Thus some of the sheep were burnt black, some got red, some snuff-coloured patches and so on in various shades of colour [the origin of the colour of the sheep]. Birobā decided that the Khuṭekars were not able to keep the sheep properly and he called for the Haṭkars and entrusted them with the care of the sheep, whereas the Khuṭekars were to weave clothes [i.e. the *ghoṅgaḍīs*] out of the wool of the sheep. But the Khuṭekars objected and said that they had been in charge of the sheep from the beginning and that they would not leave their ancestral profession. To resolve the dispute between the two groups Birobā resorted to an ordeal. Haṭkars and Khuṭekars were to stand side by side and the one to whom the sheep would turn, to him would go the right of keeping the sheep: the sheep went to the Haṭkars.

One may also see some historical element of the origin of the Haṭkars in this legend. The Haṭkars were not sheep-keepers originally, but, if not husbandmen, then Khilārīs, migrating cattle people, who for one reason or the other took to sheep-keeping in our area. We shall return to this point.

Sometimes the number of the endogamous divisions is given as 'three and a half', including the Haṭkars, Mhaskars, Khuṭekars, and the Khāṭīks as a 'half caste'. The Khāṭīks are also called Kasāis, according to Enthoven, and seem to have been recruited from Marathas and Dhangars who apparently originally sold only the meat of sheep and goats, but who eventually took to butchering as well, like the Muslim members of the same caste.[2] The number 'three and a half' is not chosen at random,[3] but it is auspicious, the 'half' indicating the somewhat qualified auspiciousness of that caste.[4] The *endogamous* divisions of the Dhangars thus vary in different areas and the names given by Enthoven are probably not exhaustive, nor are the *exogamous* divisions given by Enthoven, which are identical with the surnames, exhaustive.[5]

We did not come across the word 'Bargi Dhangars'='Dhangars with the spear' as another name for the Haṭkar Dhangars, although it is mentioned in Syed ul Hassan's '*The Castes and Tribes of H.E.H. The Nizam's Dominions*'.[6] Many of the Dhangars do carry spears, with or without a knot on the tip of the blade.[7] These spears are now only objects of worship. They are often kept in ancestor shrines and are worshipped in the morning. But once a year their chief, original function seems to come to life again at the big Somvatī pilgrimage/fair (*jatrā*) at Jejuri in the month of Śrāvaṇa (August/September). One of the favourite gods of the Dhangars, Khaṇḍobā is taken in a hunting procession to the Karha River two miles from the temple. He is received at the outskirts of the little town by a huge gathering of Dhangars equipped with spears who then troop at fast speed ahead of the *pālkhī* (palanquin), to be on time to participate in the ritual bath of the god. A person who kills a hare or a deer on the way—the latter a rare feat now in view of the lack of game and the large crowd attending the fair—is considered to be especially lucky, and some blood from the animal is put on the god's (the *mūrti's*) forehead. The connection between Khaṇḍobā, the Dhangars, and the annual hunt is further reflected in a very rare pictorial representation of Khaṇḍobā who generally carries a sword, but in this case in addition holds a spear of exactly the type used by the Haṭkar Dhangars.[8] Though there is an element of hunting and war in the past of the Dhangars—an element they share with the Rāmośīs, the ex-brigands and ardent devotees of Khaṇḍobā who have the special right to carry the *pālkhī* of the god at the rear during the Somvatī festival—, the Dhangars are pastoralists who now tend sheep and goats. We do not mean to include here those Haṭkar Dhangars who are settled farmers.

The nomadic, pastoral Haṭkar Dhangar men (and boys, as soon as they are able) wear a typical dark-red turban, a *langoṭī* (loin-cloth, which is gradually being replaced by the *dhotar*), and heavy *cappals* suited for the life of a shepherd. They carry a *kāṭhī*, a staff, which not only serves obvious worldly purposes, but tends to have ritual purposes as well, and the *ghoṅgaḍī*—the coarse blanket which provides protection against rain, wind, and sun and is courteously spread as the seat for a guest if no felt (*jen*) is at hand. Most of the men wear earrings for which the upper part of the ear is pierced, finger-rings, and occasional anklets and the *kargoṭā*, a silver chain around the waist. Not so much the dress as rather a more generous number of necklaces, nose-rings, arm-rings, and anklets distinguishes Dhangar women from those of the Kuṇbīs/Marathas, Māḷīs, and other castes.

If we use the word 'Dhangars' in the following discussion we are aware that there exist many other endogamous 'Dhangar' groups with exogamous divisions, including nomadic pastoralists and settled farmers, who live in Maharashtra and share many common material, cultural, religious and other traits, even though these groups may not be of the same ethnic stock.[9] In short, there is sufficient variation to deal with these groups in a broader context, but their description and discussion would go far beyond the scope of this paper. By sometimes using the term 'group' or 'community', we seek to avoid a narrower discussion of where to place the Haṭkars on the 'tribe-caste continuum'.[10] The substantial part played in India by groups of nomadic shepherds and cattle-herders[11] and village-based cattle-herders, especially the fact of their long existence side by side with the settled agricultural communities, their spatial separatedness,[12] their economy, and their contributions to the formation of Indian culture, have been generally ignored in scholarly discussions. Their existence in Indian history, if not their survival today, may justify (at least in the historical approach) their recognition as another group between the 'tribe' of the forest on the one hand and the interdependent, local 'caste' at the other extreme.

THE HABITAT OF THE DHANGARS—OUR AREA OF INVESTIGATION

The seasonal monsoon camps or settlements of the group described are roughly situated beyond a vertical line drawn about 10-20 miles east of Poona. The northern area includes the southern part of Ahmednagar District and is delimited to the south by the Mahadev Range and the valley of the Man River (dominated by the hill temple of the Mahadev of Shingnapur) and in the south-east by the Khanapur- and Jath-Plateau. In the east we shall not go beyond a vertical line drawn from Pandharpur in the south to Parenda in the north-east. We are here especially concerned with the Dhangars living in the high valley of the Karha River (Sasvad Basin), and in the foothills and the hill range (Phaltan Range) which separates the Nira Valley from the Man Valley. The area is part of the so-called Desh (*deś*), that is, the Deccan Plateau, and does not belong to the Maval (*māvaḷ*), the area near the Western Ghats, nor to the Konkan, the coastal region. The Census of 1961 shows that the districts in this area, namely Poona, Satara, Ahmednagar, Sangli, and Sholapur, have the largest number of sheep in Maharashtra, each having 200,000-300,000 sheep.[13] Though many Dhangars migrate from this area after the end of the rainy season and stay near the Western Ghats and in the Konkan (Kolaba District) for seven months, their traditional habitat is the area just outlined.

Other nomadic or semi-nomadic groups live in the north-western part of the Sangli District, the eastern part of the Sholapur District and the south-western and north-western parts of the Osmanabad District. Though their migration patterns differ from those of the groups described here, and their ethnic origin may be different, they are inhabitants of a traditionally pastoral area rather than of a traditionally agricultural area.

ENVIRONMENTAL FACTORS IN THE AREA, ESPECIALLY RAINFALL

One important factor in tracing the culture and economy, the annual migrations and the temporary settling—now in more or less fixed settlements—of the Dhangars, is rainfall.[14] The area receives rain mainly from the south-west monsoon, which lasts from the beginning of June to the end of October. In the Poona District we can distinguish three zones. The western zone, reaching up to Poona, has an average annual rainfall of 4,500 mm in Lonavla, situated in the Western Ghats on the Bombay Poona railway line. Poona, situated in the central zone, has an annual average of 750 mm, and the talukas of Baramati and Indapur in the east can expect an annual average of less than 500 mm. The Poona area gets most of its rainfall from the south-west monsoon. There is a sharp decrease in the amount of rainfall if we go from the western zone towards the east into the central zone. A further decrease is found in the eastern zone, comprising the talukas of Baramati, Dhond, and Indapur and the eastern part of the Haveli, Junnar, Shirur and Purandar Talukas. Often, heavy rains in Poona do not reach the eastern zone. The north-east monsoon also rarely sends sufficient showers to the eastern zone; they remain few and erratic. *A Fact-finding Committee* on the reliability of rainfall in the Poona District appointed by the then Government of Bombay reported in 1960 an estimated frequency of scarcity conditions once each three years or six years exactly in those talukas, or parts of them, where we find an abundance of Dhangar settlements (*vāḍīs*).[15]

The pattern of rainfall is not much different in the Satara District. The talukas of Khatav, Man, and Phaltan, that is the eastern zone of the district, have an average annual rainfall of less than 600 mm, much less than the central zone, which receives an annual average rainfall from 600 mm to 1,200 mm. In the Phaltan Taluka the soil is poor and stony in the vicinity of hills, but there are good black soils along the Nira and its tributary streams. In the Khatav Taluka, soils are of intermediate depth and more widely spread than in the Man Taluka, but not as rich as in the Koregaon Taluka. In the Man Taluka, the soils are extremely poor and shallow. Good soil is found only in narrow strips along the streams. Between those streams lie wide stretches of *māḷ*, fit only for poor crops like *bājrī* (*Holcus spicatus*) or for grass. Grass grown on *māḷ* land is, however, of a good quality and accounts for the large number of cattle and sheep bred in the taluka. The most remarkable fact is that in the two eastern talukas of Khatav and Man, with their uncertain rainfall, water is reached at a moderate depth when wells are sunk.

If we shift to the Sangli District, we find again that the north-eastern part, which includes the talukas of Khanapur and Jath, has the lowest amount of rainfall of the district, with an annual average of about 500 mm. The eastern zone is again a scarcity area and has low rainfall in the western talukas of Sangola and Karmala, and in the southern part of the Malshiras Taluka, though the eastern talukas, with somewhat assured rainfall, have not been free from droughts and famines in the past. In fact the whole district is generally a scarcity area. The annual average rainfall is 625 mm. The Barshi Taluka, which is situated in the north-east, has an annual average of 725 mm. The major parts of the Osmanabad District in the north-east of our area are under the influence of the north-east monsoon, namely the talukas of Latur, Udgir, Ahmadpur, Tuljapur, and Osmanabad, though the Parenda Taluka and Bhum Mahal, which are situated in the rainshadow of the south-west monsoon, get only about 600 mm of annual average rainfall.

In the north of our area a major portion of the Ahmednagar District lies in the zone of low rainfall, and receives an annual average of 508 to 638 mm. Only six out of thirteen talukas are free from scarcity conditions. These six are situated in the west (Akola Taluka) and in the north (Godavari Basin).

Our area is characterized, generally speaking, by irregular rainfall, black soils along the rivers which need cultivation with 8, 10 or even 12 bullocks, and *māḷ(-rān)*, that is, elevated stony land, hilly tracts, and the skirts of the mountains, which are suitable for pasture or the growing of *bājrī* (*Holcus spicatus*) and *jvārī* (*Holcus sorghum*). It was an area which would probably have prompted the classical Tamil poets to describe it as *mullai* or a pastoral region[16], except that here, for jasmine creepers, we would find the characteristic *bābhūḷ* (*Acacia arabica*) tree, favoured by sheep, and *hivar* (*Mimosa tomentosa*) or *neem* (*Azadirachta Indica*) trees. Some parts of the area correspond with the Tamil description of *pālai*, a region which emerges in the hot season and is devoid of vegetation, with dry lakes and tanks, where caravans and merchants are endangered by marauding tribals, as, e.g., by the Koḷīs or the Rāmośīs.[17] Partially this was the past, because the spreading of agriculture supported by irrigation has now turned the area more and more into one of settled farming. But the point we want to make is that in Indian history—at a time when the pressure on land was less than what it became after the advent of the Pax Britannica—there were areas which were the habitats of forest tribes (food-gatherers and hunters, with or without slash- and-burn cultivation), of pastoral nomads and cattle-based villages, of settled communities with regular plough cultivation (primarily the rice area), sea-fishermen (Konkan), and even robbers. The poetic conventions which divided Tamilnadu into five regions had a basis in fact that may also be discerned in the past of Maharashtra and in the survivals of today.

SOME HISTORICAL REFERENCES

Though we find towns in the area, they do not yet share the importance of the larger cities of Poona, Satara, Karhad, and Kolhapur in the west, or Sholapur in the east, nor do they belong to the earliest settlements in these districts. Phaltan, e.g., known from an inscription of the seventh century, is now a rising agricultural centre because of the Nira canal system, but in 1854 it was primarily a trading post for the exchange of goods from the interior and the coast, the goods being carried by bullocks.[18] The route led from Sholapur and via Pandharpur, Phaltan, Bhor and the Varandha Pass, to the coast. One of the earliest towns is Mhasvad (in the Man Taluka), which is mentioned in an inscription of the twelfth century (AD 1138), when this place was ruled from Mangalvedha (in the Sholapur District) by an ancestor of the Kalachurya king Bijjala of Kalyana.[19] Mhasvad itself is mentioned as Mahiṣa-vāḍā in G.H. Khare's *Persian Sources of Indian History*[20] and has been, as the name suggests, a settlement of people with buffaloes. According to the oral tradition of the temple, Mhasvad was a settlement of Gavḷīs, i.e., cattle keepers. The first inscription relating to the god Khaṇḍobā of Jejuri (in the Purandar Taluka of the Poona District) dates back to the year 1246,[21] and a tradition written down in approximately the year 1750 tells us of cowherd boys who first saw the god.[22] The popular god Someshvar at Karanje near Nira was brought, according to a tradition, by a Gavḷī woman from Saurashtra (Somnath).[23] The list could be increased considerably to show that many cults in this area originated from pastoral cults which developed into cults of settled castes, often with the pastoralists having an acknowledged part in the 'history' of the temple and in the ritual of the cult.

Regular plough cultivation does not seem to have been introduced successfully in a large area or for a long period before British times. Though we have in many places Hemāḍ Pantī temples which suggest some regular cultivation at some nuclear settlements, they have become abandoned or adapted to the service of more popular cults.[24]

The area encompasses the 'famous' famine tract and has seen many famines, of which the Durgā Devī-Famine (1396-1407) was the first recorded.[25] There are still many local traditions which tell the story of past famines. The wars between Marathas and the kingdom of Bijapur or the Mughals and others did not promote the extension of regular plough cultivation. Sometimes a 'scorched earth' policy was resorted to, for example by the kings of Ahmednagar, Vijayanagar and Bijapur, around 1562[26], or the armies of Yaśvant Rāv Hoḷkar in 1802.[27] Periods of famine, which often resulted in political unrest and exaction by rulers, discouraged regular plough cultivation. Cattle, which could be moved to another area if there was a drought, or hidden in a ravine if there was a threat from enemies, were therefore equally, if not more, valuable than land[28] (see. Plate III, a and b). As V.T. Gune remarks, it appears that after the fall of the Yādavas of Deogirī and during the Sultanate of the Deccan, no attempt was made till the middle of the fifteenth century to settle the proper revenue divisions. The land was covered with grass and the occupation of the people was cattle breeding.[29] It is small wonder that Dādajī Kondadev (d. 1647), the regent of Shāhjī and guru of Shivājī who was reputed to have tried to bring land under cultivation, should have concentrated on the Maval rather than on the east, 'either because the māvals, i.e. the western portion of the Poona District, were politically more important or because they had a comparatively secure agriculture', as the *Poona Gazetteer* suggests.[30] The whole western part of the Poona, Satara, and Kolhapur Districts, the Maval,[31] and the western part of Ahmednagar District was more populous than the east and the density of population still reflects this today. In his *Memoir* on the Satara Territory, T. Ogilvy said in 1854:

> The entire territory of Satara is divided into two distinct and very dissimilar parts, by a chain of hills branching off from the Mahadev Range near Phultun, and running from north to south for fifty or sixty miles nearly to the banks of Krishna near Walwa. The district lying to the west. . . . This portion of the territory is well peopled with industrious agriculturists, is well cultivated, and productive, and is rendered fertile and salubrious by seasonable showers. The division of the territory to the east of that chain of hills is, though still intersected by spurs, more flat and barren, and it is ill cultivated by a thin, unsettled, and in some degree predatory population. The fall of rain is scanty and precarious, and the climate is hot and insalubrious. These districts yield, however, excellent pastures, which have encouraged the breeding of horses, celebrated among the Marathas, and they maintain numerous flocks and herds.[32]

When the British government, that is the East India Company, took over the rule from the last Peshvā, it inherited a traditional Indian problem, which was not so much the lack of land, but the lack of people to cultivate it. It was not only the lack of population which the Indian king faced, but the problem of inducing the cultivators by wise and just taxation to cultivate. 'The people are few compared to the quantity of arable land . . .', Mountstuart Elphinstone said in his *Report*[33] in 1826, and H.D. Robertson in his account remarked on the achievements of Ṭoḍar Mal and Malik 'Ambar:

> . . . That prince (or rather proprietor), therefore, whose country was better peopled than the country of his neighbours, would be richer than they. Riches give power (especially to sovereigns); and a wise prince who was, or considered himself to be the proprietor of the soil of his kingdom, would readily perceive that his ambition would be best gratified by an indulgent consideration towards (even if he did not share his right of proprietorship) those who laboured on it. . . .[34]

Within a century after his statement the population increased beyond expectations and the spread of agriculture was not stopped even by serious setbacks such as famines and peasant riots.[35]

THE DHANGARVĀḌĪS (SETTLEMENTS) ON THE DESH (DECCAN PLATEAU)

The Dhangarvāḍīs, with which the present author is well acquainted are situated on the hilly pasture grounds (*māḷ*) separating the Karha Valley (Sasvad Basin) from the lower Nira Valley to the south. These *vāḍīs* are situated beyond Jejuri to the south-east in an area which has been declared a scarcity area in 1960.[36] Other *vāḍīs* are scattered over the northern range of the Karha Valley; the range which separates it from the lower Upper Bhima Valley. Again, many *vāḍīs*, which we have frequently visited and stayed in are situated in the foothills which merge into the ranges separating the Nira and Man Valleys. The *vāḍīs* differ in their composition:

(i) Some *vāḍīs* are part of a village, that is, they are situated at the outskirts of a village inhabited by other communities. Here we often find that some of the Dhangars concentrate on agriculture, whereas other families are nomadic.
(ii) Some *vāḍīs* are entities entirely inhabited by Dhangars, though some inhabitants devote themselves to agriculture.
(iii) Other *vāḍīs*, however, are still entirely populated by nomadic Dhangars with their characteristic red turbans.

Instead of describing in detail all the *vāḍīs* with their variations—to which we shall, however, when necessary, refer in the following—a closer look at a large *vāḍī* (A) situated about six miles to the south-east of Jejuri and at a smaller *vāḍī* near Shingnapur at Javali beyond the Nira Valley (B) may suffice (Fig. 1). The first, *vāḍī* A, consists of 20-23 families (Plate I, b). The number of families varies from year to year, as one or two families may leave the *vāḍī* for a year to work on the sheep farm of a wealthy landowner in Baramati. The reason is poverty, because, once the number of sheep a family owns has decreased to 20 or even 10, the male members, including boys from about 10 years of age, are forced to seek employment as shepherds. On the average each family (parents with unmarried and in some cases married children) owns between 50 and150 sheep and 2 to 5 goats. When such emigrants have enough money, they will invest in sheep and rejoin the *vāḍī*. Characteristically, the red-turbaned (i.e. nomadic) Dhangars are slow, in times of distress, to resort to other work such as farm labour, work in sugar factories, or relief work (road-building). But some members own two bullocks, a bullock cart and a plough, and they cultivate besides their own fields those of other Dhangars for half of the crop. These cultivating Dhangars tend to be settled permanently, though they may be

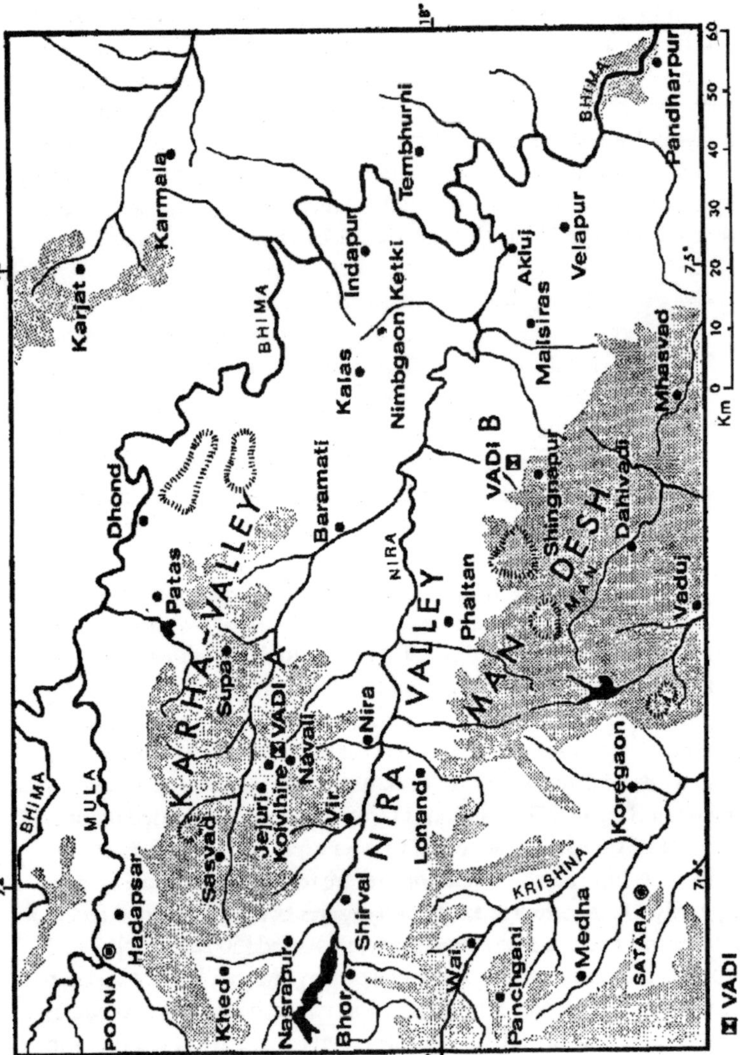

Figure 1: Map showing the main area of the monsoon camps of the nomadic Haṭkar Dhangars and the location of *vāḍīs* A and B.

foiled in dry years. This is not a case of transhumance, as the cultivating Dhangars do not belong to the same family and are separate in property. Nor can we say that cultivation is the economic base of *vāḍī* A, as only three families out of 23 concentrate on agriculture.

The families of *vāḍī* A belong to nine exogamous groups, that is, there are no marriages among families with the same surname and, normally, with the same *devak*. *Devak* amongst Dhangars is mostly a tree which is worshipped in the form of a leaf at the time of the marriage. There are said to be 32 or 34 exogamous groups of Haṭkars, each group comprising several sub-groups with different surnames. Each of the 32 or 34 exogamous groups has its own *devak*. Cross-cousin marriages (mother's brother's daughter) are practised, though not obligatorily. Bride-price (*dyāj*, written Marathi *dej*) is widespread,[37] though richer families who are particular about being 'respectable' give *huṇḍā* ['dowry'] in the form of money. For example the *mirdhā*, the leader of our *vāḍī* A, at the time of his sister's marriage, gave money to the bridegroom's father: 'We thought that we should not sell our sister. We wanted to buy the boy.' A married son may build a small hut close to the hut of his parents. After the death of the father, the mother may continue to live with one of her sons, but the sheep belonging to the father are divided amongst the sons, if the number of sheep after partition would not be too small to be economical. Many of the *vāḍīs* are linked by marriage, and members of the nine exogamous groups belong to other *vāḍīs*. The farther the distance, the weaker these concentric circles of marriage bonds become. Thus, the *vāḍī* B has marriage relations with a *vāḍī* at Valha on the Poona-Bangalore railway between Jejuri and Nira, and the Valha *vāḍī* which is closer to our *vāḍī*, in turn has frequent marriage relations with our *vāḍī*, and, of course, marriage relations within our *vāḍī* are preferred, if a suitable match is possible. Divorce and widow remarriage are allowed by custom. Polygamy may occur, though there is at present no case of it in *vāḍī* A.

The second *vāḍī* (B) would probably combine with other *vāḍīs* nearby and form a large *vāḍī* and thus differ little from A, but the pastures of the *vāḍīs* are scattered, making separate living areas necessary. The members of B are three brothers (X, Y, Z). X, the eldest and the leader of the group, has married again after the death of his first wife. His two sons of the first wife are separated from him and have their own unmarried children. Each of the two sons has about 50 sheep. X has one son by his second wife. There are many children of Y and Z, some of them married boys, but still young. The eldest member is the mother of X, Y, and Z. There are some other dependents who are employees. The pasture and some 'arable' land (a euphemistic description) is the joint property of the *vāḍī*. In all, the *vāḍī* owns about 300-400 sheep.

THE HISTORY OF THE *VĀḌĪ*

Vāḍī A has within living memory been twice shifted farther away from the little village of Navali. Navali itself is not a very old village and, according to village tradition, has developed out of 'jungle'. This certainly did not mean dense forest, as one can see if one looks at the prevailing shallow soils and stony *māḷrān* near the *samādhi* or *dargā* of a Muslim *pīr* who is worshipped by the whole village population, not only by Muslims. The village has mainly been settled by Marathas with the surname Mhaske.[38] This surname makes one suspect that the original settlers were themselves pastoralists with cattle. There is no direct proof of this, but we find a group of cattle herders called Mhaske Dhangars living in the Koyna Valley in the Western Ghats, where the forest still provides pastures which can sustain cattle herds. This does not mean that in our present case a change of profession from preponderantly pastoral to preponderantly agricultural pursuits had the consequence of a change of caste from Gavḷī/Dhangar to Kuṇbī/Maratha. We have to keep in mind that we are in an area which had been typically pastoral and that even Maratha/Kuṇbī-immigrants followed pastoral pursuits rather than regular plough cultivation. A living illustration is the village Mhasobavadi near Baramati. This particular Mhasobā came from Konkan. His vehicle is a Khilārī bull. The pastures, some 2,500 acres, are better than in the area of our *vāḍī* and sustain about 4,000 sheep and 1,500 cattle.

We cannot assume that the Mhaskes have adopted the name of their pastoral predecessors in the area, though such cases may happen as well. In the village Gavlyanci Undavdi near Baramati, one expects to find, as the name of the village suggests, a settlement of Gavḷīs. The village tradition throws a clearer light on the situation. The following translation of it is as literal as possible and should reflect something of the entangled, redundant style with which a villager makes his point:

> Formerly there were Kāsār Gavḷīs [Gavḷīs with bell-metal pots] in this place. They all died of cholera. After that the Bhosles [Bhosle is a typical Kunbi/Maratha name] came. They took *dahī* and milk to Shingnapur and that is why the Bhosles got the name Gavḷī. Before that the Gavḷīs had cows and she-buffaloes and traded with *dahī* and milk. After some days they died of the disease. After that the people by name Bhosle came. They pursued the very same trade and that is how the name Gavḷī originated. . . . The god was brought by the 'original' Gavḷīs.[39]

The predecessors of the Dhangars of our area were Gavḷīs. That is what the oldest inhabitant of our *vāḍī* A maintained.[40] Near Gulunce, between our *vāḍī* and the town Nira, there is a *vāḍī* of Dhangars attached to a tiny settlement of Marathas. The inhabitants of this *vāḍī* could point out the ruins of a formidable *Gavḷī vastī* on a foothill of a mountain comfortably overlooking a terrain which must once have been vast pastures. Instances could be multiplied. The history of the other side of the valley at Javali, near Shingnapur, in the area of our *vāḍī* B, has not been much different. From the foothills up to the Pandharpur road there have been pastures of Gavḷīs. The *vāḍī* B, which is situated near Javali, originally came from Limbut near the town of Nira. The *kulasvāmī*, i.e. the family deity, is the Bhairavnāth of Limbut, 'who had been brought by a Dhangar on a horse from Kāśī'.[41] The family tradition says that the headmanship (the pāṭilship) of the village belonged to the family. There were no canals and no dam (that is, the Nira Dam at Vir) at that time. The land belonged to this family group.[42] Then a quarrel developed with the Maratha family K . . . over the land. Finally the Dhangars left, saying to the Marathas: 'You eat this *jamin* [land].' A famine and marriage debts owed to the Marathas seem to have additionally contributed to this decision. The family tradition continues to relate the quarrels with the Gavḷīs in the new area near Javali, from where the Gavḷīs ultimately left and disappeared.[43]

There are further facets to the oral history of *vāḍī* A. In the village of Kolvihire, in the vicinity of *vāḍī* A, Dhangars with the same surname as those of the present *vāḍī* B and surely of the same stock arrived after the Gavḷīs had left the area. These Dhangars still have a reputation in the village for having been very wealthy. They owned bullocks, cows, and buffaloes; one of them even built a temple, which is still known as the Dhangar's temple, and a fertile strip of land is similarly still known by their surname. They cultivated land, but primarily they owned 'beautiful cattle' and by this everyone means Khilārī cattle. These Dhangars disappeared. Some informants believe that they died out. But this seems unlikely, as Dhangars with the same surname are found in the *vāḍī* B and in other places and they came from Limbut, only about eight miles away from *vāḍī* A. Some say that the Dhangars went away because of a famine. Their wealth disappeared. There was 'no longer enough rain and grass'.

After that a landlord from Murti Modhve occupied the land, including the pastures as well as the garden land. The Dhangars of the present *vāḍī* A first came to Murti Modhve, where they purchased land and started some cultivation. They had sheep and bullocks. Trouble started when sheep continued to enter the fields of the landlord. But the issue was settled by giving the Dhangars 125 acres, consisting mainly of land suitable for pasture, in exchange for 100 acres of cultivable land at Murti Modhve. These pastures are situated in the present area, near the above-mentioned little villages of Navali and Kolvihire. Subsequently, after many years, the landlord decided to sell further pastures, which the Dhangars had rented from him for an annual rent of Rs. 200/-. (They had rented the pastures because of the expansion of the *vāḍī*.) In a joint effort the Dhangars bought the land for Rs. 20,000/-. Though the names of the heads of the contributing families are entered separately in the land register, the pastures are joint.

We can even go behind the Gavḷīs and Dhangars in history, as there is much evidence that tribal Koḷīs had been amongst the first in Kolvihire and elsewhere. Their main traditional profession was fishing and hunting, if not brigandage, before they became members of the settled village as a minor caste of water-carriers. Thus we have a relative sequence of

(a) Koḷīs
(b) Gavḷīs
(c) Wealthy Dhangars with cattle (Khilārī)
(d) Settled landlords claiming the land of the area along with Kuṇbīs/ Marathas and Māḷīs with regular plough cultivation
(e) The Dhangars of our *vāḍī* A, specializing in the breeding and sale of sheep.

The evidence shows how cattle people would then give up land suited for cultivation in favour of pastures because of a famine or the spread of regular plough cultivation. But the evidence also reflects a general trend in the development of the whole area. In 1881 the work on the Nira Left Bank commenced and the canal system came into operation in 1885-6. Eventually the Nira Right Bank Canal was completed in 1937-8. Within recent years the Vir Dam has been completed. A large area has been opened for regular agriculture during the last 150 years or so. Some of the Dhangars became agriculturists themselves. Further consequences were the shrinking of pasture, overgrazing, and the departure of the Gavḷīs. Naturally the remaining pastures could not sustain large cattle-herds. Not all the Gavḷīs went. In the Purandar area we still find them supplying milk to Poona. In Nhai, near Kalas, between Baramati and Indapur, we have a famous Dhangar god called Bābīr with a strongly attended pilgrimage (*jatrā*) on Ḍivāḷī. He was a Gavḷī-god and the *pujārīs* [priests] are still Gavḷīs, but the main devotee is a Dhangar—now a landlord—and the majority of the devotees are now not Gavḷīs but Dhangars. The old cult has continued, but the devotees have changed. The further we get to the east the more we still find Gavḷīs keeping herds of buffaloes, especially around Pandharpur.[44] Here more regular and sufficient rainfall would make this possible.

As we noted in the beginning our Dhangars call themselves not only Haṭkars, but also Khilārīs, and this name requires explanation in this context. Khilārī Dhangar, according to Molesworth, means 'a keeper both of herds and flocks (of buffaloes and cows and of sheep and goats)'.[45] The *Sholapur Gazetteer* of 1884 informs us that the Dhangars own cows and buffaloes besides goats and sheep and that the oxen of that name (*khilārī*) are the best.[46] Today important cattle fairs at which Khilārī bulls and bullocks are sold are Karkhani, Kharsundi and Dighanci in the Sangli District, Mahud, Piliv and Sangola in the Sholapur District, and Cincli in the north-east of the Belgaum District.[47] The Khilārī ox enjoy great popularity among the farmers for their beauty and their capacity for heavy and transport work. Many a cultivator makes his living by rearing Khilārī animals in the Satara District, and the Man and Khatav Talukas are considered to be the home of the Khilārī animals, though many are imported from the Sangli and Sholapur Districts. One wonders, then, whether the breeding of Khilārī cattle has been discontinued by the Dhangars in our area. Even in the Satara District we did not come across Khilārī Dhangars having Khilārī herds.

Besides, we have traditions that, e.g., a Dhangar 'came with his *cattle* and sheep' to the village of Vir in the Purandar Taluka of the Poona District [emphasis added].[48] The late, eighty-year old *pāṭīl* of the village confirmed without our trying to elicit the answer that formerly the Dhangars had Khilārī cows, but that the pastures decreased and became over-grazed. Only occasionally may one still see a nomadic Dhangar having a cow. If, however, we move farther to the east, out of the 'famine tract', towards Mangalvedha and Pandharpur, the rainfall becomes more secure and one finds much better pastures and markedly more Khilārī cattle, often kept by *settled* Dhangars. Perhaps some cattle keepers left the area, as did the famous devotee and disciple of the god Birobā in Hunnur (Mangalvedha Taluka of the Sholapur District) 'who had come with his cows from Baramati'. He came from the 'famine tract' and out of a taluka of which the southern part is now a heavily developed agricultural area because of the Nira canal system. Cattle breeding and keeping ceased to be the domain of the Khilārī Dhangars and shifted to the settled cultivators of whatever caste. What was left to the nomadic Khilārī Dhangars in our area was sheep herding. The limited and deteriorated pastures would at the most sustain sheep but not cattle.

The growth of population, along with the recent extension of agriculture since 1947, has increased the pressure on land. The little village of Navali and the larger village of Kolvihire show an increase of population from 477 to 692 and from 1423 to 2018 respectively between 1951 and 1961 according to the *District Census Handbook* (Poona of 1961). There are many areas, e.g., between Jejuri and Nira, which are now under the plough but are said to have been *jungle* or *māḷrāṇ* 30 years ago. What was a very rare sight only ten years ago, namely a red-turbaned Dhangar laying his hand on a plough, can now be seen more often in the very same area.

During the last 10 or12 years, especially during the last three or four years, one could notice a generally increased agricultural activity in our area. Since 1962 the road between Hadapsar (a south-eastern suburb of Poona) and the town of Nira has received a metalled, tarred surface. Similarly, a metalled, tarred or partially concrete road connects Mahad in the Konkan and Bhor with Baramati and Phaltan. The village of Kolvihire—originating from a hide-out of Koḷī brigands—and Navali, right in the middle of the 'Famine Tract', have been connected by bus with Nira and Jejuri since 1970. Electricity was introduced to Kolvihire a few years ago, and to Navali in 1971. The demand of the growing industrial centres of Poona and Bombay for vegetables, fruits and grain has certainly acted as a stimulus on the agriculture of the area, the produce being carried to market by an increasing fleet of private and public trucks.[49] Where the area is not covered by the canal system, wells have been or are being built and the traditional method of irrigation by means of the *moṭ*, the bullock-drawn bucket, is steadily giving way to the oil or electrical water pump. The *moṭ* in itself provides an illustration of the change in agriculture. The water container used to be made of buffalo hide, then it became a (or two) square, heavy metal container(s) drawn sometimes by up to six bullocks. One may soon miss the typical song with which the driver at the well would cheer up himself and the bullocks, but the villager certainly does not regret that the bullocks will now be freed from this work, which consumes more of their energy than ploughing.

An instance which was related to me, but which I have not yet been able to check, comes from the Dhond Taluka where, Dhangars of three villages, namely Khoravadi, Patas, and Girim, have been affected by afforestation. The forests were closed for grazing in order to protect the newly-planted trees. Moreover, *gāyrān*, that is 'cow pasture', which probably ranks under 'cultivable waste' in the statistics, was given to Mahārs, Māngs, and Rāmośīs for cultivation.[50] Luckily for our two *vāḍīs*, their rights in land are well-settled. But elsewhere the notorious quarrels between nomads and farmers do occur, whether these refer to alleged intrusions into fields or disputes over lands. In one case, such a dispute has been carried up to the Bombay High Court.

THE MIGRATION TO THE KONKAN

When the end of the rainy season approaches, the pastures wither. Between the Dasarā and Divāḷī festivals, but definitely shortly after Divāḷī (October/ November), the Dhangars are forced to vacate their temporary settlements on the Plateau. Thus '*vāḍī*' (or '*vāḍā*', which is, however, often a walled enclosure) not only means a 'settlement, hamlet, cluster of houses', but 'a settlement, a unit of Dhangars *on the move*', and such double meanings can be traced back in Indian history.[51] A special worship of their gods, who are represented by *ṭāks*, small silver-embossed plaques placed on a *ghoṅgaḍī*, which is spread on the floor, marks the end of the stay. A dance is performed in front of them and a *devruṣi* (soothsayer, exorciser) goes into a trance and answers questions about the exact date of departure, about sickness, stolen property, the prospects of rain in the coming year and so on. The movement up the valley towards the west, the Maval, seems the natural destination, and from prehistoric times men and their domesticated animals or the wildlife have moved westward.[52] Some Dhangars (or Bangars, as they are called by surname) in the south-east corner of our area, that is around Mhasvad and to the south of Mhasvad,[53] move towards Marathvada and the Osmanabad District after Divāḷī and come back with the rainy season. Women, small children and the aged drive the horses packed with household utensils, poultry and the smallest children. This part of the *vāḍī* is accompanied by the dogs, which are never used for driving the sheep, but for protection. The horses or ponies have remained indispensable for the Dhangars, who would not have any other pack animals. But they are more and more difficult to procure.[54] The extension of roads and railways and the spread of motor rikshas have decreased their numbers. A few years ago a disease killed all the horses of *vāḍī* A and forced the Dhangars to carry their belongings on their heads to the Konkan. A still curious sight was the transport of baggage on cycles alongside horses by a *vāḍī* from Ravangav in the Dhond Taluka on the Poona-Sholapur Road. To go to the Konkan another *vāḍī* from the same area uses bullock carts, which are returned by members of the *vāḍī* who look after the fields on the Plateau.

The women and girls of our *vāḍī* A go ahead of the men and boys who drive the sheep. Each household has its flock driven separately by two people, one in front and one behind the flock. By the time the men arrive with the flocks the tents have been pitched (*vāḍī* A has no tents), and the *bhākrī*—a flat bread made of *bājrī* or *jvāri*—is prepared for a dinner supplemented by onions and perhaps some chili sauce (see Plate I, a). The camp sites on the route are the same every year and are chosen so that after the sheep arrive and prior to departure the next morning, they can graze on some *māḷrān* fallow land, or on any uncultivated strip where they might find food. Sometimes this is 'unculturable' waste land, sometimes this happens without the permission of the owner of the land. Grazing might be supplemented by leaves from trees. Increasingly the camp sites are endangered by agricultural expansion, and, especially around Poona, by new housing areas, factories, etc. (Plate II, a and b).

The first stop of *vāḍī* A is at Jejuri. Here some sheep which cannot stand the migration to Konkan are sold, mainly to Khāṭīks. The next stops on the migration are Śasvad, Hadapsar, Cincvad, Dehu Road, Talegaon, Khamset, Lonavla (via the Bor Ghat), Khopoli, Pali into the Roha Taluka of the Kolaba District. The trip takes about 10 or 12 days and covers a distance of roughly 150 miles.

Vāḍī B proceeds to the Konkan up the Nira Valley. Already the grandfather of X, Y, and Z migrated towards the west. We do not know whether he went to the Konkan, and in fact he died during one of the migrations. The stops on route are Vadale, Phaltan, Kalaj, Lonand, Bhade, Sikhmirvadi, the *copāḷā* near Shirval, Rajvadi, Bhor, Apati, Hirdoshi, Manjari via the Varandh Pass to Varandh in the Kolaba District, Birvadi, Kambala via Mahad to Vaur, Devli, etc. The *vāḍī* B does not pen the sheep on the route to the Konkan, because the *kharif*-crop (*jvārī, bājrī*) is not yet harvested or is just being harvested, or the *jvārī* fields for the *rabi*-crop are just being sown; similarly, the paddy is being harvested and the sugar cane is being harvested or planted and earthed up. Thus there is no interruption in the migration to the Konkan. The camp sites are on slightly elevated ground, i.e., on the *māḷ*, which provides some grazing for the sheep. The ground around the *copāḷā*[55] near Shirval is a typical camp site. Here is also an ancestor shrine (*deuḷ*) for the grandfather of X, Y, and Z and some other relations. On the way to and from the Konkan one or two rams are sacrificed and some *bhākrī*, rice, liver, and heart are offered to the manes.

After Divāḷī (October-November) all the roads towards the west and up the river valleys are thronged by the flocks of migrating Dhangars. We do not know when the Dhangars entered the Konkan for the first time. The late eldest member of *vāḍī* A said that some members of the *vāḍī* had worked for a *khāṭīk*, a Muslim sheep trader, driving his sheep to the Konkan. There the Dhangars saw much better pastures than on the Plateau. Characteristically for the Dhangars, it was not the possibility of penning the sheep which attracted them first to the Konkan, but the possibility of grazing. This need to graze the sheep and the scarcity of pastures preoccupy much of the mind of the Dhangars. The penning of sheep is considered a secondary source of income, though it has become more and more economically important.

Plate Ia: Dhangar women and children *en route* to Konkan camping in fields

Plate Ib: View of section of *vāḍi* A.

Plate IIa: Dhangars on their migration through Poona towards the Konkan. The flocks occasionally create traffic problems.

Plate IIb: A Dhangar woman at the time of migration.

Plate IIIa: *Viragala* showing a hero defending or retrieving his cattle and his ascension (near Indapur, Maharashtra).

Plate IIIb: A close-up of Plate IIIa. Heads of cattle bending over the dead hero. Such hero-stones of the medieval period are frequent in areas where the economy was primarily influenced by pastoralism.

We do not know when the members of the *vāḍī* B started migrating up to the Konkan, though, as we have seen, the grandfather of X, Y, and Z had at least gone up to Shirval. It cannot be assumed that they descended to the Konkan from the beginning of their migration westwards. Some *vāḍīs* move only up to the Maval, e.g., the *vāḍī* at Jhirap, near Gulunce, which migrates up to the Maval via Jejuri, Hadapsar, and Kotharud, up the Pauna Valley to Kasarambuli and Paund. Here the *vāḍī* splits up into two groups, the first moving to Kulaj, Kolvan, Kashik, Cavsar, and Tungi, the other moving towards Kalamshet, Disli, and Mulshi. Within seven months the *vāḍī* returns after having penned the sheep in the rice fields of the Maval.

THE STAY IN THE KONKAN AND LOCAL MIGRATIONS

The relations between the Dhangars and the farmers in the Konkan are said to be much better than those between the Dhangars and the farmers on the Plateau (Desh). If sheep enter standing crops, farmers and nomads will rarely come to blows or carry the case to the police, as happens on the Desh, but they will settle the dispute peacefully with the help of the village leaders. The relations are old, that is, at least one generation old in the case of *vāḍī* A and dating back to the father of X, Y, and Z in the case of *vāḍī* B. The Dhangars attribute this partially to the highly-valued sheep manure required for the preparation of the rice-fields and this is certainly one of the most important reasons.

In some cases the manuring of the fields was attempted with the help of artificial fertilizers. The result was one, and up to three, quick and good crops with complete failures in the following years. The rice field is first manured by the sheep overnight, subsequently covered with cow-dung, then covered with rice-straw and earth, and watered. Then it is allowed to dry. Afterwards the field is burnt. The rice is sown in May/June at the beginning of the rainy season, subsequently transplanted, and harvested in October/November. The fields are smaller than on the Desh and thus the *vāḍīs* have to split up, whereby two to three families may stay together pooling their flocks, that is about 80 to 100 sheep, for them overnight. For 80 sheep the payment will be Rs. 5/- or 5 kilos of rice. This rice is not consumed, but saved, and carried back to the Desh or sent there by trucks at the end of the stay in Konkan. For this transport special permits are obtained from the Collector of the district, as it is prohibited to convey rice from one taluka to another. Thus the Dhangars provide themselves with rice for their stay on the Desh, where it is costly and at times rare. In Konkan they buy and consume mainly *ragi* = Marāṭhī *nācṇī* (*Eleusine corocana*) or perhaps *bājrī* (*Holcus spicatus*) or *jondhaḷ* = (*Holcus sorghum*). In this way the *vāḍī* spends about $2^1/_2$ months moving to different villages. Thus, e.g., two families move to Cillha and stay there 15 days, then to Talvali with one month's stay, then to Pali with one month's stay. Afterwards they return to Cillha. There, meanwhile, the pulses like *vāl* (*Dolichos spicatus*), *pāvṭā* (*Phaseolus radiatus*), *mūg* (*Phaseolus mungo*), and *maṭkī* (a bean—*Phaseolus aconitifolius*) have been harvested and the empty fields provide further possibilities of grazing.

Before the crops have been harvested the penning of sheep requires increased vigilance during the night, as the sheep may stray into the standing crops. Besides, the Kātkarīs—the local tribals—are reputed to be on the lookout for a chance to carry away sheep whenever there is an opportunity. As the Dhangar men are exhausted by grazing the sheep during the day, the burden of watching the sheep during the night often falls upon the women. Their lot is not very easy, as the daily routine of work already burdens them with shifting the camp to another field, gathering firewood, fetching water, cooking, looking after the smaller children and so on.

Vāḍī B also splits up after reaching its destination in Konkan. Thus, for instance, the two married sons of X stay together during the whole period of six or seven months and serve the villages of Devli and Mur along with two other Dhangar families from another *vāḍī*. After the pulses have been harvested, the four households jointly camp in a field. A temporary shed of bamboo and straw protects them against the sun. The men come to the camp in the morning to take their food and return to graze the sheep. There is a limited possibility for *vāḍī* B to graze sheep on private strips of forest belonging to the farmers with whom the Dhangars have connections. The evening meal is brought to them in the field where they are penning their sheep for the night. The two sons of X each own some 100 sheep and pen them jointly—depending on the size of the field. If they pen them jointly they receive ten kilos of rice or twelve rupees per night. The exact amount of rice or money per 100 sheep and per night is fixed beforehand between the Dhangars and the villagers on the arrival of the Dhangars in the Konkan.

In February/March some of the Dhangars return to the Desh, leaving their flocks and families in the Konkan. The reason is partially their desire to participate in the *jatrā* (pilgrimage/fair) of Mhaskobā at Vīr in the Purandar Taluka, and partially to repay debts incurred for grain, clothes, etc., bought on credit during the stay on the Desh the preceding year. The money derives from the sale of sheep, which fetch a higher price in the Konkan than on the Desh.

The institution of *heḍ* (= a drove of sheep) provides another reason. Farmers on the Desh entrust their sheep to Dhangars, who drive them to the Konkan and sell them on behalf of the farmers. The proceeds of the sale are brought back by the Dhangars, who receive as commission an amount between Rs. 5/- and Rs. 15/- per sheep. Yet another reason is to check the yield of the *rabi* crops on fields belonging to the Dhangars and cultivated by Māḷīs or Dhangars not needed as shepherds (see below). After a few days the Dhangars return to the Konkan. The rest of the time in the Konkan is spent in penning of sheep. March/April is also the month during which marriages are celebrated, though some of the marriages may be celebrated after the return to the Desh.

THE RETURN TO THE DESH

Before the monsoon rains start in May/June the *vāḍīs* gather to return to the Desh. If anything is sure it is the rain in the Konkan. Generally in the first week of June the rains start. The sheep cannot stand heavy rains, wet feet, and mud. And if the rains reach the Desh and our area quickly, the *vāḍīs* without delay return along the same route to their homes and pastures on the Desh. But the rains may not yet have reached the Desh and only come up to the Maval. This provides good opportunities for penning the sheep on the fields of the Desh, which will be sown only when the rains start. The fields are larger than the rice fields in the Konkan and manuring requires the pooling of all the sheep of the *vāḍī*. The number of sheep is sufficient in the case of *vāḍī* A, which has about 700 sheep. But *vāḍī* B combines with two or three other *vāḍīs* from the Phaltan range and 1,000-1,500 sheep may be penned in one field. For 1,000 sheep the Dhangars will get Rs. 80/- to 100/-, for 500 sheep only Rs. 25/- to 30/- per night. Thus, the more sheep are kept in the field the more the Dhangars will gain.

Though the penning of sheep is not unprofitable, the Dhangars are eager to return home. Prolonged scarcity of rain may, moreover, limit the readiness of the farmers to spend money or grain for sheep manure. Besides there is hardly anything for the sheep to graze on. Therefore late rain, or rain reaching up only to the Maval, where the sowing has begun, may lead to local migrations of the Dhangars. For instance, in the Phaltan area one may see the Dhangars coming from Mhasvad who had returned to Mhasvad from the east, but who had to move on towards the west in the hope of more rain. From the west we will see the Dhangars (e.g., our *vāḍī* B) trying to return home to their settlements in the Phaltan range. Others, who stay close to the Maval, e.g., those from Shirval, have to move further away from the

Maval, because there is too much rain. At the same time we come across Dhangars from Kolhapur in the south-west who every year take their own sheep or those belonging to others towards the drier north-east up to Kurduvadi. They return after three months. Here we have a clear case of transhumance.

The situation in the Karha Valley would be similar. Some Dhangar *vāḍīs* may have returned home, but they may have to drift back towards the west because of the lack of rain, keeping their sheep in the fields for penning and grazing between Jejuri and Sasvad. In one case, Dhangars (from Baburda) were forced to return to the Maval and to the Konkan, because of the failure of rain and the dried-out pastures, which would hardly be sufficient to sustain the sheep in a normal rainy season.

Our *vāḍī* A normally returns to its home, though it may be compelled to stay in the fields of the surrounding villages until the rains are sufficient to revive the pastures.

THE STAY ON THE DESH

If the rains are sufficient, four sedentary months follow. The members of *vāḍī* A fetch the corrugated tin roofs from the farmers with whom they had been deposited before the start of the migration. Some Dhangars may use their canvas, normally used for building tents, as a roof for their stone-walled huts. Some, who may be guests, use the canvas to pitch tents. The rainy season brings cold and gusty winds and therefore some Dhangar families have *vāḍās*, enclosures of undressed stones, piled up without the use of mortar, about 2 m high and crowned by thorny bushes (*bābhūḷ*). These also serve as protection against the wolves, which must have been a big threat formerly. Even today one may meet with a pack of six or seven wolves crossing the road in the middle of the night. The sheep of those families who have no *vāḍā* are kept in a huge flock in a square in the middle of the *vāḍī*.

A DAY IN THE *VĀḌĪ* A

After the Dhangars have had their food (*bhākrī*) in the morning at about 9 a.m., the large herd of sheep in the middle of the *vāḍī* is divided into separate flocks of individual owners. These flocks are driven separately to the pastures, with one Dhangar man or two Dhangar boys accompanying each flock of about 80 to 100 sheep. The flocks from the *vāḍās* follow. The flocks are led into the pasture by two or three goats. The Dhangars find it difficult to keep many goats, as these traverse the pasture much more quickly than sheep and moreover they do not find the vegetation, especially the leaves of *bābhūḷ* trees, necessary for them. The location of the huts around the centre square of the *vāḍī* indicates the approximate direction towards which the pastures used by the respective families spread. The pastures are used jointly by the eight exogamous sections living in the *vāḍī*. The headman has some say in the assignment of the pastures in order to settle who is to graze on which pasture on a particular day. Sometimes one section may pool all the sheep and two Dhangars specially well-versed in husbandry may tend them jointly. The other male members are then free to do other work. The two Dhangars graze about 500 sheep carefully on the pasture, between standing crops, on the marginal patches between fields, between fields and roads, and on fallow or harvested land. The grazing lasts about two hours, until about 11 a.m., after which the sheep are watered and rested. After that they are grazed again until 5 p.m. Then the sheep are watered for the second time and slowly driven nearer to the *vāḍī*, which they reach after one hour, at dusk. After this the Dhangars have their evening meal, which again consists mainly of *bhākrī*, sometimes supplemented by onions, dried fish or rice from Konkan, or on special occasions eggs.

The women sweep the *vāḍās* and the square, and the manure of the sheep mixed with earth is carried to dung heaps lying to the east of the *vāḍī*. Each family keeps one or two heaps of sheep and horse manure. The women and girls fetch water and collect brush wood needed for cooking. Women or men may collect grass for the horses, which are left to graze, with their forelegs fettered, outside the *vāḍī* during the day. Some of the old women have wooden spinning wheels and occasionally the Dhangars women prepare felts.

SPECIAL ACTIVITIES AND SYMBIOTIC RELATIONSHIP WITH FARMERS

Soon after the arrival in the *vāḍī* the sheep are shorn. They are shorn twice a year, namely in the months of Āṣād (June/July) and Pauṣ (December/January). For the purpose the sheep are first bathed in a pond at some distance from the *vāḍī* which holds water during the rainy season. Subsequently the seven water goddesses (*sātī āsarās*), who might have been offended by the bathing, are worshipped with *bhaṇḍār* (turmeric powder). They are represented by seven chalcedony stones. The sheep are shorn in the *vāḍās*. The Dhangars are particular to remove their sandals while shearing, as otherwise the goddess Lakshmi might be offended. One member of almost every family takes part in the joint washing and shearing of the sheep. The fleece of the hardy and tough sheep of the *Deccani* type is of low quality, with 62 p.c. hair.[56] The wool is sold in the bazaar at Lonand, at the big weekly cattle market on Thursday. The fleece of about five sheep amounts to one kilo of wool, which is sold at the rate of about Rs. 2/-.

After the sheep of the *vāḍī* are shorn, those of the farmers of the surrounding villages follow. There are three types of farmers with sheep and goats: (i) The small farmers who own some pasture with *bābhūḷ* trees and can maintain about five, ten, or a maximum of twenty sheep. These sheep are shorn by the Dhangars of our *vāḍī*. The sheep are not driven to Konkan after the rainy season. They are often guarded by Dhangar boys who have no work in the parental home and are employed by the farmers. The shepherd boy earns about Rs. 300/- to 400/- per annum plus a set of new clothes and free food. The consideration for shearing the sheep is the fleece of the last sheep, which is said to be a gift to the god Khaṇḍobā, though the Dhangars in fact sell it. The shearing is not so much a source of income as a means of maintaining good and old relations with the surrounding villages. One may also see in it an element of the traditional village servant system, into which the Dhangars were, however, never fully integrated.[57] It also illustrates the caste compartmentalization of occupational activities and the traditional attitude of associating particular activities with particular groups. Though the shearing is certainly more difficult than it looks, there seems to be no reason why the farmers should not do it themselves. But it is the 'Dhangars' work'. (ii) Some wealthy landlords own—besides their agricultural land—big pastures and some 600 sheep. They employ red-turbaned Dhangars, who stay with their families on the sheep farm. These Dhangars do not have sheep of their own. The payment would be Rs. 325/- per annum plus 32 seers (*c*. 32 kilos) of grain (*jvārī*) per month (= *c*. Rs. 27/- per month). (iii) There are Marāṭhās who derive their subsistence to a large extent from the sheep they own and to a lesser degree from their land.

Thus, whereas the Dhangars help in shearing the sheep, the Māḷīs and Kuṇbīs help the Dhangars to cultivate their lands. Some of the members of *vāḍī* A and the Dhangars of *vāḍī* B own fields which are cultivated by Māḷīs, who are a caste of extremely versatile and active agriculturists. They receive half of the crop as a consideration. The yield of the harvest may reduce the quantity of *bājrī* which the Dhangars have to buy from the bazar, but it is never enough to make the Dhangars self-sufficient as far as grain is concerned. In a good rainy season there may even be an attempt to plough patches of the stony pastures, though the present author has never seen anything being grown on such land which was worth being called a crop.

Occasionally a rich landlord may call upon the Dhangars of the surrounding *vāḍīs* to pen their sheep jointly during one night in one of his larger fields. Thus one may see Dhangars of nine *vāḍīs* with about 10,000 sheep congregating in the dusk instead of returning home to their *vāḍīs*. The consideration for penning the sheep is a communal dinner[58] with a special sweet dish arranged in the house of the landlord. The landlord remains in the company of the Dhangars during the night and helps to guard the sheep.

The stay on the Desh is also utilized to attend *jatrās* of the *kulasvāmī*, the family deity of one's family. Each of the exogamous sections of *vāḍī* A has its family deity and worships in addition other gods, which may be the family gods of other sections or *vāḍīs*. From August to October there is much cause to attend *jatrās*, and every opportunity is seized upon to have at least one visit to the *kulasvāmī*. The location of the *kulasvāmī* deity often indicates the area from where the ancestors of a particular family came. We shall not discuss in detail here the symbiotic relationship as regards religion between the Dhangars and other communities. It may suffice to point out that soothsayers and exorcisers amongst the Dhangars are many and they are often consulted by farmers. Often the Dhangars have their own temple priests (*pujārīs*), but sometimes priests of other communities, e.g., the Guravs, officiate. The reputation of the Dhangars as soothsayers sometimes gives them a special right (*mān*) in a temple whose deity was a cattle-god brought by the Dhangars but who has since been adopted by all other castes, as, e.g., in the case of the god Mhaskobā of Vīr in the Purandar Taluka of the Poona District.

Between Dasarā and Divāḷī, as we have indicated before, the stay on the Desh comes to an end. Before the Dhangars leave their *vāḍīs* the heaps of manure and soil which have been accumulated by sweeping the *vāḍās* each morning are sold to farmers. Each heap fetches up to Rs. 150/-. The manure of 80 to 100 sheep amounts to two such heaps. Richer farmers even contrive to reach the out-of-the-way and seemingly inaccessible *vāḍīs* by truck in order to buy the manure.

THE PREDICAMENTS OF THE DHANGAR LIFE

The sketch of the Haṭkar Dhangars which we have given shows that they are not the type of pastoral nomads which we find in other countries outside

India, e.g., Turkey.[59] Though they migrate as a unit with their flocks, they are not bound to the changing location of their flocks because of direct consumption of milk or cheese. In fact, they do not prepare cheese and at most would use the milk—the yield of which is negligible—medicinally or to prepare tea. Nor is the consumption of mutton an important part of the diet. Only on special occasions, as at Dasarā, at *jatrās*, or at marriages, is mutton consumed. The food is more or less the same as that of the surrounding farmers. Moreover, the production of wool is negligible.

The Dhangars are nomads who have become heavily dependent on the farmers for their livelihood. Besides the sales of sheep as mutton, the penning of sheep in the fields of farmers has become a substantial source of income. Thus they have, in fact, benefited from the extension of regular cultivation, due to canal and well irrigation. The farmers are still convinced that this method of manuring the fields is in the long run the most successful for their soil. For this reason, the Dhangars believe that they are indispensable. On the other hand, we have the decrease and deterioration of pastures. Attempts to improve the breed by introducing rams from a Governmental sheep farm (Poona) have not been successful, the Dhangars say. It may be, indeed, true that only the Deccani sheep are able to graze on the meagre pastures and the weeds in harvested fields. The Dhangars are now aware of the lasting value of landed property and would possibly become settled agriculturists, but they are forced to live off their flocks. This they prefer, seeing that often members of settled Dhangar families have to work as agricultural labourers or in sugar factories in a bad season. They know that their flocks are a perishable source of income of which they may be deprived by disease at any moment. The scarcity of cultivable land leaves them in the position of nomads and the general attitude of leaving certain occupations to certain communities still allows them to eke out a living. Their life is a precarious balancing of the sale of sheep to butchers, mainly in the Konkan, the demands by farmers for manure, the need to obtain fodder, and the vagaries of the south-west monsoon.

POSTSCRIPT

The year 1971 was marked by a prolonged break in the monsoon. The reaction of the Dhangars differed slightly from the pattern described above. As usual good rains in the Konkan and near the eastern side of the Ghats (the Maval) set the Dhangars moving homewards. Thus, a *vāḍī* which has its home to the east of *vāḍī* A near Murti Modhve left the Konkan on the 23rd of May. The *vāḍī* consists of *c*. 1,400 sheep, *c*. 100 goats, 22 horses and *c.* 75 people. These Dhangars had as usual spent six to seven months in eighteen villages of the Thana District, near Panvel. Here the rice-fields are larger than in other areas in the Konkan. Occasionally all the sheep of the *vāḍī* are penned jointly. When the *vāḍī* reached the crest of the Ghats at Khandala, heavy rains set in. Some of the sheep died on account of cold. After reaching home the failure of the rains drove many families of the *vāḍī* to Lonand, beyond the Nira River, where the sheep were then penned on uncultivated fields, which are not reached by canal irrigation. Another section of the *vāḍī* returned to the Maval. They were admitted by special permission to the rich pastures of the National Defence Academy in Khadakvasla, about ten miles to the west of Poona. Like them, many Dhangars from the Karha and Bhima Valleys returned to the Maval and experienced great difficulties. The rains did reach the Maval, but did not go beyond Poona. Thus, the Maval had to be vacated whenever there was too much rainfall, and the Dhangars were forced to drive their sheep and carry their households through Poona towards the east (camping, e.g., to the east of Hadapsar). There, again, was neither rain nor the possibility of grazing their sheep, and they consequently had to return to the Maval. This to-and-fro migration had to be repeated several times, causing considerable hardship to men and animals.

Vāḍī A similarly returned to its home, but a large section left again and spent several weeks penning the sheep at Mandki, on the river Nira. The fields were those of wealthy landowners who also own fields not served by lift or canal irrigation. The irrigated land in this area is mostly covered by sugar-cane, and some of the starving Dhangar horses strayed into these fields. Four Dhangars were detained by the farmers and released after the other members of the *vāḍī* had collected Rs. 500/- as compensation for damages. Finally, rain came at the end of August and the *vāḍī* returned home.

Vāḍī B penned its sheep in some fields on the way home from the Konkan. A better source of water than that of *vāḍī* A, supplemented by *jovārī* stalks (*bāṭuk*) as fodder (which fetches high prices at such times of scarcity), helped to bridge scarcity conditions until the monsoon set in again. It goes without saying that in this period many a tree was cleared of its foliage in order to procure fodder.

At the time of writing these lines (the end of July 1972) the situation just described threatens to repeat itself, and indeed is more serious than in 1971.

ACKNOWLEDGEMENTS

Investigations on the origin and the development of pastoral cults in Maharashtra and Karnatak and the religion and history of the Dhangars were started in 1967. In all, with interruption, about fifteen months were spent in the field. This article is based on material collected while pursuing the above themes. I am deeply obliged to the German Research Association and the South Asia Institute of the University of Heidelberg for generous financial support.

I am especially grateful to Mr. R.P. Nene, Dr. S.N. Bhavsar, Mr. Ramdas Atkar and Mr. Rajaram B. Zagade for helping me at various stages of my research, and to Mrs. H. Werny for typing the manuscript with patience.

NOTES

1. Cp. I. Karve, *Maharashtra—Land and its People* (Maharashtra State Gazetteer), Bombay, 1968, p. 20. According to Karve, ibid., the Hoḷkars, the famous generals of the Maratha army and the rulers of Indore, were Haṭkars. However, a history (*bakhar*) of the Hoḷkar Rājās of Indore says about their origin: *mauje hoḷa muruma nīrece kāṃṭhīṃ jejorījavaḷa āhe. tetheṃ khaṇḍojī vīrkara khuṭekara dhanagara caugule rāhāta hote* . . . ['The village Hoḷ is situated on the bank of the river Nīrā, near Jejurī. There lived Khaṇḍojī Vīrkar, a Khuṭekar Dhangar, Caugule . . .']. See James Fuller Blumhardt and Sadashiv Govind Kanhere, *Catalogue of the Marathi Manuscripts in the India Office Library*, Oxford, 1950, p. 82, ms. 162. Caugule was an officer subordinate to the Pāṭīl, who also had to take care of the record kept by the Kulkarṇī.
2. R.E. Enthoven, *The Tribes and Castes of Bombay*, vol. II (1921), p. 163.
3. 'Three and a half' (*sāḍe-tīn*), 'three hundred and fifty' (*sāḍetīn-śe*), 'seven', 'seven hundred', 'seven hundred and fifty' are not mere numbers in the traditional outlook, but are entities of cosmological and religious significance. They may degenerate in daily use as ready-made answers to the interrogator. Empirical phenomena have to be subsumed under such entities. Cp., e.g. the 'twelve' sons of the Smṛtis. This was an attempt at codifying or subsuming the many possibilities according to custom of having 'sons' under the number 'twelve' and to arrange their relative preferability and priority with respect to their right of inheritance. Manu IV, 158-60, '350' happens to be the ideal number of sheep of a unit (*vāḍī*) consisting of a cluster of 5-7 families. '350' shepherd boys were outplayed by the shepherd god Birobā when he was young. Birobā's and his priests' black *ghoṅgāḍīs* have 'two and a half' white lines (that is, the half line is only half as broad as the two others), whereas the famous devotee of Birobā Mhāḷiṅgrāyā has only one line woven into his blanket, and Āmokasiddha, another famous devotee, has 'three and a half lines'. Of the famous temple of Khaṇḍobā in Jejuri the old *Bombay Gazetteer* (Poona District, 1885, pt. III) says, on p. 132, fn. 1: 'According to a saying this approach [to the temple] has eighteen arches, 350 lamp pillars, and

9,00,000 ['nine *lākh*'] steps. The number of steps is admitted to be a fancy one, but the total of the arches and the pillars is said to be correct.' All these numbers are traditional entities and, e.g. 'nine *lākh*' is added to the names of places which are considered to be exceedingly rich—or which were so at least in the past, e.g., Navlākh Umbare near Talegaon (Maval Taluka, Poona District).

4. Cp. Molesworth, *A Dictionary, Marāṭhī and English*, Bombay, 1857 (cit. by M.M. Underhill, *The Hindu Religious Year*, Calcutta etc., 1921, p. 30): *sāḍe-tīn muhūrtta* = three auspicious seasons or periods and a half-season; viz., Dasarā, Dipāvaḷī, Varṣa-pratipadā and Nāgapanchamī. The latter has only a qualified auspiciousness for the performance of any work.
5. Enthoven, op. cit., vol. I (1920), pp. 313, 315f.
6. Bombay, 1920. On pp. 248f. the observations of 'Captain Fitz Gerald, once an Assistant Commissioner of Berar,' are cited: '. . . The Haṭkars are all Bargi Dhangars, or the shepherds with the spear.' On p. 249 we read: '. . . The Haṭkars say that they formerly, when going on any expedition, took only a blanket seven hands long and a bear-spear, and that on this account they were called 'Bárgir', or Bargá Dhangars. . . .' This seems to indicate that the term *Bargi* has something to do with a spear. Enthoven, op. cit., vol. I, p. 313, however, suspects: '. . . Barges [*sic*] claim to be Maráthás, and were perhaps Bárgirs or mounted troopers during the time of the [314] Maráthás. . . .' The various spellings may be an attempt at a transliteration of Marāṭhī *barčī* ~ °*chi* ~ °*śī*. *Barcā* also occurs, all the versions of the term meaning a kind of small spear (*Mahārāṣṭra Śabdakoś*, s.v.). In the field the term *Barsā* was taken down. Cp. Kannaḍa *b(h)arjī* = spear.
7. The knot on the top is called *śikhar* and the spear is called *jheṇḍā* = 'a flag and a flagstaff' considered as one (Molesworth, op. cit., s.v.). *Śikhar* is the pinnacle of Khaṇḍobā's temple in Jejurī, against which long poles with flags or wrapped with cloth are leaned during the *jatrā* (pilgrimage and fair). The spear thus seems to represent the temple, the god, and the weapon, all in one. The small woollen wreath (*goṇḍa*) just below the blade symbolizes *Lakṣmī*, the goddess of wealth, the wealth of the Dhangars consisting of sheep and wool. The spear without a knot is worshipped by Dhangar devotees of the god Dhuḷobā. Here it is simply a weapon, worshipped as the weapon with which Dhuḷobā killed a *daitya* (demon).
8. Śrī-māṇika-prabhu-kṛta sacitra *Malhārī Māhātmya* [in Marāṭhī], *avṛtti* 1 *lī* [1st ed.], Beḷagāṃva, 1917.
9. Irawati Karve suggested in *Hindu Society. An Interpretation* (Poona, Deccan College, 1961, pp. 16, 19, 28-9) that the caste system has developed more through processes of agglomeration and labelling than of fission. See also, e.g. Syed Siraj Ul Hassan, op. cit., p. 204: 'The Gollas [a pastoral caste] are not a homogeneous race, but are composed of a large number of endogamous groups, the members of which are found to differ from one another in their features and complexion and even in their manners and usages. Their traditions tend to support the same view and to show how people of different origin have been linked together by common occupations and constitute the Golla caste.'

10. See the discussion by F.G. Baily, "Tribe" and "Caste" in India', in *Contributions to Indian Sociology*, vol. 5, 1961, pp. 7ff.
11. E.g. the Āhīrs, and Gollas/Gavḷīs, who are now mostly settled. The Nandīvālās of Maharashtra (studied by the late Prof. I. Karve and Dr. Malhotra) and, e.g. Maratha Gosāvīs from Mahud, near Atpadi (Sangli District), who wander every year with their cows to Bhimashankar and Nasik and return after six months, are survivals in the Deccan.
12. See, e.g. the remarks of T. Ogilvy, cited on p. 94.
13. Ranking of districts in Maharashtra according to the population of sheep (over one year of age) according to the Census of 1961:

			Sheep				*Goats*
1	Poona	—	320,030	1	Ahmednagar	—	501,263
2	Satara	—	271,257	2	Sholapur	—	373,661
3	Ahmednagar	—	228,888	3	Nasik	—	349,490
4	Sangli	—	227,954	4	Aurangabad	—	329,719
5	Sholapur	—	192,139	5	Poona	—	325,467
6	Nasik	—	132,410	6	Bhir	—	239,400
7	Kolhapur	—	108,075	.			
8	Osmanabad	—	7,6411	.			
.				.			
.				25	Kolaba (Konkan)	—	6,1562
24	Kolaba (Konkan) etc.	—	2,261		etc.		

If we take into account the goats the ranking is different. If we add together the number of sheep and goats, the District of Ahmednagar ranks first, followed by the Akola and Amravati Districts. But goats are kept by everybody, they being the poor man's cow. Sheep are primarily kept by professional shepherds and to a lesser degree by farmers living in the area, who often employ Dhangars.
14. I base the following remarks about the climatic-ecological factors *inter alia* on the District Census Handbooks (Census of 1961), the old and the revised Gazetteers and my own observations in the field.
15. Shirur Taluka; Dhond Taluka; the northern part of Indapur Taluka not protected by irrigation canals; a part of Baramati not protected by irrigation canals; the eastern part of the Purandar Taluka, situated to the east of the railway line and to the east of Rajevadi and Jejuri villages; and the north eastern part of Haveli Taluka.
16. See Kamil V. Zvelebil, 'Pastoralism as reflected in the classical Tamil theory of landscapes', in *Pastoralists and Nomads in South Asia*, edited by Leshnik and Sontheimer. Wiesbaden: Otto Harrassowitz, 1975, pp. 30ff.
17. See, e.g. A. Mackintosh, *An Account of the Origin and Present Conditions of the Tribe of Ramoossies . . .*, Bombay, 1833.

18. Brief Notes to the Satara Jageerdars. By T.C. Loughnan . . . and by Lieutenant H.B. Sandford, in *Selections from the Records of the Bombay Government No. XLI—New Series*, Bombay, 1857, p. 23, cp. p. 178.
19. Unpublished inscription, of which an abstract by G.H. Khare appeared in *Samartha* (Satara) on 25-7-1932. I owe the reference to Prof. G.H. Khare. A copy of the abstract was obtained with the help of Mr. K.B. Mhaske.
20. Vol. V, pt. 2, p. 202 (Bh.I.S.M. Granthamālā, Kr. 93, Pune, 1961): Mahisvar[=ḍ]ā [*sic*].
21. G.H. Khare, *Mahārāṣṭracīṃ cār daivateṃ*, Poona, 1958, p. 91.
22. See G.H. Khare, op. cit., p. 90.
23. *Śrī-Somnātha Māhātmya* [in Marāṭhī], Āmbavaḍe, 15th ed., Śake 1888 [AD 1966], ch. 1.
24. Arevadi, the centre of Birobā worship in the Sangli District, has a *jatrā* in the month of April which is attended by 20,000 Dhangars. But the neighbouring Dhalgaon has respectable Hemāḍ Pantī temples with few visitors. The Shiva temple at Palasdev, 15 miles to the north-west of Indapur, has a Hemāḍ Pantī base and a brick superstructure. A local story says that the temple was built by cowherds about 1680. See *Poona Gazetteer*, vol. XX (Poona District), p. 626. Besides, it is not necessarily justified to assume that there was any extensive regular cultivation around such temples. Often they seem to have been cattle-based rather than based on regular plough cultivation.
25. *Bombay Gazetteer*, Poona District, vol. XX, rev. ed., 1954, p. 45.
26. Ibid., p. 47.
27. Ibid., pp. 55f. *Bombay Gazetteer*, vol. XX (1884), Sholapur, p. 231. A. Mackintosh, *An Account . . . of the Tribe of Ramoossies. . .* , Bombay, 1833, pp. 70f. and fn.
28. The author has frequently seen Vīr-(hero-)stones showing heads of cattle behind or over the killed defender of the cattle, e.g., at Mahuli, 10 miles north of Vita (Khanapur Taluka). See also D.D. Kosambi, *Myth and Reality*, Bombay, 1962, pp. 36 and fn., 146f.
29. *The Judicial System of the Marathas*, Poona, 1953, p. 4, with fn. 9. For a village based upon cattle breeding, see D.D. Kosambi, op. cit., p. 146.
30. *Bombay Gazetteer*, Poona district, vol. XX, rev. ed., 1954, p. 49.
31. Molesworth, op. cit., *s.v.*: The region along the eastern side of the Sahyādri range. It is viewed as commencing at the termination of the *murheṃ*, and as extending 40 or 50 miles eastward. *murheṃ* 1 Mist. 2. The region along the summit and the levels of the waist and the immediate base of the Sahyādri range. It is considered as extending five or six miles eastward, and as then lost in the *māvaḷ*. The word is commonly known in the second sense.
32. 'Memoir on the Satara Territory' by T. Ogilvy, in *Selections from the Records of the Bombay Government, No. XLI—New Series* (ed. by R. Hughes Thomas), Bombay, 1857, pp. 3ff.

33. *Selection of Papers from the Records at the East-India House . . .*, vol. IV, London, 1826, p. 179. See also p. 142 with reference to the conditions in Khandesh and the area south to the Nīrā.
34. Ibid., pp. 409f. We do not enter the discussion whether the king *was* the owner of the soil.
35. See generally Ravinder Kumar, *Western India in the Nineteenth Century, A Study in the Social History of Maharashtra*, London, Toronto, 1968. On the development in the Taluka of Indapur (in the north-west of our area) see ibid., pp. 88f., 172.
36. See above, p. 89.
37. A more detailed account on kinship, marriage, divorce, inheritance, etc., will be attempted elsewhere.
38. From *mhaśā*, *mhais*, cf. *mhaskyā* = a buffalo-grazier, keeper. Molesworth, op. cit., s.v. There is ample evidence that the god Mhasobā, Mhaskobā, Mhatobā was a god of cattle and cattle herders and then developed into the ubiquitous field guardian deity or *kṣetrapāl*.
39. Told (in Marāṭhī) by Viṭhṭhal Dagaḍobā Gavḷī.
40. Limba Torve. He died two years ago on the migration to Konkan.
41. The 'Bhairavnāth from Kāśī' is the subsequent identification of a cattle god (mostly Mhasobā) with a god from the Purāṇas. Cp. also fn. 38 above.
42. I could not check this statement.
43. From the material related by Sakhārām Bābu Lakaḍe, one of my best informants.
44. The 'Paṇḍharī buffalo' is still famous.
45. Molesworth, op. cit., s.v.
46. *Sholapur Gazetteer*, 1884, p. 147, 14.
47. *Maharashtra State Gazetteers, Kolhapur District* [rev. ed. of vol. XXIV of the original Gazetteer], Bombay, 1960, pp. 293ff. *Maharashtra State Gazetteers, Satara District* [rev. ed. of vol. XIX of the original Gazetteer], Bombay, 1963, pp. 332f.
48. Hari Balkṛṣṇa Āroḷe, *Śrīnāth Mhaskobā Devācem Caritra* [in Marāṭhī], 3rd [unaltered] ed., Vīr, 1962, p. 4, see also p. 7.
49. It may be that some rich landlords have been specially favoured by the new changes. But one also notices the ability of some castes to exploit the new possibilities better than others, e.g. the Māḷīs, traditionally horticulturists.
50. The *District Census Handbook*, Poona, 1961, shows an increase from 26,400 acres of forests in 1950-1 to 34,700 acres in 1959-60 and a decrease of culturable waste from 26,500 acres to 2,900 acres during the same period. See pt. III, p. 248. The above-mentioned incident is said to have happened in May 1969.
51. Cp. W. Rau, *Staat und Gesellschaft im alten Indien, nach den Brāhmaṇa-Texten dargestellt*, Wiesbaden, 1957, pp. 51ff.: *grāma* = (1) group of migrating cattlekeepers (2) village. Cp. the term *gonisādiniviṭṭho gāmo* = cattle village and *vaja* = temporary cattle camps in the Pāli Canon. Cit. N. Wagle, *Society at the Time of the Buddha*, Bombay, 1966, p. 14.

52. See D.D. Kosambi, 'Living Pre-history in India', in *Scientific American*, vol. 216/12, 1967, pp. 112ff.
53. The scene of the famous novel *Bangarvāḍī* (Bombay, 1955) by Vyankatesh Madgulkar (tr. Ram Deshmukh, *The village had no walls*, Asia Publishing House, London, 1966, (repr.)), which vividly depicts the predicaments of a village nearly entirely inhabited by village-based shepherds. A popular but perceptive account of the nomadic Dhangars in Maharashtra has been published by Dr. Vasantrāv Ghāṇekar, 'Mahārāṣṭrācā Bhaṭkyā-Dhangar', in *Svarājyā*, Mumbaī, Puṇe, 29 November 1969, pp. 5, 12.
54. The Poona and Satara Districts were famous for horses, and amongst them the for Dhangar or Khilārī pony, of which many served as baggage carriers in the Persian campaign (1856-7), the Abyssinian campaign and the Afghan campaign (1879-80). *Bombay Gazetteer*, vol. XVIII, Poona District, p. 61ff.
55. For the *copāḷā* and its function see D.D. Kosambi, *Myth and Reality*, pp. 114f.
56. According to data gathered at the Government Sheep Farm in Poona. A good survey of the economy of sheep breeding among stationary and nomadic Dhangars is the *Progress Report of the Scheme for carrying out a survey to evolve a suitable technique for working out the cost of production of sheep and wool.* Published by the Govt. of Bombay, Poona, 1957.
57. See the various lists of village servants (*balutedārs*) and minor village servants (*alutedārs*) cited in Molesworth's *Dictionary*.
58. *irjīk*: this is normally a communal dinner for agricultural labourers.
59. See the definitions in Wolf-Dieter Hütteroth, *Bergnomaden und Yaylabauern im mittleren kurdischen Taurus*, Marburg, 1959, pp. 37ff.

Some Memorial Monuments of Western India

India possesses a rich variety of memorials to the dead, and this phenomenon of religion, history and many other fields of Indian culture remains to be studied comprehensively and comparatively. Prominent amongst these memorials, which can be found all over India, especially Western India, Rajasthan, Gujarat and in the Deccan, but also in Madhya Pradesh, Kashmir, and Bihar, are the ones erected for men who died as heroes in battle or who met with an unnatural death. In close connection with them figure the innumerable *satī* monuments.

This subject calls not only for systematic field research, but also for preservation, because there is the danger, as in so many fields of Indian history, of losing important source material forever. It would be a long list if examples were cited of *vīragaḷas* being used for building houses, roads and walls of forts or lying in a ditch near the road. Occasionally they attract the attention of farmers and are worshipped with *sindura* inside or outside a temple; this further hastens their decay. The present paper merely aims at drawing attention to the needs of preservation and to a neglected, but promising field of research.[1]

Before we deal with the special field of the worship of heroes and *satīs*, we want to distinguish—with the help of a few examples—the multiple forms of the general worship of those dead who died a natural death.

In wide sections of the population—leaving aside the brahmanical customs of immolation and ancestor worship—simple stones are planted for the dead, mostly in a *smaśān* outside a village and often near a river. Often small shrines are erected over such stones and, for instance, in southern Maharashtra, at Huljanti in the Mangalvedha Taluka of the Sholapur District, remind us of miniature megalithic 'burials' (Pl. I, Fig. 1). These shrines often merge into small temples corresponding to the fame of the deceased and the wealth of his relatives (Pl. I, Fig. 2). The whole group of about 100 monuments is clustered near the river to the side of the temple of a famous saint and devotee of a major pastoral god of Maharashtra, i.e. Birobā. The god annually comes at Divāḷī to visit his devotee and disciple. This is celebrated with a big fair. The larger shrines have domes resembling in style those of nearby Bijapur. The grouping of memorials around the temple of a god or the *samādhi* of a saint is frequent and Birobā, the pastoral god, has in many places of Maharashtra a huge cluster of memorial stones with representations of the ancestors of a patriliny.

A curious phenomenon are the 'clay tents' about 50 to 80 cms high, which can be found in Maharashtra and elsewhere. They are, at least in Maharashtra, historically connected with some pastoral community and have been compared with tents ('Jurten') from inner Asia.[2] Often stones are placed inside, representing the ancestors (Pl. I, Fig. 3). From such a cult develops a god of the pastoralists who in turn develops into a protector of fields (*kṣetrapāl*), especially when regular agriculture has come to stay (Pl. I, Fig. 4).

The worship of Śiva in the Deccan has frequently led to a large number of small temples accumulating near a *tīrtha*, on the banks of a river which has become more than a *smaśān* or burial and burning ground. A good example is the second capital of the Cālukyas of Badami, Pattadkal. Here, besides the imposing, well-studied larger temples on the banks of the river Malprabha, we find dozens of smaller shrines and the base of the portico, with a *liṅgam* in the middle of it (Pl. II, Fig. 1). M.S. Mate has referred to a similar accumulation of *liṅgam* shrines in Aihole. They are situated at secluded spots near the river as in Pattadkal and, for instance, at Tigowa in Madhya Pradesh.[3] He concludes that they were monuments to commemorate individuals. Again they cluster around a larger temple like the Saṅgameśvar, Vīrūpakṣa and Pāpanātha temples in Pattadkal. One need not go into inscriptions, but can refer to living practice to illustrate the process. An important pastoral god in Maharashtra, for instance, the god Bābīr in the Baramati Taluka of the Poona District, who draws a huge gathering during the Divāḷī *yātrā*, recently acquired two formidable Śiva (*liṅgam*) shrines behind his temple. The main devotee of this god caused these shrines to be built for his deceased father and for himself. If sufficient wealth were available—no doubt this was the case in places like Pattadkal—one would soon see more such shrines erected by the devotees of this god for the sake of acquiring *puṇya* and to ensure commemoration after death or the commemoration of the already deceased, or to assure one's vicinity with Śiva after death.

The desire to be near Śiva in the form of the *liṅgam* during and after life, *śivabhakti*, must have been a strong force behind the building of the *liṅgam* shrines.[4] One need not go so far to postulate the desire of the devotee to merge with the *liṅgam*, as is said of Lakulīśa, the 'founder' of the Paśupati sect, or of Basavappa, the 'founder' of the Vīraśaiva sect, who became one with their god. The idea of worshiping the god during life and of being close to him in constant worship even after life, and that perhaps on the Kailās, is ubiquitous. It occurs, e.g. in the representation of the deceased worshipping the *liṅgam* and *yoni* and *chatrīs* in Rajasthan, e.g. behind the Ekaliṅgjī temple near Nathdvara, or on nearly all the *vīragaḷas* where the hero was a Śaivite.

By far the most widespread and common memorials for the dead are the *vīragaḷas*—Skt. Ka. Ta. *vīra* = 'hero' and Ka. *gaḷa* or Ta. *kalu* = 'stone'. They are found in large numbers especially in Karnataka and southern Maharashtra. Nearly every old village in these regions owns at least a few of them. Perhaps they have their origin in the menhirs erected even today by the tribals in India. Their origin can already be traced in the old Tamil literature of the second century, in which we find the famous reference to the crossroads where the enemies of the king live and where inscribed stones were erected to commemorate the heroes and the robbers, the Malavars.[5] The question whether and how far the wooden memorial pillars, e.g. of the Bisonhorn Murias and the memorials of the Korkūs, are influenced from outside or *vice versa* has still to be mooted.

Amongst many tribes and castes we find the belief in the spirits of the deceased who have to be confined in a stone and have to be fed periodically.[6] In the upper strata of society we find the belief—leaving aside the notion of the transmigration of souls—that after a complete life, which includes the completion of all 'sacraments' (*saṃskāras*), the soul ascends to the Kailas. If a life remains incomplete, e.g. because of the omission of a *saṃskāra* like marriage, or because of a violent and unnatural death, the soul appears in dreams or hovers around as a ghost with unfulfilled desires, causing unrest and damage among the living unless it may be given a stone to rest in. Or, perhaps, a further step in the evolution of the belief, the stone has to be erected to effect the ascension to the gods. In an inscription of the year AD 1285 from Coorg we read:

> . . . Mārutamma of Kahigōḍo, joining fighting with his boasting bitter enemies, fell in the fight.
>
> In order that Mārutamma may attain to the world of gods, his younger brother Maliya-nāyaka . . . this *vīragal*.[7]

This suggests that a stone has to be erected to allow the hero to ascend to the world of gods. But the concept of hero and fame (*vīra* and *kīrti*) is also present and must have been a strong overriding motive in warring communities who did not have any claims as such to be called 'Kṣatriyas' but who aspired to rise in social and ritual rank. That the erection of a stone had at times to be approved by the ruler seems to reflect this.[8] Many a local princeling, if not dynasty, must have originated in such circumstances. If the hero survived he earned the wealth offered by Lakṣmī in the form of donations by the king etc., or he received promotions and insignia.[9] And if he died in battle his relatives were sure to receive royal gifts and insignia, e.g. the honour of a *chatrī* (royal parasol), or the honour of being carried in a palanquin.[10] Death or victory in battle or in a hunt against a tiger etc., indicated special qualification for rank and honour. Spiritually the soul of the hero was considered to migrate to the *brahmaloka* or *sūryaloka* or to the Kailās. We have the well-known Sanskrit *śloka* from an inscription of Karnataka:

dvāv imau puruṣau loke sūryamaṇḍalabhedinau /
parivrāṭ, yogabhuktaś ca raṇe cābhimukho hataḥ //

As the yogi achieves supernatural union with god by his austerities, so does the hero by his fight and death. The fight in itself becomes a kind of religious, yogic exercise for achieving the supernatural. It may be noted here in passing that even today we find so-called *vīras* effecting in themselves by self-mortification the presence of the god, by piercing, for instance, their legs with pointed iron rods,[11] or performing a kind of sword dance, striking the sharp edge against their body or holding the point of the sword against their body, etc.[12] The sacrifice of one's life or head or flesh to a deity was a frequent occurrence, besides the famous self-destruction of faithful followers (the *garuḍas*) of a Hoysaḷa general in medieval Karnataka.[13]

The *vīragaḷas* of Maharashtra and Karnataka of the time of the Cālukyas, Rāṣṭrakūṭas, Cālukyas of Kalyāṇī, Hoysaḷas and Yādavas (Seuṇas) of Devgirī generally show two to five reliefs on the front of the slab (Pl. III, Fig. 3). Sometimes we find in Maharashtra square stone columns up to two metres high which depict on all four sides the fate of heroes (Pl. II, Fig. 4).[14] Early precursors of the *vīragaḷas* can be seen in the Museum Gujari Mahal of the fort at Gwalior. Here the slab is crowned by a bust of the hero (Pl. II, Figs. 2+3). Generally, however, the stones in Northern and Eastern India have fewer panels than those in the Deccan. Mostly there is just one relief on the top of the stones, though they *may* be of the same size, like the stones in the Deccan. Thus only one of the hero-stones of Budhpur in Bihar (Manbhum District)—they are of the ninth-twelfth century and most of them seem to be in the Patna Museum—has two panels. Another stone characteristic of a *daṇḍanāyaka* is located in Cuttack and shows a small carving of a warrior below the right side of the main panel.[15] These stones are very similar to those found everywhere in Madhya Pradesh, e.g. at Lanji

(Balaghat District) within the precincts of the Gond fort, and at Barsur, at Jagdalpur (Bastar District) etc. (Pls. X and XI). Near Lanji, at Bhanutola (Gathadongri), we find also hero-stones with the depiction of *satī*. They are a Gond ancestor complex and the stones are very similar to those of Gond Rajas (seventeenth century) now in the State Museum at Bhopal (Pl. IX, Figs. 3 and 4). All these stones just mentioned clearly originated from a tribal context and concern tribal chiefs or tribal *nāyakas*. Some of the hero-stones which are combined with *satī* depiction at Bara Dongar and Chapka (both Bastar District) are perhaps influenced by Rajput invasions or may also be stimulated by 'Rajputization'. They are rather like *pāliyās* with only one relief. The single exception to the one-panelled stones of the eastern parts of India seem to be the *chāyāstaṃbhas* of Amaravati (third or fourth century), which tend to have several panels.

There are other early forms of hero-stones, e.g. in the region of Jodhpur and Bikaner, namely the so-called Govardhana-Kīrtistaṃbhas of the Pratihāra period.[16] The *staṃbhas* are crowned by a structure resembling a miniature shrine. On the four sides of this 'shrine' we find sometimes Gaṇeśa, Śiva, Devī and Kṛṣṇagovardhana (Pl. III, Figs. 1+2). From inscriptions we come to know that they have been erected for the hero defending the cattle[17]—even today the surrounding area is marked by pastoralism. It is a fair inference—as suggested to the author by R.C. Agarwal—that the hero's feat was compared with that of Kṛṣṇa protecting the cows against Indra's anger.

Later the Govardhanas tend to become simple *kīrtistaṃbhas* erected for a dead person beside a tank or a temple gifted by him. Brahma, Śiva, Devī, and Sūrya are shown and the stones are not meant to be hero-stones.[18]

In their pictorial contents the hero-stones of the western Deccan reflect in the lowest panel very often their ecological and social environment—which must have been a relatively static feature in pre-British times. In fact, we can refer to the well-known five landscapes or physiological regions of the Caṅkam literature, which implies the same static existence of the forest, pastoral, riverine (with rice cultivation), and littoral landscape besides the 'desert', which comes into origin in the hot season. Each of the five has its own peculiar fauna, flora, and people with their particular activities.[19] Thus many of the hero-stones depict in their lowest relief a cattle-raid, the hero defending the cattle, a stampede caused by the raid, the hero (or the enemy) slewn and lying on the ground and the cattle bending their heads over the dead (Pl. III, Fig. 4). Memorial stones connected with cattle-raids can be found in largest concentration in such areas as Rajasthan, Gujarat, Maharashtra, and Karnataka, which can be demarcated as traditional pastoral areas. Here pastoral communities like the Rabaris, Gujars, Abhiras, Gollas, Dhangars, Kurubas, etc. abound, or here we come across cattle-based villages[20] with cultivation of millets, and here widespread regular plough cultivation must have been introduced only after the 'Pax Britannica'. Many a famous dynasty arose from such obscure pastoral origins, whether they were the Hoḷkars, or the Gaikwāḍs, or even the Yādavas of Devgirī, who, according to a much disputed tradition, were Gavlīs/Gollas or Dhangars.[21] If one goes to South Karnataka—a typical rice area—one still comes across *vīragaḷas*, but hardly do they depict a cattle-raid, because here the cattle—often male buffaloes are used for ploughing the rice-fields—are not valued with that much exaggeration and are much less frequent than in the pastoral area, from where they tend to be imported.[22] If one goes to the coastal areas one frequently finds the depiction of sea-battles, as in the famous, but now decaying, *vīragaḷas* of Eksār, near Borivli. These are said to be from the time of the Śilahāras, of whom one branch ruled in the thirteenth century Konkan. The last king of this branch, Someśvara, was defeated by Mahādeva, the king of the Yādava dynasty of Devgirī, on land and at sea.[23] Today these stones, of which three are about three metres high, face a pond and are worshipped as the seven water goddesses (*sātī āsarās*) by the local population. There are many more hero-stones commemorating heroes in sea-battles from the time of the Kadambas.[24] Some are now in the Museum at Goa (Pl. IV, Fig. 4).

Often the lowest relief shows the death of a princeling or local ruler symbolized by a *chatrī* and there is no question of a cattle raid (Pl. IV, Fig. 3). The beautiful *vīragaḷa* from Velapur (Maharashtra, Sholapur District) (Pl. IV, Fig. 1) seems to depict the rise and death of the hero.[25] The lowest panels of the two-panelled battle scenes show first the hero fighting on foot against a large enemy force and the next panel shows him on a horse and with a *chatrī* in what is probably another battle. The hero may have acquired the honour of riding a horse, he may have become a kind of *śiledār*, a *daṇḍanāyaka*. In both of these fighting scenes blood-thirsty demons are depicted hovering around the dead and one of them is indeed seen drinking the blood of a dying enemy.[26] To the right of the lower panel (Pl. IV, Fig. 2) we find what must have been an auxiliary tribal force, equipped with bows and arrows, some of them having *tutārīs*—war bugles. Velapur has a large concentration of *vīragaḷas* and so has the nearby village of Mhalung. But whereas we find the depiction of a great number of cattle-raids in Mhalung, Velapur has more battle scenes. Perhaps it was one of those important crossroads between north and south and west and east and a scene of frequent battles

The middle panel shows as a rule *apsaras* carrying the hero towards heaven, and a hero-stone from the Museum at the Gol Gumbaj in Bijapur seems to indicate a cloud. Such clouds are also found on the hero-stones at Bettigeri (Gadag), which belong to the Rāṣṭrakūṭa period, and on hero-stones on the Dharwar-Goa road (124 miles before Goa). Sometimes we have celestial musicians and spirits. Sometimes a palanquin or a shrine is shown in which the hero (with his wife) is carried towards heaven. The topmost panel depends on the religion of the hero.

(a) In most cases the hero worships Śiva, represented by the *liṅgam* to which the *nandī* is sometimes added. To the right of the *liṅgam*, seen from the viewer, the priest is seated. There is a great variety in the types of priests. In their left hand they mostly hold a *ghaṇṭā*—a bell—most common amongst the Liṅgāyats, the right hand holds a *dhupārtī* = censer. On the *liṅgam* a garland of flowers is often placed.
(b) If the devotee was a Jain, the topmost relief depicts the worship of Mahāvīra or a Tirthaṅkara.
(c) In the Kolhapur Museum some stones, which were found near the temple of Mahālakṣmī, show in their topmost panel the hero worshipping this famous goddess.

In the topmost panel or above it the sun on the left and the moon on the right are often depicted. According to Kannaḍa inscriptions, this would mean that the glory of the hero would last as long as the sun and the moon.

The hero-stone is often topped by the *kalaśa*, and in fact the whole stone is often fashioned like a temple or a shrine. Sometimes two or three *kalaśas* are sculptured and the panels below accordingly show the death of two or three heroes. At several places hero-stones vertically divided into two identical sequences showing the fate of two heroes have been found, e.g. in Kikli (Satara District) and Limbut near Nira (Poona District) (Pl. VI, Fig. 1).

It would be interesting to know whether one could see an origin of the *kalaśa* in the urn-burials of megalithic tombs. In some places of Western India the *kalaśa* resembles the Buddhist *stupas* and in any case many of the ancestral memorials of this area resemble the cluster of *stupas* at the Bhājā Caves.

The custom of *satī* existed from earliest times, e.g. the Greeks noticed it amongst the Scythians, though it was rare in ancient Indian literature and is unknown amongst the tribals. Perhaps it was a custom imported from inner Asia which was maintained among such warring tribes as the Gujar, Rajput, Saka, Hūna and Turuṣka and eventually became respectable among the gentry or the people aspiring to become gentry. It may have been strengthened by the brahmanical bar to divorce and remarriage of widows in the upper castes. Apart from the usual hand- and arm-symbol, which is found rather early amongst the stones of the late Gupta period at the Gwalior fort, we want to draw attention to a twelfth century or eleventh century stone which combines the death of the hero and *satī*. The stone is in Bid near Kolhapur (Pl. V). The first panel from below shows the usual fighting scene, the second husband and wife lying on the pyre; wood and flames are indicated (Pl. V, Figs. 1-3). The third panel shows the couple in a kind of palanquin, shrine or celestial vehicle ascending to heaven, and the top panel shows the couple in front of the *liṅgam* and *yoni* (Pl. V, Figs. 4 and 1). In Kumbharvalan (Purandar Taluka, Poona District) an otherwise ordinary hero-stone with several panels shows in its lowest panel the widow seated on the pyre beside her dead husband. Her arm is stretched towards heaven as if she were blessing the living. Eventually the depiction of arm and hand of the *satī* bent at the elbow and emerging from a post prevails (Pl. VI, Figs. 2 and 3). The post has never been properly explained, because the explanation that the wife was tied to a post and that this is indicated by the post seems unlikely. That fact that a right arm and occasionally the left arm is shown may have something to do with the caste of the wives. It could not have simply been a first and a second wife of the same caste, as there are stones—indicating the simultaneous immolation of two wives—which show two right arms and hands (Pl. VI, Fig. 2). The wife, becoming a *satī*, i.e. the 'pure' or 'faithful', does not really 'die' and does in fact not become a widow, but ascends with her husband to the Kailās or becomes his wife in the next life. Thus the 'wife' ascends the pyre fully adorned and only the one who stays alive to become a widow has to break the bangles. The bangles are invariably depicted on the raised arm of the *satī*. Her actual identity may be forgotten and she often becomes a goddess in local belief. A *satī*-stone in the Gwalior Fort Museum shows the couple in the typical pose of Umāmaheśvara, indicating a close identification of the dead couple with Śiva and Pārvatī. This depiction on *satī*-stones is very widespread in Madhya Pradesh. 'Arm and hand' indicates, according to Kannaḍa inscriptions, that she extended 'arm and hand' to her husband.[27] The hand may signify blessing and has the effect of magical power to resist evil spirits, as do the handprints on walls or entrances of houses all over India. Handprints of hands dipped into turmeric powder (Marāṭhī = *bhaṇḍār*) and printed onto the shirts of devotees of a god, as at the *yātrās* for Khaṇḍobā in Maharashtra, are taken as the handprints of the god himself. They have a very auspicious strength. In Rajasthan eventually only the red handprints of the *satī* on a wall prevailed.

Not only the suicide of *satī*, but also the suicide of servants and faithful followers of a nobleman or king seems to have reached a fanatical climax in the medieval Deccan. Suicide could take place also in the fulfilment of a vow to sacrifice one's life, if the king wins a war, gets a son, etc. Interesting samples of this are again found in Velapur (Pl. VII, Fig. 1) and other places nearby with a beautiful antecedent from Mangalvedha (Sholapur District) of the time of the Western Cālukyas of Kalyāṇī.

The last multipanelled hero-stones are of the Vijayanagar period (Pl. VII, Fig. 2). But it seems that, corresponding with the conquest of the Deccan by the Muslims, their cavalry and Rajput garrisons, the simple, smaller one-panelled *pāliyā* (Pl. VII, Fig. 3) with the depiction of a horseman replaces the multipanelled hero-stone, though the slab without panels showing the hero killing an animal or depicting a hunt was even before never completely absent (Pl. VIII, Fig. 1). But with the arrival of the *pāliyā*—the term itself is unknown in the Deccan—the notions of ancestral worship, hero worship and commemoration of respectable, powerful personages seem to combine (Pl. VIII, Fig. 2). The dead warrior is shown with his weapon and on a horse carrying him and his wife (or his two wives) much in the same fashion as the god Khaṇḍobā (Pl. VII, Fig. 4 and Pl. VIII, Fig. 4) or the legendary heroes of Rajasthan are depicted. Very frequent are the ancestor slabs showing the deceased standing with hands folded and flanked by his wife or wives (Pl. VIII, Fig. 2). Perhaps the multipanelled, wooden funeral pillars of the Korkus and Bisonhorn Murias[28] and the wooden memorial *khaṃbas* in Gujarat[29] reflect the earlier multipanelled *vīragaḷas*. Similarly the *chatrīs* of the Rajputs also entered Maharashtra, whereas in the *chatrībāgs* of Rajasthan it becomes difficult to make out whether a memorial is a Śiva temple or a cenotaph of a king, e.g. that of Ajit Singh at Mandor, which was completed in 1793. In the sanctum there is no *mūrti*. On the *śikhara* we find the *kalaśa* or the *amulatā* (Pl. VIII, Fig. 3).

Only a few samples of the material collected could be given here to show the relevance of a little-explored subject, which may offer contributions to the history of the warring groups in the West and South of India. Of them the Āryan *kṣatriyas* of the Sanskrit texts are only one successful group. Research beyond the texts throws light on the role of those groups of nomads, pastoralists and forest tribes in India as warriors and soldiers aspiring to rise and responsible for the making of many a dynasty.

ACKNOWLEDGEMENTS FOR PLATES

The photographs are by the author except Fig. 4 on Plate II and Fig. 1 on Plate VI, which were photographed by Mr. L.R.A. Jamsandekar, Dept. of Archaeology, Maharashtra State. These two photographs are reproduced by courtesy of the Director of Archives and Archaeology, Maharashtra State, Bombay. Figs. 2 and 3 on Plate II are published by courtesy of the Dept. of Archaeology and Museums, M.P., Bhopal; Fig. 4 on Plate IV by courtesy of the Curator, Museum, Goa; Fig. 3 on Plate IV, Fig. 4 on Plate VI and Fig. 2 on Plate VII by permission of the Director General, ASI, New Delhi. Figs. 1 and 2 on Plate IV are published by courtesy of the Trustees of the Prince of Wales Museum, Bombay.

NOTES

1. A Seminar in Dharwar, organized by the University of Karnataka, Department of Archaeology and History, and the present author, has recently drawn attention to these needs.
2. See Walter Ruben, *Eisenschmiede und Dämonen in Indien*, Internationales Archiv für Ethnographie, Leiden, 1939, pp. 165f.
3. M.S. Mate and Shobhana Gokhale, 'Aihole: an interpretation', in *Professor P.S. Desai Felicitation Volume, Studies in Indian History and Culture*, Dharwar, at p. 503.
4. See also B.S.L. Hanumantha Rao, *Religion in Andhra*, Guntur, 1973, p. 268 on the installation of *bāṇa liṅgas* in honour of the deceased.
5. *Caṅka Ilakkiyam, Malaipaṭukaṭām*, pp. 387ff. (ed. S. Vaidyapurippollai, 2nd ed., Madras, 1967).
6. Thus, e.g. a passage from a poem of the Caṅkam literature says that the hero became a stone and was fed with sacrificial food and the stone was adorned with a peacock feather. *Puram* 243 cit. by Vanamamalai, 'Herostone Worship in Ancient South India', *Social Scientist*, vol. 34 (May 1975) 40-6, at p. 41.
7. *E.C.* I. Coorg 86(7) and 85(6).
8. N. Kasturi, 'The Hero Stones of Mysore', in *Professor K.V. Rangasvami Aiyangar Commemoration Volume*, 1940, p. 204.
9. Ibid., pp. 207f.
10. Ibid., p. 207.
11. In Devaragudda at Ranebennur (Karnataka) during Dasarā.
12. At Vir in the Purandar Taluka of the Poona District.
13. Kasturi, op. cit., pp. 205f.
14. Kikli. (Satara District), Bavde (Sholapur District), Gulunce (Poona District), Bid (Kolhapur District), Precincts of the Bharatiya Itihas Samshodhan Mandal in Poona.

15. Excavated by K.N. Mohapatra. See A. Das, *The Orissa Historical Research Journal*, vol. XV 1/2 (1967) p. 59 and Pl. III.
16. Ratnacandra Agravāla, 'Paścamī Rājasthān ke kuch pāraṃbhik smṛti stambha', in *Varadā*, April 1963, pp. 68ff., 73ff.
17. Ratnacandra Agravāla, op. cit., pp. 74ff. They are found without *govardhana* carvings up to Panchmarhi and Chindwara (Museum) in Madhya Pradesh.
18. See H. Goetz, *Art and Architecture of the Bikaner State*, Oxford, 1950, pp. 87f. Kīrtistaṃbhas may be seen in the town of Amber, one e.g. in the precincts of the Gaṇeśa temple.
19. See generally Xavier S. Thaninayagam, *Landscape and Poetry*, London, 1966, pp. 99f.; Kamil V. Zvelebil, 'Pastoralism as Reflected in the Classical Tamil Theory of Landscape', in: L.S. Leshnik and G.-D. Sontheimer, *Pastoralists and Nomads in South Asia*, Wiesbaden, 1975.
20. As e.g. at Koregaon-on-Mul in the Poona District, which has numerous hero-stones depicting cattle raids, as in many villages to the east of Poona.
21. *Cāryugācī Bakhar* (Madras Govt. Oriental Manuscript Library, MS 1799-1802). According to Jain traditions, the first Yādava of Devgirī who made a mark on history was Dṛḍhaprahāra, by rescuing the village kine. As a reward he was made city-guard by the Brāhmans and other inhabitants, who accepted him as their leader by paying him taxes. *Siṃdhī Jaina Granthamālā, Granthāṅka* 10—*Vividha-tīrthakalpa*, pp. 53-4, cit. in O.P. Verma, *The Yādavas and their Times*, Vidarbha Samshodhan Mandal, Nagpur, 1970, pp. 14f.
22. K.V. Ramesh, *A History of South Kanara*, Karnatak University, Dharwar, 1970, p. xxv.
23. R. Cousens, *Medieval Architecture of the Deccan*, 1931, ASI, New Imperial Series, vol. 48, p. 21. *Maharashtra State Gazetteer. History*, pt. I—*Ancient Period*, Bombay, 1967, p. 261.
24. G.M. Moraes, *The Kadamba Kula*, Bombay, 1931, p. 261. Memorial stones with the depiction of a ship are also found in Kathiawar, e.g. near Dwarka in the village of Ārambhaḍā (fourteenth century). See Candramauli Majumdar, *Lokagurjarī*, Annual No. 4, March 1969, pp. 15ff. See also H. Goetz, 'Rajput Reliefs—I', *Oriental Art*, vol. X/3 (1964) 163-8 and Fig. 2.
25. The stone comes from Velapur originally and is now in the Prince of Wales Museum, Bombay.
26. There is another unnoticed stone with similar representations of *bhūts* in Mhalung; the significance of the scenes in this stone remains obscure.
27. Kasturi, op. cit., p. 205.
28. Verrier Elwin, *The Tribal Art of Middle India*, rev. ed., Bombay, 1949, pp. 90ff. Ajit Mookerjee, *Indian Primitive Art*, Calcutta, 1959, pp. 62-6.
29. See Eberhard Fischer and Haku Shah, '*Vetra ne Khambha*', *Memorials for the Dead*, Gujarat Vidyapith, Ahmedabad, 1973, pp. 25ff. and plates 29ff. This book and the same authors' *Rural Craftsmen and Their Work*, Ahmedabad, 1970, give interesting details on the religious and social functions and living traditions of memorials.

Plate I, Fig. 2.

Plate I, Fig. 1.

Plate I, Fig. 4.

Plate I, Fig. 3.

Plate II, Fig. 2.

Plate II, Fig. 1.

Plate II, Fig. 4.

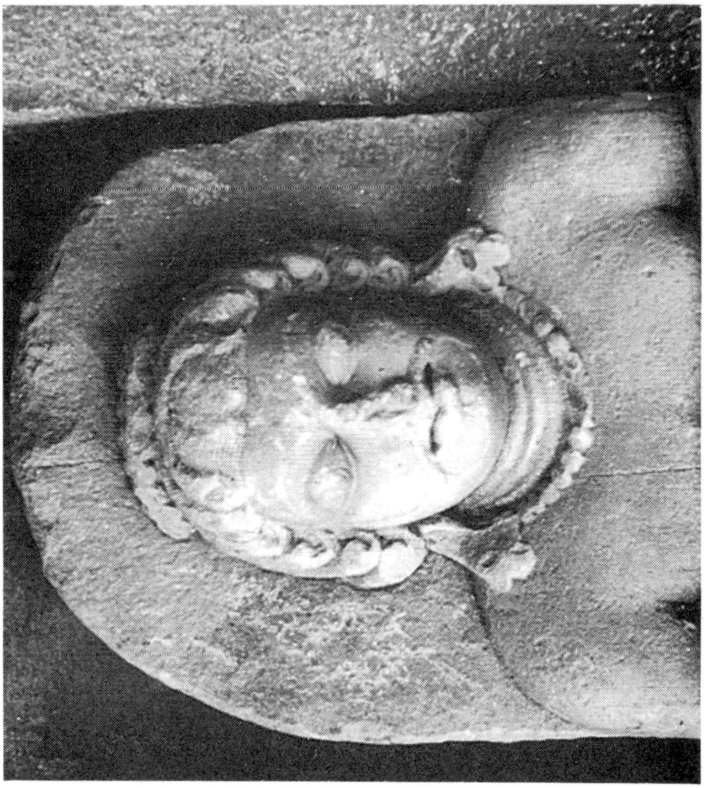

Plate II, Fig. 3.

Plate III, Fig. 2.

Plate III, Fig. 1.

Plate III, Fig. 3.

Plate III, Fig. 4.

Plate IV, Fig. 2.

Plate IV, Fig. 1.

Plate IV, Fig. 4.

Plate IV, Fig. 3.

Plate V, Fig. 2.

Plate V, Fig. 1.

Plate V, Fig. 3.

Plate V, Fig. 4.

Plate VI, Fig. 2.

Plate VI, Fig. 1.

Plate VI, Fig. 4.

Plate VI, Fig. 3.

Plate VII, Fig. 2.

Plate VII, Fig. 1.

Plate VII, Fig. 4.

Plate VII, Fig. 3.

Plate VIII, Fig. 2.

Plate VIII, Fig. 1.

Plate VIII, Fig. 4.

Plate VIII, Fig. 3.

Plate IX, Fig. 1.

Plate IX, Fig. 2.

Plate IX, Fig. 4.

Plate IX, Fig. 3.

Plate X, Fig. 2.

Plate X, Fig. 1.

Plate X, Fig. 4.

Plate X, Fig. 3.

Plate XI, Fig. 2.

Plate XI, Fig. 1.

Plate XI, Fig. 4.

Plate XI, Fig. 3.

Prehistoric Background to Pastoralism in the Southern Deccan in the Light of Oral Traditions and Cults of Some Pastoral Communities

with M.L. Murthy

INTRODUCTION

The Kuruvas (or Kurubas) are a shepherd community inhabiting the semi-arid regions of Karnataka and Andhra Pradesh in Southern India. Like some groups of Kurubas (as they are called in Karnataka) and some groups of Dhangars in Maharashtra (Sontheimer 1975: 139-70), who live in a similar semi-arid environment, they are either nomadic or practise transhumance, moving with large flocks of sheep from one pasture to the other. They now lead a symbiotic life with the settled farmers and maintain themselves by the sale of sheep and goats and through folding of their herds in the fields to provide dung, which is used as manure. As a result of the gradual disappearance of pastures and of the extension of regular cultivation, they are also adopting agriculture and are settling down in villages. Each pastoral group represents a single little community, and, more often than not, forms an isolated whole, being a homogenous, more or less self-subsistent unit, retaining some distinctive qualities. None the less, as a result of constant interaction with predominantly Hinduized societies, their religion has been subjected to continuous Sanskritization, probably over the last three thousand years. Owing to the spread of Sanskritic rites and the increasing Sanskritization of non-Sanskritic rites, one finds, as has been observed by McKim Marriott (1955: 171-222) in an Indian village, a transmutation and transformation of great and little traditions resulting from upward universalization (carrying forward of religious contents which are already present in the little traditions to the levels of literate Sanskritic great traditions of Hinduism under the influence of the latter) and parochialization (downward devolution of great traditional elements and their integration with the little traditional elements), although it is difficult to know whether the present religious traditions of these communities are the result of one, and not also the result of the other, of these two processes.

All these pastoral communities are Śaivites. The Kuruvas in south-western Andhra Pradesh worship *Mallikārjuna*; the Kurubas in north-western Karnataka and north-western Andhra Pradesh are devotees of *Mailār*; the Gollas in Andhra Pradesh, another pastoral community, of *Mallaṇṇa*; and the Dhangars of *Khaṇḍobā*—all said to be incarnations of *Śiva*. These four important gods, though they are not completely identical, share many common features. Historically, they may be traced back to a prototype god who made his appearance in the early Tamil (Caṅkam) literature of the second to fourth centuries AD, in which he is called *Murukaṉ*. *Murukaṉ*, who is later identified with *Kārttikeya* or *Skanda*, has especially one feature in common with the other gods, namely that they all have two wives. One of these wives comes from either the settled, advanced communities, who were agricultural groups, but with a propensity towards cattle keeping, or the once influential merchant groups. Under the latter can also be included the itinerant Banjaras (also called Lambadas and Sugalis) with pack bullocks, who played a very important role in the trade of cattle, food grains, salt, etc., even until the end of eighteenth century AD. Thus *Khaṇḍobā's* first wife, otherwise identified with *Pārvatī*, is also considered to be the daughter of a Liṅgāyat Vāṇī (merchant), the Liṅgāyats in general being a predominant agricultural community of Karnataka. *Mallaṇṇa's* first wife at Odela near Sultanabad in the Karimnagar District of Andhra Pradesh is *Madala Devī*, who belongs to the Balijas or Baṇajigas, another agricultural Liṅgāyat caste, also traditionally associated with trade. The second wife of the god, often regarded as a concubine by the settled, advanced and Sanskritized castes, comes either from the pastoral communities or from the forest tribes, which must have had much in common, or lived in symbiosis, with the village-based societies, as the archaeological evidence discussed below would suggest, and as is also evident from the early Caṅkam literature (Sontheimer 1976: 18f.). Accordingly *Khaṇḍobā's* second wife comes from the Dhangars, *Mallikārjuna's* favourite wife is a Ceñcū tribal, *Murukaṉ's* beloved is the famous *Vaḷḷi* of the Kuṟuvar hill tribe (see for details Vaiyapurippilai [edit.] 1967: 101f.), *Mallaṇṇa's* second wife at Odela is *Ketamma* of the pastoral Golla tribe, and *Mailār's* second wife at Devarguḍḍa in Karnataka is *Kurubattyavva* of the Kuruba tribe.

This instance in the religious history of these pastoral groups—the god having two wives, one from an advanced community and the other from a hill tribe or a pastoral tribe—presupposes acculturation of communities of different subsistence systems who were drawn into each other's fold in an ecosystem which, as archaeological reasoning points out, induced the development of an economic system that tended to be dyadic. This is reflected in a corresponding dichotomy of traditions which not only are orally transmitted but also found their way into the Purāṇas or local Māhātmyas.

Though *Mallikārjuna*, in the legend narrated below, apparently does not have two wives, he maintains his relationship with the pastoral Kuruvas through his special devotee *Bīrappa*, who is the exclusive god of the pastoral communities of the Deccan. In fact, one may detect in this legend instances pointing out that a lower culture was in continuous interaction with the higher culture. The legend of *Bīrappa* records an interesting situation with which communities like the Kuruvas must have been confronted time and again. Further, the evidence from northern Karnataka and Maharashtra corroborates such a persistence of homogeneity between oral traditions, incidents of cults, and archaeological findings in areas which, for ecological and culture-historic reasons, predetermined the economic systems and to a great extent the religion of the pastoral and peasant populations inhabiting these areas. In Karnataka and Maharashtra also, the oral traditions involve communities which were, on the one hand, at least in the past, either settled farmers with a bias for a cattle economy or respectable merchant castes like the Baṇajigas (Liṅgāyats), and on the other hand, pastoral nomadic groups based on a sheep/goat economy. The latter also include communities like the Gollas/Gavḷīs, who were once primarily cattle keepers maintaining cattle camps in the forests (Sontheimer 1976: 101ff.), as well as Rāmośīs and Koḷīs, who constituted the predatory and tribal elements in Maharashtra.

It is also interesting to observe that a binary economic system embracing both pastoralism and agriculture may at times permeate groups and even families. For instance, Haṭkar Dhangars are settled farmers, but one part of the group, or one member of a family, or a relation by marriage may be a nomadic shepherd wearing the typical red turban of the nomadic Dhangars. Such a practice evidently came into vogue due to ecological stresses and greater economic advantages. All the same, the ecological necessities (deterioration of pastures due to overgrazing, population concentration in the potential ecological niches suitable for agriculture, etc.) drove away a segment of the population into the interior forested zones and, in course of time, they lost trace of any links with the parent stock. There is evidence to this effect in the oral traditions; and, moreover, such a group, which became distinct by exclusively adopting a sheep/goat pastoral system and a 'life in the forest' (as the legends tell us), suffered social degradation and ritual impurity.

An endeavour is made here to trace to the cultural history of the Kuruvas and the prehistory of pastoralism in the Deccan by evaluating a Kuruva legend in the light of archaeological and ethnohistoric evidence. This legend was recorded at Balapālapalle (15°28': 78°7'), a village 70 km to the south-west of Kurnool town (Kurnool District, Andhra Pradesh), predominantly inhabited by members of the Kuruva community.

THE GEOGRAPHICAL BACKGROUND

The region where the concentration of Kuruvas is found broadly comprises the eastern part of Karnataka and the western part of Andhra Pradesh (for more details on geography see Singh 1971: 791-850; Spate 1972: 700-7, 715-27). The average elevation of this region ranges between 300 and 600 metres above sea level and forms a plateau country broken up by hills, sluggish rivers, small streams, and tanks. While the Karnataka part is characterized by castellated granite hills of the Archean series, in south-western Andhra Pradesh, apart from the extensions of the former, there are several chains of hills, namely, the Velikondas, the Palakondas, the Erramalais, the Nallamalais, etc., of the Cuddapah and Kurnool series. The Karnataka part of this region is drained by the Manjira, the Krishna, the Bhima, the Tungabhadra, and the Cauvery river systems. In south-western Andhra Pradesh, there are the tributaries of the Krishna, the Tungabhadra, and the Pennar. Although deep black, medium black, and mixed red and black soils are found in several parts of Karnataka and Andhra Pradesh, the region inhabited by the Kuruvas is mostly characterized by red soils and red sandy loams, both types being unsuitable for agriculture. While the hilly regions support dry deciduous forests, the low hills and plains have a scrub jungle and the peneplained rocky open country with a poor soil cover has a thin grass growth with occasional xerophytes. Excepting the areas subjected to dry cultivation in the vicinity of tanks and both dry and wet cultivation in the well-watered river basins, the rest of the region, including the hilly and forested zones, has good pastures and is well suited for a pastoral system.

ARCHAEOLOGICAL AND ETHNOHISTORIC BASIS

There is enough archaeological evidence to know the prehistory of early human populations that inhabited this region. In Pleistocene and early Holocene times, they were conditioned to a nomadic food procuring system based on a hunting and food gathering economy. The evidence for the food procuring system is available from scores of Palaeolithic and Mesolithic find-spots scattered along the river valleys, foothills, and forested zones. The faunal remains from some of the excavated Upper Palaeolithic cave sites (for a detailed account and references see Sankalia 1975; Lydekker 1886: 23-58; Murty 1975: 132-8) and a late Mesolithic rock shelter site[1] in the limestone escarpments of the Kurnool region testify to the ecological potential offered by the ecosystem for the primitive food procuring societies. The faunal remains from these sites include some of the favoured game animals, like porcupine (*Hystrix crassidens*), black naped hare (*Lepus nigricollis*), nilgai (*Boselaphus tragocamelus*), black buck (*Antilope cervicapra*), chinkara (*Gazella gazella bennetti*), four horned antelope (*Tetracerus quadricornis*), sambar (*Cervus unicolor*), chital (*Axis axis*), barking deer (*Muntiacus muntajak*), mouse deer (*Tragulus meminna*), ox (*Bos* sp.)/buffalo (*Bubalus* sp.), and Indian wild boar (*Sus scrofa cristatus*). Some of these animals survive even to this day in the higher forested hilly ranges, and tribes like Yerukulas, Boyas, Ceñcūs, Yanadis, etc. practise primitive hunting.

By around the third millennium BC, a food producing system based on a pastoral-cum-agricultural economy was introduced into this hunting and food gathering ecosystem by communities who moved in from elsewhere and raised villages in the favourable ecological niches. Some of these excavated settlements—the Neolithic-Chalcolithic sites—in the Andhra-Karnataka zone, such as Brahmagiri (Wheeler 1947), Sanganakallu (Subbarao 1948; Ansari and Nagaraja Rao 1969), Tekkalakota (Nagaraja Rao and Malhotra 1965), Piklihal (Allchin 1960), Maski (Thapar 1957), Hallur (Nagaraja Rao 1971), Utnur (Allchin 1963), Kodekal (Paddayya 1973), Palvoy (Rami Reddy 1968), and T. Narsipur (Seshadri 1971), have shown that their economy was chiefly based on cattle pastoralism supplemented by agriculture and hunting.

Even after the introduction of this pastoral-cum-agricultural system into this area, the Mesolithic cultural system based on hunting and food gathering continued side by side, as is known from the aforementioned Mesolithic rock shelter site in the Kurnool area. Here the microlithic industry occurs continuously in a deposit of 1.60 m thickness, but in the upper levels, pottery and a couple of copper objects are also found, the latter making their first appearance in the southern Deccan in the Neolithic-Chalcolithic levels falling in the time range of *c*. 1800-1500 BC. (Allchin 1968: 163). Further, from the middle levels there occur a few osteological (metapodials and phalanges) and dental remains of domesticated *Ovis*/*Capra* group along with wild fauna.[2] A few other late Mesolithic sites in the country, like Adamgarh, Madhya Pradesh (Joshi 1968: 245-54) and Bagor, Rajasthan (Misra 1973: 92-110), have already yielded the remains of domestic sheep, and they preponderate at the latter site. At Adamgarh and the Kurnool rock shelter site, while the microlithic industry and the remains of wild fauna prove beyond doubt that hunting and food gathering was the mainstay of the economy, the occurrence of the remains of domesticated sheep/goat alongside point out that the late Mesolithic communities adopted sheep/goat domestication from the advanced societies into their economic system as a result of contact diffusion.

As mentioned earlier, the faunal remains and other evidence from the excavated Neolithic-Chalcolithic sites in the area under discussion make it clear that these village-based groups were primarily cattle-keepers (Allchin 1963). The oral traditions of the existing shepherd castes, moreover, explain that a group of the original cattle-keeping-cum-farming stock branched off into new habitats, resorting to increased reliance on sheep pastoralism. In the light of the archaeological evidence and the oral traditions of the pastoral groups, it can be conjectured that the operational advantages offered by the sheep/goat pastoral system in this semi-arid grassland ecosystem induced its development as a distinctive economic system, inducting into its fold populations from the then surviving Mesolithic groups and the newly introduced Neolithic stock. The enactment of rituals associated with hunting and hunting expeditions, in the otherwise predominantly Śaivism-oriented religion of the Kuruvas and the allied groups, plausibly was the resultant product of integration, in the prehistoric past, of the cultural contents of the native hunting Mesolithic bands and the predominantly sheep pastoral offshoots of the alien Neolithic population. In this context, it is worthwhile to make note of an inscription (Sircar 1961: 8-9, 21) dated as late as Śake 1291 (AD 1369) on a pillar in the compound of the Malleśvara (also called Mailāradeva) temple at Ainavolu near Warangal in north-western Andhra Pradesh, which until recently was a predominantly pastoral area. About five stanzas (verses 23-7) in this inscription, which is in Telugu and Sanskrit, narrate that god *Śiva*, in order to protect Arjuna, assumed the form of a hunter (*Śabara*), fought with the demon *Malla* and killed him, thus acquiring the name *Mallāri*, which in course of time became *Mailāra*. The goddess, who accompanied her consort in the form of a huntress, is said to have been given the name *Māḷāchī*. This evidence implying the association of the 'great traditional' god *Śiva* with 'hunting', 'demon' and the 'forest' is suggestive of an upward universalization of the deep-rooted importance attached to hunting and forest tribes in antiquity by these pastoral castes (regarding Mallāri and Khaṇḍobā cf. Sontheimer 1976: 92, 124, 179, 189f.).

It also becomes evident from the oral traditions that the groups who adopted a sheep/goat pastoral system, in due course lost trace of any links with the parent stock and became so distinctive that their subsequent interaction with the ancestral village-based societies was that of initial conflict and eventual enculturation—in this instance a group from the higher culture taking up the life ways of the lower culture. There may thus be a change over from cattle-keeping to sheep pastoralism, as happened with the Gollas (Hassan 1920: 204) and the Haṭkar Dhangars (Sontheimer 1975: 139f.).

Keeping in view the above-mentioned considerations, it would be of great value to attempt an appraisal of the legend of *Bīrappa* for an understanding of the interplay of the ecological and socio-economic motive forces that shaped the culture, economy, and religion of the pastoral communities of the Deccan.

THE LEGEND OF BĪRAPPA

There was a Kāpu couple: *Ādireḍḍi*,[3] the husband, and *Ādemma*, the wife. They had seven sons. Their last son, *Elanāgireḍḍi*, was a *varaputra* (blessed son). He had *vaikunṭha rēkha* in his palm, *vinjāmari* on his back, *amruta rēkha* in his navel and the crown of a serpent on his head,[4] and he used to look after seven villages as a village head. The six elder brothers felt envious of *Elanāgireḍḍi*, and, to get rid of him, asked him to procure his own bullocks and proceed to a place where they had about a hundred acres of land. The place where *Elanāgireḍḍi* was asked to go and cultivate was situated north of Balapalapalle, somewhere near Srīśailam, in the same district. The local landmark of the area where *Elanāgireḍḍi* was to cultivate was known as *munimōdakamānu puṭṭa*, because of the presence of a tree (Telugu: *ceṭṭu*) known as *munimōdakamānu ceṭṭu* in that area. The belief in vogue was that in this *munimōdakamānu puṭṭa* god *Śiva* kept a *brahma rākṣasī*[5] (demoness) which was guarding this place which fell under its territory. *Elanāgireḍḍi*'s brothers thought that he would fell this tree while clearing the land for cultivation, as a result of which the demoness would get enraged and would kill *Elanāgireḍḍi*. Unmindful of this foul play he proceeded to the place with an iron axe. When he approached the tree to fell it, the children of the demoness challenged him and he killed them with his iron axe. The demoness went to *Śiva* and complained about the intruder and his killing of her children. *Śiva* told the demoness that the intruder (*Elanāgireḍḍi*) was a *varaputra* and that from then onwards that place would belong to him.

Some time ago in Kailāsa, Pārvatī asked *Śiva* for a sheep. The latter for the pleasure of his consort created one (or two). In due course, these multiplied into large numbers, overrunning Kailāsa and dirtying the gardens. Then *Śiva* brought all the sheep to the *munimōdakamānu cēnu* (the area of land recognized by referring to the *munimōdakamānu ceṭṭu*), created a *nāgalōka* (another world under the earth), drove all the sheep in, and covered the entrance of the *nāgalōka* with a stone slab. It was in this area that *Elanāgireḍḍi* started ploughing the land, and as he did so his plough hit the stone slab. His curiosity aroused, *Elanāgireḍḍi* lifted the stone slab, thus uncovering the entrance of the *nāgalōka*, and to his surprise heard the bleating of sheep. *Śiva* appeared at this moment and told *Elanāgireḍḍi* that he should take away the sheep and rear them. *Śiva* further told him that he should proceed to Kalyāṇapaṭnam,[6] which is situated in the west, followed by the sheep and without looking back, for, if he looked back, the sheep would stop coming out of the *nāgalōka*, and also that, among the sheep concealed therein, there was a golden *gorre* (ewe) and a golden *poṭṭelu* (ram) which would come out last. Unfortunately, *Elanāgireḍḍi* looked back when the golden sheep were about to come out, and they stopped. *Śiva* at this juncture asked *Elanāgireḍḍi* to go to Kalyāṇapaṭnam with the rest of the sheep. When *Elanāgireḍḍi* reached the outskirts of Kalyāṇapaṭnam with the flock of sheep, he was not allowed by the king to enter: as a result *Elanāgireḍḍi* spent about twelve years in the forest leading a nomadic life with his sheep.

In Kalyāṇapaṭnam everyone was wearing a *liṅga*,[7] every article was tied with a *liṅga* and even the animals had *liṅgas* tied to their horns. Every day *nandī* (*Basavanna*) (the humped bull), the *vāhana* (carrier) of *Śiva*, came to Kalyāṇapaṭnam from Kailāsa and, after receiving the worship from the people, it returned to Kailāsa. Since the practice of keeping sheep flocks was disliked by the king and people of Kalyāṇapaṭnam (as it was not their tradition), *Elanāgireḍḍi* was not allowed into the city: he was considered filthy!

Śiva, who from Kailāsa had been observing *Elanāgireḍḍi* spending about twelve years in the forests, took pity on him. *Śiva* decided that *Elanāgireḍḍi* should find a place in Kalyāṇapaṭnam where he could lead a comfortable life. To facilitate the entry of *Elanāgireḍḍi* into Kalyāṇa-paṭnam, *Śiva* planned a strategy. He made one of the rams of *Elanāgireḍḍi* and the *nandī* worshipped at Kalyāṇapaṭnam die simultaneously.

The people and the king of Kalyāṇapaṭnam were shocked and grieved at this mishap, for *nandī*, the *vāhana* of the god, died at the time of worship; and they started chanting prayers to bring it back to life. As soon as the ram of *Elanāgireḍḍi* died, *Śiva* appeared before him and told him to go to Kalyāṇapaṭnam with the dead ram and to sell its wool and meat to the people of Kalyāṇapaṭnam. Following these instructions, *Elanāgireḍḍi*, along with his seven sons, carried the dead ram to Kalyāṇapaṭnam. The people there, let alone buying the meat or wool, once again refused to admit them into the city.

Elanāgireḍḍi, being helpless, carried the dead ram to the outskirts of the city and put it on a pyre. The fumes and smoke coming off the burning animal started blowing over Kalyāṇapaṭnam when its inhabitants were still engaged in prayers to please *Śiva* so that he would revive *nandī*. Enraged by this deed of *Elanāgireḍḍi*, as this had rendered the ritual to revive *nandī* impure, the people of Kalyāṇapaṭnam threatened him with dire consequences. *Elanāgireḍḍi*, unperturbed, threw a challenge: if they failed to make the *nandī* alive, they should let him make his ram alive, in which case they should accept the meat and woollen blankets offered by him. The people of Kalyāṇapaṭnam, despite their best prayers with all music and dance, failed to revive *nandī*. Frustrated, they asked *Elanāgireḍḍi* to try his luck with the ram.

Then *Elanāgireḍḍi* took out of the pyre what remained of the ram and wanted to cut it into pieces, for which he needed a wooden plank. The people of Kalyāṇapaṭnam told him that since every article had a *liṅga* tied to it he could not use anything, as it would become impure. He asked them to dismantle one of the doors of the main entrance to the city and take away the *liṅga* from it so that he could use it as a plank. They obliged him finally. *Elanāgireḍḍi* cut the half burnt animal into pieces, collected them in a big pot and started cooking. *Śiva*, who had been observing from Kailāsa all that was happening, sent down *Rēvaṇa Siddēśvara*[8] to Kalyāṇapaṭnam to help *Elanāgireḍḍi* succeed in his attempts. *Rēvaṇa Siddeśvara* descended on the scene at Kalyāṇapaṭnam with his paraphernalia, and at the cross-roads of the city he stopped to buy *pasupu* (turmeric powder) and *kumkum* (red ochre) from the shops. He found to his surprise that in those shops which were selling *vajramulu* (diamonds) and *vaiḍhūryamulu* (gems), *pasupu* and *kumkum* were not available. He told those *vartakulu* (traders) to look into their bags. When they did so, however reluctantly, they found to their dismay that the bags which had been filled with *vajramulu* and *vaiḍhūryamulu* contained only *pasupu* and *kumkum*. They apologized to *Rēvaṇa Siddēśvara* for failing to recognize his greatness right in the beginning. He took from them a bit of *pasupu* and *kumkum*, gave them back their *vajramulu* and *vaiḍhūryamulu* and started for the place of conflict.

When *Elanāgireḍḍi* noticed *Rēvaṇa Siddēśvara* coming, he and his sons started drumming, dancing, and chanting prayers. *Rēvaṇa Siddēśvara* sprinkled the *pasupu* and *kumkum* into the cooking pot containing the dead animal cut into pieces. Owing to the chanting of prayers and the sounds of the musical instruments, and with the addition of *pasupu* and *kumkum* by *Rēvaṇa Siddēśvara*, the pieces in the cooking pot joined together and the ram sprung to life. It jumped out of the pot and ran amuck in Kalyāṇapaṭnam, destroying everything and killing everyone in its way with its horns and by dashing its head. Even the king, scared out of his wits, ran to a spot called *sūdiguṇḍu rayi* (a circular boulder with a conical projection on the top) and sat on it to save his life. The ram chasing the king started hitting the boulder, and with this impact the boulder started shaking. The king then requested *Elanāgireḍḍi* to bring the ram under control and promised that he and his people would take the meat and woollen blankets offered by *Elanāgireḍḍi* and also that they would follow his traditions. But *Elanāgireḍḍi* had no powers to control the ram, which was endowed with supernatural powers. Hence *Rēvaṇa Siddēśvara*, who alone was capable, curved the straight horns of the ram with his golden hand-stick: as a result the ram died. (The Kuruvas believe that since then rams have only curved horns.) Most of the inhabitants of Kalyāṇapaṭnam, as they were deeply moved by the greatness of *Elanāgireḍḍi*, threw away their *liṅgas* into water and adopted the way of life of *Elanāgireḍḍi* and his group. The others, not willing to change to the new tradition, migrated to Srīśailam, a pilgrimage centre dedicated to the god *Mallikārjuna*, and remained Liṅgāyats.

Because of the association of *birudulu* (musical instruments) in the prayers of *Elanāgireḍḍi* for the invocation of *Śiva*, and also because he won the challenge using *birudulu*, *Śiva* confered on him the title *Bīradēva*.[9] *Bīradēva* is popularly called *Bīrappa*. The descendants of *Bīrappa* are the present day Kuruvas, as *kuru* in Kannaḍa (the language of Karnataka) means wool. The Kuruvas of south-western Andhra Pradesh also call themselves Elanāṭi Kāpus. The Kuruvas in this area, as elsewhere in this region, identify themselves in two groups, namely, Uṇṇikankaṇam Kuruvas—the descendants of the first wife of *Elanāgireḍḍi*—and P(H)aṭṭikankaṇam Kuruvas—the descendants of the second wife of *Elanāgireḍḍi*. These two groups do not intermarry, as they consider themselves to be parallel cousins.

Kuruvas spread over several villages in the Kurnool District are almost acculturated into the agricultural society. Some of them keep flocks of sheep and migrate seasonally (once or twice a year) to the neighbouring villages within a radius of 150 km. For instance, the Kuruvas of Balapālapalle migrate during the drier summer months to the adjacent villages Maddūru, Togarcēḍu, Anapūru, Bāpanapalle, Yāluru, and Ṭanguṭūru. They return to Balapālapalle with the onset of monsoon. All these villages mentioned above are known as *rēnāḍupallelu* (Telugu *rēnāḍu*: red soil, *pallelu*: villages).

THE FESTIVAL OF BĪRAPPA

At Balapālapalle, there is a temple dedicated to *Bīrappa* which is a small modern structure built of bricks and limestone slabs. The sanctum sanctorum is a square room (approximately 2 m in length, 2 m in width, and 5 m in height), and facing it is a rectangular hall (8 m in length, 3 m in width, and 5 m in height). The devotees sit in this hall and perform *bhajan* (singing of songs dedicated to *Bīrappa* and from the themes of Ramāyaṇa and Mahābhārata to the accompaniment of music) on festival occasions.

Bīrappa is an ardent devotee of god *Mallikārjuna* and leads the god, who sits on a horse. There are two bronze figurines of *Mallikārjuna*. He has four hands, the posterior right hand holding a trident and the anterior right hand holding an umbrella; with his posterior left hand he holds *Mallikādēvi*, his consort, who is seated on his left thigh, while his anterior left hand is free. In one of these figurines, *Mallikārjuna* with *Mallikādēvi* is on the horse's back; this figurine, including the horse, is 10 cm tall and 6 cm broad. The other figurine is of the same size but without the horse.

The bronze figurine of *Mallikārjuna* with *Mallikādēvi* on the horse, on the day of the *jātra*, will be placed on an *ambhāri* (canopy) mounted on a wooden horse. In some places, as at the neighbouring village of Betamcherla, a bronze horse is used instead of the wooden horse. The wooden horse at Balapālapalle is 60 cm tall at the shoulder, painted in red, and to its right side stands the wooden figure of *Bīrappa*. *Bīrappa* has a beard and moustache, wears a *ṭopi* (cap), *jubba* (shirt), and *kurta* (trousers) and is bare footed. His *jubba* is green coloured and is painted with yellow flowers. He has a garland of flowers around his neck and a loin girdle around his waist. In his right hand he holds a sword upright and with his left hand he holds the reins of the horse. The belief is that *Bīrappa* leads the horse with the god sitting on it: they travel during the nights and take rest during the day.

Bīrappa's festival (*jātra*) takes place on the night of *caitra suddha vidiyā* and on the evening of *tadiyā*, the two days immediately following the Telugu New Year's day, which usually falls at either the end of March or the beginning of April.

On the evening (around 4 p.m.) of *caitra suddha vidiyā*, before the real *jātra* begins, the Kuruva men, women and children, dressed in their best attire, go in bullock carts (the bullocks are also decorated with floral designs in polychrome) to the *Sunkalamma*[10] temple, which is situated in the outskirts about 2 km away from the village. Each bullock cart is accompanied by music, and, after reaching the temple, makes three clockwise perambulations around the temple and stops in front of it. Music is played in front of the goddess for a considerable time, picking up a rhythm which induces some of the women to get possessed. Immature goats and sometimes hens are sacrificed by individuals as per their vows to the goddess. After the sacrifice they return to the village to participate in the *pāruvēta* (Telugu *paru*: to run, *vēta*: hunt), the ritual connected with the hunt, that takes place before the sunset. For this, a couple of hares (which abound in the neighbouring hilly scrubby jungle) are kept in captivity a day or two beforehand. These two hares, each held by a village elder, are let free in the presence of a crowd, keeping a distance of a few metres from the men who stand making more or less a straight line, ready to chase the animals. The scared animals run helter-skelter in a bid to escape the chasing crowds, and rarely do they succeed in running to safety. The two successful men who capture the hares enjoy a feast that night with their respective family members and friends. In case no hares are available, as happened at the nearby Betamcherla village on one occasion, a ram is let loose for the *pāruvēta* festival. In order to make the ram run as fast as it can, its tail is cut and *chunum* (calcium hydroxide) is applied to burn the wound. As is the case with the hares, the one who gets the ram celebrates the occasion by making a feast of meat with his family members and friends.

After witnessing the *pāruvēta*, most of the women return to their homes to finish the household chores early so as to assemble at the *Bīrappa* temple for the *bhajan* (singing of devotional songs) which precedes the procession. The men on the other hand proceed to the village meeting place, where the singers among them form a group and sing songs rendered in Telugu in colloquial Kuruva folk style of themes from the Ramāyaṇa and the legend of *Bīrappa*. The singing is accompanied by music and dance. This continues for about an hour and a half, after which they return to their homes for supper by around 8.30 or 9 p.m.; those who perform the worship strictly fast for the whole day.

Although no strict time schedule is observed, all the men, women and children gather at the temple by 10 p.m. By now all is ready for the procession. While some of the men (especially the aged), women and children do *bhajan* in the hall of the temple, there goes on in the front yard an incessant beating of drums and playing of flute and other favourite musical instruments of *Bīrappa.* When the beating of drums and the playing of flute reaches a climax, some men get possessed. When they get possessed, they become ferocious, and bellowing with rage, they fiercely brandish the *alugu* (sword) (also a spear sometimes) and hit with the pointed tip of the sword on their own person, on either the head or the abdomen. This display of savage fierceness is called *ugram* (infuriation) and scars left by this act can be seen on those persons who have gone through this experience. There is always an aide standing by with a bowl of turmeric powder (which has antiseptic properties), applying it to the wounds; in case an individual starts hitting himself too hard with the likelihood of a serious injury, the onlookers will hold him back and give him a lemon. The possessed individual, keeping the lemon in one palm, pierces the sword into it with the other hand, cutting it into two pieces: his *ugram* is thus relieved. Those who get possessed and experience *ugram* are held in high esteem in the society because it is believed that only those who are pious, truthful, and virtuous get possessed. It is also not uncommon to see young boys and women getting possessed: while the former behave like their elder counterparts in all respects, the latter on the other hand, go into trance and dance swaying their hands and bodies.

Amidst the beating of drums and other fanfare, the god—the small bronze figurine of *Mallikārjuna* (with *Mallikādēvi* in his lap) sitting on the horse, placed in the canopy on the wooden horse with *Bīrappa* leading it—is brought out into the front yard and mounted on a pedestal to be taken out to the outskirts of the village. Before the procession starts, the god is profusely garlanded, coconuts are offered, lemons are cut and a *mēkapilla* (immature goat) is sacrificed. The procession now proceeds through the important lanes, accompanied by the people singing devotional songs to the beating of drums and playing of musical instruments. It has become customary to hire a *natch parte* (dance party) to dance in front of the god in the procession.[11] As the procession moves into the spacious yard on the outskirts of the village, which is the usual meeting place for all the village festivals and functions, the pedestal carrying the god is brought to rest on the ground. A ceremonial bath is then given to the figurine of *Mallikārjuna* (and *Mallikādēvi*) and the wooden figure of *Bīrappa*; they are anointed with sandalwood paste; incense is burned; the god as well as *Bīrappa* and the wooden horse are decorated with flowers and garlands; coconuts, plantains and other fruits are offered; lemons are cut; and an immature goat is again sacrificed. While the priest (of the Kuruva caste) and other devotees are engaged in the worship, beating of the drums continues with occasional spells of silence, and it is a common scene to see both men and women getting possessed. This goes on until the early hours of the morning (with the *natch parte* entertaining the enthusiasts not very far from the place of worship), and the procession returns to the village before sunrise. Another immature goat is sacrificed before the procession enters the village, and the *jātra* comes to an end with the placing of the idols (the bronze figurines, wooden horse and *Bīrappa*) in their original positions in the temple. The next day is the day of *mokkubaḍulu* (offerings) and *uggupālu* (feeding milk to the new born child), which take place only in the evening (around 3 p.m.) in front of the temple. For the *uggupālu* ceremony, a *kambaḷi* (woollen blanket) is spread on which is placed a rectangular bowl filled with about two litres of coconut milk; according to the original practice, the bowl should be filled with sheep's milk. The devotees have to drink all the milk without lifting the bowl with their hands and without spilling even a single drop of milk on the *kambaḷi*. Before drinking the milk, the devotees, moving on all fours, perambulate thrice around the bowl, barking and biting each other like dogs. In the same kneeling position they bend their heads to the bowl, one after another, and, holding the bowl with the teeth on a corner, drink the milk, slowly lifting it up. The *uggupālu* ceremony is over by about 6.30 p.m., and this marks the ends of *jātra* for that year.

ANALYSIS OF THE LEGEND AND THE CULT OF BĪRAPPA

The story begins with the Kāpu couple, *Ādireḍḍi* and *Ādemma*. The prefix *ādi* of these names, meaning the earliest or most ancient, considered in the context of Indian tradition, implies reference to the foremost ancestral communities from whom the Kuruvas have descended. The episode by which *Elanāgireḍḍi* was asked to procure his own bullocks and clear a particular area of land for cultivation in a new territory suggests the gradual expansion of agricultural communities into regions hitherto uncultivated. The belief that a *brahma rākṣasi* was the guardian of the forest in which *Elanāgireḍḍi* was to clear a specific area of land for cultivation, underlines the awareness of the forest tribes possibly having territoriality, when these new communities started moving in. These forest tribes can be no other than the Mesolithic groups whose continued survival into the Neolithic-Chalcolithic times is attested by the archaeological evidence.

Tradition tells us that *Elanāgireḍḍi* comes across a flock of sheep in the forest. This is of great significance in the light of archaeological evidence. In the excavations of the cave sites in the Kurnool region, dental remains possibly belonging to wild sheep are found along with those of the other wild fauna falling in the time range of Late Pleistocene (Murty 1975). The expression in the tradition that the sheep are found concealed in the *nāgalōka*, and that *Śiva* asks *Elanāgireḍḍi* to rear them, seems to highlight a surprise discovery of a potent domesticate in the forest. Pending confirmation of the identification of the remains of wild *Ovis/Capra* group among the Kurnool cave fauna, it can be provisionally stated that the precursors of the domesticated sheep/goat species were probably extant during Pleistocene times in this hilly and forested country. The legend moreover tells us that *Elanāgireḍḍi* leads a nomadic life (for twelve years) in the forest along with the flock of his sheep, which is a clear confirmation of adoption of sheep pastoralism as a distinct economic system by a community. Further, the refusal of entry to *Elanāgireḍḍi* and his sheep into Kalyāṇapaṭnam; the aversion shown by the inhabitants of Kalyāṇapaṭnam towards keeping sheep; the religious importance bestowed on *nandī*, the humped bull, at Kalyāṇapaṭnam—all add up to indicate that cattle played a predominant role in the economy of Kalyāṇapaṭnam, which originally must have been a prototype settlement of the Neolithic-Chalcolithic type. It is said that *liṅgas* were worn by the inhabitants of Kalyāṇapaṭnam and that even the animals therein were tied with *liṅgas*. This religious tradition continues to be practiced by the agricultural Liṅgāyat community of Karnataka, revealing their ancestral relationship, and thus lends support to the belief that the economy at Kalyāṇapaṭnam was cattle-keeping and agriculture. The oral traditions augmented by the archaeological findings thus suggest that a nomadic or semi-nomadic pastoral system based on sheep herding and a sedentary village system sustained by cattle-keeping and agriculture were in vogue in this geographical area.

The struggle between *Elanāgireḍḍi* (and his group) and the inhabitants of Kalyāṇapaṭnam, portrayed in the oral tradition by reference to: (1) the death of the sheep of *Elanāgireḍḍi* and the *nandī* at the time of worship at Kalyāṇapaṭnam; (2) the challenge thrown by *Elanāgireḍḍi* as to which group would be able to revive the respective animal; (3) the success of *Elanāgireḍḍi* in bringing his sheep to life; and (4) the ultimate victory of *Elanāgireḍḍi* in making the inhabitants of Kalyāṇapaṭnam follow his traditions, altogether point to the initial conflict and final enculturation between two groups having different economic systems. This evidently took place due to the operational advantages of the sheep pastoral system over cattle-keeping and agriculture in this semi-arid grassland ecosystem most suitable for grazing.

It is interesting to note that god *Mallikārjuna* has two carriers, as he is worshipped by two types of communities. In the case of the Kuruvas, a horse is the *vāhana* of the god, whereas for the settled agricultural communities, the humped bull is the god's carrier. Archaeologically, the knowledge of the domestic horse (*Equus caballus*) is attested from Harappan times, at a rough estimate from around 2000 BC, and in the Deccan, a few remains of horse—one molar and a second phalanx in the Neolithic-Chalcolithic levels (*c*. 1500-1100 BC) and a splint bone in the early Iron Age levels (*c*. 1100-800 BC)—were found at Hallur, a site in the Tungabhadra valley of Karnataka (Alur 1971: 107-24). At the present state of our knowledge regarding the association of horses with the prehistoric cultures of India, it is difficult to know at what stage the horse became the *vāhana* of the god. The horse, however, seems to have assumed great significance as an animal of mobility from the Iron Age (*c*. 1000 BC), and the Deccan is rich in Megalithic grave complexes, some situated in the sheep pastoral area. A few of the grave sites have yielded horse bits, horse burials and iron implements (Leshnik 1971: 141-50, 1975: 40-67; Deo 1970), suggesting the importance attached to the horse. The adoption of the horse by the Kuruvas, to begin with, must be due to its mobility, and to this day some groups of Kuruvas and Dhangars use the horse as the transport animal when they go on their annual migration. Secondly, it is considered prestigious to have the horse as the riding animal, as is the case with the Śiledārs of Maharashtra. Thirdly, this indicates that the humped bull, and consequently cattle, played no significant role either in the economy or the culture of Kuruvas.

REFERENCES FROM KARNATAKA AND MAHARASHTRA

Versions basically analogous to the aforementioned *Bīrappa* legend, but with some differences, are available from eastern Karnataka and southern Maharashtra. They centre on the origin of the *uṇṇikaṅkaṇ* and *hattikaṅkaṇ* groups of the Kurubas. *Uṇṇi* (Kannaḍa) refers to the wool bracelet (*kaṅkaṇ*) worn by the members of the group which, according to tradition, subsists on a sheep/goat economy. The *uṇṇikaṅkaṇ* is tied during a marriage ceremony performed in the forest, no *hatti* (Kannaḍa: cotton) being available. The *hattikaṅkaṇ* group depends primarily on agriculture, with a strong preference for a cattle economy. This brings them nearer to the other agricultural-cum-pastoral communities like the Vakkaligas and Gāvaḍās (Gāvuṇḍas) of Karnataka and the Kāpus (Reḍḍis) of Andhra, who similarly had a strong leaning towards a village-based cattle economy. In all versions, it is told that the original and actual occupation of the mythical ancestors of the Kurubas was considered to have been agriculture and that they belonged to one or the other of the above-mentioned groups.

The tendency of fission in these groups, leading to the formation of a distinct group with a sheep/goat economy, is an intrinsic reflection of the man-land relationship and seems to have occurred repeatedly from prehistoric times. According to the legends it is always the younger brother, depicted as 'brave', 'lazy', or 'stupid', who is connected with the tending of sheep and migrations—the elder members of the family staying back at the village. This can be corroborated by the annual migration of the Dhangars in the Kolhapur area of Maharashtra. In this region, even to this day, the younger members of the settled Dhangar families join together for the long transhumance towards the drier north-east, up to Kurduvadi in the Usmanabad District, at the beginning of the monsoon. As maintenance of large flocks of sheep requires considerable territories for grazing, such transhumance was obviously necessitated by the increasing pressure exerted on land due to the extension of agriculture and over-grazing in their native habitats. It is plausible that in ancient times such transhumant groups eventually got disassociated from the parent sedentary stock once they moved into new habitats which offered better pastures but no scope for agriculture. The oral traditions in the Kolhapur area itself provide a culture-historic explanation for such a disassociation. Firstly, it is believed that the *uṇṇikaṅkaṇ* Kurubas are the illegitimate children of an ancestor who had extramarital relations with a demoness during his migrations in the wilderness. This once again implies a reference to the forest tribes, who must have been the then Mesolithic populations. Secondly and generally, it is the filth and bad smell attributed to the sheep and the shepherds, their association with the 'forest'—which means any unsettled, uncultivated, potentially dangerous, and ritually unclean area—and the consumption of sheep's meat (if not the slaughter of sheep), which tended to cause fission. The oral traditions apart, sheep pastoralism none the less becomes an important adjunct to settled agriculture under conditions of drought and other ecological restraints which render the maintenance of large cattle herds impossible. There may thus have been a change-over from cattle-keeping to sheep economy, as happened in the case of the Gollas or the Haṭkar Dhangars.

The enculturation of shepherds in the settled system is reflected in the legend by the arrival of the Kuruvas and their sheep in Kalyāṇapaṭnam, notwithstanding the initial culture-clash. In other versions, as found in the *Hālumatada Caritra* (Attikolla 1949), Kalyāṇapaṭnam is the famous capital Kalyāṇi of king Bijjala of the Kalacuri dynasty. His minister Basavesvara, who is reputed to be the famous restorer of the Liṅgāyat faith, calls the Kurubas with their herds of sheep to Kalyāṇapaṭnam. But they are repelled by the people of the city for the same reasons indicated in the Balapālapalle legend. Later the Kurubas return to Kalyāṇapaṭnam at the instance of *Maruḷasidda*—a saint like *Revaṇasiddha* claimed by Kurubas as well as Liṅgāyats. The miraculous revival of the dead animal by the Kurubas convinces the inhabitants of Kalyāṇi and facilitates their settling and 'the sale of milk and milk products'. The Balapālapalle legend is more straightforward: the Kurubas want to sell meat and woollen blankets.

The arrival of shepherds in a settlement and their enculturation is also the central theme in the legend of Pattan Kudoli, a large village sixteen kilometres to the east of Kolhapur in Maharashtra. Their arrival is marked by the arrival of their gods *Viṭṭhal* (*Viṭhoba*) and *Bīrappa* on horses, who are accepted into the village only after they have performed some miraculous feats. In fact, the *Viṭṭhal/Bīrappa* cult is the most important cult today at Pattan Kudoli. Owing to the influence of the Liṅgāyat god of Pattan Kudoli, the Dhangars in the area have given up sacrificing sheep to their gods. Nor is the sound of the '500' drums (drums also play their magical role in the legend of Balapālapalle) of the Dhangars and Kurubas who come for the annual *jātra* allowed to disturb the peace of the Liṅgāyat god: thus the drums are said not to be audible in the temple. Kurubas in northern Karnataka were inclined towards the Liṅgāyat faith and their saints are claimed by both the groups, but what generally prevented Kurubas from becoming Liṅgāyats was their occupation and the consumption of meat. *Bīrappa* often becomes a vegetarian under the influence of Liṅgāyat faith.

Some Dhangars also maintain the belief that their original *dharma* (tradition) was Liṅgāyat, which they lost because they turned to keeping sheep and the consumption of meat (Sontheimer 1976: 121). This is reflected in the episode at Kalyāṇapaṭnam which indicates a reversal to the pastoral life amongst the Liṅgāyats, who are said to have adopted the way of life of the Kurubas, whereas some of them unwilling to accept this change migrated to Śrīśailam to continue their Liṅgāyat tradition.

Bīrappa/Birobā has been exclusively a god of the Kurubas and

Dhangars. According to some legends, he is said to be *Vīrabhadra* and lives in the forest, and there are also clear-cut accounts explaining his association with hunting. For instance, he is said to have been found as an abandoned child in a forest by two huntresses. According to one version, these huntresses are the daughters of *Bāṇāī*, the female head of a large cattle and sheep camp and the second wife of *Khaṇḍobā*. A hunting background is also mentioned in an account of the Haṭkar Dhangars of Berar, who carried bear spears on their expeditions. This spear is still carried by many Dhangars and is conspicuous in the Somavati Amāvasyā festival in Jejuri (Pune District, Maharashtra). Here the Dhangars consider the procession of the god *Khaṇḍobā*, from his temple on the mountain down to the river a hunting expedition. The corresponding god *Mailār* in Devaragudda near Ranebennur in Karnataka has his hunting excursion on the eve of the Dasarā festival. The Kurubas have a prominent role in this ritual and one of their elders climbs a high bow to make predictions at the climax of the ceremony. The Kurubas have a special right to this bow, which is usually kept in the temple. On the Dasarā day, the enormous *cappals* (sandals) of the god and the goddess are kept ready by the side of the temple to protect their 'pure' feet in the hunting expedition. A similar tradition connected with *Murukaṉ* occurs in the *Paripāṭal* (XXI) of the Caṅkam age, indicating how widespread and persistent certain incidents have been (Sontheimer 1976: 190). In some of these rituals, as at Devaragudda for instance, the *bhaktas* (devotees) consider themselves horses (the *vāhana* of the god) and beat themselves with whips, an act showing their devotion to the god, while some others consume offerings of milk and bananas, acting like dogs, as at Balapālapalle. Such practices are also common in the cult of *Khaṇḍobā*. Moreover, in the *jātra* of *Khaṇḍobā* at Pālī (Satara District, Maharashtra), the *vāghyās* (*bhaktas*) enact a ritual in which they imitate the dogs of the god and kill sheep by tearing their throats with their teeth. The Kuruvas in the Telangana region of Andhra Pradesh were known to have sacrificed sheep and other animals in the same fashion; but such practices are fast disappearing in almost all the regions.

The crystallization of the pastoral (and forest) and the settled agricultural (and merchant) communities is not only shown by the two wives of the god, but also borne out by the *vāhanas* which have clustered around the cults of the god. *Khaṇḍobā* rides a horse. *Śiva/Mahādev/Śaṅkar* has a *nandī*, at times several of them, or even a herd of cattle of votive stone figurines. *Birobā* tends to have a horse and/or a ram. There are also a few bronze figurines of rams with a disproportionately small human figure (*Birobā*?) leading the ram. This can be interpreted, as in the case of *nandī/Basava/*

Basavanna, which is worshipped by the Liṅgāyats, that the ram in all likelihood must have been worshipped by the shepherds. These suggest that before the gods emerged in the form of *mūrtis* (images), their *vāhanas* were the objects of worship. In the case of *Birobā*, who is primarily the god of the shepherds, the *nandī* is conspicuous by its absence; the 'horse with the rider' is ubiquitous. During the *jatrā* at Pattan Kudoli each Dhangar family keeps its individual bronze figurine of 'horse with the rider' in the temple—a veritable army. As a matter of fact, this deity seated on a horse is one of the most widespread and common presentations in the Deccan: he may be *Mailār*, *Mallikārjuna*, *Khaṇḍobā*, *Mallaṇṇa*, *Birobā* or any similar god often identified with *Bhairav*. He has two (as in the case of *Birobā*) or four arms; one of his wives is seated before him or in his lap; and he may be accompanied by a dog. *Khaṇḍobā* has either stone or wooden horses, sometimes a multitude of them; *Mallikārjuna* has several wooden horses (as at Uravakonda near Bellary in the borders of Andhra Pradesh and Karnataka, one of the most typical sheep pastoral areas), or even a bronze horse, as at Betamcherla; and these recall the clay horses of the Tamil god *Aiyaṉār*, who, it is believed, keeps a vigil by his nocturnal rides and protects the village (though at times he may be dangerous to the villagers). At some places, a living horse is kept ready, as for the god *Jyotibā* (near Kolhapur), and a horse is led in front of the ceremonial hunt during the Somavati Amāvasyā festival of *Khaṇḍobā*.

As outlined earlier, the importance of the horse had been realized by the Iron Age times and both these nomadic and village-based communities living in the semi-arid, millet-growing and pastoral area found much use for the horse. For the nomadic pastoralists like the Kuruvas and the Dhangars, the horse is of utmost importance as a pack animal. For the settled farmers with large herds of cattle, the horse was of greatest use in petty warfare, especially over pastures. These groups were always ready for a feud, which generally began with a cattle raid, and such cattle raids and warfare over pastures, as for instance in the Palnad region of Andhra Pradesh, are known even in the late Medieval times. Thus there is no wonder that the *mūrti* of the god *Śiva* is generally equipped with a sword and a shield and is mounted on a horse. Moreover, groups from both types of communities formed an important element in the Medieval armies. Many of them rose high in rank as polygars of Śiledārs, and the horse became a prerequisite for honour and booty. The invasion of the Muslims or the influence of the Rājputs only enhanced the predilection for horses, and, during the Maratha period, much of the pastoral area in Maharashtra was used not only for pasturing cattle and sheep but also for rearing horses.

CONCLUSIONS

In the oral traditions and cults of pastoral communities like the Kuruvas/Kurubas and Dhangars is preserved valuable information for understanding the origins of the sheep pastoral system in the Deccan. Plausibly, the sheep pastoral system developed as an offshoot of the food-producing system which was introduced by the Neolithic-Chalcolithic communities who moved into this region from elsewhere. The earliest manifestations of these new societies are apparent in the village-based, primary Neolithic sites like those of Hallur, Kodekal, and Palvoy in the southern Deccan ascribable to *c.* 3000 BC. The economy of these village settlements was characterized by animal husbandry (predominantly by cattle-keeping), supplemented by agriculture and hunting. The evidence available from the excavated cave sites is suggestive (though not as yet conclusive) that the wild ancestors of the domestic sheep were extant in this region during the Pleistocene times; and the oral traditions imply that these were domesticated by a branch of the Neolithic-Chalcolithic stock who moved into the forested areas. A branch of this original population must have moved into the forested areas under ecological pressures and, realizing the suitability of semi-arid pastures for grazing, specialized in sheep pastoralism. It is perhaps for this ancestral relationship that the Kuruvas of Kurnool district call themselves Elanati Kāpus: Kāpu being a traditional agricultural community. It can be postulated on archaeological reasoning that the sheep pastoral system, since its inception in this area, drew into its fold some of the surviving Mesolithic populations as a result of contact-diffusion in a common geographical area. This is attested: (1) by the two wives of the god, one belonging to a settled agricultural/merchant community and the other to a hill/forest/pastoral tribe; (2) the importance attached to rituals associated with the hunt and hunting expeditions of the god, in the otherwise Sanskritized religion of the Kuruvas; and (3) other episodes narrated in the oral traditions connected with the 'forest'. Moreover, the present habitats of the Kuruvas are characterized by innumerable Mesolithic find spots indicating that sheep pastoralism was introduced into the structure of a hunting and food gathering ecosystem.

The populations who adopted the sheep pastoral system, in due course, broke away from the ancestral village-based stock and became so distinctive that they came to be regarded by the latter as socially degraded and ritually impure, as a result of their association with sheep and consumption of sheep's meat. But at the same time, under conditions of ecological duress, cattle-keepers like the Gollas and agriculturists like the Haṭkar Dhangars resort to sheep pastoralism, and such a change-over is portrayed in the oral traditions by an initial culture clash and eventual enculturation of the village-based cattle-keeping societies into the shepherds' cultural and economic system. Such a process must have occurred recurrently and even reversibly from prehistoric times, striking a balance between economic-cultural systems and the eco-climatic systems in the geographical area which had supported populations of three modes—(1) nomadic hunting and food-gathering type, (2) sedentary cattle-keeping-cum-agricultural type, and (3) sheep pastoral type—all at one time. The resultant integration of cultural elements from the three types of systems, as well as Sanskritization of non-Sanskritic rites, is explicit in the religious traditions of the shepherd groups. The adoption of the horse for various uses by both the agricultural and pastoral groups might have taken place with the spread of Iron Age culture into the Deccan, although the possibility of a slightly earlier date for the use of the horse exists on theoretical grounds.

Abstract: The oral traditions and religious cults of pastoral communities like the Kuruvas (Kurubas), the Dhangars, and the Gollas of the Deccan are centred on themes which provide evidence to reconstruct the development of their economic and cultural systems. It is endeavoured here to make an appraisal of the oral traditions and cults of the Kuruvas, the sheep pastoralists inhabiting the semi-arid regions of the southern Deccan, in the light of archaeological evidence. These studies point out that the antiquity of the sheep pastoral system in this region plausibly goes back to the Neolithic-Chalcolithic times, in that it developed as an offshoot of the sedentary village-based cattle-keeping-cum-agricultural system. The sheep pastoral system, since its inception, also drew into its fold the hill and forest tribes, and this is evidenced by the enactment of rituals associated with hunting, in the otherwise Sanskritized religion of these communities, as well as one of the wives of their god, who belongs to a hill forest tribe.

NOTES

* The authors express their thanks to Messrs. B.S. Muralidhar Reddy and E.V. Rajendra Sarma, Mine Owners at Betamcherla, whose local help made these investigations possible. Thanks are also due to Mr. E.V. Sujata Sarma, Managing Partner of the South Indian Mineral Co., Betamcherla, who took a keen interest in our work and helped us in several ways in the study of Kuruva traditions at Balapālapalle. G.-D. Sontheimer is obliged to the Deutsche Forschungsgemeinschaft for financial help received in the year 1977.

1. This cave site, locally known as Muchchatla Chintamanu Gavi, was jointly excavated by the first author and Dr. K. Thimma Reddy of Andhra University.

2. Thanks are due to Dr. A.T. Clason of Biologich-Archaeologich Institut, Groningen, for identifying the remains of domestic *Ovis/Capra* group in this collection.
3. Kāpus are the chief landholding and cultivating caste of Telangana. They rear milch cattle and bullocks which are employed in agricultural operations. Kāpus also claim their descent from *Ādireḍḍi*, from whose seven sons the whole Kāpu race is said to have sprung (Hassan 1920: 306).
4. These are some birth marks which, according to ancient tradition, are expected to be found (though not always) on the person of individuals endowed with supernatural qualities. This is a good example of later interpolation whereby *Elanāgireḍḍi* was raised to a suprahuman status.
5. The name *brahma* may actually have been derived from *bhram*: 'to wander around' (Sanskrit, Kannaḍa, Marāṭhī). There is a god in Karnataka and elsewhere known as *Bharmappa/Bharma/Bhramā* etc. who roves on horseback during the nights guarding the village. The *brahma rākṣasī* is a typical tree or forest demoness who lives on trees and roves around guarding the forest. The same demoness occurs in the traditions of Dhangars/Kurubas around Kolhapur, and she is called *Yeḷamakkaḷtāī* (Kannaḍa, the mother of seven children). She inhabits a tree the cutting of which results in harmful consequences (Sontheimer 1976: 38ff. [cp. English version: *Pastoral Deities in Western India*, pp. 34ff.]; Settar 1971: 17-34).
6. Kalyāṇapaṭnam is situated to the north of the Pune-Hyderabad road, about 160 km to the west of Hyderabad. Also known as Kalyāṇa, this place seems to have been involved in social upheavals. The Liṅgāyats, a Śaivite sect who experienced a flourishing period in the twelfth century AD under their spiritual leader Basavappa, the minister of king Bijjala, had been attracted to Kalyāṇa, which was first the capital of the Cālukyas and then of the Kalacuryas. As they seem to have posed a threat to Jainism and Brahminism, they were subsequently forced to leave Kalyāṇa and were dispersed in different directions.
7. The phallus shaped object, or its symbolic representation, worn by the Liṅgāyats.
8. The Vīraśaivas (Liṅgāyats) claim *Revaṇasiddha* as one of their *pūrvācāryas* and the Kurubas equally claim him as one of theirs. According to an inscription of the twelfth century AD, one Revaṇagavaḍa, belonging to the Haṇḍe-Kuruba caste, built a temple when the Cālukya king Someśvara was ruling in Kalyāṇa (Kalyāṇapaṭnam). This Revaṇagavaḍa became Revaṇasidha (see Hanumanthiah 1958: 77), or *Rēvaṇa Siddēśvara*.
9. There are various explanations for *Bīradeva/Bīrappa/Birobā*. Some derive it from *vīradeva* (*vīra*: hero; *deva*: god). This belief is in vogue in Karnataka, where *Bīrappa* is also associated with *Vīrabhadra*. In the legend quoted here, *Bīradeva* is associated with musical instruments (*birudulu*). This corresponds with southern Maharashtra, where *Birobā* is associated with *bāvan birudeṃ*, which are 52 magical cult objects, the drum being the most important (Sontheimer 1976: 193 [cp. *Pastoral Deities* . . ., p. 199]). But *Birobā* is also said to have '52' *vīrs* (*bīrs*)—godlings or spirits—under his control.

10. *Sunkalamma* is a village goddess, and her temple is a small modern structure of 2 x 2 m dimension standing 1.5 m high. The deity is represented by an elongated conical black limestone rock of 0.5 m height.
11. The dance troupe consists of a couple of young Bogum girls and their male colleagues who, standing on a well illuminated high rostrum erected on a bullock cart (which proceeds slowly in front of the procession), dance to the tune of gramophone records blasting at the maximum volume. This undoubtedly is the impact of Indian cinema and understandably, although regrettably, provides one of the rare occasions for amusement to the otherwise monotonous routine of the Kuruva village. None of the Kuruvas, unfortunately, know whether the practice of having dancing girls in the procession of the god has a high antiquity. In point of fact, the Bogum caste (Hassan 1920: 91-8) represents an order of Telugu dancing girls. Some of them, belonging to Munnur and Telaga Bogums, are recruited from the Munnur, Kāpu, Golla, Telaga and other castes of the same social standing. There are also Balija Bogums, known as Basavīs, who belong to the Liṅgāyat caste and are chiefly found in Karnataka. The Basavīs, being devotees of *Śiva*, are also called Liṅga Basavīs; they abstain from eating meat and drinking intoxicating drinks. The Bogums are professional dancers and musicians who enjoyed royal patronage during historical times. They were originally attached to the temples of *Śiva* and *Viṣṇu* as servants of god. The duties assigned to them were to fan the idol, to carry the sacred light, and to sing and dance before the god in a procession and in the temple. They now earn their living by singing and dancing, prostitution and concubinage.

REFERENCES

Allchin, Bridget and Raymond, 1968, *The Birth of Indian Civilization*. Harmondsworth: Penguin Books.

Allchin, F.R., 1960, *Piklihal Excavations*. (Andhra Pradesh Government Archaeological Series, 1.) Hyderabad: Government of Andhra Pradesh.

——— 1963, *Excavations at Utnur*. (Andhra Pradesh Government Archaeological Series, 5.) Hyderabad: Government of Andhra Pradesh.

———1968, *Neolithic Cattle Keepers of South India*. Cambridge: Cambridge University Press.

Alur, K.R., 1971, 'Skeletal Remains (Vertebrata)'. In: M.S. Nagaraja Rao, *Protohistoric Cultures of the Tungabhadra Valley. A Report on Hallur Excavations*, pp. 107-24, Dharwar.

Ansari, Z.D. and M.S. Nagaraja Rao, 1969, *Excavations at Sangankallu, 1964-65* (*Early Neolithic House at Bellary*). (Deccan College Building Centenary and Silver Jubilee Series, 64.) Poona: Deccan College.

Attikoḷḷa, Yallangavḍa Ph., 1949, *Hālumatada Caritra*. Dhārvād.

Deo, S.B., 1970, *Excavations at Takalghat and Khapa*. Nagpur: Nagpur University.

Hanumanthiah, V.R., 1958, *Bharatadesada Kurubara Caritra* (The History of Shepherds in India), Bangalore.

Hassan, Syed Siraj ul, 1920, *The Castes and Tribes of H. E. H. The Nizam's Dominion*, Bombay.

Joshi, R.V., 1968, 'Late Mesolithic Culture in Central India'. In: *La Préhistoire-problèmes et tendances*, pp. 245-54. Paris: Editions du Centre National de la Recherche Scientifique.

Leshnik, L.S., 1971, 'Some Early Indian Horse-bits and Other Bridle Equipment'. *American Journal of Archaeology* 75/2: 141-50.

——— 1975, 'Nomads and Burials in the Early History of South India'. In: L.S. Leshnik and G.-D. Sontheimer (ed.), *Pastoralists and Nomads in South Asia*, pp. 40-67. Wiesbaden: Otto Harrassowitz.

Lydekker, R., 1886, 'The Fauna of Kurnul Caves', *Palaeontologia Indica*, Series C. 4/2: 23-58.

Marriott, McKim, 1955, 'Little Communities in an Indigenous Civilization'. In: McKim Marriott (ed.), *Village India*, pp. 171-222. Chicago: The University of Chicago Press.

Misra, V.N., 1973, 'Bagor: A Late Mesolithic Settlement in North-West India', *World Archaeology* 5/1: 92-110.

Murty, M.L.K., 1975, 'Late Pleistocene Fauna of Kurnool Caves, South India'. In: A.T. (ed.), *Archaeo-zoological Studies*, pp. 132-8. Amsterdam: North Holland Publishing Co.

Nagaraja Rao, M.S., 1971, *Protohistoric Cultures of the Tungabhadra Valley. A Report on Hallur Excavations*. Dharwar.

Nagaraja Rao, M.S. and K.C. Malhotra, 1965, *The Stone Age Hill Dwellers of Tekkalakota*. Poona: Deccan College.

Paddayya, K., 1973, *Investigations into the Neolithic Cultures of the Shorapur Doab, Southern India*. Leiden: Brill.

Rami Reddy, V., 1968, *Pre- and Protohistory of Southwestern Andhra Pradesh*. (Ph.D. Thesis, Poona University).

Sankalia, H.D., 1975, *Prehistory and Protohistory of India and Pakistan*. Poona: Deccan College.

Seshadri, M., 1971, *Report on the Excavation at T. Narsipur*. Bangalore: Government of Mysore.

Settar, S., 1971, 'The Brahmadeva Pillars'. *Artibus Asiae* 33: 17ff. and 34ff.

Singh, R.L. (ed.), 1971, *India: A Regional Geography*. Varanasi: National Geographic Society of India.

Sircar, D.C. (ed.), 1961, *Annual Report on Indian Epigraphy for 1957-58*. Delhi: Government of India Press.

Sontheimer, G.-D., 1975, 'The Dhangars: A Nomadic Pastoral Community in a Developing Agricultural Environment'. In: L.S. Leshnik and G.-D. Sontheimer (eds.), *Pastoralists and Nomads in South Asia*; pp. 139-70.

Wiesbaden: Otto Harrassowitz. [Editors' note: Also in the present volume, pp. 87-122]

——— 1976, *Birobā, Mhaskobā und Khaṇḍobā. Ursprung, Geschichte und Umwelt von pastoralen Gottheiten in Mahārāṣṭra*. Wiesbaden: Franz Steiner. [Editors' note: English version: *Pastoral Deities of Western India*, New York 1989.]

Spate, O.H.K. et al., 1972, *India, Pakistan and Ceylon*. Bombay: B.I. Publications.

Subbarao, B., 1948, *Stone Age Cultures of Bellary*. Poona: Deccan College.

Thapar, B.K., 1957, 'Maski 1954: A Chalcolithic Site of the Southern Deccan'. *Ancient India* 13: 4-142.

Thurston, E., 1909, *Castes and Tribes of Southern India*. Madras.

Vaiyapurippilai, S. (ed.), 1967, *Caṅka Ilakkiyam*. Madras.

Wheeler, R.E.M. (Sir), 1947-8, 'Brahmagiri and Chandravalli 1947: Megalithic and Other Cultures in Mysore State'. *Ancient India* 4: 130-310.

King Vikram and Kamaḷū Śinde, the Shepherd: *Bhakti* Episodes from an Oral Epic of the Dhangars of Maharashtra

INTRODUCTION

From the vast oral literature of the shepherd communities of Maharashtra (comprehensively called Dhangars) we want to present just one excerpt in summary which deals with the relationship between a *bhakta* and his god. The episodes presented here are part of a long *ovī* which one may call an oral epic, composed in a rural Marāṭhī idiom. The *ovī* runs into nearly 500 note book pages transcribed from tapes. The hero of the episodes is Kamaḷū Śinde, a legendary ancestor of the Śinde family whose descendants are still living as shepherds—mainly in the Sātārā District of Maharashtra.

Kamaḷū Śinde's memorial—resembling a Muslim tomb—is still shown near Phalṭaṇ in the Sātārā District in the vicinity of the temple of the god Dhuḷobā. Dhuḷobā is the family god (*kulasvāmī*) of the Śindes and other Dhangar clans. He is a god of Śaivite provenance whom Kamaḷū Śinde had won by his strenuous and sincere *bhakti*. The epic of Dhuḷobā and his *bhakta* bears some semblance with the 'history' (*caritra*) of another famous Dhangar god, Mhaskobā of Vīr (Purandar Taluka, Puṇe District).

The 'history' of this god was printed at the end of the last century.[1] A comparison of the lively, at times dramatic *ovī*, which one must hear and see being performed, with the printed, somewhat tedious version of Mhaskobā's *caritra*, makes one realize how much will be lost when the vast oral literature of India eventually fades out of existence.

The singer and narrator of the *ovī* of Dhuḷobā is a blind Dhangar, Dājī Rāmā Pokḷe, about 60 years old. He belongs to those Dhangars who traditionally serve in the temples of one of the Dhangar family gods like Birobā, Satuśā, Khaṇḍobā or Dhuḷobā. These Dhangar 'priests' (*pujārīs*) periodically visit the various families who are traditional followers of the particular family god. The singer, in a way, acts as a kind of medium of the god, not only by serving the god and the *bhaktas*, but also by singing and reviving the memory of the god amongst his Dhangar 'clients'. Simultaneously, his performance also teaches the Dhangars to sing the *ovī*. Some of them, in fact, become better performers than their *guru*. Perhaps we should add that for the Dhangars the mythical contents of the *ovī* are not 'tales' or 'fairy stories', but *true* events which took place in the *satyayuga*, the golden age of truth.

THE FORM OF THE *OVĪ*

The *ovī* primarily consists of free verse with an occasional rhyme. It is unlike the literary, classical *ovī*[2]—a '*janapada*' *ovī*—a folk *ovī*, constituted of cycles of eight syllables or *tāla-mātras* (= drum beats), e.g.

mé - gha - rā́ - jyā pít - yā - cáṃ (va)
mé- gha - rā́ - jyā pít - yā - cáṃ

A syllable like 'va' links the two lines. The verses are often interpreted by prose which some Dhangars would call *saṃpādanī*. According to Molesworth's *Marathi-English Dictionary*, this means 'the dressing up (... of any legend-exposition) with rhetorical embellishment'. Thus the *ovī* in this form resembles somewhat the medieval *campū*, which Apte in his Sanskrit Dictionary calls *gadya-padya-mayam*, following the *Sahitya-darpaṇa* (569).

The *campū* is—Apte continues—a kind of elaborate and highly artificial composition in which the same subject is continued through alterations [*sic*, alternations?] in prose and verse. A Dhangar would normally describe the prose parts of the *ovī* simply with the phrase '*ovī toṇḍāṇeṃ sudhārūn karāycī*'—'improving the *ovī* by making it intelligible'. In fact, it is not only a device to make the audience and the nascent performers catch the meaning of the *ovī*, but it also carries the story on and at times delays it, arousing curiosity for the further development in the story. The present *ovī* comes from the Haṭkar Dhangars, who are mostly nomadic. Two Dhangars sing the first two lines, one of them being the expert in singing *ovīs*, whereas two more Dhangars repeat the first two lines. The *ovī* is mostly sung, but in the districts of Kolhapur, Satara, and Sangli, where the Dhangars are more or less settled, it is also accompanied by musical instruments, namely one or more drums (*ḍhol*), cymbals (*jhānj*), and flutes (*pavā*).

PERFORMANCE AND CONTEXT OF THE *OVĪ*

LOCALE AND TIME

During the rainy season, from the middle of June till about the Divāḷī festival in October/November, the nomadic Haṭkar Dhangars stay in their *vāḍās* (monsoon camps) on the drier parts of the Deccan plateau (the Deś) eastwards of Puṇe. After their four months' stay they migrate to the west, most of them to the coastal area (the Koṅkaṇ), from where they return after eight months as soon as the rains start. Their stay on the plateau near the shrines of their ancestors and their family god is a time of relaxation after the arduous migration. It is also the occasion to celebrate.

One day after the new moon day (*amāvāsyā*) of the month of Āśvin (October/November) and nine days before the Dasarā festival the Dhangars 'establish the pot' (*ghaṭasthāpanā*) in the huts and the temple of their *vāḍā*. An earthen pot is placed on a bed of leaves from the Banyan tree on which a layer of earth is spread. Grains of wheat, millet, and gram, like the intercultivated fields of traditional Maharashtra, are sown in it. The pot is filled with water, which percolates into the earth, and eventually the seeds sprout. In front of the pot established in a household all the gods worshipped by the Dhangars are placed in the form of small silver plaques. In the temple of the *vāḍā* the pot is established for the *kulasvāmī*.

Every night during the nine nights before Dasarā all the gods, like Birobā, Mhaskobā, Khaṇḍobā, etc., are worshipped with vegetarian offerings in addition to the *kulasvāmī* in the temple of the *vāḍā*. Many of the Dhangars, at least one member of each household, observe a fast. After the evening worship the *ovī* of the *kulasvāṃī* is sung and continues to be sung for the rest of the nine nights. The Dhangars may also perform a dance. The purpose of the *ovī* and the dance is to keep the god awake. On the ninth day the vessel of the god is worshipped by shaking it with the exclamation '*ude, ude*' (*uday* = arise! awake!). By shaking the pot the god is released from his nine days' presence near (?in) the pot. On this day the Dhangars perform a dance before the god and in the evening after the *āratī* ceremony—a platter with five lights is waved around the god—the *ovī* is completed. On the next morning the god is bathed and sheep are sacrificed for the god: an offering of the cooked liver and meat of the sheep is 'shown' (*nivad dākhavtāt*) to the god before a communal dinner and dance follows.

The second occasion for the *ovī* is the *kheḷ*. This is a festival performed by each clan separately some time after Divāḷī. It marks the end of the stay in the *vāḍā*. In the evening before the day of the great dance the ancestors are worshipped and a part of the *ovī* is sung in front of the ancestor shrines so that the ancestors may be pleased. The next day after the dance and the worship of the family god, of the other gods, and of the ancestors, the *ovī* is sung in the evening. The *ovī* is not always necessarily about the family god, and *ovīs* of the other gods, e.g. the so-called 'guest gods' who may have come with relations by marriage, are also performed.

Another occasion for singing the *ovī* may be during a *jatrā* (pilgrimage and fair) to the main shrine of the *kulasvāmī*. Besides, at any time, whether in the monsoon camp or on migration, one can hear a Dhangar or two loudly singing an *ovī*, perhaps just to keep themselves awake while guarding their sheep in the night.

FUNCTION OF THE *OVĪ*

The *ovī* is part of the *navrātra* rites and the *kheḷ*. Much of the *navrātra* consists of a vigil (*jāgaraṇ* or *jāgar*), and the purpose of the *ovī* is to invoke the god by remembering him and to strengthen the link with the god anew. Thus it is not only the *bhakta* who opens himself for the arrival and presence of the god by keeping awake, but the purpose is also to activate and awaken the god (*devālā jāgvāycem̧*). In addition the daily routine of the frugal and at times strenuous life of the Dhangars becomes enriched by remembering the god in an *ovī* which tells of his wonderful deeds and of the beautiful things he owns or creates. The fun and enthusiasm derived from singing and hearing the *ovī* is matched by the knowledge one has gained about the god. The god himself, on the other hand, feels that his *bhaktas* are devoted to him (*devālā vāṭṭem̧ bhagat āplī bhaktī karat āhet*). The audience does not consist only of the men of the *vāḍā*. The women in the nearby tents, huts or houses also hear the *ovī* and are amused and heartened by the description of the birth of the god, the exploits of the little child, the description of the cradle, etc.

The ancestors housed in little shrines in the *vāḍā* still have a very strong influence on their descendants, which expresses itself especially at the *kheḷ*. They are also pleased to hear the *ovī*. However, Kamaḷū Śinde is a legendary ancestor whose fame has transgressed the limits of the particular clan and who is popular amongst the 'twelve' clans who are by privilege worshippers (*mānkarīs*) of the god Dhuḷobā. Kamaḷū Śinde's behaviour is exemplary and sets norms, though the Dhangars feel that nobody behaves like that nowadays (*tyāpramāṇem̧ vagāylā pāhijem̧, paṇ vāgat nāhī*). Yet a well-performed *kheḷ* and *ovī* leaves an impression to the observant and unbiased outsider that the social, religious, and spiritual homogenity of the *vāḍā* is not only intact but, in fact, reinforced.

One may venture the hypothesis that the cohesion and harmony of a *vāḍā* is reflected by a good *ovī* and by the well-performed *kheḷ*. However that may be, in one rather big *vāḍā*, which is inhabited by members of different clans and is nearer to the influence of the modern age, nobody can sing an *ovī* properly and the *kheḷ* normally ends in a quarrel due to drunkenness. Thus conversely the *ovī* is not just oral literature and art, but also a rite which fulfils religious, psychological, entertaining, social, and self-regulating functions.[3]

SUMMARY OF THE *OVĪ* IN TRANSLATION

Ovī: The remembrance is set (*sumbarāṇeṃ*[4] *māṇḍileṃ*)
On the Mother Earth
On the Father who rules the clouds
On Bhoḷā, the Innocent, who is my god
And the Lady Pārbatī
On Bhoḷā who is my god
The Lord of the Kailās
The Incarnation of Śambhu
On the mountainborn [wife] of Bhoḷā
She is my little mother
She is [the wife] of Bhoḷā
On the Nine Nāths
On Śrīguru Datta
Remember the name of the guru
He is my fortitude
He is with me
Is on the stony heath of Masūr
In the forest of Tārgāv
Kāśīliṅga Birāppā
On the bank of the Gaṅgā at Kāpurhoḷ
[Who is] the source of water for the Tuḷśī shrub
On the top of the Banyan tree
On the stony heath [called] Toraṇ
In the frightful forest
In the Tamarind forest
He has taken the seat in the mind
Has filled the mind
[He is] in the hole of an anthill
A round stone coloured with red
Turmeric powder on it as valuable as gold
With a woolen blanket as his seat
And a woolen banner
With turmeric powder as an ornament
With a woolen blanket over his head

And a garland of flowers
My Lord is gold
Pure as water from a spring
The god is my prince
[Is the] husband of Kāmābāī
. . .
They are the couple in this life
[She gives] five betel leaves to her lord
And applies *kuṅkū* on her forehead
On the day of Saṅkrānt[5]
Sign for the happy state of wifehood
Birāppā belonged to his queen
The girl Kāmāvatī
[He was] of youthful age
Yellow with turmeric powder
Kāśīliṅga Birāppā
The remembrance is set
[On him] on the mountain of Śiṅgṇāpur
On Bhoḷā who is my god
On Girjā, the mountainborn [wife] of Bhoḷā

Prose: What did Girjā say to Śaṅkar? 'My God, you may pervade the three storeys (*tāḷ*) of heaven and the seven underworlds (*pātāḷ*), you have the knack of making and destroying, but I have only one request: let me be presented with a child, but not even the shadow of a male should fall on my body. And it should become a hero of a child, superior to the 33 crores of gods. Such a child should be given by your divine powers.' Śaṅkar was in a difficulty: 'The queen who shares my throne wants a child and the shadow of a man should not fall on her. This is her request.'
Śaṅkar with his miraculous powers—what did he do? He retired. And muttered a mantra. He broke a burning piece of Khair wood and threw it on the body of Girjā. It hit her on the left side and a blister sprang up. And she became pregnant because of it.

Ovī: She became pregnant
The miraculous powers of my Lord
One month passed
Two months passed
Three months passed
In the third month

The colour of her body changed
In the fourth month
Her body became rounder and rounder
Her eyes and eyebrows became heavy

Prose: [Repetitious] . . .
She began to eat less food and drink less water.

Ovī: In the fifth month
The child in the womb
The boy in the womb
His body branched into shape

Prose: In the fifth month the boy in the womb branched into five limbs [legs, arms and face]. The child in the womb grew fully. In the sixth month six folds of her sari could be seen [because of the expanding waist of the Girjā]. In the seventh month seven folds were visible. The child in the womb grew. In the eighth month eight folds were visible. The child in the womb grew.

Ovī: The child started moving
In the ninth month
Nine months were over
Nine days were left
On Monday
Between nine and ten o'clock
The womb of Girjā
Began to pain
Girjā began to weep.

Prose: [Repetitious] . . .
Śaṅkar understood. He blindfolded her eyes and held her at her arms. He led her around in the temple. He laid her down placing her head towards the north and her feet towards the south. And Girjā went to sleep by the miraculous powers of the Supreme Lord. And the child in womb—

Ovī: Was in great difficulties
Which way to go
If I shall go this way
They will call me 'Sinner'

If I go by the right side [of the body]
They will call me 'Right Side-born'
If I go by the mouth
They will call me 'Mouth-born'
If I go by the ear
They will call me 'Ear-born'
If I go by the nose
They will call me 'Nose-born'
If I go by the eyes
They will call me 'Eye-born'

Prose: [Repetitious] . . .
The piece of burning ember had left a blister on the left side. On that spot the god tore open the left side. And the Parameśvar emerged. Śaṅkar opened his two eyes to see the boy. What was the boy like? A god superior to the 33 crores of gods was born: His feet on lotus, a diamond on his navel, with golden hair. The irises were like burning Khair wood, the pupils were like red berries, the eye-balls were like slices of lime. The nose had a ridge like that of a date-fruit. The tongue of the god was shaped like a betel-leaf, the teeth like the seeds of the pomegranate, the lips like creepers, the fingers like the capsules of green beans. They tell the sun 'don't rise' and the moon 'don't set', such was the lustre of the boy whom he had made his progeny and son of Girjā. Now, Parameśvar had presented her with a boy. What did Girjā do in her temple? On the fifth day she performed the rites of the fifth day,[6] on the seventh day those of the seventh, on the eighth those of the eighth, on the ninth those of the ninth, on the tenth she worshipped the ten incarnations, on the eleventh she made him cry.[7] On the twelfth she performed the rites of the twelfth day.

Ovī: On the thirteenth day
In her temple
She tied a cradle

Prose: A cradle with a railing and a golden canopy, small posts of silver (carrying it), silken ropes, a golden rope for swinging it.

Ovī: The cradle with the wooden railing
The golden rattles [were tied to it]

The cradle with the wooden railing
A bunch of pearls [was tied to it]
And the Rāghu and Mainā pair of birds.
Pictures of Rāma and Sītā were painted
And the digit of moon
Toys were bound to the cradle
The miraculous doings of my god
In our temple
The cradle of the god
Girjā began to say
Took the rope
Swung the cradle.
On the thirteenth day
She had a great problem
What name should be given
The astrologer has to be consulted
One must go to the settlement of the Meḍhaṅgī[8]
To them who know
His name has to be settled
[A name]which should shine in the world
Such a name has to be given

Prose: Thus she created a make-believe aunt [who was to give] ornaments and clothes to the boy. A make-believe aunt she created. This aunt placed her ear near the ear-pendant of the boy. From the ear of the boy a humming sound emerged. It settled down in the mouth of the make-believe aunt.

Ovī: A name has to be given
To shine in the world

Prose: The make-believe aunt whispered the name in the ear of the boy.[9]

Ovī: Mhaṅkāḷ is the boy's name
A difficult (*ignā*) time (*kāḷ*) has come.[10]
His name has been set.

Prose: Mhaṅkāḷ, the boy, [his] name is set. And day by day he began to grow. The one month old boy looked like two months old. When he was two months old he looked like four months old. The four months old boy looked like eight months. The eight months old boy looked like one year old. The one year old boy looked like two years old. He grew miraculously. He stood up in the cradle, Mhaṅkāḷ, the boy. A time of difficulty had come [for him].

Ovī: He started walking
Wore the cap with the four tassels
Began to speak

Prose: Day by day he grew. The Mhaṅkāḷ became a boy of six years, seven years . . . a boy of twelve years. What did Mhaṅkāḷ, the boy, say to Girjā: 'Whatever I wish to play with I want to have—a ball of silver, a toy beset with pearls, a staff of silver.'

Ovī: The boy was allowed to play
Mhaṅkāḷ, the boy started playing
Some days passed by
The miraculous doing of the god
The miraculous doing of Śaṅkar
He saw the whole world
[And saw] the wealthy (*nav lākh*) city of Ujjain

Prose: Now Śaṅkar had a look at the world. And he saw the city of Ujjain. In this city there ruled King Maṅkāvatī. The throne of the Sātārā kingdom and the throne of Ujjain were comparable. Except Ujjain there was on the nine parts of the world and on the tenth part, namely Kāśī, no other throne that equalled the throne of Sātārā.[11] On the throne [of Ujjain] Maṅkāvatī ruled. How did he rule? He who did evil things, who was a sinner, would get rewarded and commended. He who behaved honestly, did not do harm to anybody, who would not tell a lie, he would get a three months' imprisonment and would be fined 500 rupees. Such was the rule of the kingdom. The affairs were upside down. Mhaṅkāvatī ruled wrongly over the city of Ujjain. Śaṅkar assessed the world. There was no god in this city of wealth. Why wasn't there a god? Thus he told Mhaṅkāḷ, the boy.

Ovī: I show you the world
I show you the city
O god, go to the wealthy Ujjain
Establish a just rule

Establish a just place [town]
Appoint a true king
On the throne
Look for a king
Seat him on the throne
His fame should be established
That what is true, but turned into false
That what is false, but declared to be true
Should be crushed, o god.
That what is true should be set afoot
Mhaṅkāḷ, boy,
Set out and go
To the wealthy Ujjain
Ujjain is in your charge

Prose: . . . [repetitious] Mhaṅkāḷ, the boy, reflected. He put on wooden shoes, put on breeches, tied bells to his waist, wore a gown reaching from neck to the heels, hung the magic bag under his arm, took the conch into his right hand and the *triśūl* into his left. He smeared ash across his forehead, put on the necklace and wore the earrings. [Opening the topknot] he let down his load of hair on the back. On the Mountain of Śiṅgnāpur the god dressed. The guru of Mhaṅkāḷ was Śaṅkar and Girjā was the mother. 'Alekh' he shouted. The god blew his conch. By its sound the Mountain of Śiṅgnāpur trembled. He said to his guru: 'Now that I go to Ujjain, whenever I face a difficulty there, I shall come to you. And my difficulties should be removed.' 'Go,' Śaṅkar said, 'your wish is granted.' Śaṅkar placed his hand on his head.

Ovī: The god set off
. . .

[In the following the itinerary to Ujjain in Mālvā is described. The subsequent events are summarized here.]

When Mhaṅkāḷ approached the city of Ujjain, auspicious *omina* appeared. A pair of foxes and a pair of Piṅgaḷā birds[12] said to each other: 'A true god (*kharā bhagavān*) has come to Ujjain. There will be justice (*nyāy*) in Ujjain.' The god went one and a half miles east to the city. There was a deep waterhole and on its side an anthill. The god disappeared and stayed in the pond. He took the form of a seven hooded cobra. The hair on the neck of the cobra had the length of the span of a hand. In the night at ten o'clock he set off towards the city. The city and the palace were guarded by sentries. The palace was locked. When Mhaṅkāḷ emerged from the waterhole he took the ruby from his head and kept it on the black rock. Its red light fell upon the gates of Ujjain. The god realized that he would be hewn into pieces if the guards discovered him and he assumed his third form—a small cobra. He entered the palace through a small window. Inside he again assumed the form of the big cobra and killed king Mhaṅkāvatī. Unnoticed by the guards be returned to his waterhole. During the day he would sit in the anthill. When at dawn the soldiers unlocked the door to the king's room they found that the king had followed 'god's order'.

[In the following the mourning celebrations are related.]

Navlākh Ujjain was now devoid of a king. There were the five wise men (*pāc panc*) who convened in order to choose a new king. The relatives of the king meanwhile started quarrelling for the right to ascend the throne. But Mhaṅkāḷ killed them one after the other as soon as one of them had occupied the throne. They were not qualified to bring justice to Ujjain. After all the relatives of the late king had died, the five men decided that one of the sons of each of the five wise men should be enthroned one after the other. But all of them were killed in turn by Mhaṅkāḷ in his form of a cobra. Nobody was now ready any longer to ascend the throne. Thus the five wise men hit upon the idea that two *Mhetras*[13] should throw a stick (*daṇḍkeṃ*) in front of the houses of one of the castes according to a fixed turn—Mahārs, Māṅgs, Teḷīs, Tāmboḷīs, Dhangars, Saṇgars, Vāṇīs—and the man chosen in this way had the 'permission' to ascend the throne.

There was a mother with a son called Vikram. They lived in poverty and drudgery. Nobody had any pity for them (*dāndharm kuṇi vāḍhinā*). The little Vikram suggested that he should ask the various castes to entrust to him their cows so that he could graze them. The two annas he would get from grazing their cows would suffice for their maintenance. Vikram thus grazed a hundred or two hundred cows on the bank of the river Yamunā. There were two Paḷas trees near the river. At noon he would let the cattle drink and let them rest on the bank of the river. Meanwhile he would clean the place under the tree by smearing fresh cow dung and make a *liṅgam* (*piṇḍ*) of Mahādev out of sand. Then he would circumambulate the *liṅgam* five times. He would decorate it with various flowers and then break his millet bread into four pieces, place one piece in front of the *liṅgam*, offer one to the river and one to the cows and eat one himself.

For twelve years members of all castes who had tried to ascend the throne and rule over Ujjain, died. Only one house was left where the stick had to be thrown as a last resort: the hut of Vikram and his mother. When his mother discovered the stick she broke into tears and wondered why the god was angry in spite of their miserable state. Meanwhile the little Vikram returned from the pasture and he questioned his mother: 'Tell me the truth of what has happened, tell it to the son of a Vāṇī (merchant).' She told him what had happened and consolingly he embraced and kissed her. The mother suggested that they should flee in the middle of the night, but Vikram answered that one cannot escape one's fate, which is written by the goddess Saṭvī on the child's forehead on the sixth day after birth.[14] And he told her story of Mariāī, the goddess of smallpox and cholera. Once Mariāī, entered a village. She had eyes on all four sides of her head. People started dying. There was an old woman. When she saw everybody was dying she became afraid and went to a distant mountain in the middle of a dark forest and sat down there. She wanted to return when the people in the village had all died and Mariāī had left. She had a great thirst for life and that was why she had gone to the mountain. But Mariāī knew that this woman had gone to the mountain.

Ovī: Whoever fears me
That person I pursue.

Mariāī came to the old woman taking the form of a woman collecting firewood. The old woman explained to her that in her village people were dying like flies and that she had come out of fear of Mariāī. 'I have a thirst for life' (*malā jagāycī āśā he*). Mariāī asked her to search for lice on her head and the old woman agreed. She sat in front of Mariāī and began to look for lice—and she saw that Mariāī had eyes on four sides. 'O dear, there are no lice on your head, there are eyes. How is this?' She became afraid. And Mariāī said, 'I am she from whom you were running away. I have come to devour you.' And she devoured the old woman instantaneously.

After this story Vikram told his mother not to weep. If he had to die he had to die. He set off for the palace. There he did not take his seat on the throne as the others before him had done, defiling thereby Mhaṅkāḷ's throne. He circumambulated the throne five times and then stood in front of it folding his hands in worship. Then he sat down behind a pillar. Vikram's mother meanwhile had gone to the flower-garden and brought various kinds of flowers. From the palace up to the waterhole she made a bed of flowers, lighted incense and placed pots of curds and milk. She thought that an enemy of her son would be distracted by this and her son's life would be saved.

From each household one person had died. Śaṅkar/Mahādev, whom little Vikram had worshipped for twelve years now, intervened with a divine messenger who carried a message saying: 'If anything is great it is his devotion (*bhakti*) to me. God thirsts for *bhakti*. Twelve years he has done *bhakti* for me. His life should be spared. Navlākh Ujanī should be given to him and he should be enthroned.'

Mhaṅkāḷ, on his way to the palace, was surprised about the bed of flowers leading from his waterhole to the palace, the fragrance of incense sticks, and the pots of curds and milk. 'A great, kind, motherly woman must have done this.' He met the celestial messenger who asked him to read the letter in which it was also indicated how Vikram's mother should be rewarded. When Mhaṅkāḷ entered the palace he rolled up into a coil and sat on the throne. He noticed that for the first time the throne had not been defiled by anyone sitting on it. He called out for the invisible person and said he would spare his life. When the boy behind the pillar heard this, he thought it might be a trick and he perspired for fear. Somehow he gathered courage, thinking, 'Sometime my turn to die will come', and he embraced the huge cobra. The cobra licked him from his toes to his hair and he was transformed into a splendorous young prince. Mhaṅkāḷ handed over the kingdom to him.

The god, however, asked Vikram to worship him to the west of the city where two Nāndruk trees and two Banyan trees had grown in close embrace. He prescribed the mode of worship. For twelve years the king was to worship Mhaṅkāḷ on that spot whereupon the god would tell him in a dream what to do next. Then the god disappeared in his waterhole.

When the morning dawned the Mhetars were called and they were asked to take shovel, hoe, etc. and to bury the boy, who was presumed dead. Now besides him there was nobody left to be buried and the very existence (*sattva*) of Ujjain was at an end. For twelve years they had buried dead bodies and now their trouble of burying was over. When the king heard the voices, he woke up, stretched his limbs and yawned. When the Mhetras saw the 'king' alive they dropped their shovels, hoes, etc., and, terrified, ran to the five wise men. These and the whole city went to see the new king, Vikram. His mother also went to see whether her son was not, in fact, dead. But there he was—safe and sound and a king.

[The coronation festivities are described.]

The king was aware of what the god had told him to do. Restless, he got up from his throne. He went to the spot which the god had indicated and where he could find him. On the side of the city in the direction towards the west he found the place where the four trees grew intertwined with each other. He swept the place in front of them and sprinkled water from the seven pots. He placed seven flowers and lighted incense sticks. Then he circumambulated the trees five times and folded his hands in worship. He read seven pages [from a sacred text] and returned back to the palace, where he had his food. Henceforth this was his daily worship for twelve years. For twelve years King Vikram was the servant (*sevak*) of Mhaṅkāḷ. Then the god appeared before Vikram in a dream and ordered him to bring water from Kāśī and to build a temple without cupolas unlike the temples of the 33 crores of gods, because if people see cupolas they tend to be distracted from seeing the god. King Vikramāditya built a temple with three doors on three sides but without a cupola. The god sat in his temple in his form of a seven-hooded cobra. He demanded constant worship, seven times at night and seven times during the day. Each time the remnants of the previous offering were to be removed.[15] He also ordered Vikramāditya not to show any pride towards the citizens of Ujjain nor towards the god. He should talk even to an urchin and not harbour any pride or deceit in his mind. Thus his kingdom would flourish. But eventually Vikramāditya forgot the words of the god and did become affected by pride and arrogance. He told the god that there was no greater *bhakta* than himself on the nine continents of the earth and in Kāśī who would serve him better. The god felt challenged. He told the king that he would go in search of a *bhakta* greater than him and return to Ujjain only if he found one. The god put on his breeches, his wooden chappals, a girdle of silver and his long gown reaching from the neck to the heels. Around the neck he wore a necklace, in the ears his earrings and under the shoulder the magic bag (*jhoḷī*). He opened his topknot and his hair fell behind, reaching down to his knees. With the right hand he took the conch and with the left the *triśūl*. He smeared ash across his forehead and shouted '*alekh*', blew the conch so that the temple and the whole city of Ujjain began to tremble. Then he set off towards the west in search of a *bhakta*. He left the Deś[16] and went to the Koṅkaṇ, nowhere finding a *bhakta* that satisfied his mind. Then he turned to the Kānāḍā-Land [Karnāṭaka], but did not come across a satisfying *bhakta*, nor did he understand the language spoken there, Kānāḍī. In vain he searched for a *bhakta* in the Telaṅganī-Land [Āndhra]. Then he reached the Land of the Horse-faced, where men and women are horse-faced. Then he turned to the Goat-beard-Land, where men and women have goatees, but he could not get a true *bhakta*. Then he went to Gujarāt, where men and women wore robes reaching from neck to feet. But he did not follow their language nor could he find a *bhakta*. This made the god think. Had he not been himself proud like Vikramāditya? He had to go to the Mountain of Śiṅgṇāpur. He had to ask his guru, who was Śaṅkar, the god with three eyes and Gaṅgā in his hair. He reached Śiṅgṇāpur, shouted '*alekh*', and blew the conch. Surprised, Śaṅkar opened his eyes—Mhaṅkāḷ, the boy, had come. Śaṅkar enquired why he had left Ujjain, and Mhaṅkāḷ told him of the pride and the arrogance of Vikramāditya and his search for a true *bhakta*. He requested him to show him a true *bhakta*; otherwise he would not return to Ujjain. Śaṅkar indicated a true *bhakta* who lived near Vaḍgāv Paṅgare, where the god Birāppā/Birobā had his temple and where on a hill nearby lived the god Satuśā. To the west of it there was the Mountain of Hārāḷī and at the foot of the mountain was the *vāḍā* (shepherd settlement) of Kamaḷū Śinde and his wife Lāhubāī.

Lāhubāī was a barren woman, yet always richly adorned, with shoes on, a horizontal streak of red *kuṅkū* powder on her forehead [like the Dhangar and Māḷī women and not a simple dot as women of other castes have it]. She would never go without a nosering, beset with jewels, never go without the necklace. Her daily life was devoted to Kamaḷū, her husband. Before sunrise she would get up, wash her hands and feet, apply the horizontal streak of *kuṅkū* and worship her lifelong spouse, who was for her not only a husband, but a god. The 33 crores of gods supported this marriage; therefore she had to worship the feet of Kamaḷū, and spoke politely, having her meal only after Kamaḷū had taken his. If he had not eaten, she would fast.

He owned nine lākhs of sheep and goats, not to count the horses and foals. 370[17] households of Dhangars were in the *vāḍā*, and they followed the dharma [social and religious practices] of his family. Also the family of Śendge was in the *vāḍā*. The *vāḍā* had five raised platforms [near the five entrances]. There were five platforms, each around a Nāndruk tree, for the council of the five wise men. There were stone vessels and pots in Kamaḷū's household, with stone lids. He had an imposing moustache and a beard which had never been touched by a razor. He wore a girdle made of wool around his waist. A woolen shred served as his handkerchief. His shirt was tied with twelve strings. Around his head he had wound a turban worth 52 lakhs of rupees. Over the shoulder he had thrown a blanket. In the hand he held a staff made of Khair wood. It was curved on the top and points were projecting from it. He was a man of 'truth and importance' (*ek tattvācā ek mhatvācā*). With his shoes he would never touch the droppings of the sheep [as they are sacred]. He would hold goats and sheep by their neck and let the goat kids and the lambs drink to their hearts' content and not separate them from their mother. In his plate there was milk, butter, buttermilk, curds and ghee. And he would take lumps of food and even if it was tasteless he would eat ferociously. Alone he would herd the goats and sheep. Kamaḷū's wife would spin the wool of the sheep. She called the wool 'gold in the basket', which should not be weighed and sold. Thus she was a woman of 'sincerity and importance' (*aśī ek tatvācī ek mhatvācī*). She was a queen in her house and by following dharma earned a good reputation and fame. She would not sell *amṛt* [i.e. curds, milk and ghee]. But if any poor being came, he would drink milk and eat curds to his heart's content. Though worldly riches were plentiful, there was no son to inherit the wealth. As God had set their lot so it was to be borne. The milk was boiling and clouds of smoke would reach Kailas.[18] [The way to the *vāḍā* and the encounter with various gods is mentioned, cp. above, pp. 197f. Then Mhaṅkāḷ reached the Mountain of Hārāḷī.]

For twelve *koś* (2 x 12 miles) there was no village, no village boundary, and not even a shepherd settlement. Then suddenly Mhaṅkāḷ saw the impressive *vāḍā*, and he was sure he would meet a *bhakta* there. It was noon and all the sheep had gone grazing. Only the women were in their huts. Mhaṅkāḷ, the 24 years old god, climbed down the mountain and changed his form. He became an old man, ugly-looking, a hundred years old. His legs were such that 'the ankles were outside and the knees inside'. He wore a small shred of a loincloth, a torn shirt with the twelve strings to tie, a turban of pitiable length. He had no teeth and had watery eyes. The mucus of his nose and spittle would drop on his navel, he had long nails and scratches all over his body. Boils as large as onions and mangoes were all over his body and they were bandaged with strips of cloth through which pus was oozing. There were flies and gadflies on his body. With his magic power he created a blanket over his shoulder the ends of which were dusting the floor before and behind him. In his hand he held a branch from a Khair tree. Even that was crooked with points projecting from it. He created a magic bag and carried it [in the typical fashion of Śaivite Gosāvis] under his armpit. Limping he came wearing shoes which were held together by strings. The sound of his stick was 'tap, tap' and the blanket was dusting the floor before and behind. His size was that of a child. That was the form which Mhaṅkāḷ assumed in search of a *bhakta*. He sat down on the platform, his tongue was hanging out, he stretched his legs and let his head hang down panting like a dog. It looked as if he were dying. The wife of Kamaḷū had never seen such an apparition. It was midday. She waved to him and went to him. All the 360 shepherd women gathered and enquired about his village and family. But it turned out that he was a destitute old man who lived in a forest, thirsty and starved. The rumour of her *dharm* (*dharmācī āvāī*) had traversed the nine continents and because of her fame he had come to her *vāḍā*, he explained. To test whether there was any substance in this rumour he had come (*kas baghāylā ālā*). The god asked for water and she went to fetch it. But the god threw a fistful of ash and there was not even a drop of water. Not to lose her reputation of being a righteous, hospitable wife, she quickly went to the well to bring water. The god spoke a mantra and there was not a drop of water in the new well nor in the old one and she returned with an empty pot. The god continued to test her genuineness like the goldsmith who tests the genuineness of gold. She wanted to give him a pot of milk, but there was no milk, nor ghee, nor butter.

Lāhubāī was in a fix. If she said 'no' her *sattva* (trustworthiness) would be drowned and if she said 'yes' there was nothing with which she could keep her promise and her *dharm* (= *puṇya*) accumulated over 2 x 12 years. She sank into silence and pondered over the god who had come to test her and take away her *sattva*. The god would say why was she hankering after riches and what had Parameśvar possibly not given her in abundance! Though he asked for water, food, milk and curds she would not give it! Thus she did not say 'no' to him nor 'yes'.

The god said, 'Don't forget me because of others. One must know thirst and hunger. One should be aware of the hunger and thirst of a poor man. Go back to your hut the roof of which is carried by five beams. Look whether there is something.' When she entered the hut all the pots were full again and now she knew that never in the 2 x 12 years had there been such a miraculous sight (*camātkārī nadar*) in the *vāḍā* and that with the arrival of the old man fortune had come (*hyo mhātārā ālyavāneṃ aslā pāyguṇ lāglā*). Lāhubāī spread a felt on the ground for him and gave him curds and buttermilk. She asked him to sleep until he would get a meal on the return of her husband. In the evening Kamaḷū returned with his goats, sheep, horses and foals. Along with him the 370 shepherds also returned. As usual he drove goats and sheep into the sheep-pen and closed the entrance with a thorny shrub. Then he let the kids and lambs drink from their mothers. Finally he went to his hut to have his evening meal.

[His wife told him of the old man sleeping under the Nāndruk tree and of the strange happenings.]

It was a principle of Kamaḷū that whenever somebody came to his *vāḍā* hungry he would feed this person before he would eat himself. He got up from his stone dish, went to the old man and saw that he was sleeping. Not to disturb him he lay down beside him and went to sleep hungry. The god reflected. He only wanted 'to test the mind' (*man tyāceṃ bhagtoy*), but he now felt guilty to have let him go to sleep hungry (*pāp basleṃ śirimastaki*). Instantly Kamaḷū woke up and told the old man to dine with him in his hut.

The god asked him to dine first because of his leprous condition. But there was only one stone dining plate and on Kamaḷū's insistence the two ate together from the same plate. The god thought, 'My servant is really open-hearted' (*ovī: manāyācā mokaḷā/kharā mājhā sevaka*). Kamaḷū decided that the old man should stay with them forever. His *karma* and *daiva* (fortune) had turned well. The old man was to be protected like a father. In the morning husband and wife heated water, bathed the old man and fed him curds and milk. Thus the old man spent his time in the *vāḍā* of Kamaḷū Śinde. One day the god told him that he would come along to graze the goats and sheep. Lāhubāī and Kamaḷū warned him of the strenuous excursion of 12 *koś*, where he would surely die. But the old man insisted that he show him how to protect the goats and sheep. Lāhubāī gave them food for the day. They went into the lonely, frightful forest. The god asked him to either lead the herd or to follow it. Kamaḷū chose to go in front. The god challenged him, 'If an untoward incident happens while you are guarding the sheep in front I shall give you five lashes'. Kamaḷū agreed. 'To test the mind of Kamaḷū the god took five pebbles out of his magic bag and threw them in front of Kamaḷū. Five leopards appeared in front of him. He pondered while resting his bearded chin on his staff.[19] As long as he could remember, he had not seen such animals in the forest. 'Whether they will devour me or whether they will keep sitting, who knows?' The leopards tore the throats of the animals and killed them one after the other without devouring them. Kamaḷū requested them not to just kill all of them, but to satisfy their hunger and if that was not done to kill another one. But the god brought the animals back to life, putting the five pebbles back into his magic bag. Kamaḷū was now ready to receive his blows, having lost the challenge because of the mishap. He looked forward expecting the blows and the god behind created a whip magically, raised his hand—and disappeared. He had met a real *bhakta*. The god returned to Ujjain and took his seat in the temple. King Vikram realized that he must have found some *bhakta*.

Meanwhile Kamaḷū was searching for the old man. He thought the leopards might have devoured him. When he returned to his *vāḍā* his wife enquired about the old man. They would not eat and were full of sorrow, because they had lost the old man whose presence had made them pass their time pleasantly. While they were sleeping in the middle of the night the god remembered that he had been to their *vāḍā* without disclosing his 'village and name'. He returned to the *vāḍā* and told them his desire for a true *bhakta* after Vikram had disappointed him by arrogance. Instead he wanted Kamaḷū to worship him in Ujjain and to destroy Vikram's *pūjā*. He instructed him to go every evening after the day's hard labour 350 *kos´* to Ujjain and to again resume his work after returning in the morning. He was to bring a pot of curds and a pot of milk decorated with flowers of the Tarvāḍ tree, to circumambulate him and to worship him with folded hands.[20] Kamaḷū told his wife of their unique chance of serving the god and doing *bhakti*. The god asked a promise from Kamaḷū that he would serve him, and Kamaḷū placed his hand on the head of the god to seal the promise. The god in return blessed him. But Kamaḷū had a reservation: was not Vikram the first *bhakta*, who moreover offered a lavish and highly pure *pūjā*, whereas his, the Dhangar's worship, was rather defiling (*amaṅgal*)? But the god dispelled his apprehensions. He returned to Ujjain. The next day in the evening Kamaḷū set out, though the night was dark and one could not see the thorns which would pierce the feet and in spite of his sleepiness which made the eyelids heavy. He carried pots of curds and milk.

[The itinerary to Ujjain is again described, which also involved the crossing of the river Nīrā at Kāmbaḷeśvar near Phalṭaṇ, where there is a temple of the seven water nymphs or the goddess Bhivāī on the black rocks of the bank.]

The god actually devoted to Kamaḷū (*Kamaḷucyā pāyāt*) tested him by blowing wind which made Kamaḷū sleepy. He eventually reached the city gate of Ujjain and went to the temple of Mhaṅkāḷ. He approached the god and saw that King Vikram had already performed his lavish *pūjā*. The god said to himself, 'My confirmed *bhakta* (*nirdhār bhakta*) has come'. Kamaḷū cleansed the floor and the god by sprinkling a mouthful of water which he had brought all the way from the river Nīrā. After all, he was a simple Dhangar right from the forest. He poured the curds and milk over the god after having removed the worship of Vikram. He placed the flowers of the Tarvāḍ tree on the head and the shoulders of the god. He circumambulated the god five times and threw turmeric powder on him and stood looking at the god (*darśan*). Then he left, reaching the Mountain of Harāḷī in the morning.

When the king went to see the god he discovered the strange, defiling kind of *pūjā* which had been performed.

[He reinstalled his own mode of worship. But the 'defilement' occurred again and again every night.]

Then the king posted heavily armed soldiers near the temple to find out who disturbed his *pūjā* and to kill that person. But the god protected his *nirdhār bhakta* and made the soldiers blind and deaf. When the god restored their eyesight they saw the old man leaving Ujjain and wondered who he was.

The month of Jyeṣṭha (May/June) arrived with rainfall. The Nīrā river was flooded. This was an opportunity for the god to test Kamaḷū's fearlessness while crossing the river and whether he was a true *bhakta* (*Śindyācem̥ man dev baghto*). The depth of the river could not be fathomed and Kamaḷū pondered, 'Should my twelve years' effort in serving the god be in vain? But if the god really supports me (*dev mājhyā pāṭiva aslā*) he will carry me to the opposite bank, otherwise I shall be drowned in the floods.' At least the memory of dying for the sake of the god would survive in the world.[21] To the east of Kambaḷeśvar, on the black rock there was the home of the water goddess Bhivāī. In front of this spot there was a deep pond which could not be fathomed even 'by the rope used for twelve rope-woven bedsteads'. These seven nymphs, i.e. [as they are also comprehensively called] the water goddess Bhivāī, was a kind of 'fictitious' elder sister (*māvācī bahiṇ*) of Mhaṅkāḷ, the 'boy'. She would be disgraced and her *sattva* (trustworthiness) would vanish if she did not help her brother and his *bhakta*. Thus she placed lights on the rocks of the opposite bank and when Kamaḷū resolutely jumped into the river she created a huge wave which carried him to the opposite bank. When Kamaḷū looked back, he realized the real terror of the floods and exclaimed, 'If the god really supports me he should support me as he has done'. When Kamaḷū reached Ujjain he was caught by the soldiers. They tied him to a post. He remembered and remonstrated with the god whom he had served twelve years, having come a thorny way, defying the floods of the river, tending sheep and goats during the day and spending the whole night to perform the service of the god. 'And why did he now allow them to beat me in his temple? He could not be a supporter of his *bhakta*.' Then the god arose in living form from his pedestal,

[a description of the god as given before follows]
because

Ovī: The *bhakta* is there for the god
The god is there for the *bhakta*

The god told the soldiers to stop beating his fearless *bhakta* and to release him. He invited Kamaḷū to join him on his pedestal, but Kamaḷū declined. 'I do not want fame (*kirit*)'. Meanwhile the soldiers reported that they had caught the culprit, and King Vikram came to the temple. Kamaḷū and Vikram quarrelled in the temple as to whom Mhaṅkāḷ belonged to. The god thought that Kamaḷū was by far a superior *bhakta*. With his miraculous powers he caused lightning to strike the temple which was followed by thunder so that the whole temple trembled. Vikram took to his heels, but Kamaḷū, fearing that the god might be hurt by the falling debris, slung his arms around the god and protected him. When the danger was over and the temple had not collapsed Vikram returned and the god gave his verdict. Kamaḷū was his true *bhakta* and not Vikram, who had run away fearing to lose his life. The god now asked Kamaḷū to shift his *vāḍā* to Viḍhṇī, one and a half miles from Phalṭaṇ. There was a heath and a terrifying forest with crickets chirping and the wind whistling. After the Hoḷī festival, on Monday, on the fullmoon day of the month of Śimgā, on the day of Dhuḷvaḍ,[22] he would appear. The day was fixed and the god confirmed by a 'letter' that he would come to the *vāḍā*. Kamaḷū transferred his *vāḍā* to Viḍhṇī, on the east of Phalṭaṇ. He told his wife that he would go to Ujjain to bring the god. She doubted whether the god would come to their *vāḍā*, but Kamaḷū chided her and asked her not to say anything inauspicious. Then she worshipped the sheep and her husband with a platter of lights and requested him to go and bring the god. Kamaḷū went to Ujjain.

[The description of the itinerary is repeated.]

When he reached the temple, the god told him to wind the end of his turban around his five fingers and light them with the help of a censer.[23] He told him to go ahead and not look backward as otherwise he would disappear at that spot.[24] He then took his usual form [see above] and when he passed the gate of Ujjain Vikram intercepted him, requesting him to stay back and not to follow a mad man. But Mhaṅkāḷ retorted: 'It is my lot to go. I go for the sake of *bhakti*. What else does the god starve for if not for *bhakti*? He has served me better than you (*malā jāṇeṃ bhāg hye. kā jāto ta bhakticyā pāyāt. dev kaśālā bhūkyālā tar bhaktilā bhūklelā. tyānī mājhī sevā tujhyāpekṣā cāṅglī kelī*).' Vikram requested him to leave at least some sign of his disappearance. Mhaṅkāḷ told him that for three days there would be burning a *nandādīp*[25] in the temple. This light would be burning without oil at the tail end of a seven-hooded cobra. But after three days it would get extinguished and the cobra would collapse. The fourth part of Ujjain would be under water and the twelve city gates would sink into ruins. At that time Vikram would realize that Mhaṅkāḷ had left Ujjain following his *bhakta*. Another two and a half parts of the city (out of nine *lākhs*) would be in flames. From the second day onwards 'Nine Lākh Ujjain' would be called the 'Burnt Ujjain'. With these words the god left.

In front of Kamaḷū goblins and demonesses were dancing. Lions were roaring. There were lumps of snakes intertwined with each other. But Kamaḷū went ahead.

[The return itinerary is described.]

In the bed of the river Nīrā the god stopped and looked towards the east. There he saw on the black, rugged rock the temple of Bhivāī. There was a huge, unfathomable hole in front of it, belonging to Bhivāī, with fish as big as elephants which nobody was allowed to catch. They were the wealth (*dravya*) of Bhivāī. In their nose they wore huge noserings beset with pearls. Bhivāī was like a Brāhmaṇ woman and would not tolerate pollution nor a Caṇḍāl. She was well-dressed and adorned with heavy ornaments. She wore a white sari and a green blouse. A horizontal streak of *kunkū* was on her forehead. She had tied her hair in a knot which was decorated with pearls and corals. She wore silver anklets and had lampblack applied to her eyes. Her golden hair was as soft as that of a child before the first cutting of hair. Such was the manifestation (*avatār*) of Bhivāī at Kambaḷeśvar. It was night when the god saw her and he told Kamaḷū to go ahead and tell his wife that the god had been held up on the bank of the Nīrā and to arrange the Hoḷī festival: 'Tell your wife to have a bath and ask her to arrange the Śimgā festival.' At 8 o'clock in the morning seven pots of curds and milk have to be sprinkled on a spot to the east of the *vāḍā*. 360 cow dung cakes have to be collected and placed there for the Hoḷī fire. Sugar-cane stalks should be pulled out by their roots as well as castor oil plants and they should be erected. On this spot five rupees should be placed and milk and curds should be poured. Five gates with coconut branches should be erected, vessels filled with coconut kernels and turmeric powder should be kept. And the Hoḷī fire should be lighted. The whole night a vigil (*jāgar*) should be observed. Then in the morning the god would appear, but Kamaḷū should not *wait* for him. Kamaḷū asked the god to promise that he would really come, as he was afraid he would disappear. The god promised. Kamaḷū went ahead to prepare the festivities. When he reached home, his wife enquired (somewhat mockingly) where the god was. He told her that the god was held up at Kāmbaḷeśvar and that he had told them to prepare for the Hoḷī festival.

Meanwhile the 2 x 12 years old god reflected which form he should assume in the presence of the water nymphs, who were not even ready to mention the name of a man. If an adult man were to intrude he would be burnt to ashes. He decided to become their brother in the form of a three years old child [a description of which follows]. With his magic power he created a cradle, beautifully adorned. And the cradle floated in the pond of Bhivāī. The god's magic power put the whole pond ablaze and the light fell on Bhivāī's temple and her throne. The seven goddesses were seated in the temple [saying], 'O woman, who has shaken this forsaken place and what enemy has come?' They came out and stood on the wall of the temple.

'Who could possibly be there besides them? Who has polluted this place? Who was the hero who had come and who was now to fight them?' Bhivāī took the form of a star between the clouds and threw light like an 'electric torch' held in a hand. Her brightness dimmed the light of Mhaṅkāḷ. It was then that she saw the child in the water near the opposite bank. 'Bravo' she said and decided to make it the eighth sister if it were a girl and a brother if it were a boy. But could the child come into her hands? It would come towards her if it was a blessed child, but if it was a child of sin it would burn to ashes and drown. She tied up her sari, went down the stairs and folded her hands. As soon as Bhivāī's feet touched the water the cradle reached her hands. Their eyes met and Bhivāī began to laugh and Mhaṅkāḷ began to laugh. While she laughed jewels came out of her mouth. Jewels also came out of Mhaṅkāḷ's mouth. Bhivāī took the cradle out of the water and placed it on the wall. The seven sisters gathered around the child and admired it [saying], 'God has given us a brother out of water.' They heated seven pots of water and bathed it. It was great fun.

The event of the three years' old boy floating on a cradle made Mhaṅkāḷ give a prediction (*bhaviṣya*) which Bhivāī understood intuitively. Henceforth a *jatrā* (*yātrā*) would take place at Bhivāī's pond attended by those for whom she is a family god (*kulasvāmī*). For the son of such a family—three years, two years, six months, five weeks, seven years or ten years of age—the fishermen (Koḷīs) of Kāmbaḷeśvar would make a raft out of reeds from the castor-oil plant. And they would place the child on the raft and drive it around in a circle. And this custom is still practised today.[26] Bhivāī enquired about the reasons of his coming and he explained her that Kamaḷū had served him as a *bhakta* for twelve years. He told her that he himself had no support (*ādhār āsrā*) of anybody, unlike the other gods, e.g. Birāppā, who has his sister Māyavvā or Mhakubāī.[27] Bhivāī admonished him for going to a Dhangar *vāḍā* for the sake of a silly Dhangar—to the Dhangars 'who eat stale food, bathe in cold water and eat half-cooked meat. They milk their goats and sheep and do not care whether it is rotten because of the hair or sheep droppings in it. They may cook the milk or just swallow it hastily. Every day there is pollution and they do not observe rules of pollution on account of menstruation, childbirth, birth of foals, kids and lambs. They take the beestings and cook it. And when animals die or even men die they do not observe the periods of pollution.' Bhivāī tried to persuade him not to go and defile himself. But if he really decided to go she would have to come. He chided her for her mistaken view: 'Why should I not go just because of their habits of eating and drinking? What is great and important if not *bhakti*? For the sake of my *bhakta* I go to the *vāḍā*.'

He told Bhivāī that he would take the form of a child there and that she should present herself on the thirteenth day after his 'birth' for the name giving ceremony.

[We further summarize the *ovī*]

After this the 'birth' of Mhaṅkāḷ in the form of a newborn boy in the ashes of the Hoḷī fire took place on the day of Dhuḷvaḍ [the day of throwing ash and dust after the burning of the Hoḷī fire], one day after Hoḷī. He adopted the name of Dhuḷobā, 'Father Ash', because he was born in the ashes of the Hoḷī fire. Kamaḷū and his wife first thought that the god had sent an ordinary child to them, the childless couple. But the miraculous growth of the boy and his exploits made them eventually realize that he was the god himself. The god grazed and protected the goats and sheep, then he created two goblin soldiers, Yetāḷ (Vetāl) and Khaṅkāḷ, then the god married the 12-year old daughter of the Rājā Vāghmoḍe of Māḷśiras (Sholāpur District). The girl had been born miraculously from a blister in the burnt palm of Vāghmoḍe's hand. Vāghmoḍe having received a lot of riches, i.e. a bride price, from Kamaḷū, and finding that the bridegroom (changing his form) was an old, haggard man with festering boils, tried to foil the marriage. The marriage was set to take place on the heath of the goddess Saṭvāī, which was a lonely place. The hope that the old man would be devoured by a tiger on the night before the marriage proved abortive when the god tied five tigers in front of the temple of Saṭvāī. During the marriage ceremony the god changed into his original form, his splendour being equal both to the sun and the moon, so that one can describe him by the saying 'the sun need not rise and the moon need not set, such was his lustre'. Then the god went to Mahādev of Śiṅgṇāpur, took up the challenge of a monstrous *daitya* (demon) and went to defeat him. Finally, he settled with his wife Mitābāī in the temple at Viḍhṇī near Phalṭaṇ.

BHAKTI ELEMENTS IN THE *OVĪ*

The present *ovī* has some typical (Śaivite) folk elements, e.g. the frequent play with the numbers 'five' and 'twelve'. Twelve years are also the cycle of *tapas* which occurs in one or the other form in the *ovī*, e.g. in the form of the twelve years of nocturnal and arduous travels of Kamaḷū Śinde in order to worship Mhaṅkāḷ. Śiva appears as the Mahādev of Śiṅgṇāpur (Phalṭaṇ Tālukā, Sātārā District). He is similar to the classical, philosophical Śiva of the Śaivite Purāṇas who lets others act for himself and is absorbed in meditation. Only occasionally he acts at the instance of Pārvatī. He is also a last resort and a source of inspiration for his creations. Here his creation is a Bhairava-like god, a Mahākāl, who is not only fearful, death-bringing and awe-inspiring—as in the Purāṇas—but is also a very human god. He is close to his devotees and is involved in their life and in establishing royal justice on earth. This is, incidentally, paralleled in the historical development of religion in Maharashtra, because after the fall of the Yādavas and the rise of the Muslims we find that gods like Bhairavnāth, Birobā, Mhaskobā, Khaṇḍobā and even Viṭṭhal, etc., eventually become more popular than the 'high-gods' Śiva and Viṣṇu.[28] Mhaṅkāḷ is also like a Śaivite Gosāvī who imitates or identifies himself with Śiva (*sarūpya*). He has the typical magic bag filled with ash under his armpit, wears a *triśūl* and shouts *alekh* (*alakṣya*), referring to the *nirguṇa* form of Śiva of whom he himself is a *saguṇa* form. He communicates with people and is susceptible to his own faults, e.g. to his pride. He feels guilty of letting Kamaḷū Śinde sleep hungry.

The relationship between 'devotee' and god is a kind of *do ut des* on the *bhakti* level. 'The *bhakta* is there for the god and the god is there for the *bhakta*.' The god starves for a 'devotee' and his search for him is rather pathetic. The truer the 'devotee' the more the god supports him and becomes conscious of his own responsibility for trustworthiness (*sattva*). When he has found a candidate a number of tests follow to see whether he is a *true bhakta*. The god tests his *bhakta's sattva*, his genuineness and his true mind. He appears as an old repulsive man, makes the *bhakta* cross the dangerous river, demands full trust by asking him not to turn around to see whether the god is coming, etc. Absence of fear is one of the criteria, as the story of the deadly Mariāī and the episode of crossing the river reveal. A true *bhakta*, moreover, has time for his domestic world and yet is fully devoted to his god: Kamaḷū Śinde looks after his worldly duties during the day and manages to go to Ujjain every night to worship Mhaṅkāḷ.

True *bhakti* is also devoid of any elaborate ritual, and a lavish *pūjā* does not impress the god. The question of pure and impure does not arise. Poverty does not matter—on the contrary: Vikram was a poor cowherd. Nor does *bhakti* permit of arrogance and pride as the fate of Vikram makes so clear. A sincere *bhakta* is also likely to come from an out-of-the-way place, from the forest, the *vanam*, where a Kamaḷū Śinde lives. Yet life there, away from 'civilization', does not mean unbounded freedom without rules governing behaviour. It is shown that life there may be impure and yet in consonance with *dharma*, because *dharma* must be based on *sattva*, pure motives, otherwise *dharma* will remain an empty shell.

Pure *bhakti* is also not carried by any *sakāma* motives. One would have thought that the childless Dhangar couple worships the god for the sake of a son, but this is nowhere indicated. Ultimately they win much more with their artless *bhakti*, namely, not just a child but the god himself born as a child in the ashes of the Hoḷī fire. Thus the god yields to Kamaḷū's combination of *tapas*, *sattva*, and *bhakti* and comes towards his devotee, meeting him halfway. He comes from Ujjain to the new *vāḍā* near Phalṭaṇ, relieving Kamaḷū of a twelve years' cycle of *tapas* which meant going to Ujjain every night.[29]

ACKNOWLEDGEMENTS

The German Research Association has sponsored various stays in Maharashtra, Andhra Pradesh and Karnataka between 1967 and 1978, during which a large collection of oral literature was built up. The author of the epic dealt here with is Dājī Rāma Pokḷe, to whom I owe special thanks, as well as to Sakhārām Bābu Lakaḍe, who introduced me to the author.

Ramdas S. Atkar and Rajaram Babu Zagade were as usual indispensable aides while on field research or transcribing tapes.

NOTES

1. *Srīnāth Mhaskobā Devācem̩ Caritra*, 4th edn., Vir, 1972 (tr. into German in G.-D. Sontheimer, *Birobā, Mhaskobā und Khaṇḍobā. Ursprung, Geschichte und Umwelt von pastoralen Gottheiten in Mahārāṣtra*, Wiesbaden, 1976). [Editor's note: English version: *Pastoral Deities of Western India*, New York, 1989.]
2. For the classical *ovī* see: Shankar Gopal Tulpule, 'Classical Marāṭhī Literature' in: Jan Gonda (ed.), *A History of Indian Literature*, vol. IX, Fasc. 4, Wiesbaden, 1979, p. 451.
3. These aspects are dealt with more closely in: G.-D. Sontheimer, 'Ritual und Recht im traditionellen Indien. Gottesurteil und Entstehung von Eigentum'. Paper given at the 'XV. Religionswissenschaftlicher Kongress' at Bad Soden-Allensdorf (March 1980, unpublished). [Editor's note: The paper has not been published.]
4. *sumbarāṇem̩* comes from *smaraṇa*, cp. the *nāma-sumirana* 'the remembrance of the name of God'. See: Ch. Vaudeville, *Kabīr*, vol. I, Oxford, 1974, pp. 140f. Here Dhangar gods are 'invoked' or 'remembered'.
5. This ceremony takes place at Makar Saṅkrānti, in the middle of January, when the sun leaves Sagittarius and enters Capricorn.
6. Worship of deities on the fifth day of the birth. The sixth day is not mentioned. On this day the goddess Saṭvāī or Saṭvī = *ṣaṣṭhī*, the 'sixth' is worshipped. The goddess comes and writes the fate and character of the child on its forehead in invisible, immutable words. See: D.D. Kosambi, *Myth and Reality*, Bombay, 1962, p. 88. But in the case of a god who is essentially Śiva and above *karma*, it would hardly be appropriate to refer to this rite. So the singer omits to mention it.

7. There is a lot of punning and alliteration without much meaning in the enumeration of the rites, e.g. *ákroś*-'loud-crying', is connected with *akarā* = eleven.
8. A class of fortune-tellers, diviners, presagers, astrologists (Molesworth's *Marathi-English Dictionary*, s.v.).
9. An aunt has to whisper the name into the ear of the new-born child. Actually it is Mhaṅkāḷ who suggests the name.
10. Normally the name should be derived from Mahākāl = Śiva as the destroyer, Time personified.
11. There were historical connections between the Marathas and Ujjain. The singer may refer to the rule of King Śāhū of Sātārā (1709-49). But Ujjain was also the headquarters of the Śindes (Scindias) during Śāhū's time. In 1801 Yaśvant Rāv Hoḷkar (a Khuṭekar Dhangar) pillaged Mahādjī Śinde's capital Ujjain, *Maharashtra State Gazetteers, History*, pt. III, Maratha Period, Bombay, 1967, pp. 61, 114. The Śindes originally came from Kanherkheḍ in the Sātārā District and were *pāṭils* (headmen) or *gāvḍās* (headmen of a village with a preponderant pastoral economy).
12. *piṅgalā*: 'little, spotted owl, Noctua Indica' (Molesworth). The speech of this bird is believed to be intelligible to human beings and its prophecies to become true.
13. *mhetar*—a cleaner or sweeper; a term for the hereditary Mahār of a village (Molesworth).
14. Cp. fn. 6.
15. This happens in quick succession on the special days of Śiva: the *liṅgam* is covered with flowers and three horizontal marks of ash are made by three fingers, and milk, etc., is poured over it. The next worshipper immediately removes the flowers etc. and begins to worship anew.
16. The Plateau eastwards of the Western Ghāṭs.
17. Such numbers are mostly stereotypes.
18. This is how Śiva realized the existence of Kamaḷū.
19. The typical relaxed posture of a shepherd.
20. Shepherds (Kurubas) still bring pots of milk to bathe the god on their pilgrimage to Viṭṭhal-Birāppā in Patan-Kudoli (Kolhapur District).
21. The death-defying attitude of Śaiva Bhaktas even led to religious suicide in former times. See: G.-D. Sontheimer, 'Some Incidents in the History of the God Khaṇḍobā.' In: *Asie du Sud. Traditions et changements*. VI European Conference on Modern South Asian Studies, Paris, 1978, p. 116. [Editor's note: reprinted in EK, New Delhi, 1997, 19-33.]
22. Śimgā is the Hoḷī festival, as well as the month in which it is held, i.e. Phālgun (February/March). Dhuḷvaḍ is the day after Hoḷī, i.e. the first day after the full moon of Phālgun. Dhuḷvaḍ is the day of throwing dust and ashes from the Hoḷī fire.
23. Similar kinds of *tapas* may still occasionally be seen in the field.
24. This is a very common temptation the god poses as a test of the restraint and trust of a *bhakta*.
25. A light kept burning night and day before the god.

26. On Bhivāī and her *jatrā* see: G.-D. Sontheimer, *Birobā, Mhaskobā und Khaṇḍobā*, op. cit., pp. 77f. [*Pastoral Deities* . . . , pp. 75f.]
27. The famous goddess Māyavvā/Mhākubāī/Mahākālī of Cinclī (Belgaum District) is Birobā's foster sister, having found the little boy in a thicket on a tree, very much like Kārttikeya, who is also called *śarabhū* = 'reed-born', 'born in a thicket'.
28. G.-D. Sontheimer, 'Some Incidents in the History of the God Khaṇḍobā', op. cit., p. 115 [cp. p. 28 in EK].
29. The motif of the god coming towards the *bhakta* after the latter's lifelong, strenuous *bhakti*, e.g. by going to a far-away mountain to worship him daily, is quite frequent. See: G.-D. Sontheimer, *Birobā, Mhaskobā und Khaṇḍobā*, op. cit., pp. 202f. (Mhaskobā) [*Pastoral Deities* . . . , pp. 210f.] M.S. Mate, *Temples and Legends of Maharashtra*, Bharatiya Vidya Bhavan, Bombay, 1970, p. 167 (Khaṇḍobā).

On the Memorials to the Dead in the Tribal Area of Central India

In a volume dealing with the memorials to the dead in India a reference to the considerable variety of memorials in Middle India should find a place. Over the years a number of authors have commented on particular cases and W. Koppers especially has given a valuable synopsis of the funeral rites and hero-stones to the dead amongst the Bhīls, Korkūs, Santāls and the Māḍiyās;[1] E. Fischer and Haku Shah have given detailed information on the erection and worship of memorials to the dead amongst some tribal groups in Gujarat;[2] and there are many other, often incidental contributions, but the general picture remains disjointed and discordant, and the rather selective pre-occupation with either 'tribal' or 'Hindu' phenomena may deprive us of supplementary evidence. The present note intended to provide some additional material is a preliminary to a more comprehensive treatment of the subject.

MEMORIALS IN BASTAR

In the Bastar District, various types of memorials exist. The small Hindu kingdoms which were under the influence of the South have left their traces in the form of ruined temples at Bārsūr, Bhairamgaḍh, and Dantevāḍā. Bastar was raided from the ninth century by the Eastern Cālukyas, Coḷas, Western Cālukyas and Hoysaḷas.[3] There was a strong Telugu influence, though the Telugu village population was eventually 'tribalized' and even adopted the Goṇḍi dialects of the surrounding tribals.[4] The great temples more or less decayed. But amongst the ruins a considerable number of hero-stones can be found. They generally appear to be of a pre-Muslim and pre-Rājput period. These hero-stones are similar to the early hero-stones found scattered all over eastern Madhya Pradesh, Andhra, eastern Maharashtra, Orissa, and Bihar. They are heavy, thick slabs of about 1 m. to 1.2 m. in height. Sometimes they are exquisitely carved, like the sculptures of the temples in the vicinity of which they may be found, but we also meet with rough versions. Both types generally depict a warrior on foot who holds a sword and a shield (Figs. 1 and 5) or is equipped with bow, arrows, quiver and a dagger. Rarely do we find that the early stones are connected with a *satī*. However, two hero-stones outside Bastar in the Goṇḍ Fort at Lānjī (Balaghat District) show a miniature female figure with a prominent depiction of her hand standing behind the fighting hero. But the emphasis is on the commemoration of the hero. The custom of commemorating *satī* does not seem to have been prevalent at a time when these memorials—called here 'old hero-stones'—were erected. The 'old' hero-stones generally are a single-panelled slabs as we have indicated. In the eastern half of India they rarely have several panels, unlike the hero-stones of western Madhya Pradesh (Terahi, Sivapuri Districts), now in the Gujarī Mahal Museum in Gwalior, which are of the late Gupta period, and unlike the multi-panelled hero-stones of Maharashtra and Karnataka. This does not preclude the possibility that multi-panelled *wooden* pillars carved on four sides like those of the Bisonhorn Māḍiyās might not have been more widespread. The wooden memorial tablets of the Korkūs and the wooden multi-panelled memorials in Western India indicate a wider distribution. Koppers also points out that 'a change in the material of which the monuments are made (wood for stone or *vice versa*) was accepted as a matter of course'.[5] However, multi-panelled memorials always seem to have been concentrated in the western half of India. Occasionally, we may find hero-stones with more than one panel in Eastern India, e.g. one stone from Budhpūr (Manbhum District, Bihar, tenth century, now in the Patna Museum)[6] or the stone in the State Museum at Bhubaneswar, where we find a hero-stone with two panels, in the upper panel of which the hero worships Ekapāda Bhairava.

Two hero-stones at Bārsūr show royal heroes on horse back. Both the heroes have a royal parasol; one stone shows the hero with an attendant who holds the *chatrī* over him, similar to depictions of Revanta for which hero-stones are sometimes mistaken.[7] One of the 'old' hero-stones at Bārsūr shows the hero with the shaven forehead and short pig-tail still common amongst the Māḍiyās and also found on the more recent wooden '*urasgatta*' pillars erected for prominent Bisonhorn Māḍiyās. At the bottom of the stone a small seated figure is carved, representing probably the son or the wife of the hero, who may have arranged for the erection of the stone. Bārsūr also has a memorial of a chieftain with sword, shield, *chatrī*, and his dog (Fig. 1). The hero wears as usual big ear-rings, and a bead head-band. This type of head-band is still characteristic of the Muriyās. Two longish sculptures, *c*. 1.20 m. high, showing warriors with a 'Muriyā' bead head-band and their hand resting on a spear appear to be memorials, but may have been part of a temple (Figs. 25 and 26). In Dantevāḍa the connection with the South is clear: here we find a hero offering his head, probably to the goddess Danteśvarī, because the stone is found at the entrance gate to the precincts of the Danteśvarī temple. I have not seen such stones elsewhere in Madhya Pradesh. The representation is similar to the hero-stones from Nalgoṇḍa (now in Hyderabad) except that the hero holds the sword on his neck and not on his throat.[8] In the old temple complex of Mārkaṇḍī in the Candrapur District of Maharashtra, adjacent to Bastar, a similar depiction of head-offering can be seen.[9] Mārkaṇḍī also houses a few remarkable 'old' hero-stones. S.B. Deo assigns these temples on stylistic and other grounds to the late eleventh century,[10] which must be also the approximate date of these hero-stones. They suggest a tribal context. At Bārsūr a singular *satī*-stone is available (Fig. 4). But it does not appear very old and compares with the stones from Baḍeḍongar and Capkā (Bastar District), described below. Ajit Mookerji describes it as a specimen of folk-art and assigns it approximately to the eighteenth century.[11] It shows a couple sitting in a pyre pit, and two water-pots; on one of them the wife rests her right hand. Over the couple are shown a *kīrtimukha*, the ornamented left arm and hand of the *satī*, and the sun and the moon.

Baḍeḍongar, in the northern part of Bastar, was also an ancient headquarters of a Hindu ruler. We find 'old' hero-stones without the hero's wife, besides others which are smaller in height; they are topped by the arm of the *satī* and show the couple seated in a pose similar to that of Umāmaheśvara, the wife holding her arm and hand (with a pot?) upwards. Often *liṅga* and *yoni* are present (Fig. 6). In one case the horse of the hero is added in a relief below (Fig. 7). In another stone an undulating *chatrī*-like roof with pillars, similar to Rājput memorials in north-western India, frames the couple and indicates northern influence. One rectangular stone shows a 'Revanta' hero with the *satī* facing the horse (Fig. 27). A water-pot is in her raised hand. Besides there are some more memorials in Baḍeḍongar which are *satī*-memorials as found in north-western Madhya Pradesh, e.g. on the way to Udaygiri, at Vidiśā near Sāñcī on the river Betuā. About 1.50 m. high, they depict the *satī's* arm and hand, various symbols like the sun and the moon, a water-pot, and five humps (*pañcaliṅgas*). The couple would be standing in a relief below, the *satī* holding a water-pot (Figs. 8 and 9).

In an *āśram* at Capka, not far from the road between Jagdalpur and Koṇḍagaon, we find a number of small memorials for heroes with their *satīs*.[12] Though smaller they resemble those stones at Baḍeḍongar which show seated couples. In one case the deceased is flanked by two wives (Fig. 11). Another shows the couple seated on a lotus pedestal in a kind of temple which has three or four storeys (Fig. 10). The top of the temple seems to have been moulded with the help of plaster into a pointed dome at the time when these stones were found in the surrounding fields and set up in the precincts of the *āśram*. The *satī*, seated to the left of her husband, is resting her right arm on what seems to be the usual *kalaśa*. Two stones show horsemen. In one case it is definitely a *rājā* who is charging with his horse (Fig. 12). He holds a spear and is surmounted by a *chatrī* flanked by the moon and the sun. Apart from northern, Rājput influence, the stones at Capka remind us of hero-stones at Jajpur in Orissa, and they may be similarly attributed to Rājput influence, as also a series of stones in the district of Durg.[13]

The best-known memorials of Bastar are the wooden *urasgattas*, as Grigson has called these funeral pillars, but which are now called simply *mūnde* or *khaṁba*.[14] According to Verrier Elwin, they are not substitutes for the stone menhirs (*uras-kal*) but are erected in association with them; an important man gets his stone to rest his uneasy ghost in the next world and his pillar to promote his reputation in this.[15] The upright stone pillars or menhirs (*uras-kal*) are erected by some of the Māḍiyā clans. Others have instead the so called *danya-kals*. These large horizontal slabs are supported by a number of smaller stones. At the head of such burial places we may find wooden pillars which roughly resemble the shape of a human being and have at times horns similar to the headdress of the Bisonhorn Māḍiyās.[16] Sometimes only small stones are erected, but they are expected to grow in course of time. The erection of the menhir is necessary to placate or lay at rest the *hanal*, the departed. The laying at rest of the 'shadowy soul' or the 'erecting of the power' of the deceased in a stone monument which is worshipped as if it were a living being is a widespread custom of popular belief in the southern half of India and has already found expression in the early hero-stones mentioned in the Caṅkam literature. These were not only 'memorials', but were worshipped as if they were 'gods' and, in fact, it is said that for some communities they were the only 'gods'.[17] The worship of the hero-stone involved its decoration with peacock feathers, and spears were erected around it like a fence. The bow and the shield were added. Toddy was poured over the stone and a ram sacrificed.[18] The aid of the hero-stone could be enlisted by worshipping it for victory in war, for rain and fertility.[19] The worship of the hero-stones (actually *naṭu-kal* = 'the stone which has been erected') mentioned in the Caṅkam literature resembles the bilateral relationship and interdependence of the living with the dead prevalent in the Bastar area and adjacent tribal parts.[20]

The memorial which proclaims the fame of a particular person in this world is the wooden *urasgatta* or *khamba*. It gives a kind of biography of the deceased. Longish, vertical panels show the fauna surrounding the deceased, e.g. the animals he hunted. Another base panel shows only aquatic animals—ducks, frogs, fish, tortoise, crocodile, etc. Others show the objects used by the deceased, e.g. the typical tribal knife, the headgear of a Bison Māḍiyā and the drum. Other panels show the dance of the Bisonhorn Māḍiyās with their drums and their typical hair style, and the dancing tribal women. Invariably *lāndā*, the rice beer, is being prepared or procured. The deceased might be shown seated on an elephant, ploughing a field, or with a *triśūl*. At Bastenar, near Gidam, a swing is shown, indicating that the deceased was a shaman (Figs. 14-18).

These pillars are not many and are mainly found between Jagdalpur and Gidam and between Jagdalpur and Citrakoṭ. There are three carved panels on the four sides which resemble the wooden, quadrilaterally carved pillars found in western India.[21] Koppers as well as Elwin hold that the *urasgattas* were made under 'Hindu influence' and were, in any case, prepared by extra-tribal craftsmen.[22] This may well be so, considering that they are worshipped as actual 'memorials'. They are erected in honour of important people and *prima facie* do not seem to have the same function as the *uraskals* or the early *naṭukals* of the Caṅkam literature, namely the worship of the dead to appease them and to enlist their co-operation in the world of the living, or, in the case of the *naṭukals*, to enlist their help for victory in a battle.

THE KORKŪ MEMORIALS

There are different types of memorials, called *mūndas*, which are attributed to the Korkūs. Firstly, we come across the wooden memorial tablets with panels, e.g. near Pañcmaḍhī in the Pancmadhi District of Madhya Pradesh. They are up to 1.20 m. in height, but we find also very small ones, about 25 cms. in height, said to be for women. The panels show the sun and the moon, and the waning moon is carved above the sun and encircles half of it. This is said to be a sign of death. 'The panels show horsemen, men dancing and the sides are cut with a chevron pattern' (D.H. Gordon).[23] Often a tree is carved on the reverse. Sometimes the names of the deceased are carved on the top of the tablet. At the bottom (presumably) the son responsible for the erection of the tablet is depicted. Sometimes identical horsemen are carved in different panels. It may be that several deceased are commemorated by one tablet in the case of poor persons as suggested by Russell and Hiralal.[24] Nowadays the *mūndas* at Pañcmaḍhī and Tāmiā are apparently just dumped on one heap, which may suggest a togetherness of the ancestors who lived as one family; it may also reflect neglect, because the pointed tablets are supposed to be planted into the soil (Figs. 21 and 22).

Gordon and Koppers also refer to the stone pillars at Pañcmaḍhī and Tāmiā.[25] Though the wooden tablets have several panels, Gordon is inclined to derive them from these stone pillars. But only two of the stone pillars at Pañcmaḍhī have several panels and the others are very similar to the *kīrtistambhas* known in Rajasthan from as early as the eighth century[26] (Figs. 19 and 20). They are also found between the Narmadā and Taptī rivers, e.g. at Dhumkal, with inscriptions dated in the thirteenth-fourteenth century. Some of them simultaneously commemorate Bhīl chiefs and their *satīs*.[27] The pillars at Pañcmaḍhī must have similarly originated in the context of memorials for chieftains. Similar memorials are also found in the museum at Chindvāḍā. The hero is shown on horseback, fighting against an enemy horseman, or he is fighting with sword and shield against a bowman. The pillars are otherwise shaped like the pillars of temples deriving ultimately from, or being reminiscent of, the ornate pillars of the Gupta period and, as we said, of the (*govardhana*) *kīrtistambhas* in Rajasthan.

The *mūndas* of the Korkūs (made sometimes by Goṇḍs) in the former Berār region of Maharashtra, e.g. at Cikaldā (described by Koppers),[28] are again different. Being thin stakes carved on four sides, they very much resemble what was described to me as a marriage pole in the Chindvāḍā Museum. The marriage pole is a very widespread, essential item of the marriage ceremony in Central India. The upper storey of the two-storeyed memorial pillars frequently has, though not invariably, the forms of a wedding hut.[29] Much of the *sidoli* (the celebrations accompanying the erection of the *mūnda*) is connected with the wife of the deceased or some near female relative and reflects incidents of the marriage ceremony.[30] Life after death is very much the same as life in the world of the living amongst the Korkūs[31] and the Rāj Goṇḍs.[32] Amongst the Rāj Goṇḍs every man and woman is believed to live with his or her original marriage-partner, even though there is remarriage of widows. A woman can be married only once with full wedding rites and it is these rites which determine her status in the society of the departed.[33] In this context the very widespread *satī*-pillars with the arm and the hand of the *satī* may actually be considered as identical with the marriage pole, though *satī* amongst tribals was confined to chieftains who were under the influence of 'kṣatriyazation' or 'rājputization'. The 'marriage pole' frequently appears on hero-stones in

Western India up to Karnataka, and sometimes the couple is seated beside it as in a marriage ceremony.

The close connection between the marriage bond of the couple in this world and the continuing bond of the couple based on the first marriage in some ancestral world or Land of the Dead suggests that the marriage pole and the memorial pillar are identifiable. The marriage pole is a symbol of the lasting bond between husband and wife, and in fact it represents the bridegroom. The wife's arm and hand emerging from the pole indicate her immolation and blessings. In a *satī*-stone relating to a Bhīl chief the wife is carrying what seems to be a marriage pole.

As the couple is reunited amongst the ancestors, the *satī* is reunited with her husband in heaven[34] and some features of the *satī* immolation reflect a marriage ceremony.[35]

The *satī* pillar is not only found on the *vīragalas* in Western India, but a tall *satī* pillar of about 2.50 m. may be seen in the Museum at Rāypur (in the Mahant Ghāsīdās Smārak Samgrahālaya). It resembles a temple pillar and has *kīrtimukha* and goose motifs. The bangles on the top two right hands remind us that it is a *satī* memorial for two wives. The memorial has been classified as belonging to the period of the Goṇḍ *rājās*.[36]

THE MEMORIALS OF THE GOṆḌ *RĀJĀS*

Finally we should refer briefly to the memorials of the Goṇḍ *rājās*. Some of them were in the Museum of Rāypur and have been shifted to the State Museum at Bhopal.[37] A Goṇḍ ancestor complex may be found near the village of Bhānutola at Gāthadongrī near Lānjī in the Balaghat District; these memorials are in an advanced state of decay. Yet one may still discern the vigorous popular folk style and attention to detail in these hero memorials, many of which are associated with *satīs* if the hero was a royal personage. Simpler stones without *satī* seem to have been erected for Goṇḍ soldiers. One stone shows shield and spear set up besides the soldier, who sits with his hands folded in worship (Figs. 23 and 24).[38]

NOTES

1. W. Koppers, 'Monuments to the Dead of the Bhils and Other Primitive Tribes in Central India', *Annali Lateranensi*, vol. VI, 1942, pp. 117-206.
2. Eberhard Fischer and Haku Shah, '*Vetra ne Khambha*', *Memorials for the Dead* (Gujarat Vidyapith, Ahmedabad, 1973).

3. W.V. Grigson, *The Maria Goṇḍs of Bastar* (OUP, 1938), pp. 3ff.
4. Grigson, op. cit., p. 3. For the modern period see e.g. S.L. Kalia, 'Sanskritization and Tribalization', in: *The Changing Tribes of Madhya Pradesh*, ed. T.B. Naik, Govt. of Madhya Pradesh, Dept. of Tribal Welfare (Indore, 1961).
5. Koppers, op. cit., p. 202.
6. Upendra Thakur, *The History of Suicide in India* (New Delhi, 1963), pp. 151ff., Pls. I-IV. Slides of the hero-stones in the Patna Museum were shown to me by H. Kulke.
7. B.N. Sharma, *Iconography of Revanta* (New Delhi, 1975), Fig. 33. The monument showing 'Kaśyapa (?) and Revanta' (Fig. 33) resembles memorials in the Gujarī Mahal Museum in the Gwalior fort. There the stones are crowned with the busts of the heroes exactly in the same way as in Fig. 33. The horseman in Fig. 33 is again the hero rather than Revanta. A similar depiction of the hero occurs on the double-panelled hero-stone from Budhpūr—see Thakur, op. cit., Pl. IV, No. 2. The sculpture of Fig. 33 is of *c.* tenth century, according to B.N. Sharma. The hero-stones in the Gujarī Mahal Museum are probably of the eighth-tenth century, according to H. Goetz, 'Rājput Reliefs', *Oriental Art*, X, 3 (Autumn, 1964), p. 166. The earliest hero-stone in the Gujarī Mahal Museum is of the sixth century.
8. For illustrations and the literary background see Jean Filliozat, 'L'abandon de la vie par le sage et les suicides du criminel et du heros dans la tradition indienne', *Arts Asiatiques*, vol. XV, 1967, pp. 65ff. Figs. 10-5. See also M.L.K. Murt[h]y's essay, 'Memorial Stones in Andhra Pradesh', in *Memorial Stones; A Study of their Origin, Significance and Variety*; eḍ by S. Settar and G.-D. Sontheimer (Dharwad/New Delhi, 1982).
9. Shantaram Bhalchandra Deo, *Mārkaṇḍī Temples* (Nagpur, 1973), Pl. XLVII, Fig. 3.
10. Deo, ibid., p. 57. V.V. Mirashi dates them to the eighth-ninth century. V.V. Mirashi, *Literary and Historical Studies in Indology* (New Delhi, 1975), pp. 239 ff., 253.
11. Ajit Mookerjee, *Indian Primitive Art* (New Delhi, 1953), Pl. XXVI.
12. Mr. Rajendra Kaicker drew my attention to these stones and also visited Capkā with me.
13. Slides pertaining to Jajpur were shown to me by H. Kulke.
14. Verrier Elwin, *Maria Murder and Suicide* (OUP, repr. 1977), p. 32.
15. Verrier Elwin, *The Tribal Art of Middle India* (OUP, 1951), p. 91. Figs. 101-2.
16. Cp. also W. Knabe, *Untersuchungen über die Grundlagen der Maria-Religion*, Ph.D. thesis, Köln, 1978, *passim.*
17. *Puranānūṟu* 335: the inhabitants of the *mullai* (pastoral) region consider the hero stones as the only gods.
18. *Akanānūṟu* 35 (hero-stones are decorated with peacock feathers, offerings of ram with toddy). *Paṭṭinappālai* 78-80, *Akanānūṟu* 131 (around the hero-stones a shield is kept and spears form a kind of a fence for the hero-stone). *Pur.* 268:

a stone under a thatched roof is erected on the seventh day after the death of the hero (the phrase is *kallukku vaippatu*—to plant a stone). *Pur*. 268: a nomad asks the bard to worship the stone, implying that it will cause rain. See V. Mahadevan, 'The Worship of Hero Stones' (in Tamil), R. Nagaswamy (ed.), *Seminar on Hero Stones*, State Govt. Dept. of Archaeology, Govt. of Tamil Nadu (Madras, 1974).

19. *Puranānūrū* 329: the relatives of the dead consider him as a wargod and worship him at dawn. *Pur*. 306: a woman worships a hero-stone for the success of her husband in the war. *Akanānūrū* 297: warriors sharpen their arrows on the stones. *Malaipaṭukaṭām* 394-6: people believe that 'gods' (*kāṭavuḷ*) are living in the hero-stone.
20. See the discussion by Louis Dumont in connection with the Guar ceremony—the second obsequies—amongst the Saoras as described by Verrier Elwin, *The Religion of an Indian Tribe* (OUP, 1955), in: *Contributions to Indian Sociology*, vol. III, 1959, pp. 68ff.
21. See Koppers, op. cit., Figs. 38, 39 and 40.
22. Verrier Elwin, *The Tribal Art. . .*, pp. 93ff.
23. D.H. Gordon, 'Korku Memorial Tablets', *Man* (London, 1936), No. 19.
24. Russell and Hiralal, *The Castes and Tribes of the Central Provinces of India* (Delhi, 1975) (repr.), vol. III, p. 565.
25. Koppers, op. cit., p. 177.
26. See G.-D. Sontheimer, 'Some Memorial Monuments of Western India', *German Scholars on India*, ed. by the Cultural Department of the Federal Republic of Germany (New Delhi, 1976), p. 269 and Pl. III, Figs. 1 and 2. [Editor's note: Also in the present volume, p. 127.] See also R.C. Agarwal's contribution on the *Kīrtistambhas* in *Memorial Stones: A Study of their Origin, Significance and Variety*, edited by S. Settar and G.-D. Sontheimer (Dharwad/New Delhi, 1982).
27. A.V. Pandya, 'Some Newly Discovered Inscriptions from Gujarat', *Vallabh Vidyanagar Research Bulletin*, vol. 1, issue 2 (International Language Section), pp. 1ff., 11: Dhumkal inscriptions 10 and 11 on *satī pāliyās*, AD 1323 and 1387 (Pl. 15B shows, however, a *kīrtistambha* pillar and in another figure, a cluster of memorial pillars, again in the style of *kīrtistambhas*), pp. 19f.: Two inscriptions (16-17) at Maṇḍālā for Bhīl headmen, AD 1354 and 1458. Another inscription (18) also relates to a Bhīl headman and is of AD 1420. See Pl. 16A which shows a multi-panelled pillar depicting incidents of his life. Inscription 19 is from Paṭāvalī near the Dhāmaṇmāḷ peak of the Satpuras. Date AD 1425. Pl. XXI A shows the Bhīl chief with sword and shield and his wife, obviously a *satī*. She holds a water-pot in her right hand and in her left hand she carries what could be a marriage pole.
28. Koppers, op. cit., p. 172.
29. Ibid., p. 180.

Cf. also the wooden mortuary monuments (*bṛṣakāṭh*) in Bengal. Ajit Mookerjee, *Folk Art of Bengal* (University of Calcutta, 1946), p. 47 and Pl. XIII, Figs. 18

and 19 and Pl. IV, Fig. 20. B.K. Chaudhuri, 'A Preliminary Study on the Bṛṣakāṣṭha of Bengal', *Proc. of the 25th Indian Science Congress*, Calcutta, 1938.

30. Koppers, op. cit., pp. 179f., gives evidence from the Bhīls and Korkūs.
31. Russell and Hiralal, op. cit., p. 566.
32. Christoph v. Fürer-Haimendorf, 'The After-Life in Indian Tribal Belief', *Journal of the Royal Anthropological Institute*, vol. 83, 1953, pp. 37-49, at p. 39.
33. v. Fürer-Haimendorf, ibid., p. 39. Cf. also Verrier Elwin, *The Religion of a Tribe* (OUP, 1955), p. 282 on the influence of the deceased husband on the living widow and her new husband; pp. 250ff. on the demand of the deceased to have his widow with him in the underworld.
34. See, e.g. P.V. Kane, *History of Dharmaśāstra*, vol. II, pt. I, 2nd ed. (Poona, 1974), p. 631: *Mitākṣarā* on Yājñavalkya: Śaṅkha and Aṅgiras say 'she who follows her husband in death dwells in heaven for as many years as there are hairs on the human body, viz., $3^1/_2$ crores of years. Just as a snake-catcher draws out a snake from a hole by force, so a woman draws her husband from (wherever he may be) and enjoys bliss together with him. In heaven she being solely devoted to her husband and praised by bevies of heavenly damsels, sports with her husband for as long as fourteen reigns of Indra. Even if the husband be guilty of the murder of a brahmana or of a friend, or be guilty of ingratitude, the wife who dies (in fire) clasping his body, purifies him (of the sin) . . .' This contrasts considerably with the view of the Goṇḍs. Though according to tribal belief the deceased husband may still have a claim on his wife on account of his marriage with her, there is no question that she could 'purify' him from his 'sins'. At the most she could look out for his material well-being in his afterlife by taking care that he is properly fed and by trying to appease his restless spirit from causing nuisance as a *bhūt* to the living. But the notion of 'purification' as stated above must have been attractive for those attempting to rise in spiritual and social status. The *Mitākṣarā* significantly adds that *satī* was a *sādhāraṇa dharma* to all castes from brahmaṇa down to cāṇḍāla. But there were many other commentators who disapproved of *satī*.
35. See Russell and Hiralal, op. cit., vol. II, p. 366 for the importance of the *kalaśa* in the marriage ceremony: . . . 'In front of the wedding procession are carried *kalaśa* or earthen jars filled to the brim with water, and with green shoots and branches floating on the top. The *kalaśa* is said to represent the universe and to contain the principal gods and divine mothers, while the waters in it are the seven seas. All these are witnesses to the wedding.' The water-pot is ubiquitous in the *satī* and other memorial stones. Russell and Hiralal, op. cit., p. 371 (on *satī*): . . . 'The widow next walks round the pyre seven times, as she did round the marriage-post at the wedding. . . .'

    For the marriage pillar standing in a water-pot—this arrangement is said to be a modern introduction—see John Irwin, 'Aśokan Pillars: a reassessment of the evidence', pt. IV: Symposium, *Burlington Magazine*, vol. CXVIII (November 1976), pp. 734ff., at p. 742.

36. See Bālcandra Jain, *Purātatva Upavibhāga meṃ saṁgrahīta vastuoṁ kā sūcīpatra bhāg 2*, Mahamta Ghāsīdās Smārak Samgrahālay (Rāypur, 1960), pp. 40f. and Pls. 22 and 23.
37. See ibid. for plates of these memorial stones.
38. I wish to express my thanks to the German Research Association (Deutsche Forschungsgemeinschaft), which provided financial assistance for visiting some of the locations mentioned in this note. I am also grateful to Mr. Rajendra Kaicker, New Delhi, and Professor B.D. Chattopadhyaya, Jawaharlal Nehru University, New Delhi, for accompanying me on a trip to Bastar in 1974.

Fig. 2: A hero-stone, Bārsūr.

Fig. 1: 'Old' hero-stone, Bārsūr (Bastar District) *c.* 10th-11th century.

Fig. 3: A hero-stone, Bārsūr.

Fig. 4: *Satī*-stone, Bārsūr. *c.* eighteenth century.

Fig. 5: 'Old' hero-stone, Baḍeḍongar (Bastar District)

Fig. 6: Hero-stone with the *satī* (in imitation of Umāmaheśvara), Baḍeḍongar

Fig. 7: Hero-stone with *satī*, Baḍeḍongar

Fig. 9: *Satī*-stone, Vidiśā, *c.* eighteenth century.

Fig. 8: *Satī*-stone, Vidiśa near Sānchī, *c.* eighteenth century.

Fig. 10: Memorial of a *satī* with her husband, Capkā (Bastar District).

Fig. 11: Memorial of a hero with two *satīs*, Capkā.

Fig. 12: Memorial of a *rājā* or chieftain, Capkā.

Fig. 13: *Satī* memorial, Capkā.

Fig. 14: Wooden memorial of the Bisonhorn Māḍiyās (Marias) on the Jagdālpur-Gidam Road (Bastar District).

Fig. 15: Detail of Fig. 14: aquatic animals in one of the base reliefs of the pillar.

Fig. 16: Detail of Fig. 14.

Fig. 17: Detail of Fig. 14.

Fig. 18: Detail of Fig. 14.

Fig. 19: Memorial pillar, Pañcmaḍhi (Pañcmaḍhi District).

Fig. 20: A memorial, Pañcmaḍhi, *c.* tenth century.

Fig. 21: Memorial tablet (*mūnda*) of the Korkū tribe (Pañcmaḍhi).

Fig. 22: Memorial tablet (*mūnda*) of the Korkū tribe.

Fig. 23: Memorial of a Goṇḍ chieftain with *satī*, Bhānutola near Lānji (Balaghat District).

Fig. 24: Memorial of a Goṇḍ warrior, Bhānutola.

Fig. 25: A warrior with a *muria* head-band, Bārsūr

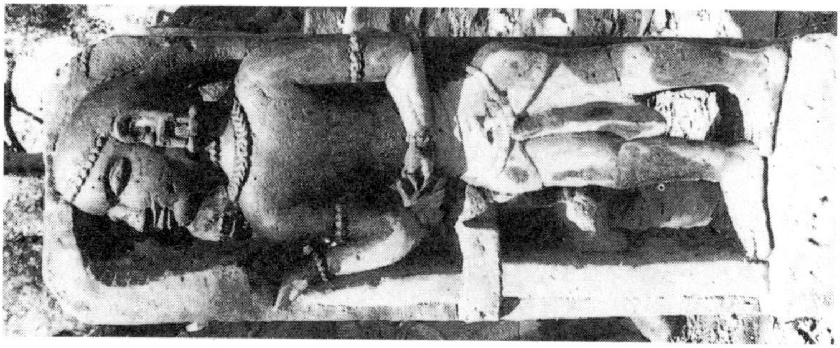

Fig. 26: A hero-stone, Bārsūr.

Fig. 27: 'Rēvanta' hero with the *satī* facing the horse, Baḍeḍongar.

Hero- and *Satī*-Stones of Maharashtra

Systematic investigation of the hero- and *satī*-stones of Maharashtra should be a substantial contribution to the religious, social and economic history of this region, and—linked with a similar study of this phenomenon in other parts of India—to the history of India in general. The enormous quantity of archaeological remains in India may have caused the neglect of memorial monuments like the *vīragals*, the ancestor shrines, etc. They were either noticed sometimes in passing or utilized (provided they were inscribed) for the purpose of reconstructing dynastic history. Though the hero-stones of Maharashtra, with a few exceptions, do not have inscriptions, their sheer multitude, a certain uniformity and at the same time a remarkable variety in detail (obviously in response to particular events or the wishes of the sponsors of the stone), would make them an urgent case for detailed study. This urgency is also enhanced by the fact that, more than other archaeological remains, they are in danger of destruction by road-building, wall-building, simple neglect and what not. Illustration of such neglect would demand too much of our space.

Naturally the explanation of the silent memorials of Maharashtra—silent as far as inscriptions are concerned—would need supplementation by local history, literary evidence and comparison with other areas, especially Karnataka. The instances we refer in this note mainly come from the districts of Poona, Sātārā, Sholapur, and Kolhapur. In a considerable number of villages we find clusters of hero-stones which may have, however, been recently collected by villagers, as e.g. in Kiklī (Wai Taluka, Satara District), or in Nāygāv Peṭh (Haveli Taluka, Poona District), Mhāḷuṅg, and Veḷāpūr (both Malsiras Taluka, Sholapur District), to mention some remarkable assemblages of hero-stones.

The hero-stones are invariably found in old villages which existed in the pre-Yādava times, e.g. in Corācī-Āḷaṇḍī (Āḷaṇḍī of the 'brigand') and in Koregāv-on-the-Mūḷā which are both mentioned in a copper-plate charter of the Rāṣṭrakūṭa king Kṛṣṇarāja I, dated 23 March 768, donating the village of Koregāv-on-the-Mūḷā (Kumārī-grāma) to a group of Brahmans from Karhāḍ.[1]

In the following study we shall place lesser emphasis on the art styles of the stones than on the contents depicted in these stones in the context of other extraneous evidence like historical, social, religious references, physical ecology and literary sources.

VĪRAGALS DEPICTING CATTLE-RAIDS

Though the Rāṣṭrakūṭa copper-plate inscription is symptomatic of the beginning of a steady, but slow (and, at times, relapsing and stunted) expansion of regular agriculture eastward of Poona, especially near river-beds, this was a process which was actually accelerated and brought to near completion only after the 'Pax Britannica' and during post-Independence developments. The area to the east of Poona included the notorious famine tract and was traditionally a pastoral, millet-growing land. Villages like Koregāv-on-the-Mūḷā remained essentially based on cattle-economy and thus two out of three stones in this village (built into the wall of a Mahādev temple) show, in their lowest relief, heads of cattle bent over the hero, who was killed while defending or retrieving cattle, or have some similar scene depicting a cattle-raid. The nearby Nāygāv Peṭh shows an even larger concentration of hero-stones with depiction of cattle (Fig. 1). Interestingly enough, in Nāygāv Peṭh there is a near absence of the otherwise familiar panel with *apsaras* carrying the hero to Kailās—it may have been too sophisticated an idea for the inhabitants of this pastoral village. The panels with cattle and the dead hero, the fighting scene, the hero worshipping a *Śivaliṅga* with *yoni* in the uppermost panel, popular in the depictions of the stones of Nāygāv, make them somewhat unique.

To whatever old villages or hamlets of the famine tract we turn, these cattle-raid stones are found, that is, in the valleys of the Bhīmā, Karhā, Nīrā, and Mān. Invariably, oral traditions and historical sources point to a continuity of pastoral life in these villages and hamlets up to modern times. Though the contents of the *vīragals* are forgotten by the villagers, the oral pastoral traditions persist and there is sufficient evidence (e.g. in the Śāhū Daptar records of king Śāhū of Sātārā, referring to prominent Dhangars in the area east of Sātārā) of the continued tradition of cattle-raids, and the existence of professional cattle-lifters. To cite a few instances:

(a) *Corācī-Āḷaṇḍī*: This village has three beautiful cattle-stones outside and one (out of two) inside the Mahādev temple which is situated at the edge of the older ruined settlement. It is associated with 'brigands', i.e. Rāmośīs or Beraḍs, and the pastoral Gavḷīs who brought the worship of the cattle-god Mhātobā (Mhasobā). He has remained the most important god in the village.

(b) *Koḷvihīre*: Situated in the Purandar Taluka, Poona District, this village has two cattle-raid stones in front of the temple of Bhairava (originally a *kulsvāmī* of a pastoral, exogamous Haṭkar-Dhangar group). More stones have recently been unearthed by the villagers which show a high percentage of cattle-raids. The village tradition refers to the presence of Vālmīki Koḷī, the erstwhile robber, and to Gavḷīs and Dhangars, both groups remembered to have owned herds of large cattle.

(c) *Mūrti Moḍhve*: Not far from Koḷvihīre, it has about five cattle-raid stones (Fig. 2). One is a square pillar, later used to support the '*sabhā-maṇḍapa*' of a small Mahādev temple. Mūrti Moḍhve was an *inām* of the More family obtained during Śāhū's times.[2] They are Haṭkar-Dhangars. Not far off are the ruins of a Gavḷī settlement, deserted because of deteriorating pastures and expansion of agriculture during the last hundred years or so.

(d) *Guḷuñce*: Situated in the Purandar Taluka, Poona District, it has two exquisite hero-stones, one possibly depicting the hero being killed in a stampede of the cattle-herd. Nearby there is a deserted settlement of Gavḷīs with their deities still being worshipped by the Dhangar shepherds.

(e) *Bhāde on the Nīrā River*: This village near Vīr in the Purandar Taluka, Poona District has broken pieces of hero-stones at the Bhairava temple. Pastoral traditions are continued by the nearby temple of Birobā and Iṭhobā (Viṭhobā), the famous Dhangar god and his 'elder brother'.

(f) *Mhasvaḍ*: Etymologically derived from Mahiṣavāḍā ('the camp of the buffalo demon'), this village is mentioned in an unpublished Kannaḍa inscription[3] of the Siddhanāth temple. The inscription of the year Śake 1060 (AD 1138) mentions the donation of some land to a Brahman for the performance of the daily *naivedya* by a predecessor of the Kalacūrya king Bijjaḷa of Kalyāṇī, who ruled from Maṅgaḷveḍhā as a subordinate of the Cālukya king Jagadekamalla of Kalyāṇī. But in spite of the settlement of Brahmans, the place has retained its pastoral traditions.[4] The oral traditions refer to a Mhasojī Gavḷī, who first had his *vāḍā* there. The legends relate to a Gosāvī or Kāḷbhairava who killed a demon Mahiṣa here, whence the derivation of the name of the place. The only extant hero-stone in the precincts of the temple, in a small so-called 'father-shrine', shows the hero defending cattle. Mhasvaḍ eventually became the headquarters of the Māne family, who were *śiledārs* (cavaliers), and the whole valley of the Mān river remained an area for grazing flocks of sheep, herds of cattle, and horses, and was reputed to be inhabited 'by a thin, unsettled, and in some degree predatory population'.[5]

(g) *Dolāsaṇe*: Situated on the Nāsik-Puṇe Road (Sangamner Taluka, Ahmednagar District), we find here a hero-stone depicting a cattle-raid. It is built into the back wall of the Kāḷbhairava temple (Fig. 3). As so often, Kāḷbhairava is here connected with the pastoral Gavḷīs who are said to be the 'first' settlers.

(h) *Paṇḍharpūr*: Instead of multiplying the same instances, we may refer to the role of Viṭhobā of Paṇḍharpūr, who has been portrayed as a cattle-lifter in a thirteenth century literary work of the Mahānubhava sect.[6] This role assigned to their god in the *Līḷācaritra* might, no doubt, enrage and wound the feelings of the Vārkarīs, the devotees of Viṭhobā. While there is every justification for such a possible reaction of the Vārkarīs, I feel that this problem needs to be studied in its historical context, not forgetting the social values of the time. From the religious point of view, Viṭhobā could have, of course, no connection with the cattle thief. The Viṭhobā of the Vārkārīs is different from the one who lived at the time when the cult was not fully evolved. One of the great achievements of Indian religion is its ability to transform a rustic, or somewhat gruesome, cult into a sober and peace-loving sect, and this is most often done by slowly shifting the original beliefs and practices. The cult of Viṭhobā was evolved at a time when no outright social disrepute was attached to cattle-raids. It was considered a formal invitation to a feud or a war and an act of bravery, according to the Caṅkam literature.[7] Even today, we hear of traditions in Rajasthan and Gujarat of cattle-raids marking the beginning of a feud. The *daṇḍanāyakas* of the time when Viṭhobā took his form seem to have liberally indulged in robbing cows and women.[8] Then the 'thief' also had a claim to a hero-stone when he died in a raid,[9] if only in order that his spirit might be laid to rest and not haunt his relatives. Thus the *Līḷācaritra* (*Uttarārdha*, *līḷā* 411) may have, in the hitherto easily accessible version,[10] plausibly explained to the Mahānubhāvas the origins of a very popular cult by referring to circumstances prevailing at that time in a way which was persuasive and sufficient to discredit the cult in their eyes. Because whatever bravery the hero may show—and bravery and prowess were the prime criteria to qualify him for being commemorated by a hero-stone—the *defence* of cows tended to be spiritually and religiously meritorious and prestigious. The really blasphemous passage in the *līḷā*, which represents a third layer, should have convinced nobody and is contained in a variant reading relegated to a footnote by S.G. Tulpule. Viṭhala vīru, the 'hero' Viṭhala, as he is called in the *līḷā*, is another indication that the worship of a hero was initially involved. But the argument that it could have well been a cattle-thief who was initially involved in the cult has become somewhat otiose, because meanwhile the new and final edition of the *Līḷācaritra* (ed. by Dr. V.B. Kolte) contains the original, rather short *līḷā* and it is clear that the present version in Tulpule's edition must be a later accretion, twisting the original *līḷā* beyond recognition. As a matter of fact in the original *līḷā* Cakradhara, the founder of the sect, answers the question of Mahadāisā as regards the festive show (*naḍanācu*) and attachment (*upādhi*) displayed in Paṇḍharī thus: 'My lady, this hero died in the cause of (defending) cows. His name is Viṭhalu. In his name this hero-stone was erected (*bhaḍakhaṃbā māṃḍīlā*). There the deity viewed it as belonging to itself. [or: The deity apprehended identity with the *bhaḍakhaṃbā*: *tetha devatā abhimānu ghetalā*]. He (i.e. the *bhaḍakhaṃbā*) fulfils the wishes [of the devotees]'.[11] One more fact makes the story that Viṭhobā died defending cows more likely: an unnoticed *vīragal* of the Yādava period is actually found on the side of the *samādhi* of Cokhāmeḷā. The stone is near the spot which must have been, according to Tulpule, the original site of the original shrine of Viṭhṭhala.[12] It is built into a wall and heavily covered with oil and soot. The scenes show a fight, heads of cows, and the usual *apsaras* accompanying the hero. The top portion is apparently broken off, but there can hardly be any doubt that it must have contained the panel which is never absent on hero-stones of that period in the pastoral area, namely the hero worshipping the *liṅga*.[13] This may reinforce the view that there was a popular pre-Vaiṣṇava cult, before the Vaiṣṇavas and their Bhakti arrived.[14] Even today, Viṭhal or Iṭhal is, in the eyes of the pastoral groups, rather not a Vaiṣṇava Kṛṣṇa, but a pre-Vaiṣṇava pastoral Gavḷī, who came from Karnataka. He is considered to be a brother of the pastoral god Birobā/Bīrappa worshipped by the shepherd communities of the Deccan. Sometimes Bīrappa is said to be in the form of a *liṅga* and is carried by Viṭhobā around his neck.

The 'local deity' mentioned in the original version of the *līḷā* may have been the pre-Vaiṣṇava Śaivite cult. The later, twisted and inflated, version of the *līḷā* says that the mother of Viṭhobā consecrated a *liṅga* at the *bhaḍakhaṃbā* of Viṭhobā. For all the twisting, this may correctly echo that it was originally a place of Śaivite worship assimilating Viṭhṭhala, whence the Śaivite cult received its name. Subsequently, the Vaiṣṇava Bhakti must have emerged in the foreground and the fact that Viṭhobā had been protecting cows must have made this easier—Kṛṣṇa being the 'protector of the cows' *par excellence*.

It may be said that the *Līḷācaritra* is rather late, but the date of its composition given by Tulpule as Śake 1205 (AD 1283)[15] would still allow us to say that the passage retains a memory of the real origin of the cult.

(i) *Veḷāpūr, Mhāḷuṅg*: Veḷāpūr is situated in the Malsiras Taluka, Sholapur District (Fig. 5). About sixty known hero-stones, including fragments, form a remarkable assemblage, but equally striking is the relatively small percentage of stones (five) depicting cattle-raids. Veḷāpūr was situated at an old cross-roads between north and south, west and east. It reminds one of the passage in the *Malaipaṭukaṭām*,[16] where it is said that at many cross-roads, where the enemies of the king live, inscribed stones can be seen which are reminders of the dead heroes and of the Maḻavars (the robber tribe). It was probably a border town where many a battle must have been fought between the powers of the south and the north. Veḷāpūr was probably attacked and defended by the *daṇḍanāyakas* of the border area. Two villages on the road to the north, Mhāḷuṅg and Bavḍā, and the town of Āklūj on the way to Indāpūr may have had the function of securing this road. In each of these places we find hitherto unnoticed stones which show the hero conquering a small fort which must have been the local fortified *vāḍā* (Figs. 6, 7 and 8). In Bavḍā, the local *vāḍā* has disappeared, whereas in Mhāḷuṅg and Āklūj the forts exist, and, in fact, hero-stones have been used for their walls. Bavḍā, and especially Mhāḷung, again have 'cattle-raid stones' in their sizeable collection: in Bavḍā, three out of 21 hero-stones, and at Mhāḷung, four out of 50 hero-stones are cattle-raid stones.

Many of the stones in Veḷāpūr show "*daṇḍanāyakas*" or some royal heroes with *chatrīs* and in one case with a banner bearing an unidentified symbol. One of the most impressive stones has been moved to the Prince of Wales Museum in Bombay, according to Cousens.[17] It has four panels, and the two lower ones represent fighting scenes. The second panel from below shows the hero as a *daṇḍanāyaka*, or high-ranking officer on horseback and with a *chatrī*; the lowest panel shows him on foot. Maybe the stone depicts two battle scenes wherein the hero rose in rank. Even more interesting are the *bhūts*, or goblins, which hover around the battlefield. One of them has a Bhairava-like halo, a dagger and a *kapāla*, the other actually sucks the blood of a dying enemy.

Such *bhūts* frequenting the battlefield are well known to literature, and the nearest reference comes from the *Śrīśivabhārata*.[18] The depiction of '*bhūts*' is also found at Mhāḷuṅg on stones showing the same style and craftsmanship as those in Veḷāpūr (Fig. 12). On the lowest panel of the stone in the Prince of Wales Museum we also come across a group of four warriors with bugles and bows. They probably represent a contingent of tribals having hooked noses familiar from depictions of *yakṣas* or tribals. The villages around Veḷāpūr, again, show a high percentage of cattle-raid stones, e.g. Khūḍūs, Paṭvardhan Kurolī, Mīre, etc.

(j) *Kiklī, Wai Taluka, Sātārā District*: Kiklī is situated on the eastern fringe of the Wai Taluka, and on the border between the richer rainfall area to the east of the Ghāṭs and the dry 'pastoral area'. About fifty remarkable hero-stones, including fragments, are scattered in this village. Some of them were submerged in the soil to support the side of a steep access to the remnants of an old 'Hemāḍpant' temple which was re-erected nearby.[19] One of the steps of the access to the former temple turned out to be a *vīragal*. The others were recently retrieved by the villagers and re-installed near the village square as they were in danger of being destroyed by the pressure of the access path.[20] More *vīragals* were used in house-building and may be retrieved from ruins. Initially, no cattle-raid stones were thought to be extant, but excavation unearthed some.

VĪRAGALS OUTSIDE THE 'PASTORAL AREA'

(a) *The Kolhāpūr Museum and Bīḍ* (*Karavir Taluka*): If our theory is correct, namely, that social and physical ecology is reflected in the contents of the hero-stones, we should not find stones depicting cattle-raids to the west of Poona, the area up to the Ghāṭs (Māvaḷ), or the area around Sātārā and Kolhāpūr, i.e. an area receiving sufficient rainfall and traditionally more an area suited for rice cultivation. There are, indeed, only one or two hero-stones depicting a cattle-raid in the beautiful collection of hero-stones of the Śilahāra and Yādava period in the Kolhāpūr Museum. It may be said that this collection only contains selected stones and, therefore, none of the humbler cattle-raid stones. But if we go to Bīḍ in the Karavir Taluka, to the south-east of Kolhāpūr, we come across approximately a hundred *vīragals*, most of them built into a wall facing the entrance to the Lingāyat Mahādev temple. None of them shows a cattle-raid. And though the Kolhāpūr farmer is proud of his Khilārī oxen, the Gazetteer informs us that they are mainly imported from cattle-fairs held annually in the classical pastoral area of the eastern parts of the Sātārā District, from the cattle-fairs of the Sholapur and Sangli Districts, and from the eastern part of the Belgaum District.[21]

Sāvantvāḍi, the small former princely state, has similarly a large number of hero-stones. Most of them are of the Vijayanagara period and do not contain depictions of cattle-raids. Many of them indicate that the wife (or wives) committed *satī*, symbolized by an arm emerging from a pillar (Fig. 16).

Kolhāpūr being one of the oldest and most famous *śaktapīṭhs*, the goddess Mahālaksmī figures in the top panels of two *vīragals*. They are exhibited in the Kolhāpūr Museum. Here, the hero does not worship the *liṅga* and *yoni*, but he worships the goddess.

(b) *Sea battles*: It is quite natural that in a coastal area like Koṅkaṇ and Goa we would not find any depiction of cattle-raids, but rather depiction of sea-battles. The famous stones of Eksār near Borivḷī (Thana District),[22] and the stones of the Kadamba period in the Goa Museum are proof of their existence. But this does not preclude the existence of the usual hero-stones depicting a fight in the lowest panel, e.g. at Lahore, near Mahāḍ in the Kolaba District, though the present author has seen none depicting a cattle-raid. This corresponds with the lesser importance of cattle in an area where rice is cultivated with male buffaloes as the plough animal.

RELIGIOUS SUICIDE

Veḷāpūr and Mhāḷuṅg have hero-stones depicting suicides. In one case the head of the hero is carried on a platter in front of his just decapitated erect body, which in turn is followed by the decapitator and an army. Maybe this refers to a vow of the hero to offer his head in return for a victory of his master. This very depiction in stone has a precursor in an extremely elaborate stone of the Cālukyas of Kalyāṇī at Maṅgaḷveḍhā (Fig. 17). The lowest panel has disappeared, but probably contained a battle scene. On the second panel from below, the hero is seated on an elephant and is received and accompanied by musicians, etc. On the third panel, his head is cut off and carried away on a platter. Again, this seems to be in consequence of a vow; on simpler stones at Mhāḷuṅg, Toṇḍale and Boṇḍale—all in the Malsiras Taluka—we see a man who has also just been beheaded. There are two stones from Kiklī which show the hero in front of a low pillar from which three spears emerge on top, similar to the points of a *triśūl* (Fig. 20). This may indicate his imminent suicide, as we know of the suicide of heroes by throwing themselves on a bundle of *śūlas*, or spears.[23] Even today, the devotees of the god Mailār on Devaraguḍḍa, who are called *kañcavīra*, and the Gorappas (the equivalents of the Vāghyās of Jejurī) of the Kurubā community perform their self-mortifications in front of a huge stone *triśūlam* which is also used for tying the iron chains which the Gorappas have to break. The pillar resembles the one depicted in Kiklī.

Here we may also refer to peculiar memorials which are found in Karnataka[24] and in Maharashtra, e.g. in the Khaṇḍobā temple of Jejurī. Under the pavilion-like structure for the hook-swinging ceremony in Jejurī (*bagāḍ*) we find a small carved stone-plate with footprints of a saint (or Khaṇḍobā?) surrounded by heads of four rams (Fig. 21). Rams are still sacrificed by the Dhangars to Khaṇḍobā (or the goddess Bāṇāī) and other *kulsvāmīs* in a ceremony called *dāvaṇ* = 'a string of five rams': for five years a ram is set aside each year for sacrifice. According to the *Mhaskobācem-caritra*, the god tested the *bhakti* of the founder of the cult and his five sons by asking for the sacrifice of the latter.[25] The sons agreed to be sacrificed but the god revived them, or rather replaced the human victims by rams. There often is a close identification of human beings with the animals of the god, e.g. as the god's horses and the god's dogs, which are indispensable requisites for a warring and hunting god like Khaṇḍobā Mailār. *Bhaktas* behaving like barking dogs and eating from a wooden bowl without using their hands or behaving like horses by whipping themselves can still be seen on Devaraguḍḍa during the Dasarā festival.[26] The idea of suicide in order to obtain a god's response or merger with him may be one of the reasons for going to the extent of considering oneself a sacrificial animal. It is the idea of Paśupati taken literally on the popular level. Eventually, the animal sacrifice completely superseded this identification, but the presentation of the *pādukās* and the heads of rams may still reflect an earlier identity of human and animal sacrifice. This identity seems to be indicated on a similar memorial in front of the Khaṇḍobā temple at Āklūj (Malsiras Taluka) (Fig. 22). Here, the *pādukās* rest on a *nandī*, who in turn rests on a *yoni*-shaped pedestal. The *nandī* is flanked by two human heads and two heads of rams. A similar memorial is found in one of the small shrines at an entrance to the Hoysaḷeśvara temple at Haḷebīḍ. Here, the *pādukās* are flanked by two beheaded human figures and various animals in addition to heads of rams. The *pādukās* seem to rest on a snake.

THE CONCEPT OF *VĪRA*

The emphasis on the fortunes obtainable on the battlefield, but even more, the emphasis on the ephemerality of life, is well known from Kannaḍa inscriptions. Earning fame and immortality and nearness to gods like Śiva and Mahālakṣmī, and the ascension to *brahmaloka* or *sūryaloka* must have been powerful ideas. It was not just the idea of being commemorated as an ancestor, but, in addition, the idea of a *hero* which found emulators from all castes, at least in Karnataka. The hero, on account of his *vīrya*, had immediate access to the god. In that respect he resembled the *yogī*, who became a *siddha* by attaining *siddhis*, or who, by controlling the spirits of the 'fifty-two *vīr*' (Mar. *bāvan vīr*), could realize his god or merge with his god, or could attain a supernatural, godlike position. This would allow the *yogī* to use the spirits of the fifty-two *vīrs*. They are all heroic gods or godlings, like Bhairava, Mārutī (Hanuman, Mahāvīr) or Vikramāditya (of whom it is said, according to legend, that he prayed to the Mahākāl of Ujjain for victory, thus borrowing his powers).

What combines the hero and the *yogī* is the heroic and unconditional acceptance of suffering, pain and death. We have noticed above the *kañca-vīras* of Devaraguḍḍa. Similarly, even today, the descendants of the founder of the Mhaskobā cult in Vīr (Purandar Taluka, Poona District) combine the martial and yogic aspects of the hero and the *yogī*: they strike themselves with swords to effect possession by the god Mhaskobā. They are called *siddhas*, but also *vīras* according to the old District Gazetteer.[27] Thus the famous *śloka* from inscriptions in Karnataka:[28]

dvāv imau puruṣau loke sūryamaṇḍalabhedinau
parivrāṭ yogayuktaśca raṇe cābhimukho hataḥ

may relate to the close similarity of the hero and the *yogī* as far as their motivations and aims are concerned.

FORM AND CONTENT OF THE HERO-STONES

(a) Normally, the *vīragals* have three, four or five panels. The middle panel shows the *apsaras* carrying the hero towards heaven. Sometimes, he sits in a celestial *pālkhī* with or without his wife. The topmost panel shows the hero as the devotee of some deity, generally Śiva in the form of the *liṅga* with *yoni*, attended by some priest. But the hero may also be the devotee of a *devī*, e.g. of the Mahālakṣmī of Kolhāpūr, a Jina, or a *tīrthankara*, or of Gaṇeśa, whom we accordingly find at times depicted in the top panel.

Sometimes, the hero is shown lying prostrate on the battlefield with *apsaras* descending to garland him. On one hero-stone we find the *apsaras* descending with garlands and the wife sitting near her slain husband raising her hand indicating that she is a *satī* (Fig. 7).

More often the hero is lying prostrate with heads of cattle bent over him in a small panel below the battle scene.

On some hero-stones, the story of the fate of the hero attracted much admiration, and this has normally led to an increase in the number of panels to five. Each of the three lower panels may describe different stages of the battle or different battles and, at times, the subsequent suicide of the hero. The above-mentioned hero-stones describing the conquest of a fort (Figs. 6, 7 and 8) tend to enlarge the size of the panel with the battle scene or scenes at the cost of the other panels. The hero-stone of Āklūj (Fig. 8) actually foregoes the normal partition into panels to save space and most of it is used to accommodate, in one large square, a battle, the subsequent attack on the fort, and the carrying away of the 'dead' hero in a palanquin. That the slain hero is carried away from the scene of the fight, seated in a palanquin to become a god, or—in the present case—to join Śiva, is reflected, e.g. in oral traditions of Rajasthan.[29] The next panel, showing the hero, his wife (a *satī*?), *apsaras* and saluting elephants, is very small, and so is the topmost panel, where the hero has joined Śiva.

(b) The front of the slab is sometimes divided vertically to accommodate two sequences for two heroes (Fig. 28). The top panel, with *liṅga*, may or may not be divided. In the latter case, the heroes are shown worshipping together.

(c) Accordingly, the top of the stone may be crowned by two *kalaśas*.

(d) In several places (Kiklī, Lohare, Mūrti-Moḍhve, Bāvḍe, Guḷuñce, Phalṭaṇ), we find a quadrilaterally carved *vīragal* which shows three panels of identical size with, sometimes, varying scenes. Probably, these are memorials which commemorate four heroes on the same stone. An exception to this is the stone in the garden of the Bhārat Itihās Samśodhan Maṇḍal in Poona, where the hero is depicted in larger size, stretching over one side of the stone.

In Phalṭaṇ (Malṭaṇ) two remarkable hero-stones of the Yādava period maybe seen outside the gate of the town wall near the Khaṇḍobā temple. Topping the vigorous battle and *apsara* scenes we find on the first stone (I) each of the four heroes apparently worshipping his particular deity, e.g. Viṣṇu with Garuḍa, Śiva, Sūrya (two horses are carved below the deity) and what is probably also Śiva seated on a demon (Fig. 29a-i). The second stone (II) is crowned by slightly receding rectangular panels. On one side of them the hand and arm symbol with a *kalaśa* and one *pādukā* are shown. The opposite side is occupied by the sun and the moon, and on the other two sides *kīrtimukhas* have been carved. It is worth mentioning about this stone—situated as it is near the walls of the town—that it depicts the conquest of a fort by some princely hero with a *chatrī*. Phalṭaṇ has always been an important trading town for the exchange of goods on the west-east route leading to Veḷāpūr (see above, i).

(e) A trilaterally carved fragmentary hero-stone may be seen in the open-air museum at the Devgiri Fort near Aurangābād.

(f) Multi-panelled hero-stones are known from the late Gupta period (the earliest being of the sixth century AD) at the Gwalior Fort (Gujarī Mahāl). We can perhaps assume that the custom of carving panels came from there to Maharashtra and Karnataka, except for the representation of the hero on the top of the stone in the form of a bust, which seems to have been common in Madhya Pradesh in the post-Gupta period. The earliest multi-panelled hero-stones in Maharashtra and Karnataka seem to be those at Paṭṭadakal and belong to the Rāṣṭrakūṭa period. The early Dravidian hero-stones are not divided into panels.[30]

(g) The more we turn to the north-east from the southern districts of Maharashtra, e.g. to the Usmanabad District, and again in the Candrapur District, and to the east towards Andhra Pradesh, the number of multi-panelled stones as well as the number of panels of the stones decreases. Here we come across hero-stones which are not divided into panels (Fig. 41). On the stone, which is generally about one metre high, the warrior is carved in action holding a shield and wielding a sword, a bow, a battle-axe, or a spear; occasionally, the sun and the moon are shown. Sometimes the hero is confronted by smaller-sized foes. Though from the artistic point of view the stones are at times quite elaborately carved (e.g. in the precincts of the temple complex at Mārkaṇḍī in the Candrapur District), one hardly hesitates to assign them to a tribal context. Unlike the hero-stones of southern Maharashtra and Karnataka (Figs. 42 and 43), only in rare cases is a top relief indicated with the hero worshipping the *liṅga* (as, e.g. in the Museum of the Bīdar Fort). We find a number of memorials in areas which belonged and still belong largely to the forested tribal belt, and these stones probably commemorate tribal chiefs. This type of hero-stone links up in its form and content with those of the Bastar District (Madhya Pradesh) and eastern Madhya Pradesh. Similarly in Andhra Pradesh the same type of memorial occurs, and it is continued into the Vijayanagara period, where the memorials, however, tend to be much larger in size.

SATĪ

Much has been said about this institution, but many problems remain, not least in the area under discussion. There are essentially three ways of representing *satī* in our area:

(a) The symbol of hand and arm with bangles, emerging from a pillar, is carved on a slab of stone. The arm is bent at a right angle at the elbow. Often, the couple, or the husband and two wives, are depicted on the slab. To this the *liṅga* and *yoni* as well as the sun and moon are usually added. The origin of the pillars seems to have been in Madhya Pradesh or Rajasthan, where we find the *govardhana-kīrtistambha* for heroes, e.g. in the Jodhpūr area, but even up to Pañcmāḍhi in Madhya Pradesh. In the Raipur Museum a pillar with a *kīrtimukha* and goose motif shows two right hands and arms carved in the upper part of the pillar. The pillar is otherwise similar to the *govardhana-kīrtistambhas* and, though said to be of the seventeenth century AD., gives the impression of a much earlier date, though perhaps not contemporaneous with the *govardhana-kīrtistambhas*. The pillar as a memorial for *satī* and heroes seems to have been introduced from the North to Maharashtra, and the word used instead of *vīragal* was *bhaḍa-khamba*.[31] The presentation of the pillar on *satī*-stones, i.e. slabs, gives the appearance of a relatively later date than the presentation on the multi-panelled hero-stones. Pillar and arm are common in the presentation of *satī* on the Vijayanagara memorials. The representation of pillar and arm in a *vīragal* is found on the stone in Māṭhgāv and is found on nearly all hero-stones at Sāvantvāḍi.[32] Notwithstanding the necessity of further exploring the meaning by intensive local field research and literary studies, the representation of the hand with arm and bangles may be explained as the *satī* giving her blessings. But the significance of the pillar still awaits explanation. It may, however, be a marriage pillar which represents the lasting union of the couple. The wife is not separated, and she does not become a widow if she 'commits' *satī*. That the classical *vīragal* was considered to be a kind of *stambha* can be seen in Vālhā (Purandar Taluka, Poona District,) where the arm is carved as an adjunct to an otherwise common hero-stone (Fig. 33). Another intermediary stage between the classical *vīragals* and the more simple *satī*-stones concentrating on 'pillar and arm' may be found in a fragmentary piece at Rāśīn (Karjat Taluka, Ahmednagar District). Here the top of the hero-stone is still carved in the classical fashion, showing a panel with the *liṅga* and the hero, whereas the lower part of the stone seems to be resolved into the arm, hand and pillar symbol with no further panels.

(b) The depiction of the wife in the act of committing *satī* is found occasionally on normal *vīragals*, e.g. on a *vīragal* at Bīḍ (Karavir Taluka, Kolhāpūr District) where the couple is shown lying on the pyre.[33] In another hero-stone, located at Kumbhārvaḷaṇ in the Purandar Taluka of the Poona District, the wife is seen about to lie down beside her dead husband. Both are engulfed by the flames of the pyre and the left hand of the *satī* is extended towards heaven as if she were blessing the living (Fig. 31). The middle relief on the *vīragals* normally shows *apsaras* carrying the hero to heaven. Occasionally, some celestial vehicle is carried by them in which husband and wife are seated in a manner similar to the Umāmaheśvara pose. This presumably indicates that the wife has joined the dead hero as a *satī*.

During the times of the Yādavas *satī* was still confined to royalty and the gentry. According to the *Smṛtisthaḷa* of the Mahānubhāvas, Kāmāīsā, the queen of Rāmadeva Yādava (1271-1310) was forced to commit *satī*.[34]

In the *Jñāneśvarī* reference to the *satī* rite could serve as a simile for a devotee who suffers peril for the sake of god.[35] On most of the hero-stones there is not yet any indication that the wife committed *satī*. But among people aspiring for prestige and rank the custom of divorce and remarriage might have been discarded and *satī* might have spread. The simple idea of *apsaras* carrying the hero towards heaven without a celestial vehicle or palanquin—which was a sign of honour and at the same time allowed scope for the wife of the hero to be carved—seems to preclude the idea of *satī*. Yet at times we find the wife somewhat awkwardly and artificially placed beside the *apsaras* and then perched behind the hero worshipping the *liṅga* with him in the top panel (Fig. 30). Spread of the custom of *satī* accounts for the tendency to include the wife in the middle panel besides the *apsaras*, and to show the couple worshipping in the top panel. However, such depictions may not yet imply that *satī* was actually committed. On modern ancestor memorials (e.g. of the Dhangars in Maharashtra) the wife is also shown, though she may be alive. But even if she remarries she will be united after death with her *first* husband, with whom she was first united in marriage. Thus it would not be premature to show her on the ancestor stone at the death of her first husband.

Generally the evidence shows that the symbol of 'hand and arm' and/or pillar is a later development, and is rarely found in the pre-Yādava and Yādava periods. There is an early exception at Phalṭaṇ, where on a quadrilaterally and exquisitely carved hero-stone the arm and hand is shown without the pillar in the top panel to the left of a *kalaśa*. The right side of the *kalaśa* is occupied by one *pādukā*. The hand or arm is attached to the above-mentioned hero-stone in Vālhā (Purandar Taluka, Poona District), again indicating a transitional phase (Fig. 33). Elements of the earlier hero-*satī*-stone and the later stones with arm and pillar are combined on a big boulder found in the Māruti temple at Nārāyanpūr (Purandar Taluka, Poona District) (Fig. 34). Here, in the lowest relief the four *satīs* are seated behind the dead husband with raised arms. Such a presentation is found on earlier, more realistic hero-*satī*-stones (Figs. 7 and 31) (cp. also S.B. Deo, 'A Unique Hero-Stone of Mārkaṇḍī'). The right arms of the four *satīs* are shown emerging from a pillar. This is the later method of showing *satī*. The whole stone is carved in a style which is closer to 'folk art' than are the classical hero- and *satī*-stones. On the left of the stone horsemen are carved, perhaps members of the entourage of the hero. On the right side of the stone there is nothing but a crude Gaṇeśa, suggesting that the hero must have been a devotee of that god, and was perhaps a Brahman. The stone is probably of the early Marāthā period.

Thus *satī* seems to have been relatively rare in the pre-Yādava and even

Yādava period in Maharashtra, and when it happened it was depicted realistically. Eventually the 'classical', multi-panelled hero-stone merged into the slab showing 'arm, hand and pillar' without panels and the sculptor and the relatives of the deceased seem to have been satisfied with comparatively crude presentations of the hero and his wife or wives.

(c) The arm without pillar is also found, but this presentation seems to be a relatively recent and the carving looks simpler.

THE '*PĀLIYA*'

Probably, the last old-style multi-panelled *vīragals* in Maharashtra are of the fourteenth century, as exemplified by the inscribed and dated hero-stone of Māṭhgāv (AD 1317).[36] The *vīragals* seem to have been eventually replaced by the one-panelled *pāliya* from the north, which is rather an ancestor memorial than a hero memorial. To the horse and rider a representation of the wife of the rider is added, seated behind her husband on the horse. The representation is similar to that of Khaṇḍobā and Mhaḷsā. Khaṇḍobā's dog is also shown at times. Obviously, an identification or nearness of the couple with Khaṇḍobā and Mhaḷsā is intended, as on the *satī*-stones in Madhya Pradesh. There, the depiction of the couples resembles Śiva and Pārvatī in the Umāmaheśvara pose.

Probably we have to assign to the Marāṭhā period stone slabs found at Korṭī (Karmala Taluka, Usmanabad District) and at the Khaṇḍobā temple at Jejurī (Poona District) showing the heads of 'heroes who died in war' still remembered as such by the local population (Fig. 38). As a last trace of the old, classical hero-stones, these slabs are crowned by the *kalaśa*. The Marāṭhā period is, moreover, marked by the pavilion-like *chatrīs* from the north and by the *ghumṭas* built over the *samādhis* of heroes, saints, famous personages and prominent ancestors.

ACKNOWLEDGEMENTS

Mr. Ramdas Atkar and Mr. Rajaram Zagade, who helped me on my excursions, took a personal interest in the subject, and discovered many memorials themselves.

The Sarpanch of Āklūj, Mr. Mohite (Malsiras Taluka, Sholapur District) for permission and help to photograph Figs. 8-10.

Prof. G.H. Khare and Prof. S.G. Tulpule for discussion on the subject.

The German Research Association (Deutsche Forschungsgemeinschaft) for financing my stay in India which made it possible to supplement my work on the hero- and *satī*-stones.

NOTES

1. *E.I.* XIII, pp. 275-92; D.D. Kosambi, *Myth and Reality* (Bombay, 1962), pp. 146f.
2. Ma. Cam. Dikshita, and Vi. Go. Khobrekar, *Śāhū Daptarātīla Kāgadapatrāmcī Varṇantmaka Sūcī* (Nagpur, 1969), *daptara aṃka* 26, *puḍke* 1, 33236, p. 331.
3. An account of the inscription was published by G.H. Khare in *Samartha* (25 May 1932, published from Satara). A copy of the article was made available by the kind help of Mr. K.B. Mhaske.
4. For the traditions and history of Mhasvaḍ and the area around see the author's *Birobā, Mhaskobā und Khaṇḍobā: Ursprung, Geschichte und Umwelt von pastoralen Gottheiten in Mahārāṣṭra* (Wiesbaden, 1976), pp. 26ff. [Editor's note: English version, *Pastoral Deities in Western India*, New York, 1989, pp. 22ff.]
5. *Memoir on the Satara Territory* by T. Olgilvy, in: *Selections from the Records of the Bombay Government*, No. XLI, New Series, edited by R. Hughes Thomas (Bombay, 1857), pp. 3ff.
6. Sontheimer, op. cit., p. 72, fn. 10. [*Pastoral Deities* . . ., p. 70, fn. 10.] See meanwhile the discussion by S.G. Tulpule in 'The Origin of Viṭhṭhala—An Interpretation', in: *Annals of the Bhandarkar Oriental Research Institute, Diamond Jubilee Volume*, 1978, pp. 1005-9.
7. *Tolkāppiyam, Poruḷatikāram* 60.
8. *Maharashtra State Gazetteer, History*, pt. 1: *Ancient Period* (Bombay, 1967), pp. 350ff. *EC* VII, Sk. 256; VIII, Sb. 339.
9. *Malaipaṭukaṭām* 387 ff.: inscribed stones for heroes and the Maḷavars (the robber tribe). For the 'deification' of robbers after their decease, see William Crooke, *Tribes and Castes of the North-Western Provinces and Oudh*, vol. II (Calcutta, 1896), p. 326. For an excellent account of the transformation of a robber of the 'criminal' Mīna tribe (Rajasthan) into a 'Hindu dev', see Jyotindra Jain, *Bavaji and Devi, Besessenheitskult und Verbrechen in Indien* (Wien, 1973), pp. 44ff.
10. S.G. Tuḷpuḷe, *Līḷācaritra, uttarārdha*: *bhāga* 2 (Nagpura/Pune, 1967), p. 101. See Kolte's edn. (Bombay, 1978), *līḷā* 508.
11. V.B. Kolte (ed.), *Līḷācaritra*.
12. S.G. Tuḷpuḷe (ed.), *Prācīna Marāṭhī Korīva Lekh* (Pune, 1963), pp. 89-90.
13. Deleury's view that Viṭhobā must have been a hero who died in a cattle-raid seems confirmed. However, the hero-stone found at Paṇḍharpūr leaves the *mūrti* of Viṭhobā unexplained. Deleury traces the *mūrti* to images of Bir Kuar, the Ahir deity, and refers to similar depictions on 'hero-stones' near Wāī (Satara District), but such 'hero-stones' are of a much later (Marāṭhā) period, derive from the worship of Viṭhobā, are modelled after the *mūrtis* of Viṭhobā and Rakhumāī, and are actually ancestor memorials. G.A. Deleury, *The Cult of Viṭhobā* (Poona, 1960), pp. 197ff.
14. M.S. Mate, 'Pandharpur: Myth and Reality', in: M.S. Mate and G. Kulkarni (eds.), *Studies in Indology and Medieval History*, Prof. G.H. Khare Felicitation Volume (Poona, 1974), pp. 134ff.

15. S.G. Tuḷpuḷe, op. cit., p. 13.
16. See fn. 9 above.
17. Henry Cousens, *Medieval Temples of the Dekhan* (Calcutta, 1931), p. 63, Pl. XCVI; Moti Candra, *Stone Sculpture in the Prince of Wales Museum* (Bombay, 1974), p. 54, Fig. 160; Günther-Dietz Sontheimer, 'Some Memorial Monuments of Western India', in *German Scholars on India*, vol. II (Bombay, 1976), Pl. IV, Figs. 1 and 2. [Editor's note: Also in the present volume.]
18. *Śrīśivabhārata*, 22, 68-70 (Ānandāśrama Press edn.), p. 66.
19. *Maharashtra State Gazetteers, Satara District* (Bombay, 1963), p. 817.
20. The author wishes to record the help rendered by Mr. V.G. Khobrekar, Mr. Inamdar and Mr. Jamsandekar, and the villagers of Kiklī, especially Mr. Babar, the Sarpanch, in helping me to study the stones.
21. *Maharashtra State Gazetteers, Kolhapur District* (rev. edn., 1960), pp. 293-5.
22. Cousens, op. cit., p. 21.
23. On Śūla Brahma stones see N. Kasturi, 'The Hero Stones of Mysore', in *Professor K.V. Rangasvami Aiyangar Commemoration Volume* (Bangalore, 1940), p. 205.
24. S. Settar, *Hoysaḷa Sculptures in the National Museum Copenhagen* (Copenhagen, 1975), p. 99 and Pl. XLVIII.
25. Hari Balakrishna Arole, *Śrīnāth Mhaskobā Devācem-caritra*, 1st edn. (Pune, 1889), 4th edn. (Pune, 1972), pp. 8ff. Tr. into German as appendix in the author's *Birobā, Mhaskobā und Khaṇḍobā . . .*, pp. 200ff. [English version in *Pastoral Deities . . .*, pp. 207ff.]
26. Rā. Ciṃ. Ḍhere, *Khaṇḍobā* (Puṇeṃ, 1961), p. 140: The *bhaktas* in Khaṇḍobā's procession at Naḷdurg who whip themselves are called *vārū* (steed; war-horse).
27. *Gazetteer of the Bombay Presidency*, vol. XVIII, Poona District, 1885, pt. 3, p. 464.
28. The text may be found in the *Mahābhārata* (Calcutta edn. 5. 1031). In the critical edition the text is found in the critical apparatus after 5.33.52. See also *Pañcatantra* 1.345.
29. See fn. 9, Jyotindra Jain, op. cit.
30. R. Nagaswamy (ed.), *Seminar on Hero-Stones* (Madras, 1974).
31. S.G. Tuḷpuḷe, *Līḷācaritra* (see fn. 10 for details) and *Prācīna Marāṭhī Korīva Lekh*, p. 297. *Bhaḍ* is derived from Skt. *bhaṭa*, which means 'warrior, soldier, mercenary, outcast, barbarian', Apte, *Sanskrit English Dictionary*, s.v.
32. S.G. Tuḷpuḷe, *Prācīna . . .*, Pl. 65, panel 3.
33. Sontheimer, 'Some Memorial Monuments of Western India', Pl. V, Figs. 1-4. [Editor's note: Also in the present volume.]
34. S.G. Tuḷpuḷe (ed.), *Smṛtisthaḷa* 149 (Pune, 1969), p. 48.
35. *Jñāneśvarī* 16.185; 18.347.
36. S.G. Tuḷpuḷe, *Prācīna . . .*, p. 290ff.

Fig. 1: Cattle-raid stones, Nāygāv Peṭh.

Fig. 2: Cattle-raid stone, Mūrti Moḍhve

Fig. 3: Cattle-raid stone, Dolāsaṇe.

Fig. 4: Cattle-raid stone, Kandār.

Fig. 5: A typical hero-stone, Veḷāpūr.

Fig. 6: Defence of a fort, Mhāḷuṅg.

Fig. 7: Attack on a fort, Bavḍe.

Fig. 8: Conquest of a fort, Āklūj.

Fig. 9: Detail of Fig. 8.

Fig. 10: Detail of Fig. 8.

Fig. 11: Detail of Fig. 8.

Fig. 12: A hero-stone, Mhāḷuṅg.

Fig. 13: Detail of Fig. 12.

Fig. 14: Detail of Fig. 12.

Fig. 15: Detail of Fig. 12.

Fig. 16: A hero-*satī* pillar of the Vijayanagara period, Sāvantvāḍi (Courtesy: Lt. Col. H.H. the Rājbahādūr of Sāvantvāḍi)

Fig. 17: A hero-stone of the Cālukyas of Kalyāṇī, Mangaḷveḍhā.

Fig. 18: Detail of Fig. 17.

Fig. 19: Detail of a hero-stone at Boṇḍale.

Fig. 20: Hero-stone from Kiklī indicating religious suicide.

Fig. 21: Memorial at the Khaṇḍobā temple in Jejurī.

Fig. 22: Memorial at the Khaṇḍobā temple, Āklūj.

Fig. 23: *Pādukās* of Khaṇḍobā, Phalṭaṇ.

Fig. 24: A panel from a hero-stone, Tonḍale.

Fig. 25: Detail of a hero-stone, Toṇḍale.

Fig. 26: Another panel of the hero-stone, Toṇḍale.

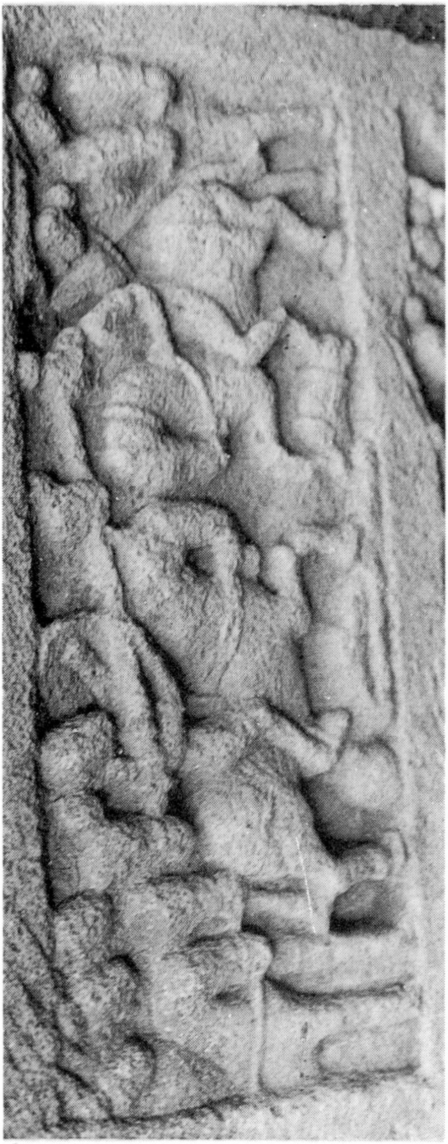

Fig. 27: Another panel of the hero-stone, Toṇḍale.

Fig. 28: Memorial for two heroes sitting beside the *Śivaliṅga* and *Yoni*, Phalṭaṇ.

Fig. 29 (a): A hero-stone of the Yādava period, Phalṭaṇ.

Fig. 29 (b): Detail of Fig. 29 (a).

Fig. 29 (c): Detail of Fig. 29 (a).

Fig. 29 (d): Detail of Fig. 29 (a).

Fig. 29 (e): Another side of the Yādava hero-stone, Phalṭaṇ.

Fig. 29 (f): Detail of Fig. 29 (e).

Fig. 29 (g): Detail of Fig. 29 (e).

Fig. 29 (h): Top panel of the third side of the Yādava hero-stone, Phalṭaṇ.

Fig. 29 (i): Top panel of the fourth side of the Yādava hero-stone, Phalṭaṇ.

Fig. 30: A broken top panel of a hero-stone, Phalṭaṇ.

Fig. 31: A *Satī*-stone, Kumbhārvaḷaṇ.

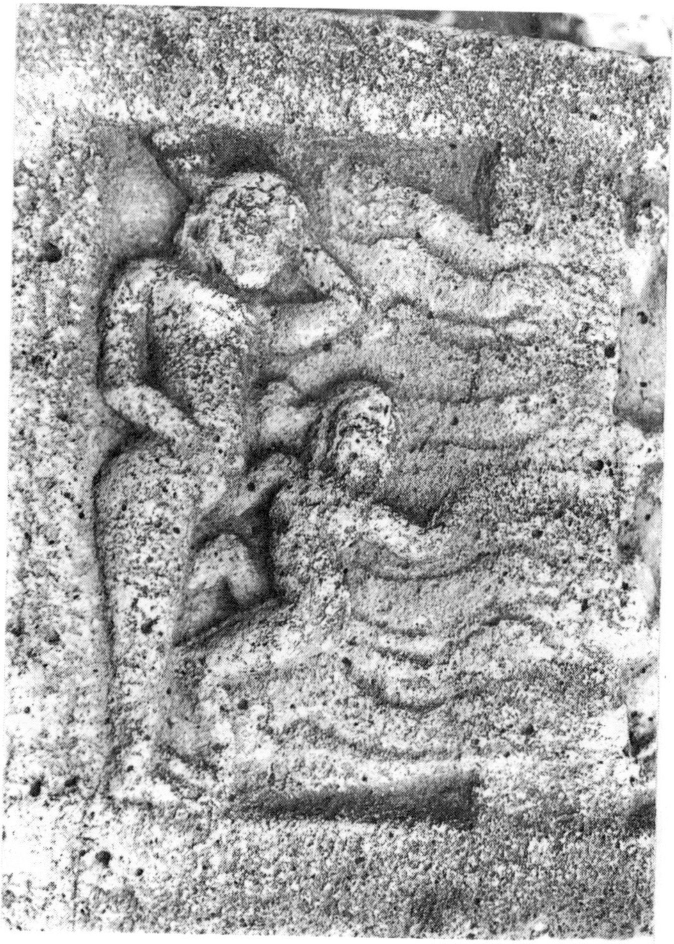

Fig. 32: Detail of Fig. 31.

Fig. 33: A hero-*satī*-stone, Vālhā.

Fig. 34: A hero-*satī*-stone, Nārāyaṇpūr.

Fig. 35: A typical *satī*-stone with pillar and arm.

Fig. 36: A *satī*-stone for three wives, Kandār.

Fig. 37: A *satī*-stone for two wives.

Fig. 38: Pillars with faces of heroes, Korṭī.

Fig. 39: A hero-stone, Veḷāpūr area.

Fig. 40: Detail of Fig. 39.

Fig. 41: A hero-stone, Ridhore.

Fig. 42: A hero-stone, Mārkaṇḍī.

Fig. 43: A hero-stone, Mārkaṇḍī.

God, Dharma and Society in the Yādava Kingdom of Devagirī according to the *Līḷācaritra* of Cakradhar

THE RELIGIOUS CONDITIONS IN THE YĀDAVA KINGDOM OF DEVAGIRĪ AND THE *LĪḶĀCARITRA*

The Yādavas ruled from Devagirī (Daulatābād) in Marāṭhvāḍā. The heartland of the kingdom was the Godāvarī river basin in northern Maharashtra, from where the kings tried to extend their rule over much of the present-day Maharashtra and other parts of the Deccan. The Godāvarī river basin can be considered a typical nuclear agricultural area forming the backbone of a kingdom, as e.g. the ancient Tamil *marutam* (riverine area) was seen as the backbone of the kingdom and characterized by the rule of Vēntaṉ (Indra).[1] The Yādava kings claimed to base their kingdom firmly on the brahmanical notion of society, that is, on the *varṇāśrama* or *cāturvarṇya* system. This was clearly expressed by Puroṣottama, one of the ministers of Rāmacandra Yādava (AD 1271-1311), shortly before the incursions of the Muslims. He claimed to be a student of Veda and *smṛti* and to have given separate courses of conduct to the various *varṇas* and *āśramas*, in other words, to have administered *varṇāśrama dharma*, *dharma* in its entirety.[2] Similarly, Kṛṣṇadeva, or Kānherdev (1245-61), as he is more popularly called in the *Līḷācaritra*, is referred to as 'intent on the restoration of the Vedas'.[3]

The Yādava kingdom saw the rise of the Marāṭhī language, which was spoken by the Yādava kings, the extension of agriculture and the spread of temples, correctly or wrongly attributed to the famous Hemādrī, the *karaṇādhīśvara* or *mahākaraṇādhipa* (chancellor) of King Mahādeva (1261-70).[4] Hemādrī was also associated with the successor of Mahādeva, King Rāmacandra (1271-1311). Hemādrī's famous *Caturvargacintāmaṇi* reflects the attempts to collect and consolidate the religious rites and observances existing at that time from a *śāstric-purāṇic* point of view and sets a guideline to the religious life for a society to be administered according to Dharmaśāstra and the *varṇāśrama* system. That the Yādava King Rāmacandradeva wanted to have control over religious matters is also indicated in the 'Inscription of the 84' in the Viṭhṭhala temple of Pandharpur in the south, on the border of the kingdom.

In this inscription, which records donations to the extension of the temple, Rāmacandradeva is called 'the chief of all (religious) groups of devotees of Pāṃḍarī (Pandharpur) and the guideline of all (religious) customs'.[5] The different sections of the *Caturvargacintāmaṇi* deal with *vrata*, *dāna*, *tīrtha*, *mokṣa*, and *pariśeṣa*.[6] Though the work deals with *caturvarga*, i.e. the four *puruṣārthas*, *dharma*, *artha*, *kāma*, and *mokṣa*, the vast population consisted of 'Śūdras', a population to which access to Sanskrit, Veda, and *mokṣa* was practically closed and which, though influential, had thus no access to scriptural religion. Moreover, the *bhakti* movements of the Āḻvārs and Nāyaṉārs in Tamilnadu and of the Vīraśaivas in Karnataka had proven to be a much more readily available access to God.

The god of *bhakti* promised more readily salvation in the form of nearness, merger, or even identity with God than the tiring and laborious migration through cycles of *saṃsāra* leading to *mokṣa* or *svarga*. Especially the two famous protagonists of *bhakti*, Jñāneśvar and Cakradhar, were aware of the religious aspirations of 'women and Śūdras', which prompted Jñāneśvar to compose his commentary on the *Bhagavadgītā* in Marāṭhī.[7] But, whereas Jñāneśvar had hardly any intention to form a threat to the existing religious and social order, Cakradhar was less careful in his dealings with the rules of society, about the demands of ritual purity, and in his considerate and 'liberal' attitudes towards women. Jñāneśvar's support of the social order is evident e.g. in his comment on the *Bhagavadgītā*, when he says (3. 169):

> *mārgadhāreṃ vartāveṃ/viśva heṃ mohareṃ lāvāveṃ/*
> *alaukika nohāveṃ/lokāṃprati/*
>
> One should keep on the traditional way of duty,
> And lead the world to progress,
> One should not do something
> Which is different from popular convention.

Nevertheless, Jñāneśvar's life and the effect of his work must have been a spiritual relief when social and ritual conditions threatened to become rigid, but his work did not seriously result in *varṇasaṃkara* ('confusion of castes'), however apprehensive the stalwarts of the *varṇāśrama* system might have been. In this way Jñāneśvar prepared the typical Maharashtrian way of the saint who may live within society as a *gṛhastha* and combines *nivṛtti* and *pravṛtti*. This attitude did not topple the conventional order of society, but rather made it workable and tolerable. Jñāneśvar, the 'outcast Brāhman', even had to get a *śuddhipatra* from the Brāhmans of Paiṭhaṇ (Pratiṣṭhāna).[8]

Paiṭhaṇ remained the seat of the *śāstric dharma* and brahmanical learning and even in later times Muslims would direct appeals to the Brahmans of that town because of their reputation of resolving cases.[9]

Cakradhar was after all not only a saint, but an *avatār* of Parameśvar, according to the beliefs of the Mahānubhāv sect. He says of himself: 'a walking and speaking god is hard to get in the world'.[10] He was elusive, wandering from place to place, first in solitude for twelve years and then attracting followers. He and his followers tended to be 'heterodox', de-emphasizing the importance of the Veda; this must have been an anathema to an orthodox believer in the Veda like Hemādrī. The followers of Cakradhar eventually became a sect with canonical ritual and ethical works, with clear features of a 'counterstructure', but with elements drawn from the structure which was actually to be rejected.[11] Yet, it would be wrong to say that Cakradhar himself openly rebelled against the conceptual or actually practised order of the *varṇāśrama* system.

In the following we give some illustrations of Cakradhar's relationship to the law, the religion, and the social order in the Yādava kingdom. The evidence is from the *Līḷācaritra*, which describes the life and teaching of Cakradhar as recorded by Mhāiṃbhaṭ with the help of informants immediately after Cakradhar's death. The whole work, edited by V.B. Kolte, contains 592 (*Pūrvārdha*) and 645 (*Uttarārdha*) *līḷās*.[12] Written in prose, it has an authentic ring and reflects realistically the social and religious conditions in a Hindu kingdom which was now identified rather with a region and its culture than with a particular dynasty. The great amount of realism in the descriptions of the life and times of Cakradhar distinguishes the *Līḷācaritra* from much other Indian hagiographical literature.

CAKRADHAR AND THE *VARṆĀŚRAMA* SYSTEM

(A) THE *SANNYĀSĪ* BEYOND THE CONVENTIONS OF SOCIETY

Though Cakradhar was the fifth *avatār* of God (*parameśvar*), he had all the characteristics of a *sannyāśī*, a renouncer of the world.[13] He was traditionally born at Broach (Gujarat) in 1194 as a son of a minister. His name was Haripāladev and he died young. When the dead body was taken to the cemetery, it was possessed and reanimated by the spirit of Cāṅgdev Rāuḷ

(*Pūrva*. 17). After spending some time as a prince at the royal household and living a married life, he grew tired of the world and left for a pilgrimage to Ramtek near Nagpur (*Pūrva*. 18-19). Then he took *sannyās* being initiated by Govindaprabhu, another *avatār* of Parameśvar according to the beliefs of the Mahānubhāv sect. With him he shared many anti-conventional attitudes.[14]

After this followed a period of twelve years of unsettledness (*Pūrva*. 21: *avasthā*), which began with indifference towards his own body (*Pūrva*. 21: *śrīmūrtīvari udāsya svīkarileṃ*) and a life in the forest (*ibidem*: *araṇyāmadhyeṃ bijeṃ karīti*). For twelve years he lived a solitary life (*Pūrva*. 21-105: *ekāṃk*) and then attracted his first follower, the elderly woman Bāisā, which was—so to say—the beginning of the 'sect'.

Curiously, during his solitary wanderings, Cakradhar married again, a daughter of a merchant, for a short while. But this only goes to show that he was God and thus beyond *jātikuḷa*, beyond caste and family restrictions (*Pūrva*. 32). Nor did he observe the rules of pollution in his dealings with women (*Uttara*. 384) and untouchables. There is a remarkable *līḷā* (*Uttara*. 72) which shows his accessibility for untouchables and at the same time reflects their longing for access to God:

Three Mātāṅgas[15] came to the Jogeśvarī temple. They stood at the door. Two of them greeted the spire of the temple. Then they said: 'Let's go.'—'No,' [said the third,] 'I shall not come without having seen this god [Cakradhar].' Thus they [the two] left. He waited. Āusā[16] came out. He said to Āusā: 'My Lady, tell the Gosāvī [that] a man belonging to an untouchable caste (*bāhīrīlu pāiku*) has come and that he says: "I shall not go without having seen this god".'

Āusā went [and said]: 'My Lord, Svāmī Jagannāth! A man belonging to an untouchable caste has come. He says: "I shall not go without having seen this god!".'

The Gosāvī asked for some sweet (*lāḍu*) from Bāisā. The Omniscient said: 'Go, give him the sweet and tell him, I have sent it.'

Āusā came. He still stood there. She gave him the sweet. 'Go away, Cakraśvāmī has allowed you to go.' He said: 'I shall not go without having seen him.' He was not prepared to listen to her.

She came back [again]. He still was standing there on the same spot. 'Why don't you go? Cakrasvāmī has allowed you to leave.'—'No mother, I shall not go without having seen this god.' Āusā told the Gosāvī: 'Oh Svāmī Jagannāth, he says: "without seeing this god I shall not go".'

So the Gosāvī came out. He stood near the door. [The Mātāṅga] put the sweet near the feet of the Gosāvī. Then he prostrated and started leaving.

The Gosāvī came back to the verandah and said: 'Oh you desirous of *prasād*, will you take some *prasād*?'—'Yes, yes [they answered]. Who will not reach out his hand for rice with clarified butter? Who will not reach out his hand for cotton and silk garments? [But that is not the real *prasād*] I shall dive deep into this pool of muddy water and then [whatever I shall bring forth, even if it is mud] *that* should be taken as *mahāprasād*. This is not the real *prasād*. How can *this* be taken as [real] *prasād*?' Thereupon he distributed the sweet amongst all.

Another incident concerns Cakradhar's meeting with a Camār, a member of the untouchable cobbler caste. The *līḷā* (*Pūrva*. 27) also discloses that the *Dharmaśāstra*, in this case a digest of *dharma*, was consulted and applied:

There was a certain village near Bīḍ. The Gosāvī went there. He sat down near a water-hut. A Camār and his wife had gone to the market. They were returning from the market. The Camār became thirsty. He came to drink water at the water-hut. At that moment he saw the Gosāvī sitting there. He came near. He prostrated, touched his feet and sat in front of the Gosāvī. He took out his betel-pouch. He cut a betel-nut into pieces [and] offered them to the Gosāvī. He folded some betel-leaves and gave them. Then the wife of the Camār came from behind. He also gave a betel-leaf [to her]. Then he took one himself. Then she said: 'Get up and move. The others have left.' He said: 'Wait a little.' Again she said: 'Get up and move. They are far ahead. [Everything] has become quiet. The cattle are on their way to the village. It is evening. Are you thinking of relieving somebody of his blanket? Get up and move.' He said: 'Wait! Wait a little.' This happened twice, thrice. But he would not get up. She said: 'Well, are you coming or not?'—'I am not coming.'—'Shall I go then?'—'Go.' She went ahead and came back again. Then she said: 'If you don't come, then release me (*tari pheḍi mājhīye māthāṃcā hātu*). He said: 'You are released. Go!' She said: 'Who is witness?'—'This Lord is witness.' She said: 'My Lord, are you a witness?' The Gosāvī nodded approvingly. Immediately she left.

The Gosāvī offered betel. And he [the Camār] held out his hands. The Gosāvī took some betel out of his mouth. He [the Camār] ate the *prasād* and got into trance (*stīti*, Skt. *sthiti*). Immediately the Gosāvī left from there. The Omniscient said: 'He came to the town Āmba of Khol Nāyak.[17] There, having become a godly man, he was having his [divine] play. He started living in a godlike manner (*isvaratveṃ varto lāgalā*). The people honoured him as is becoming for a god. In every house they gave him a bath, anointed him, made *pūjā* with sandal paste and incense, and performed *āratī*. They kept his food on a big plate placed on a wooden stand. He slept on a cot with a mattress. Thus he was sitting [once] in a house being worshipped, having his meal, anointed with sandal paste, his forehead painted with holy marks, around the neck a garland of flowers, the *āratī* being performed, when a Camār of his village had gone to the market. He said: 'Are you not so and so Camār?'

There were some Brāhmans [nearby]. They said: 'Who is this?' He said: 'He is a Camār of our village. He belongs to our clan (*āmcā gotīyā*). His parents are waiting for him.' The Brāhmans said: 'Is it so? Oh my goodness! How the people are polluted now (*kaisā loku vīṭāḷīlā*).' In this way one heard it from the other. More and more heard it. And [the Brāhmans] came to the place of Jagaḷdev and Vīṃjhadev. Jagaḷdev and Vīṃjhadev were the chief officers (*adhīkārī*) of that place. All the important people (*māhājana*) came to them. They told them: 'This Camār here has polluted the whole village. What should be done in such a case?'

Thereupon they called the Brāhman who knew the *nibandha* [digest of *dharma*] and asked him: 'This Camār has polluted the whole village. What should be done to him?' He looked into the *nibandha*. The following [conclusion] emerged from the *nibandha*: He should be placed in a heap of limestones.

Immediately they dug out a pit [and] seated him in it. On the top they kept heated limestones. They emptied bags of water over it. A crowd had collected. At that moment somebody came from the market. He saw the crowd and asked them: 'Why are there so many people?' They said: 'Don't you know?'—'I don't know.'—'The one who was playing here having become a godly man, has turned out to be a Camār. He has polluted the whole village. We have seated him in the heap of limestones.' He said: 'How can it be that you have seated him in a heap of stones? He is playing in the market. Go and see!' On this they all came to the market. And there, well-worshipped, he was playing as before. They recognized him. All over the body [he was anointed with] sandal paste, lines of sandal paste were on his forehead. [On the lines of sandal paste] rice corns were pasted. Around the neck were garlands of flowers. The Omniscient said: 'The garlands of flowers around the neck would not wither, nor would the *pūjā* [arrangement] be disturbed.' Then all repented. They prostrated [and] said: 'My Lord, we are sinners and Cāṇḍāḷas. We have harassed you.' Then they left.

Cakradhar did not think much of the impurity caused by women during menstruation and stood, like the Vīraśaiva saints, for equality of men and women, in any case in religious life (*Uttara*. 102):

Do you think that their [the men's] souls are big and theirs [the women's] are small? Is the God protecting you different from the one protecting them?

In fact, Cakradhar advises his disciples 'that the living should live like the dead' (*Uttara*. 305) and thus keeps in line with the general notion that a *sannyāsī* is considered to be dead as far as *saṃsār* is concerned. However, as has been rightly observed, the *sannyāsī* still lives in the phenomenal world, *jagat*.[18] What is meant by *saṃsār* in this context is explained in *Uttara*. 585. Cakradhar teaches his followers the *asannidhāna-dharma*, the *dharma* to be observed in the case of his absence:

. . . Bhaṭo[bās][19] asked: 'My Lord, the Gosāvī is confronting [us] with "absence of his nearness" [that is, he will leave us]. What then should be avoided by a *mahātmā* while there is *asannidhāna*?'

The Omniscient replied: 'Vānareyā,[20] one should not be a witness to money transactions (*dravyasaṃbandhā sākṣī na ṭhakāveṃ*). One should neither buy nor sell.

One should not resort to violence. One should not have "likes" and "dislikes". One should not distinguish between commandments and prohibitions (*vidhi-niṣedha*) [because a *mahātmā* is beyond them]. One should not visit *jatrās* (popular religious festivals) and *kṣetras*. One should not stay in towns and cities.'

In other words, Cakradhar equates *saṃsār* to *vyavahār*, to the involvement in worldly business and affairs (*Pūrva*. 477).

(B) CAKRADHAR'S ATTITUDE TOWARDS SCRIPTURAL AND FOLK RELIGION

Similarly, Cakradhar often turned against established ritual and religion whether based on scriptures or on folk beliefs. Thus he emphatically disclaims the need to go to *tīrthas* and *kṣetras*, because they do not lead to liberation. How could it be otherwise, if God in the form of Cakradhar is personally present? Thus when Mahādāīsā, an elderly female devotee, intends to go on a pilgrimage to Mallikārjuna,[21] after having already visited Dvārkā and Vārāṇāsī, Cakradhar holds: 'My presence and service (*dāsya*) to me give liberation; *tīrtha*, *kṣetra*, *vrata*, *dāna* are of no avail for liberation. You should not leave here.'—'Yes, my Lord.' And she touched his feet.

Thus he completely removed Mahādāīsā's faith in *tīrtha*, *kṣetra*, *vrata*, *dāna* and in Dādos.[22] We notice that these are more or less exactly the topics with which the great ritualist Hemādrī professed to deal in his *Caturvargacintāmaṇi*. But folk religion does not fare better in Cakradhar's attitude. One may, for instance, refer to *Uttara*. 316:

Afterwards [the Gosāvī] took his seat in the temple of Jogeśvarī in Vāḍegāv. A certain person brought a sheep there. Bāisā said: 'Please go. The Bābā is here.' The Omniscient said: 'My Lady, this one [the deity] says, "I shall take, I shall take [the sheep]". He [the sacrificer] says, "I shall give, I shall give". Let's leave here. One should not remain in a place which is marked by passion and darkness (*rājase tāmase sthānīṃ na baisāveṃ*).'
After that the Gosāvī proceeded to the temple of Nṛsiṃha. There he stayed for the night.

The Nṛsiṃha temple may not have been an ideal place either, because elsewhere Nṛsiṃha is considered to be a spirit (*bhūt*) rather than an *avatār* of Viṣṇu (*Uttara*. 601). Eventually the deities (*devatās*) were canonized in hierarchical order of eight classes, but God (*parameśvar*) retains his essentially monotheistic position.[23]

Cakradhar is particular to stress faith instead of ritual (*vīdhi*): 'Is there any king or master for faith (*bhāv*)? Faith is fluid [or: changing],' he says, implying that ritual becomes rigid (*Pūrva*. 395).

(C) THE *SĀDHĀRAṆA DHARMAS* AS ENUNCIATED BY CAKRADHAR

As so often in the case of renouncers of *saṃsār*, we also find in the *Līḷācaritra* ethical, exemplary attitudes and utterances of Cakradhar which were to be codified later on in the *Sūtrapāṭh*.[24] These attitudes and utterances were in demand in a society dominated by *svadharmas*, that is, rigid caste and family rules, and prescribed rituals. The roles which had to be played in *saṃsār* could be oppressive unless there existed the *sannyāsī*, saint, or god who could provide philosophical and spiritual insights which could be interpreted and applied to day-to-day life and even to juristic contexts.[25] For some only in this way could life in *saṃsār* be worth tolerating. No doubt, even the Dharmaśāstras had recognized this before and their authors had interiorized and interpreted much of the teaching as *sādhāraṇa dharmas*, which ultimately had to be the base of society and of the true *dharma*. We may refer to the famous passage of the *Yājñavalkya-smṛti* (III. 65-6)[26]:

> The (outward show of the) *āśramas* [especially of the *sannyāsī*, but *a fortiori* that of the student or house-holder] is not the efficient cause of *dharma*, for that comes about only by being *done*. Consequently whatever is not agreeable to one's own self should not be done to others: Truthfulness, not stealing, absence of anger, modesty, cleanliness, discrimination, courage, equanimity (including humility), the quality of subjugating the senses, and knowledge: these comprise all *dharma*!

It often remained the function of the saint or god who was beyond society and yet involved in it to reactivate these principles by their teaching and life. There are frequent references to Cakradhar's kindness (*dayā*), e.g. when he condones an adulterer (*Uttara*. 271), or when he stresses *ahiṃsā* by protecting a rabbit which he calls a *mahātmā* (*Pūrva*. 42) and thereby incidentally converts the hunters to follow *ahiṃsā*. He inculcates that one has to act towards others in a way to assure *abhaya*—freedom from fear (*Uttara*. 368). One should help people on one's own inspiration and there is no need that Cakradhar specifically tell one to do so (*Uttara*. 216). *dharma* and *ācāra* are his who actually practises them. 'Why do you worry about the *dharma* of others?' (*Uttara*. 403).

(D) THE SANNYĀSĪ AND LAW

It is only logical that a *sādhāraṇa dharma* emanating from the sphere of the renouncer must occasionally conflict with the rules of law administered by the state and the customary law practised by society. Cakradhar is beyond this law and there may be an appeal to his divine powers—as ordeals may be used as a last resort in resolving cases[27]—if decisions taken by courts like a *sabhā* seem dissatisfactory. One incident concerned the inheritance to a *maṭha* (*Uttara*. 72):

There was a *sannyāsī* in a monastery. He had two disciples. One of them used to serve him. The other used to study. After many days the *sannyāsī* died. His two disciples quarrelled. One of them said: 'The books of the monastery are mine.' The other said: 'The books belong to him who reads them.' Accordingly they brought the matter before a *sabhā* and presented the issue. The *sabhā* held: 'The monastery belongs to him who reads the books.' The books were brought. They were given to the one who could not read. He could not read them. Thereupon they were given to the other for reading. He could read them. They gave the books to him. The other was dismissed. The Gosāvī came to this place. He sat under a tree. That disciple came there and greeted him, touched his feet, and told him [what had happened]. The Omniscient asked: 'Is your case (*sthaḷa*) victorious?' He said: 'I can't read.' The Omniscient said: 'Call a *sabhā*. Start reading and you will read.'
He called a *sabhā*. The books were brought and given to him. He started reading. All [the members] of the *sabhā* joined [unanimously] in clapping their hands. The monastery and books were given to him. The other was dismissed. The [winner] offered the Gosāvī a meal. He [the Gosāvī] slept on a platform. Then the Gosāvī was to leave. But he would not allow the Gosāvī to leave. The Omniscient said [recalling the incident]: 'Bāi,[28] I had to quarrel with him so that I could leave.'

The presence of Cakradhar also provided safety and even impunity to all kinds of beings (*jīvas*). In the incident of the rabbit and the hunters, he is a protector of animals (*Pūrva*. 42). The hunters may be following their professional *svadharma* of a hunters' caste, but the conception of *dharma* is different on the divine level of Cakradhar, and it is the *dharma* protecting animals or human beings in the company of Cakradhar, the *sāṃghātu dharma* (*Pūrva*. 191), which applies here. Thus there is also the case of the thief whom Cakradhar saves notwithstanding the theft or robbery he has committed. On the other hand, it is the prime duty of the king to look after justice (*nyāy*) and to prosecute thieves. Thus *daṇḍa* and *sāṃghātu dharma* conflict (*Pūrva*. 57):

In a certain village the Gosāvī was seated in a temple. In this village a robbery of horses occurred. The horses of the village officer (*adhikārī*) were stolen. One of the thieves was confined in the stocks. The watchmen came in search [of the other thieves]. Then there was the Gosāvī seated in a dilapidated temple. They saw the Gosāvī [and shouted]: 'Who is he?'
The Gosāvī was desirous of keeping silence (*maunā*). Therefore he remained completely silent. They shouted: 'Catch him, catch him! He has come to free him!' They caught hold of the Gosāvī and said: 'Come on.' The Gosāvī was brought to the wooden stocks. 'Put them on, put them on.' The Gosāvī put his holy feet into the stocks. Then they tried to lock the stocks by hammering a bolt into them. But the arm

of the one who tried [to hammer] remained raised in the air. He said: 'Oh dear, I can't hammer the bolt in.' Then somebody else tried. Similarly, nobody was able to hammer it in.

They went to the village officer to tell him. 'Some other thief has come to free the thief. We have caught him. We put him in the stocks. When we tried to hammer the bolt in, the arm went up, but it would not come down.' Thus they told him this account. Then the village officer mounted a horse and came with a torch. When he saw the beauty of the Gosāvī, he said: 'What's the matter, you sinful Cāṇḍāḷas! Who asked you to act like this? What is this! You have confined the Gosāvī [in the stocks]?' He climbed down from the horse, prostrated clasping the holy feet, and requested the Gosāvī: 'Please, remove your feet from the stocks.' The Omniscient said: 'First free my companion.'—'My Lord, he has committed a grave illegal act (*eṇeṃ thorū anyāyo kelā ase*).' The Gosāvī answered: 'Well, then, I shan't remove [my feet].'—'Break his bolt!'

The carpenter was called and the bolt was removed. Only then did the Gosāvī remove his feet. Then the village officer requested to take him to his home: 'Please, come to my home.' The Omniscient said: 'First my companion.'—'My Lord, he is a thief.' The Omniscient answered: 'He is *your* thief, but he is *my* companion.'—'Let's go.' He, the thief, [went] in front. The Gosāvī followed. Thus they proceeded to the house [of the village officer]. They arranged a seat for the Gosāvī and he took his seat. He made his companion sit down. The holy feet of the Gosāvī were washed ceremoniously. The feet of the thief were also washed. Then he offered bathing clothes to the Gosāvī. The Omniscient [said]: 'First to my companion.' Thus they gave bathing clothes to him. They anointed his body. Then the Gosāvī had his massage. Water was kept ready. 'Please, come for your bath.' The Omniscient said: 'First my companion.' So he had his bath. Then the Gosāvī had his bath.

Then they brought the dinner and said: 'Please, have it.'

Again the Gosāvī said: 'First my companion.' He was served, too. He had his meal in the same row as the Gosāvī. They brought betel-leaves. Again the Gosāvī said: 'First my companion.' The Gosāvī was served betel-leaves. He [the thief] was also served betel-leaves. They kept a cot and a mattress. For him [the thief] they kept a small cot. The Gosāvī accepted to sleep (*Gosāvī pahuḍa svīkarilā*). He [the thief] slept. Then, in the middle of the night, the thief requested the Gosāvī: 'My Lord, I did a grave illegal act. The Gosāvī will go from here and they will beat me. They won't save me. My Lord, shall I leave then?' The Gosāvī gave him the permission. 'My Lord, the door is closed. How can I go?' The Omniscient said: 'Make a folded rope out of clothes, tie it to the back, and leave this way. Get down.'

Thus the Gosāvī told him a way out. Thus he went. Then next morning he [the village officer] asked him [Cakradhar]: 'My Lord, where is your companion?' The Gosāvī said: 'He has already left.' Thereupon he said laughingly to the Gosāvī: 'The Gosāvī has let his companion run away.' Then the Gosāvī put on his own clothes [and] kept the clothes [given to him by the village officer]. Then the Gosāvī left from there.

Theft and adultery are common in the Kaliyuga, according to Cakradhar

(*Uttara*. 271): 'Rare is one who does not commit theft and adultery, which is the *dharma* of Kaliyuga.' He tells this to a moneylender who has been hiding in a temple for three days because of a charge of adultery against him. Cakradhar compassionately grants him protection, saying, 'Go now, nobody will touch you!' Gratefully the man requested Cakradhar to accept refreshments.

(E) CAKRADHAR'S SUPPORT OF *GṚHASTHA-DHARMA*: THE FUNCTION OF FAMILY PROPERTY, THE NECESSITY OF THE SON AND THE POSITION OF WOMEN

Cakradhar may have been in many respects beyond the conventions and law of society, but he did not underrate the importance of family life and the *gṛhastha-dharma* which play a central role in the *Dharmaśāstra*. His *bhakta* Nāgdeo, for instance, once took a group of Brāhmans who were *mahājanas* to him and requested him to explain the *sannyāsa-dharma*, but Cakradhar refused and explained the *grahasta-dharma* [*sic*] instead (*Pūrva*. 555): 'What use is the *sannyāsa-dharma* to you? Why don't you ask me about what you are?'

Family and property are basic institutions of the life in *saṃsār*, and this commonplace is also very much evident in the *Līḷācaritra*. In the *Dharmaśāstra* the adjustment of the claims by various rival 'owners' (*dāyādas*) as regards family property is a central subject (*dāyavibhāga*). Especially the *Mitākṣarā* commentary on the *Yājñavalkya-smṛti* was a foremost authority in this field in the Deccan.[29] In the *Līḷācaritra* relatives are also called *dāyādas*, or rather *dāḷadrī* (*Pūrva*. 439) and *dāiṃ* (*Pūrva*. 387). That they could be rivals with their claims on each others' property is indicated in one *līḷā* (*Pūrva*. 387): A certain Brāhman complains to Cakradhar that his *dāiṃ* have encroached upon parts of his field, and he requests him that this encroachment should be removed.

To avoid the claims of collateral *dāyādas* must have been one of the reasons which prompted Vijñāneśvar, the author of the *Mitākṣara*, to establish the son's right by birth in the father's and grandfather's property.[30] Besides, the necessity of a son who has to continue the life in the world is another commonplace not only in general Indian belief and the *Dharmaśāstra*, but also in the *Līḷācaritra*. In one *līḷā* (*Pūrva*. 63) Cakradhar is invited home by a wealthy landlord (Ṭhākur) who is polygamous, but without son. He sends first his elder wife to him with the request for a son, but Cakradhar refuses to oblige. Subsequently, the landlord sends his younger wife to him. Again he shows his disinclination to let her in. Ultimately, the Ṭhākur comes himself and requests:

'My Lord, why does the Gosāvī not accept? I am without a son. I have no son (*mi nīputriku. mātem̩ putru nāhīm̩*). The Gosāvī should make a gift of a son to me.' The Omniscient said: 'You will have a son.' He had a son after some days and months from his elder wife. When the son was born the Gosāvī went away.

Not having a son is also a divine punishment for administering an expiation which may be justified by the *dharma* of the society, but violates divine justice and equity. Thus the Camār in the *līḷā* quoted above may have broken the rules of pollution and he may have been quite legally put to death. However, his contact with Cakradhar had deified him. On the question of Māhādaisā what had happened to the persecutors and executioners Cakradhar answered: 'My Lady, their race died out (*Bāi, teyācā nīrvam̩su jālā*).'

Son and father have joint property in whatever the father earns. This is in accordance with the *Dharmaśāstra* texts of that time, especially the *Mitākṣarā*.[31] It is reflected in a *līḷā* of the time when Cakradhar was still Haripāldev, the son of a minister (*Pūrva*. 27). The son had incurred heavy debts while gambling and the minister said to his sullen son:

. . .'Your debt is [as good as] paid off, my boy. Does not all this belong to you? For whom else have I earned it? Whose estate is this? This is all yours, isn't it?' Having said so he put his left arm under his [the son's] back and took him up, placing him on his lap. After he had seated him on his lap he fondled [and] embraced him. He kissed him. Then he made his treasurer [go and] pay off directly their [the creditors'] five hundred *āsus* (gold coins). After that the Gosāvī [*sic*] gave up his sullenness . . .

In another *līḷā* we learn that Cakradhar was very much aware that property ought to serve as maintenance for dependent female members of the family and that the male members have the duty to maintain them. They cannot prematurely renounce worldly life. Thus he sent his disciple Bhaṭobās, who had taken *sannyās*, home to his village to organize the maintenance of his wife Gaṅgāisā and to beget the necessary son! She had complained to Cakradhar with the following words (*Uttara*. 32):

. . .What shall I do? I have no wealth (*dhan*), no father, no brother. My brother-in-law doesn't give me my share of grain (*vaijobā varo na ghalī*). There is no milk for my [female] children. How can I survive with just one earthen pot with me?. . .

Cakradhar orders her husband to provide for his wife (*Uttara*. ibid.):

. . .'Take her to the village. Give to her what is rightfully due to her. Make a home for her and do what she says. A soul is waiting for you.'. . .

A number of destitute women ultimately found their security as followers of Cakradhar. This was also a cause of danger to Cakradhar's reputation and life, as we shall see. One of the causes for sonless widows to become destitute was that the sonless widow's right to property of her deceased husband was, according to the *Mitākṣarā*, dependent on whether her husband died separate and unreunited from agnatic relations, like the husband's brothers etc. This must have been a rare occurrence.[32] But even if he died separate and the sonless widow could inherit according to the *Mitākṣarā*, the danger that the king would take the estate by escheat was very near at hand.[33] This the sad case of Śāntibāisā (*Pūrva*. 217) discloses, throwing incidental light on the position of women in the Yādava kingdom:

Śāntibāisā was from Vasmatī. Her [actual] name was Māiṃbāisā. Her husband had expired. Her son had died. Whatever wealth (*dhan*, or elsewhere: *dhanakuḷavāḍī* = wealth, land, and agricultural implements) there was had been taken by the king. Her eldest daughter, Ekāisā, was a widow (or: 'empty-handed', i.e. without bangles). Her younger daughter was Jasamāisā. She became possessed [by an evil spirit]. Her husband did not like her. Her parents-in-law did not like her. Her younger brother-in-law also disliked her. They drove her away. Māiṃbāisā brought her to her place. In this way Māiṃbāisā became very miserable. When [some] people prepared to leave [for a pilgrimage] to Dvārāvatī, Māiṃbāisā said to herself: 'Now I shall go to Dvārāvatī. I shall tie one [daughter] to my back and the other in front. Then I shall enter the sea'...

Before Māiṃbāisā went to Dvārāvatī she met a sister's son, Sāraṅgapaṇḍit,[34] in Paiṭhaṇ. He advised her to meet Cakradhar on her way to Dvārāvatī. Meeting Cakradhar, her sorrow vanished and her daughter became freed from the evil spirit by Cakradhar's healing powers. Cakradhar exhorted her to proceed to Dvārāvatī. Māiṃbāisā, however, decided to stay: ...'No, my Lord, this is my Dvārāvatī. I have met our Kānhā (Kṛṣṇa) here itself. I shall not leave the nearness of the Gosāvī . . .'

Cakradhar, however, insisted that she first take her daughter home to her relatives by marriage. The daughter was miraculously received with full honours and great joy.

(F) THE INTERDEPENDENCE OF THE *SANNYĀSĪ* AND SOCIETY

Cakradhar as a *sannyāsī* and a divine personality must have functioned as a leaven in society and must have been a relief to many living in *saṃsār*. He embodied in his life and teachings the *sādhāraṇa dharmas* and had the power of healing (see e.g. *Pūrva*. 54, 92, 116, 232) and destroying *karma*

(*Uttara*. 35). On the other hand, he was likely to become dependent on society and was in danger of getting more and more involved in *saṃsār*. He must have been aware of the constant age-old tension between the demands of his initiated or uninitiated followers and the demands of a secluded sannyāsīc life. His constant wanderings and elusiveness show his attempt not to be a burden to society by attaching himself to definite villages and households for his and his followers' alms (*bhikṣā*). Accordingly, he taught his follower Nāthobā the rules of begging alms (*Pūrva*. 223: *bhīkṣāvidhi*), citing first a Sanskrit passage:

> . . . For begging food one should go to the four *varṇas* (*cāturvarṇyaṃ cared bhaikṣaṃ*). One should follow this rule of the *śāstra* (or: this principle?). One should not select a [certain] house for begging *bhīkṣā*. One should not go to a house of an acquaintance. One should enter [the village] from one side and leave it from the other.

Gifts (*dāna*) and provisions for maintenance (*vṛtti*[35]) are primarily to be given to persons and institutions which fulfil socio-religious functions according to the notions and concepts of the *varṇāśrama* society, e.g. to Brāhmans, for the building and upkeep of temples, or to established, longstanding religious orders and their monasteries. Sannyāsīc recluses at the most can claim *bhīkṣā*. Thus (*Uttara*. 306), when Cakradhar once went to the Saṅgameśvar temple on a Monday, devotees came in particularly large numbers for the *piṇḍa* and *tarpaṇa* rites. They also worshipped Cakradhar and by evening a large heap of offerings had collected in front of Cakradhar. But he admonished Bāisā to leave the offerings to the priest of the temple, because they rightfully belonged to him. For Cakradhar *bhīkṣā* represents independence and bliss (*Pūrva*. 510: *bhīkṣā rājyā*, *bāi*).

The avoidance of worldly involvements even extends to contacts with the king. Though the saint, a divine personality, a *sannyāsī* or *sādhū* may be an objective advisor to those in charge of the affairs of the world, Cakradhar avoids the contact with kings and their gifts very much as Tukārām refused the gifts of king Śivājī.[36]

One famous *līḷā* (*Pūrva*. 61) reflects the relationship between Cakradhar and the king, in this case Kṛṣṇadev (or Kānhadev):

> The Gosāvī was staying in the Bahirav (Bhairav) temple at Loṇar Kuṇḍ. The king came to the Kuṇḍ for the Monday [ritual]. With him was [his son] Mahādev, who was being caressed [by his father]. He asked the priest there:
> 'Is there some Siddha or a [*mokṣa*-seeing] ascetic (*sādhak*)?' A priest of (the Goddess) Kamaḷajai said: 'One holy man (*purukha*) has come to the Bahirav temple.

How can I tell of his handsomeness? How can I describe his intelligence? How can I express his glory? How can I tell of his generosity?' In such words he gave a description of the Gosāvī. Then it occurred to Kānhadev: 'Where can I meet this holy man?' Immediately Kānhadev went to the Tārātīrtha. There, at the Tārātīrtha, the Gosāvī was sitting under a Banyan tree. The priest had come along with Kānhadev. He said: 'This is the holy man.' Kānhadev went straight in front of him. He asked the betel servant for a purse of gold coins. He put it in front [of Cakradhar]. He prostrated. The bard and the groom said: 'Take it! Take it! Kānha, the son of Śiṅgaṇa, is pleased with you.' The king, however, said: 'Move away. King or pauper are the same to him. I am Kānha, the son of Śiṅgaṇa, only for you.' On this the Gosāvī looked at them. He also looked at the king. And [the Gosāvī, having nothing to say,] looked at the floor. The king said: 'To him gold and mud are the same. He showed me that wealth and stone are the same.'[37] Afterwards he kept a secret watch [on the Gosāvī]. For some time the Gosāvī remained sitting. Then he went forth. [The man] who had kept the watch came with the purse of gold coins: 'King, this holy man has not touched the purse of gold coins.'—The Gosāvī [recalling it] said: 'This king had full regard for me [or: is a believer]. He has not returned the wealth once assigned [to a holy purpose] to the treasury. Afterwards he built a wall for [the temple of] Kumāreśvara, and had it whitewashed.' One Mahānubhāv says: 'He built a bathing *ghāṭ*.'

In another incident we come to know about an attempt of King Mahādev (1261-70) to meet Cakradhar (*Pūrva*. 225f.), whose fame had spread to such an extent that the king one day found his court empty, because all the courtiers had left to have *darśan* of Cakradhar. King Mahādev also decided to meet Cakradhar. While on his way an inauspicious omen occurred and the king was held back: the royal elephant had collapsed. The second attempt was marred by heavy rainfall which sent the king back to his fort (*Pūrva*. 226). On the third day the king made a firm decision to meet Cakradhar. However, Cakradhar slipped away, apprehending that the king might hand over his kingdom to him (*Pūrva*. 227).

The desire of a king to hand over his kingdom to a saint or a god and then to rule on behalf of him was not an uncommon occurrence in Indian tradition. Gorakhnāth, Rāmdās, king Sivajī, and some others come to mind.[38] What is more remarkable is that Cakradhar refused this possibility. The reason is indicated in the same *līḷā*. His faithful follower Bāisā, the old widow, questioned him why after all he did not allow the king to meet him. Cakradhar retorted: 'And where will you poor, destitute people go?'

Though Cakradhar tried to keep away from involvement in the world, it is natural that his following of initiated and uninitiated eventually resulted in a 'sect', a kind of parallel society. Rules had to be evolved to regulate the behaviour of the followers, and metaphors were drawn from the institutions which rule in the *varṇāśrama* concept and in ordinary social life. The institution of marriage e.g. offered a metaphor for the relationship between alms-bag and *sannyāsī* (*Pūrva.* 223): Cakradhar gave Nāthobā an alms-bag and exhorted him:

> ...'From now onwards this bag should be married to you. It is yours. Up to your death you should protect it...'

This is reiterated in one *līḷā* (*Uttara.* 2), when another disciple, Bhaṭobās, is given a bag:

> ... 'You and this bag are married. Don't let her fast and starve. This rule (*vidhi*) should be observed up to death...'

THE ADMINISTRATION OF JUSTICE AND THE CASE AGAINST CAKRADHAR

(A) SOME REFERENCES TO LAW, COURTS, AND LEGAL PROCEDURE IN THE *LĪḶĀCARITRA*

The *Līḷācaritra* is a non-legal work. The more it is surprising to notice the number of references to *dharma* and its conception on different levels. We get the impression that the heartland of the Devgiri Yādavas must have been strictly administered in secular and religious matters. As the case of the Camār (*Pūrva.* 27) shows, the official authorities of the state supported the administering of expiation (*prāyaścitta*) by Brāhmans on the basis of the *śāstra* in cases of ritual pollution. *Ad hoc* courts existed which consisted of respectable village and town elders (*māhājanas* or *mahājanas*) who might decide in spiritual (if they were Brāhmans) as well as in strictly legal matters. For instance, the *māhājanas* may, rather informally, it seems, confirm miracles of Cakradhar (*Pūrva.* 14). Once (*Uttara.* 227) Cakradhar and his followers were accused by a Gujar (i.e. a person from Gujarat) of having taken away a coconut with a gold coin in it which was buried in a deserted hut. Cakradhar occupied the empty hut. He asked his follower Bhaṭobās to take the matter to the court (*yāsīṃ vevhāru* [Skt. *vyavahāra*] *āṁghoṃ jā*). The court consisted of *māhājanas*, that is, according to a *var. lect.*, of Brāhmans of the village (*gāvīcāṃ brāhmaṇīṃ*). Bhaṭobās effectively silenced (*nirotaru kelā*) the accuser by his *vevhāru*, which may mean in this context 'by his telling evidence as to the true facts:'[39]

> 'We have not heard about his coconut. We don't know what sort [of coconut] it is. He left a hut which was deserted.' Thus he proved it. Thereupon all the *mahājanas* said: 'What has he to do with your coconut? You lie flat in front of this Gosāvī with your body covered with cowdung and mud. Go. He will tell you of the whereabouts of your coconut.'

Bhaṭobās told Cakradhar about the decision (*vevastā*, Skt. *vyavasthā*). The Gujar acted as he was told and the coconut was retrieved from a friend of the Gujar.

In the case of the inheritance of a *maṭha* we have seen that a *sabhā* was called which also consisted of *māhājanas*. The instituting of court procedure was called *sabhā karṇeṃ* or *vevhāru sāṃghneṃ*. Legal transactions included pledges (*Uttara*. 303: pledge of an earring, *Pūrva*. 233: pledge of a betelnut cutter), loans (*Pūrva*. 452: *ruṇa*, Skt. *ṛṇa*), and even the sale of human beings (*Uttara*. 182).

(B) THE CASE AGAINST CAKRADHAR IN THE *SABHĀ* AT PAIṬHAṆ

Eventually Cakradhar came in conflict with the order of established society. According to one *līḷā* (*Uttara*. 266), he was conscious that the people might be objecting to the presence of mostly women in his following. A strange incident is told in another *līḷā* (*Uttara*. 509). The rejected wife of Hemādrī, by name Dematī, came to have *darśan* of Cakradhar. She applied sandal paste from the feet of Cakradhar to her forehead. Surprisingly, she was taken back by Hemādrī. When he wondered about the reasons of his renewed affection to Dematī, she told him of the *darśan* of Cakradhar, attributing the reason of Hemádrī's affection to this *darśan*. Cakradhar resented the rash disclosure by Dematī because he knew that Hemādrī did not agree with him and his followers. He sensed that Hemādrī might plan some mischief. Whatever the real reason had been—whether it was the objection against the (mostly elderly and destitute) women amongst his following or whether it was his life and teaching, considered to be against the principle of a kingdom ruled according to the conception of an orthodox *varṇāśrama* system—the events drew to a climax (*Uttara*. 536):

Thereupon the Gosāvī crossed the Gaṅgā [Godāvarī] river and went to Paiṭhaṇ. This was the moment when they instituted a *sabhā* in the Mudhāditya temple. [There were present] Hemādpaṇḍit (Hemādrī), Sāraṅgapaṇḍit, Māyitā Harī, Prajñāsāgar leading all the people of the town, the Mahājanas, scholars, expounders of Purāṇas, Sannyāsīs, Brahmacārīs, Jains, and members of the Nāthpanth—thus they all were assembled. They brought the Gosāvī into the Mudhāditya temple. The Gosāvī sat down in the square of the Mudhāditya temple. All said: 'So—you are a Gosāvī,[40] are you!'—The Omniscient said: 'I am a Bhikṣu Mahātmā.' 'Now you tell us [what you really are]?' 'Everyone of you who has assembled here is one by one a leading person: scholars, Brahmacārīs, Sannyāsīs, people having vowed to live only on milk (*payovratī*), exponents of the *śāstra*, expounders of the Purāṇas.' And he looked at Sāraṅgapaṇḍit, [who] avoided his eyes. 'You are the Māhājanas of the people of the eighteen "castes" (?, *aṣṭadasā prajā*),[41] Jains, Nāthapanthīs—thus all of you are assembled. You would not drink knowingly [something which is] sour. Then ask yourself what I am.' 'He has a special attraction to women, hasn't he? He behaves with women in a manner we prefer not to speak about, doesn't he?' All acclaimed: 'Yes, indeed.' There was unanimous clapping in the *sabhā*. Then everybody started whispering to one another. At that moment Māyitā Harī [and] Prajñāsāgar, both of them got up: 'That you whisper is wrong!' They disassociated themselves from the whispering. 'This is bad for the country. You are Cāṇḍāḷas!' With these words they left.

The Omniscient said: 'Each of you is a knower of the Veda. Every one of you seated here is a leading person. You ask yourself what I have done to you.' 'We have thought about it.' 'Is it so? Then *do* what you think [fit to do].' After that they took him to a small shrine inside the enclosure [of the Mudhāditya] temple. There he accepted the *pūjā* of the nose.

The '*pūjā* of the nose' is a euphemistic and reverent way of saying that Cakradhar's nose was cut, according to another source, along with his ears.[42] The description in the *līḷā* suggests that the whole procedure of the *sabhā* was premediated and manipulated. The whispering may indicate that the full truth was not brought to light. In any case two forthright members spoke out and did not lend themselves to a unanimous decision (*samaya*). They drew their consequences from this miscarriage of justice (*Uttara*. 537):

Māyitā Harī [and] Prajñāsāgar disassociated themselves from the whispering. They left [and] went home. They left their spacious and rich houses, left kith and kin, [and] wealth. They left the country. Māyitā Harī Nāyak left his mansion and went to Telaṅgaṇa. He tied a purse with gold coins to his waist. In one hand he had a sharpened stone, in the other he held his wife. With bullocks [and] a bullock cart—thus he left. One person [standing] on the upper storey [of a house] said: 'Rob him of his wife. He has not accepted our *samaya*. Throw him out, throw him out of our Maharashtra.' Māyitā Harī retorted: 'Is my wife yours or your father's? I am leaving your Maharashtra of the Mahārs on my own.'[43]

We need not unduly prolong the story. Cakradhar continued to teach and even had his nose restored miraculously. But he was resigned to leave this world, not before having forecast the incursions of the Mlecchas from the north and a devastating famine (*Uttara*. 603).[44] Both events actually occurred. Cakradhar himself was finally murdered on the instance of the king or Hemādrī (*Uttara*. 641). But according to the beliefs of the Mahānubhāvs this cannot be true. Cakradhar left Maharashtra wandering to the northland and was last seen in Ujjain (*Uttara*. 645).[45]

NOTES

1. See *Tolkāppiyam* III.5. Vēntaṉ has been identified with Indra (Intiraṉ). The term 'nuclear agricultural area' or region of settled village agriculture has been borrowed from Burton Stein's essay 'Integration of the Agrarian System of South India', in: R.E. Frykenberg (ed.), *Land Control and Social Structure in Indian History*, Madison, Wisc., 1969. Cp. also G.-D. Sontheimer, *Birobā, Mhaskobā und Khaṇḍobā*, Wiesbaden, 1976, pp. 19, 23ff. [Editor's note: English version, *Pastoral Deities in Western India*, New York, 1989, pp. 15, 19ff.]
2. J. Duncan M. Derrett, 'Law and Social Order before the Muhammadan Conquest', in: id., *Religion, Law and the State in India*, London, 1968, pp. 171ff., 175f.
3. Onkar Prasad Verma, *The Yādavas and Their Times*, Nagpur, 1970, p. 174.
4. D.D. Kosambi, *Myth and Reality*, Bombay, 1962, p. 52. P.V. Kane, *History of Dharmaśāstra*, vol. I, pt. II, Poona, 1975, p. 749.
5. S.G. Tuḷpuḷe, *Prācīna Marāṭhī Korīva Lekha*, Puṇeṃ, 1963, p. 179.
6. Kane, op. cit., p. 749.
7. See *Śrī Jñāneśvarī*, Muṃbaī, 1960 (Govt. edn.), 18.1447-9: the Veda is rich, but appeals to the upper *varṇa* and is miserly, because women and Śūdras were ignored. Therefore, the Veda appeared in the guise of the *Gītā* to remove this deficiency.
8. *Śrī Nāmadeva Gāthā*, Muṃbaī, 1970, *abhaṅg* 890, 897.
9. V.K. Rajwade, *Marāṭhāṃcyā Itihāsācīṃ Sādhaneṃ*, vol. XV, p. 6.
10. *cālatā bolatā dev to jagī durlabh. Uttarārdha* 564.
11. See Victor Turner, *The Ritual Process*, Chicago, Aldine, 1969, *passim*, as followed by A.K. Ramanujan, *Speaking of Śiva*, Penguin Classics, repr. 1979, pp. 34f. The concepts of anti-structure and counter-structure were applied to the literature of the Mahānubhāv sect by Anne Feldhaus, 'The Mahānubhāvas and Scripture', in *Journal of Dharma* (Bangalore) III (1978), pp. 295-308. We do not deal here with the fully developed phases of the sect, but primarily with its 'founder' and his relationship to the established order of religion, society and law as reflected in some of his teachings and 'divine deeds' (*līḷās*). For an introduction to the general background of the 'sect' see I.M.P. Raeside, 'The Mahānubhāvas', in *BSOAS*, XXXIX/3 (1975), pp. 585-600, also id., 'A bibliographical index of Mahānubhāva works in Marathi', in *BSOAS*/3 (1960), pp. 404-507.
12. V.B. Kolte, *Līḷācaritra*, Mahārāṣṭra Rājya Sāhitya Saṃskṛti Maṃḍaḷa, Muṃbaī, 1978, 935 pp. The abbreviations *Pūrva*. (= *Pūrvārdha*) and *Uttara*. (= *Uttarārdha*) have been used here.
13. Louis Dumont, 'World Renunciation in Indian Religions', in: id., *Religion, Politics and History in India*, Paris/The Hague, 1970, pp. 63-104, and Romila Thapar, 'Renunciation: The Making of a Counter-culture?', in: id., *Ancient Indian Social History. Some Interpretations*, New Delhi, 1978, pp. 63-104. Both works have influenced the general background of this article.

14. Anne Feldhaus, *The Deeds of God in Ṛddhipur*, New York, 1984.
15. Members of the (then) untouchable Mātāṅga/Māṅg caste (Skt. *mātaṃga*).
16. A female *bhakta* of Cakradhar.
17. Khol Nāyak or Kholeśvar was a Brāhman general of King Siṅghaṇa II (1200-46). Āmbe, Inscription, in *Ind. Ant.* VI, pp. 97-8. Verma, op. cit., p. 93.
18. Dumont, op. cit., p. 43, fn. 18.
19. Or Nāgdev, who became the first *ācārya* of the Mahānubhāv sect, having been nominated by Cakradhar.
20. 'Monkey', the nickname of Bhaṭobās, who was once seen by Cakradhar jumping from one branch of a tree to another.
21. Probably Śrīśailam in Andhra.
22. Rāmdev, who was a devotee of Cakradhar and a former guru of Mahādāisā.
23. See Anne Feldhaus, 'The *devatācakra* of the Mahānubhāvas', in *BSOAS* XLIII/1 (1980), pp. 101-9.
24. See Anne Feldhaus, *The Religious System of the Mahānubhāva Sect: The Mahānubhāva Sūtrapāṭha*, New Delhi: Manohar, 1983.
25. That *sādhāraṇa dharmas*, principles underlying the whole of Hinduism and based on philosophical and religious insights and behaviour of a high degree, should also rule in a juristic context and much more so in modern times, when the guidance of caste dharmas and caste rituals are on the wane, was emphasized by Derrett in *A Critique of Modern Hindu Law*, Bombay, 1979, p. 34ff. See also G.-D. Sontheimer, 'Die Ethik im Hinduismus', in: C.H. Ratschow (ed.), *Die Ethik in den Weltreligionen*, Stuttgart, 1981, pp. 349-436, pp. 420 ff., on the *sādhāraṇa dharmas*. There are many examples throughout Cakradhar's *līḷās* which show e.g. his kindness, patience, courage, knowledge, humaneness, obedience to his guru (Govinda Prabhū or Śrī Prabhū), though the principles do not necessarily appear *expressis verbis* and are as yet unsystematized and unenumerated. As regards *asteya* (abstention from theft) which appears in practically all Sanskrit (Dharmaśāstra) formulations of *sādhāraṇa dharmas*, Cakradhar is less emphatic: he protects a thief (see below), condones and takes the moral blame on himself of a theft of chick-pea bundles by his followers which was in excess of what he had originally connived at. He does not mind getting the chick-peas roasted rather stealthily and participating in eating this delicacy (*Uttara*. 15).
26. Cited and as translated by Derrett, op. cit., pp. 71f.
27. Witnesses and documents as evidence were preferred to ordeals by the Dharmaśāstra in legal procedure, because of the emotional element involved in ordeals. See G.-D. Sontheimer, J.D.M. Derrett, G. Smith, 'Gerichtsverfahren und Richter im traditionellen indischen Recht', in: J.D.M. Derrett, G.-D. Sontheimer, G. Smith, *Beiträge zu indischem Rechtsdenken*, Wiesbaden, 1979, pp. 74, 82, 84. In this *līḷā* it seems that *dāsya*—devoted service to God—is preferred by Cakradhar to mere *jñāna* and thus he miraculously enables the serving disciple to read the texts.

28. Bāisā, the elderly woman who was Cakradhar's first follower.
29. For the *Mitākṣarā* (between 1121-5) see e.g. G.-D. Sontheimer, *The Joint Hindu Family*, New Delhi, 1977, p. 120 ff. The commentary was written by Vijñāneśvara, a Chief Justice of the Cālukya King Vikramāditya IV, who ruled from Kalyāṇī in northern Karnataka.
30. See Sontheimer, *The Joint Hindu Family*, pp. 124 ff. *Yājñavalkyasmṛti*, with the *Mitākṣarā* of Vijñānesvara, Nirnayasāgara Press, 5th edn., Bombay, pp. 217f.
31. *Mitākṣarā*, p. 219 (H.T. Colebrooke's transl. in *Two Treatises. Mitākṣarā and Dāyabhāga*, *Mit.* I, i, 19-24, 27).
32. See Derrett, *Religion, Law and the State in India*, pp. 208, 416. *Mit.*, pp. 242f, Colebrooke's transl. II, i, 39. Sontheimer, op. cit., p. 134.
33. Śāstric law provided that property of Brāhmans would never escheat. Gautama XXVIII, 42; Baudhāyana I, 5, 119, 122; Vasiṣṭha XVII, 75; Manu IX, 189. But according to inscriptions and other sources it is clear that property was often seized by the king or his assignee in the absence of sons, grandsons, or great grandsons, and that it was a great favour on the king's part to allow property to pass to śāstric heirs. Derrett, *Religion, Law and the State in India*, p. 208.
34. A famous Brāhman with influence in the Yādava court who is to play an ambiguous role in the case against Cakradhar.
35. See e.g. *Pūrva*. 116: A *sāsan* [*sic*] enjoined a *vṛtti* to the temple of the Brāhman of Vaijanāth and provided for a field, house, bedding and cot, one (female) buffalo, a female servant, and sixty gold coins (*āsus*).
36. *Tukārāmābāvāṃcyā Abhaṃgācī Gāthā*. Muṃbaī, 1950 (Govt. edn.), *abhaṅg* 1884-97.
37. The terms used by Tukārām are similar, e.g. wealth and mud are the same to me (1897), gold and mud are the same to me (1895), ant and king are the same to me (1895).
38. Śivājī handed over the kingdom by placing a note in the alms-bag of Rāmdās (*manmatha nāma saṃvatsarī vaiśākh śuddha dvitīyes Śivājī mahārāj yaṃnī samarthāṃcyā jhoḷīt rājyācī ciṭhi tākalī*).
Vāṃkenīsicyā 26*vyā tipaṇ*, as quoted by S.K. Altekar, *Śrī Samartha Caritra*, 2nd edn., Puṇeṃ, 1974, p. 68.
39. According to Kātyāyana 26 the term *vyavahāra* etymologically means 'the removal (*hara*) of various (*vi*) doubts (*ava*)' in legal procedure.
40. 'Gosāvī' implies a person who has renounced worldly business, pleasures, and affections.
41. *aṣṭadasā* = *aṣṭadaśa*. Cp. D.C. Sircar, *Indian Epigraphical Glossary*, Delhi, 1966, pp. 31f. *aṣṭadaśa* implies 'all' and 'completeness'.
42. See fn. 4 to *līḷā* 536 (p. 670).
43. A caustic pun on the words 'Mahārāṣtra' and 'Mahār'. The Mahārs are the famous 'autochthonous' untouchable caste of traditional Maharashtra.
44. For the Durgā-Devī-Famine (1396-1407) see Sontheimer, *Birobā, Mhaskobā und Khaṇḍobā*, p. 150. [Editor's note: Cp. *Pastoral Deities of Western India*, p. 153.]

45. I am grateful to Dr. S.G. Tulpule for his help in translating the *Līḷācaritra* and his critical comments on this article. Sanskrit terms used mainly in a Sanskrit form or context (e.g. *varṇāśrama*) have been transliterated according to the usual indological practice. Marathi terms are transcribed in their spoken form or are transliterated as they appear in the *Līḷācaritra* (e.g. *stīti* instead of *sthiti*) and without the final inherent *a* (e.g. *dev* instead of *deva*).

Folk Deities in the Vijayanagara Empire: Narasiṃha and Mallaṇṇa/Mailār

THE RISE OF FOLK DEITIES

The rise of local warriors and rulers (the *nāyakas*) in the Vijayanagara Empire from the fourteenth century onwards is said to have been coupled with 'the increased tempo of expansion of settled village agriculture into what were previously forested zones'.[1] One wonders, however, whether this expansion led everywhere to an increase of settled regular agriculture as it would be practised in a nuclear agricultural area based upon irrigation with the help of rivers and tank reservoirs. Inquiries in the field and simple empirical observations in Andhra (e.g. in the Karimnagar and Kurnool Districts) make it obvious that there are large tracts which have come under systematic plough cultivation only during the last 100 or 150 years, especially since dams like the Tungabhadra Dam have been constructed. I suggest that the expansion of agriculture into forested areas resulted essentially in what the *tiṇai* theory of the old Tamil literature would connect with the landscape of *mullai*. This is a region where pastoral activities, with plough cultivation of millets and similar rainfed crops, prevailed. No doubt we have the—sometimes pathetic—evidence of dam building in the Vijayanagara Empire. Thus Paes and Fernão Nunes tell of the big tank at Vijayanagara, where, in a desperate attempt, the primordial practice of human sacrifice had to be resorted to.[2]

But the social and spatial separateness of communities living in different ecological areas, which in earlier times, did not disappear in the Vijayanagara Empire. Analogous to the rise of local rulers, folk cults typical of areas in which they were ruling began to rise with the beginning of the Vijayanagara era. Already in the thirteenth century, Cakradhara, one of the most prominent personalities—or rather the incarnate Kṛṣṇa—of the Mahānubhāva sect in Maharashtra, who prophesied just before the invasion of the Muslims that in the imminent Kaliyuga the great temples of Śiva and Viṣṇu would decay and popular deities like *kṣetrapāl* and Mairāḷ would take their place.[3] Mairāḷ is the equivalent of Mallaṇṇa in Andhra and Mailār in Karnataka. From the thirteenth century onwards the rise of folk cults as distinguished from purāṇic cults, especially the prominence given to the *devī*, is also evidenced in Tamilnadu.[4]

A complete disjunction between folk cults and rituals and the purāṇic deities did not take place in Tamilnadu. In Andhra, folk cults also rose or were emphasized at the same time, but not at the cost of the purāṇic deities who were worshipped in great and more ancient pilgrimage centres. These centres often offered a framework for universalization of folk cults. However, these folk cults were never fully or only superficially integrated into the Vaiṣṇava-Śaivite purāṇic or sectarian pattern, and their persistence to this day has to be explained.

It appears that the particular function and importance of the local gods remained valid in their social and geographical context. The local ruler in the Vijayanagara Empire was often himself a product of this environment, or, when he was an intruder, he had to adjust himself to the new environment. When the local ruler rose to regional importance or assumed or claimed imperial sovereignty, he would sponsor and worship deities of the purāṇic level.

NARASIMHA AS A FOLK DEITY

One of these typical popular gods of the Vijayanagara Empire was Narasiṃha. No doubt he was already at a very early stage considered to be an *avatāra* of Viṣṇu. He is mentioned in a list of *avatāras* in the *Mahābhārata*,[5] and the fourth-century Kondamotu panel from the Guntur District[6] points to the early worship of a theriomorphic Narasiṃha in a Vaiṣṇava context. But—as A. Eschmann has indicated—there are 169 temples of Narasiṃha listed in the 1961 Census of India, *Fairs and Festivals*, out of which roughly 70 per cent are 'Hinduized' cults with an aniconic *mūrti*, mostly a stone, and non-Brāhman priests.[7] This list does not cover some important districts like Kurnool, where we have a Narasiṃha cult in many places, including the famous temples of Upper and Lower Ahobilam, to which I will return.[8]

Whatever the period and degree of 'Hinduization' may have been—and the process is not complete even today—there was at the root a theriomorphic tribal divinity, generally originating in a forest, on a hill, in a cave or a ravine. The deity was visualized, if at all, not in an anthropomorphic *mūrti*, but by oral legends as an animal of the feline order, mostly a 'lion'. This deity was worshipped by tribals, came to be called Narasiṃha and was eventually identified with the *avatāra* of Viṣṇu. For tribals and villagers, however, he may still retain his character of a dangerous divinity or spirit (*bhūta*), and it is this aspect which is emphasized rather than the *avatāra*. A comparison with Maharashtra seems useful: there Narasiṃha received only superficial and peripheral recognition as an *avatāra* of Viṣṇu.[9] His old connection with the *gaṇas* and the world of magic was emphasized.[10] The purāṇic influence was limited. As in Andhra, he was connected with the Godavari river, where he was said to have washed off the impurity he incurred when he killed the demon Hiraṇyakaśipu.[11] Thus on both sides of the Godavari river temples of Narasiṃha originated. Here the purāṇic influence ends. Cakradhara and the other 'god' of the Mahānubhāva sect, Guṇḍam Rauḷ, used to stay in such temples. These temples were called 'temples of the king' (*rājāmaṭha*), which referred to Narasiṃha in his capacity as the leader or king of the *bhūtas* and the *vīras*;[12] Cakradhara called him an *avatāra* of a *bhūta*.[13] He was connected with the *śmaśāna*, which sometimes is homologous with the 'battlefield' and the 'forest'. Narasiṃha could be used against enemies in magic rites.[14] But it was dangerous to use him this way, because he might turn against one. Narasiṃha was also called and used as a *bhūtāstra*. His position as a leader of the *bhūtas* and his belonging to the host of 52 *bhūtas* or *vīras*, who consisted of ghosts of killed heroes, and deities like Hanumān, Bhairava, Mahiṣāsura, etc. was perpetuated in Maharashtrian *bhakti* literature.[15]

All of these were deities fit to be painted red with *śendūr* (Skt. *sindūra*) and to receive non-vegetarian offerings. Though the other female and male ghosts and spirits in whose company Narasiṃha is mentioned—e.g. Tukāī, Māyarāṇī, Mhasobā, Vetāḷ, Hanumān, Bhairava—very often became established village deities with temples and a *jatrā*, Narasiṃha remained a *bhūta*, except in a few places.[16] Narasiṃha, as king of a violent host of martial ghosts and demonised tribal deities, could have been a rallying point and a model for a king of actual warriors and of warfaring tribals. But this function was instead eventually assumed by Mailār *alias* Khaṇḍobā.

THE HUNTER AND HIS ASSOCIATION WITH THE TRIBAL WOMAN

In consonance with the continued importance of tribal and pastoral groups, Narasiṃha is considered a great hunter in Andhra, especially in the Kurnool District. The mythological association with, or the acculturation of, tribals followed a general and age-old pattern which was widespread in folk religion and goes back to the famous Murukaṉ and his beloved Vaḷḷi from the Kuruva tribe.[17] The same pattern is found in the case of Narasiṃha, Mallaṇṇa, Mailār, Khaṇḍobā and similar gods: the god falls in love and 'marries' a second wife from the tribe. Often the connection resembles marriage by elopement or capture according to tribal or predatory patterns. The god has to pass through all sorts of trials and tests.[18] It is as if the intruding god (or ruler) has to adjust himself to the environment for the time being, or, if you will, becomes 'tribalized' or 'parochialized'. Very occasionally we find the suggestion in oral literature, as it is intimated in some of the *bhakti* texts, that the adventures of the god represent his search for the soul of a *bhakta*, which he seeks in the form of a tribal woman.[19] In oral folk literature, however, the emphasis is on the erotic relationship. Narasiṃha's first wife is thus called Lakṣmī and the second wife is a huntress from the Ceñcū tribe, Ceñcū-Lakṣmī, the daughter of a Ceñcū chief or 'king'.[20]

The original cult spot of Ahobilam is an aniconic image on the slope of a hill in a cave amidst forests. A temple in the Vijayanagara style was added later. On a temple wall, a scene is prominently depicted in which a diminutive Narasiṃha is extracting a thorn from the sole of the foot of Ceñcū-Lakṣmī. She is of huge size compared to Narasiṃha, wears a leaf-skirt and supports herself on a tall bow. (Pl. I, 1) It is said that one day Ceñcū-Lakṣmī saw a lion and shot him: from the dying lion the beautiful Narasiṃha arose. They fell in love with each other and Narasiṃha wanted to marry her. Ceñcū-Lakṣmī wanted to see whether he was a suitable husband, and put him to tests, e.g. climbing trees, jumping over the river, collecting wild honey, and finding a golden, life-bringing insect in a termite mound. It is in upper Ahobilam that non-vegetarian offerings are made to Narasiṃha. He is called a *vīra* there, and in more classical (here Vaiṣṇava) terminology he is considered *ugra*. Narasiṃha in Ahobilam is said to be a brother of the Narasiṃha of Madduleti near Betamcherla. Here we find him even further removed from the classical *avatāra* of Viṣṇu. There is hardly any influence of Vaiṣṇava sectarians or the central state in this very popular cult situated in a ravine. Only in recent years a *devasthānam* (temple committee) has been trying to dissuade people from sacrificing animals to the god, with little success so far. The *jatrā* is celebrated on Saturdays. Many people get possessed by Narasiṃha on that day. On Sundays Narasiṃha is said to go on a hunt and no living creature is supposed to approach the temple. For his hunting excursions devotees offer wooden *cappals*, which are said to be worn out after the god has returned. To keep *cappals* ready for the hunt of the god is a widespread practice, e.g. in the Murukaṉ and Mailār cults.

The god is considered to be an *avatāra* of Viṣṇu until 12 o'clock noon on the day of the *jatrā*, and he is supposed to receive vegetarian offerings. After noon he receives sacrifices of he-goats and rams as Narasiṃha. But many people do not stick to this rule, and offer he-goats and rams before 12 o'clock.

In Kandagiri in the Kurnool District, Narasiṃha—said to be one of the seven Narasiṃha *avatāras* of Viṣṇu in the district—is a hunter and a thief who is after the 10,000 sheep of the Vempalas. The Vempalas are a community of pastoralist farmers. Narasiṃha stole their sheep and was seen carrying two sheep on his shoulders, two in his arms, and one in his mouth. When he was chased by the 26 dogs of the farm labourers, he jumped over the river, hurting his knee. But the dogs could not cross the stream. And he persuaded the people that it would be much more useful if they worshipped him by sacrificing rams, and in turn gained the prosperity of their herds.

The legend of Narasiṃha and his second wife is widely diffused, e.g. the second wife is also called Saddalakhamma, who comes from the Motādi Kāpu community. A comparison with the oral literature on Khaṇḍobā in Maharashtra shows the close parallels of these cults with respect to their gods' acceptance or worship by ecologically separated people. We summarize a legend very popular among the Dhangar shepherds in Maharashtra:

Khaṇḍobā goes on a hunt. Exhausted and thirsty, he comes to a Dhangar camp headed by a beautiful shepherdess called Bāṇāī. He changes his form into that of an old man and is employed by Bāṇāī. After acquitting himself miraculously of all his tasks, he finally kills all the nine *lakhs* of sheep. Bāṇāī now recognizes the god in the old man and agrees to marry him. He revives the sheep. He changes his form and exceeds the sun and the moon in lustre and beauty. After a rather rustic ceremony which lacks all the respectable elements of a 'sanskritic' marriage, Khaṇḍobā and Bāṇāī settle on the 'hill-fort' of Jejuri, much to the chagrin of his first wife, Mhāḷsā *alias* Pārvatī. Ever since, because of Bāṇāī's link with Khaṇḍobā, the shepherds have been worshippers of the god.[21] This worship also includes the sacrifice of rams. In another version Bāṇāī is said to be the head of twelve shepherd (Dhangar) camps and to have two daughters who went hunting daily.

The pattern of marriage with a girl from a tribe or a pastoral community is the same in the case of Mallikārjuna of Śriśailam. It is widely diffused throughout the cult of Mallaṇṇa, Mailār, and Khaṇḍobā. When Mallikārjuna/Śiva went on a hunt in the forests around Śriśailam he met a Ceñcū girl, fell in love with her, and married her. Ever since then, the Ceñcūs have been the special devotees of Mallikārjuna/Mallaiah and have special rights in his temple in Śriśailam. The pattern is spread all over the Deccan. The first wife, Pārvatī, may be identified with an important local goddess like Māḷacī/Mhāḷsā and considered to come from an influential group, e.g. Liṅgāyat merchants. The second wife comes from the Gollas, the Kurubas, or the Dhangars, and the god is a special god of pastoral groups, forest tribes, fishermen, robbers, and warriors, of rulers and those who wanted to be rulers.

NARASIṂHA AND HIS RELATIONSHIP TO HAMPI

It has been suggested that it was as part of the policy of furthering the cohesion of the empire that the kings supported such famous temples and pilgrimage centres as Ahobilam, Simhacalam, Kandagiri, etc., in the eastern region of their empire. Kṛṣṇadeva Rāya (1509-29) is said to have visited these centres before and after his war with the Gajapatis.[22] The Sāḷuva dynasty came from the eastern part of the empire. The first king of the Sāḷuva dynasty was called Sāḷuva Narasiṃha (1486-91), and the Portuguese called the kingdom after him.[23] In fact, it is said that the family god of the Vijayanagara kings was Narasiṃha, and during the time of Kṛṣṇadeva Rāya the monumental monolithic statue of Lakṣmī-Narasiṃha was built in the capital of Hampi.[24] (Pl. I, 2). It is plausible to say that what was on the *local* level, as in upper Ahobilam, a *miniature* Narasiṃha in a *tribal* context had turned into the *purāṇic avatāra* Lakṣmī-Narasiṃha represented in *colossal* style.[25] The tribal huntress of great *local* importance, Ceñcū-Lakṣmī, also occurs in Hampi, but she has been relegated to a minor position and is depicted in a relief on a wall amongst the popular royal scenes of the 'King's Throne' or *mahānavamī* platform (Pl. I, 3).

MAILĀR/MALLAṆṆA AND NARASIṂHA: THE PERSISTENCE OF FOLK CULTS

Sometimes Narasiṃha is said to have come in the disguise of a Dāsarī, one of the special itinerant devotees of Narasiṃha. The Dāsarīs have a yellow-coloured robe, peacock-feathers, a tiger skin, *śankha*, *tālam*, and *tambūra*, and sing legends of Narasiṃha. Mallaṇṇa's special devotees—who resemble the Dāsarīs of Narasiṃha—are sometimes called Gattu-Mallayyas or Vaggayyas in Karnataka and Vāghyās in Maharashtra. These devotees imitate dogs in their rituals and performances and carry a pouch made of tiger skin filled with turmeric powder. Sometimes the 'dogs' are compared with tigers in literature and pictorials, and this comparison dates back to the Caṅkam literature.[26] In their attitudes they present a mixture of tigers and dogs. We detect behind this cult the ageless Rudra described in the *Śatarudrīya*, with his hosts of outlandish folk, especially the *vrātyas*. The dogs, of course, are also mentioned.[27] Mallaṇṇa is a great hunter accompanied by dogs, who was slowly metamorphosed into an *avatāra* of Śiva during the Maratha period. He transcended, so to speak, his own asuric form and became Mallāri—the enemy of Malla—who defeated the demon Malla or Mallāsura, or the two demons Maṇi and Malla. In this capacity he was already the *kulasvāmī* of the Kākatīyas of Warangal, as we are told by the *Krīḍābhirāmamu*.[28]

Mallaṇṇa in Andhra or Mailār in Karnataka was, according to the *Krīdābhirāmamu*, the god of those 'who hunt with the spear'. He was also the god *par excellence* of heroes. These heroes were called Mailāra-Vīrabhaṭṭas or Vīramuṣṭis in the *Krīdābhirāmamu*. They survive in the Kañcavīras of Karnataka, who still practice self-mortifications resembling the ritual self-immolation by heroes which was widespread in medieval South India.[29]

Very near to Hampi, that is, in Ādimailār (Hadagalli Taluka, Bellari District), as well as in Devaraguḍḍa near Rānebennūr (Haveri Taluka, Dharwad District), there are two famous centres of Mailār. In Ādimailār this god is said to have first appeared in a termite mound. Mailār was also called Mārtaṇḍa Bhairava. The termite mound indicates the origin of the god in the forest. He is worshipped, like many folk deities of this kind, in his *ugra* form. Mailār was not the somewhat tendentious version of a purāṇic Śiva, who tended to be sometimes banalized and ridiculed. He was rather the descendant of a popular Rudra, close to outlandish and unintegrated people beyond the *varṇa* system. Often he was identified with a local hero who established Mailār's cult. The stern and uncompromising Vīraśaivas, as well as the Jains, took exception to this god, whose followers claimed that he was the true Rudra.[30] Śaṅkarācārya is also reported to have attempted to convert Mallāri's followers—who even included Brahmans—from their strange rites.[31] But in vain. The Vīraśaivas had to acknowledge Mailār and Mallaṇṇa in popular practice and the Jains lost their importance.

When the Vijayanagara Empire was overthrown and scattered, Narasiṃha and Mallaṇṇa/Mailār continued to flourish. They even grew in importance—true to the prophecy of Cakradhara that the popular gods would rise. Maharashtra inherited Mailār.[32] He became Khaṇḍerāyā/Khaṇḍobā and inspired the dynasties of the once obscure Holkars and Gaikwads as their family god.

Whereas Vaiṣṇava theology could maintain purāṇic and sectarian Vaiṣṇavism and Narasiṃha remained a god of famous Vaiṣṇava pilgrimage centres in Andhra, the *popular* Narasiṃha folk cult also continued to exist. In the case of Mailār/Khaṇḍobā, the Brahmans tried to encapsulate Khaṇḍobā in the *Mallāri-Māhātmya* and to enlist him into their fold.[33] Mailār/Khaṇḍobā became a purāṇic *avatāra* of Śiva called Mārtaṇḍa Bhairava, who saves the Ṛṣis, their womenfolk and the cows from the depredations of two notorious robber kings and heroes, called Maṇi and Malla. But, in practice, he remained a god of peasants, tribes, merchants, robbers, heroes—dead or alive—and rising kings. Amongst them there was little cognizance of the brahmanical content of the *Mallāri-Māhātmya*.

These gods represented the parochial and heterogeneous religious element in the religion of the Vijayanagara Empire with which the king had to reckon. They are parallel to the local rulers, whom the king constantly had to watch. One of these local rulers is mentioned in the *Virūpākṣa Vasantōtsava Campū* by Ahobala, who—according to the editor of the work, R.S. Panchamukhi—lived in the beginning of the fourteenth century.[34] The particular chief is said to attend the car-festival of the God Virūpākṣa at Hampi along with other chiefs and kings.[35] He was the *adhipa* of Bhujanganagara (Havanur in the Haveri Taluka of the Dharwad District) and was a devotee of 'Mallārigiri Mahādeva'. The followers of this god are said to have been 'seven crores' (*saptakoṭa*) and to have carried torches at the festival (*yātrā*) of their god, Mallārigiri.[36] To this day the pilgrims carry torches at the *yātrā* of Mallāri/Mailāra, especially at the *dasarā* festival at Devaraguḍḍa. But this is also a custom in the Khaṇḍobā cult. Their victory cry, '*yeḷkoṭi, yeḷkoṭi*'—'seven crores'—also refers to the enemies of the god Mallāri who became devotees of the god after their death in battle. The victory cry is still an essential feature in the worship of Mallāri in Karnataka, Maharashtra and Andhra.

THE *MAHĀNAVAMĪ* AND ELEMENTS OF FOLK RELIGION

B. Stein draws our attention to the nine-day *mahānavamī* and the *dasarā* festival in Vijayanagara.[37] He shows the importance of this festival, which was celebrated in the light half of the month Aśvin (October/November) rather than in the month of Caitra (March/April). It combined the aspects of Rāma's victory and the worship of the warrior goddess Durgā.[38] Stein shows the festival's 'overwhelmingly royal character and symbolically incorporative character'.[39] Perhaps this festival, with its ancient, if not primordial, precursors, was also equally suitable to integrate the heterogeneous folk elements, the folk deities, and the popular-religious atmosphere surrounding the royal rituals in the Vijayanagara Empire. Stein suggestively compares the festival with the ancient *aśvamedha*, but hesitates to fully accept the comparison. Such a comparison, he suggests, might be 'anachronistic' and 'flawed in being an apparent violation of the Vedic prohibitions as well'.[40] Perhaps, then, the festival should rather be compared with the more popular rituals which the classical *śrauta* ritual tried to eliminate, as Heesterman has shown.[41]

The classical *śrauta* rituals 'eliminated' or 'assimilated away' the 'pre-classical' rituals based on communal celebrations, agonistic dualism and competitions, song, music, dance, ritual abuse and ritual copulation.[42] It purified and individualized the 'pre-classical' rituals by breaking the dualistic pattern and cyclical exchange that made the *yajamāna* the centre of the ritual. The sacrifice became independent from ritual rivalry and the complementary pattern of purity and impurity. The classical *śrauta* ritual became the domain of absolute purity.[43] But this development did not *abolish* the parallel popular versions of rituals connected with the king, of which the *mahānavamī* and the *vijayadaśamī utsavas* or *vratas* have features from primordial times and occur in the late texts like the *Devīpurāṇa* and the great ritual compilation of Hemādri, the *vratakāṇḍa* of the *Caturvargacintāmaṇi*. Perhaps the 'popular' side of the *aśvamedha* and the reservation against it from the point of view of the classical *śrauta* ritual that caused even two early texts to declare it 'abolished' or 'decayed' (*utsanna*).[44] This aversion may be the reason why the *mahānavamī*, though very auspicious for popular festivals (*utsavas* and *vratas*), may have been considered inauspicious for reading the Veda (*anadhyāya*).[45]

Manu says that the recitation of the Veda must not be disturbed or defiled on account of, e.g. the sound of a flute (*vāṇa*: IV. 113), or by the voices of dogs, asses and camels (IV. 115), or by sitting on a horse, an elephant or a camel, or by a verbal altercation, by staying in a camp, or by a battle (IV. 121) and so on. That the Brahmans did not dominate the *mahānavamī* rituals—as Stein notices—also probably indicates the popular, inherently 'impure' nature of the festival and its emphasis on the king as the greatest of the warriors, who was nearly 'homologized . . . if not equated with god'.[46] The highest position in the ritual hierarchy, with its implications for the realm and the social system, was certainly occupied by the king, and not—in this context—by the Brahmans.[47] The festival strengthened his royal divinity and power for the coming year and brought prosperity and victory to the realm until it was repeated the next year. The popular character of the festival may also be indicated by the public (ritual) reviling of Brahmans.[48] Ritual reviling is still common all over the Deccan in popular festivals. It was even part of the 'classical' *aśvamedha*.[49]

The reports of the foreigners on the *mahānavamī* and *dasarā* festival are supplemented by the scenes on the walls of the 'Mahānavamī platform'. These scenes also suggest a popular, modified version of the *aśvamedha* ritual: we notice the display and the worship of the royal horse, though with one umbrella instead of the two mentioned by Paes,[50] the hunting of elephants,[51] wrestling and pugilistic bouts,[52] hunting with traps, dogs and bows, fights against tigers, some rather stylized and in the Hoysaḷa tradition, female and male dancers, camel riders with drums, fencing or stickfighting—all features still common in one way or the other in popular religion, especially as features in the *yātrās* of Karnataka, Andhra Pradesh, and Maharashtra (Pls. II a to d). These ritual games would be an *anathema* in the classical (*śrauta*) ritual. That the *mahānavamī* festival could be an equivalent or a substitute of the *aśvamedha* is also expressed in the version of the *Mallāri-Māhātmya* (1697) by the poet Mādhava, an author from Tanjore: the *mahānavamī yātrā* is the most auspicious for the worship of Mallāri and his wife, and the *yātrā* is as good as the *aśvamedha*.[53]

THE HORSE IN THE CULT OF MAILĀR

The significance of the horse as an embodiment of the king and his power in the ritual, royal and martial sphere, and especially in the *mahānavamī* festival, was noticed by the foreign travellers.[54] A good horse was still a precious animal owned by nobles and the enterprising, like the later *śiledārs* of Maharashtra. Its worship as an embodiment or a *vāhana* of the god was also an important part of the cult of Mailār/Khaṇḍobā. The mythological opponent of Mallāri/Mailār/Khaṇḍobā was Malla or Mallāsura; he was very much modelled on the example of a king trying to usurp the world and to overthrow the traditional order, and as such he is inseparably associated the horse and with the elephant. Especially the *asura's* horse eventually became the *vāhana* of the god, an *avatāra* of Śiva. A live horse of the god is still displayed in many temples of the god.[55] Many of the *bhaktas* of Mailār act as horses of the god, galloping and whipping themselves during the festival of the god.[56] Thus the annual *jatrā* in Ādimailār, a place which is not very far from Hampi, and the annual *dasarā* festival in Devaraguḍḍa, both centres of Mailār worship in Karnataka, are also called *kudurahabba*—'the festival of the horses'. It is interesting to note that this festival dates back at least to the reign of Deva Rāya II. Amongst the beautiful *mūrtis* of Mailār and his first wife, Maḷavva, there is one (see Pl. III, 1) which has an inscription engraved on the pedestal. It records that the *mūrti* was consecrated as a *kudureya utsava mūrti*—'a *mūrti* for the horse festival'—in the year AD 1518.

CONCLUDING REMARKS

What seems important in our context is the far-reaching cohesion and similarity between the folk Murukaṉ, Narasiṃha, Mallaṇṇa, Mailār, and Khaṇḍobā as far as mythology and ritual are concerned. What emerges from this are the contours of a parallel, cohesive folk culture which was no doubt interlinked with the Purāṇas. But, on this level, purāṇic and sectarian Śaivism and Viṣṇuism were not in focus.

Our written sources know relatively little—or consist of partial or tendentiously edited records—of this culture, which had no immediate need of written texts. It was mainly based on a vast body of *oral* myths and legends, rituals, and practices handed down orally since primeval times. The king and the *mahānavamī* ritual took account of this pervasive and heterogeneous, basically non-scriptural folk religion and folk culture. The festival provided the local chiefs prestige and ritual rank under the umbrella of the Vijayanagara king, as the reports of the European travellers suggest. The parallel is found in folk cults, for instance, in the cult of Mailār in Karnataka or in the cults of Khaṇḍobā and Mhaskobā in Maharashtra. There is a strong ritual of the devotees and of their privileges (Marāṭhī: *mān*) which is not based on ritual purity according to the *varṇa* system, but on their degree of devotion or their often extreme feats of bravery.

The situation in which the Vijayanagara king was placed amidst his chiefs, nobles, and heroes can be expressed in the terms of the *Mārtaṇḍa Vijaya*, an early-nineteenth-century work on the Khaṇḍobā cult: 'For the hero (*vīra*) the king is god.'[57] The reverse may have been emphasized when there was no strong ruler personifying the god: then the god—who was a deified hero/ruler and often a manifestation of Śiva—became a king on earth and was treated like a king. According to legend, 'King' Mārtaṇḍa Bhairava or Khaṇḍerāyā miraculously drove away the emperor Aurangzeb.[58]

The second marriage of the god, with a tribal woman, often a daughter of a 'chief' or 'king', may indicate, on the mythical plane, apart from themes of hunting and eroticism, the extension of the spiritual sovereignty of the god, who now combines, for instance, the upper world (by his first wife) and the lower world (by his second wife). On the more mundane level of the king the second marriage may reflect the extension of royal sovereignty into the pastoral and forested areas. The defeat of the *asura* or *daitya*, in our case Malla or Maṇi *and* Malla, indicates the rise of the god and the extension of his spiritual power. The god defeats Malla, and the demon becomes a *bhakta*, or the loyal follower of the god, e.g. his *dvārapāla*.[59]

On the mundane level this may correspond to the victory over the local ruler and the extension of royal sovereignty into the pastoral and forested areas, with the resulting shift towards the king's paramountcy. In practice the defeated enemy would often be reinstated as a subordinate ruler.[60] The ritual of the *mahānavamī* festival would annually restate this sovereignty of the king over his subordinate rulers, whose loyalty would be on test.

In conclusion, we may say that our picture of Vijayanagara will be incomplete if we do not take notice of the fervent and exuberant, but essentially non-scriptural, non-sanskritic folk culture.

NOTES

1. Burton Stein, 'Interpretation of the Agrarian System of South India', in: R.E. Frykenberg (ed.), *Land Control and Social Structure in Indian History* (Madison, Wisc., 1969), pp. 175-216, at p. 195.
2. Robert Sewell, *A Forgotten Empire, Vijayanagar* (Delhi, 1st Indian edn., 1962), p. 237 (Paes), 345ff. (Nunes).
3. Vi. Bhi. Kolate (ed.), *Līḷācaritra*, Maharashtra Sahitya Mandala (Mumbai, 1978), p. 613 ["Uttarārdha", *līḷā* 436].
4. Burton Stein, 'Devī Shrines and Folk Hinduism in Medieval Tamilnad', in: Edwin Gerow and Margery D. Lang (eds.), *Studies in the Language and Culture of South Asia* (Seattle: University of Washington Press, 1973), pp. 75-91.
5. Suvira Jaiswal, *The Origin and Development of Vaiṣṇavism* (Delhi, 1967), p. 120. *Mbh*. 12. 337.36 (crit. edn.).
6. A.W. Khan, *An Early Sculpture of Narasiṃha* (Hyderabad, 1964) (Andhra Pradesh Govt. Archaeological Series, 16).
7. A. Eschmann, 'The Vaiṣṇava Typology of Hinduization', in: Anncharlott Eschmann, Hermann Kulke and Gaya Charan Tripathi, *The Cult of Jagannāth and the Regional Tradition of Orissa* (Delhi, 1978), pp. 99ff., at p. 108.
8. Cf. Madeleine Biardeau, 'Narasiṃha et ses sanctuaires', in *Puruṣārtha* (1975), pp. 49-66.
9. See Rā. Ciṃ. Dhere, 'Rājāmaṭhāce rahasya' in: idem, *Lokasaṃskṛtīcī Kṣitīje* (Pune, 1971), pp. 47ff.
10. Dhere, ibid., pp. 50ff.
11. See Dhere, ibid., p. 48, citing Dāsagaṇu, who composed the *Godāmāhātmya* (25: 40-1) on the basis of the *Brahmapurāṇa*.
12. See Dhere, ibid., pp. 53f.
13. *Līḷācaritra*, *līḷā* 318, cf. 601.
14. Dhere, ibid., p. 51, citing *Śalyaparvan* by the Mahānubhāv author Navrasnārāyaṇ: Śakunī using the *narsiṃhasādhana* in the *śmaśāna*, raising all kinds of *bhūtas* and *vīras*.
15. Dhere, ibid., pp. 54f.

16. For example, Narsingpur on the confluence of the rivers Bhima and Nira. The temple is surrounded by walls and bastions, giving it the appearance of a fort. The original place is said to have been a little further away at a crossroad, the natural abode of *bhūtas*. The present '*mūrti*' of Yogāsana-narasiṃha is rather rough and *ugra*-like. Another noteworthy temple is at Kole-Narsingpur in the Sangli District, near Karad.
17. G.-D. Sontheimer, *Birobā, Mhaskobā und Khaṇḍobā* (Wiesbaden, 1976), pp. 21, 61ff. [Editor's note: English version: *Pastoral Deities in Western India*, New York, 1989, pp. 17, 58ff.] K. Zvelebil, 'The Va̤l̤i-Murugan myth—Its development', in *Indo-Iranian Journal* 22 (1980), pp. 113-35.
18. See Sontheimer, ibid., pp. 61ff. [*Pastoral Deities* . . ., pp. 60ff.]
19. See K. Zvelebil, 'Shaktic features of Aruṇakiri's Bhakti', in *South Asian Digest of Regional Writing*, vol. 6 (1977), pp. 85-96.
20. The author wishes to thank Mr. B.S. Murlidhar Reddy and E.V. Rajendra Sarma, Betamcherla, for their kind help while he was studying the Narasiṃha cult at Madduleti and Ahobilam together with Dr. M.L.K. Murty, Deccan College, Pune. He is also grateful to Dr. Murty for transcriptions and translations of oral texts told by local informants, especially Dāsari Rāmu, a Golla Dāsari from Puttagummi, near Ramallakota, Kurnool District.
21. Sontheimer, op. cit., pp. 63ff. [*Pastoral Deities* . . ., pp. 60ff.]
22. K.A. Nilakanta Sastri, *A History of South India—From Prehistoric Times to the Fall of Vijayanagara* (Oxford University Press, 1966), pp. 280f. His predecessor Vīra Narasiṃha (1505-9) made donations to many pilgrimage centres, ibid., p. 277.
23. Ibid., p. 273. Sewell, op. cit., pp. 229, 231.
24. Sastri, op. cit., p. 285, calls it the last monument of Kṛṣṇadeva Rāya's reign (1528).
25. There is nothing to suggest among the broken pieces that Ceñcū-Lakṣmī rather than the classical Lakṣmī could have been part of the statue (to be restored by the ASI). If one sees the enormous sized *liṅgam* in the adjacent temple absolutely untouched, one wonders who the actual vandals were who destroyed the statue.
26. See Hart, George L. III: *The Poems of Ancient Tamil* (Berkeley: University of California Press, 1971), p. 193. See Sontheimer, 'The Mallāri/Khaṇḍobā myth as Reflected in Folk Art and Ritual', in *Anthropos* 79, 1-3 (1984), pp. 155ff. [Editor's note: Also in EK, pp. 34ff.] See also Sontheimer, 'Dasarā at Devaraguḍḍa: Ritual and play in the cult of Mailār and Khaṇḍobā', in: L. Lutze (ed.), *Drama in Contemporary South Asia: Varieties and Settings* (*South Asian Digest of Regional Writing*, vol. 10 (1981), 1984, pp. 1-2), *passim*. [Editor's note: Also in EK, pp. 63-6, *passim*.]
27. *Taittirīya-saṃhita* 4.5.4 For the connection of Rudra with the *vrātyas* see, e.g. Asko Parpola, *Arguments for an Aryan Origin of the South Indian Megaliths* (Madras [?]: Govt. of Tamil Nadu, 1973), pp. 34ff.
28. *Krīḍābhirāmamu*, by Viṣṇukonda Vallabhārayadu, 145 (Secundarabad, Andhra

Pradesh Book Distributions, 1972), pp. 35f.: Mailara Deva dwells in Orugallu (i.e., the present Warangal). See D.C. Sircar (ed.), *Annual Report on Indian Epigraphy for 1957-58* (Delhi: Govt. of India Press, 1961), pp. 7f.; cf. also Census of India, 1961, vol. II, *Andhra Pradesh*, pt. VII-B (18: Warangal District), pp. 24f.: 'Vidhyanada, the great poet, also wrote in his book *Prataparudrīyam* that the family deity of Kakatiyas [*sic*] was Mylaru Deva'. The actual temple is near Warangal at Iloni.

29. *Krīḍābhirāmamu*, 141-2. Cf. Sontheimer, 'Dasarā at Devaraguḍḍa . . .', op. cit., *passim* [Editor's note: Also in EK, pp. 63-86.]. S. Settar and G.-D. Sontheimer (eds.), *Memorial Stones, a Study of their Origin, Significance and Variety* (Dharwad/New Delhi, 1982), pp. 209ff. (M.L.K. Murty), 271ff. ['Hero- and *Satī*-Stones of Maharashtra', also in the present volume, pp. 252ff.] *et passim*.
30. M. Cidanandamurti, 'Kannaḍa Kāvya, Śāsanagaḷalli Mailāra mattu Māḷaci', in *Prabuddha Karnāṭaka* 48-3 (1966), pp. 41-62. I am grateful to Mr. R. Zydenbos for procuring a transcript of this article and to Mr. Rajaram R. Hegde for help in translating. See, e.g. the Jain work *Samayaparīkṣe* by Brahmaśiva (*c*. 1150). Mailār is a *kṣudradevatā* who cannot give boons (9. 128), a Jain who died in battle (2. 71), and people who perform *vratas* for this god are not true Jains, but are *kāḷa*, which means 'sınful' (4. 125). In the *Śaṅkaradāsimayya-purāṇa* (ed. V.B. Halabhavi) by Mallikārjuna (seventeenth century), Mailāra is claimed by the Goravas to be the true Śiva, who kills Malla, but Śaṅkaradāsimayya, who was a great Śiva *bhakta* and was believed to be an *avatāra* of Śiva, held Mailāra to be a *graha* (a malevolent spirit). He was a Jain *muni*, called Mallideva, who fell from his vow. He became a servant holding the *chatri* for Śaṅkaradāsimayya.
31. See N. Veezhinathan (ed.), *Śrīśaṅkaravijaya of Anantānandagiri* (Madras: Univ. of Madras, 1976), Ch. 29, p. 117. Sontheimer, 'Dasarā at Devaraguḍḍa . . .' op. cit., *passim* and idem: 'The Mallāri/Khaṇḍobā myth . . .', op. cit., p. 166 [cp. EK, p. 52], and on the dispute between Śaṅkara and the Brahmans see also G.H. Khare, *Mahārāṣṭrācīm cār daivateṃ* (Puṇeṃ, 1958), pp. 133 ff. R.C. Dhere, *Khaṇḍobā* (Puṇeṃ, 1961), p. 79, identifies Ujjayinī and Mallapattana, both mentioned in the *Śrīśaṅkaravijaya*, respectively with the Vīraśaiva centre (*pīṭha*) Ujjayinī (one of the five Vīraśaiva centres) in Karnataka and with Mailār in the Bellari District, situated to the north-west of Ujjayinī.
32. Ekanāth (2nd half of the sixteenth century) called him the Kānaḍyā Khaṇḍerāyā—the Khaṇḍerāya from Karnataka. See Kāśināth Anaṃta Jośī (ed.), *Śrīsakalasaṃtagāthā, Khaṃḍa dusrā, Śrī ekanāthamahārājāṃce abhaṃga*, 3730 (Puṇeṃ, 2nd. edn., 1967).
33. For some versions of the myth of Mallāri, see Sontheimer, 'The Mallāri/Khaṇḍobā myth . . .', op. cit., p. 155, fn. 1 [cp. EK, p. 59, fn. 1]. The Ṛṣis and their *āśram*, which have to be protected, are hardly ever given in oral accounts as reasons for the interference by Śiva. It is simply 'for the sake of the oppressed bhaktas' that Śaṅkar took the form of Mārtaṇḍa Bhairava and defeated the demon(s). Thus the Dāsī of Jayarāma, an authoress and student of Jayarāma

(AD 1599-1673), says in one of her *abhaṅgas*: For which purpose did Śaṅkar assume the *avatāra* of Mārtaṇḍa Bhairava? The *bhaktas* had fallen into distress. With the sword in his hand he punished the *daityas* Maṇi and Malla. *Guruvaracī pade va abhaṃga* by Dāsī of Jayarāma, *ravivāraceṃ abhaṃgacapade* 11. (From a Siḷā press copy, no date).

34. R.S. Vidyaratna Panchamukhi, *Virūpāksha Vasantōtsava Champū* (Dharwad: Kannaḍa Research Institute, 1953), p. ix. I owe the reference to Dr. M.S. Nagaraja Rao.
35. Ibid., p. xi.
36. Ibid., p. 19.
37. Burton Stein, *Peasant State and Society in Medieval South India* (Delhi: Oxford University Press, 1980), pp. 384ff.
38. This pattern was followed in post-Vijayanagara days in the famous cult of the goddess Bhavānī or Tukāī (Durgāmahiṣāsura-mardinī) of Tuljapur in Maharashtra. She was the family goddess of many Maharashtrian nobles, including King Śivājī. Dasarā was and still is the most important festival. It is said that the goddess accompanied Rāma and Lakṣmaṇa up to a certain spot in Tuljapur (the *ghaṭaśīla*) on their way to the south. Whereas the two brothers proceeded to Lanka, Tukāī waited here for their return. See D.R. Amladi, *Tuḷajāpūr Bhavānī* (Bombay: Govt. of Maharashtra, 1961), pp. 4, 7. G.H. Khare, *Mahārāṣṭrācīṃ cār daivateṃ*, pp. 176f.
39. Stein, *Peasant State and Society*, op. cit., p. 389.
40. Ibid., p. 388.
41. My summary remarks are based on J.C. Heesterman, 'Vrātya and sacrifice', in *Indo-Iranian Journal* 6/1 (1962), pp. 1-37. Idem: 'Brahmin, ritual and renouncer', in *Wiener Zeitschrift für die Kunde Süd- und Ostasiens*, 8 (1965), pp. 1-31. Idem: 'Die Autoritat des Vedas', in: Gerhard Oberhammer (ed.), *Offenbarung, geistige Realität des Menschen* (Wien, 1974), pp. 29-40.
42. Heesterman, 'Brahmin, ritual and renouncer', p. 12.
43. Ibid., p. 16.
44. *Taittirīya-saṃhitā* v. 4.12.3; *Śatapathabrāhmaṇa* XIII, 3.3.6. Cited P.V. Kane, *History of Dharmaśāstra*, vol. II, pt. 2 (Poona, 1974), p. 1237.
45. Burton Stein, *Peasant State and Society*, op. cit., p. 388, citing Aparārka's commentary.
46. Ibid., p. 390.
47. It may be, following Richard Burghart, 'Hierarchical Models of the Hindu Social System', in *Man* (N.S.), vol. 13, pp. 519-36, that the king occupied the highest position in the hierarchy of the empire on account of the deification of his kingship or the ritual equation with the deity of the realm, whereas the Brahmans claimed their superiority on the basis of the *varṇa* system. A third hierarchical model was that of the ascetic (or *bhakti* saint, who claimed superiority over the king and the Brahmans (especially the Purohita) because he had transcended the world of sentient beings. Burghart, op. cit., p. 533: 'The Brahman, the ascetic, and the king

each absorbed elements of the other two codes into his own code and then claimed the absolutely supreme rank in the social system.'

48. As reported by Nicolo Conti, cited by Stein, op. cit., p. 388. Cf. *Kālikāpurāṇa* 63: 11-25.
49. See Kane, *History of Dharmaśāstra*, vol. II, pt. 1, pp. 1234f.
50. Sewell, op. cit., pp. 262, 267.
51. Cf. the title of Deva Rāya II: *gajabeṭekāra* ('Hunter of Elephants'). Sastri, op. cit., p. 269.
52. Cf. Sewell, op. cit., pp. 258, 359. The *mallas* (wrestlers) are ubiquitous in villages and village festivals in the Deccan and are already mentioned in the *Līḷācaritra*, *Pūrvārdha* 30. Thus Mailār/Mallāri also means 'the enemy of Malla, the wrestler'. See further Sontheimer, 'The Mallāri/Khaṇḍobā myth . . .', op. cit., p. 157 [cp. EK, p. 37].
53. *Śrīmallāri Māhātmya*, by the poet Mādhava (Śake 1619 = AD 1697) from Tanjore, 21.26-8. Besides *mahānavamī*, the festival on the sixth day of the light half (*campaṣaṣṭhī*) of Mārgaśīrṣa (November/December) is the main festival associated with Mallāri according to the texts.
54. Sewell, op. cit., pp. 115, 254, 354, *passim*. Hemadri, the chancellor of the Yādava king Mahādeva (1261-70), stresses the importance of the worship of the horse in the *durgāpūjā* and the *vijayadaśamī*. See Kane, *History of Dharmaśāstra*, V, pt. 1, pp. 184, 191. For the importance of the horse in the capital of the Kākatīyas, Warangal, see *Līḷācaritra*, *Pūrvārdha* 31.
55. On the *mahānavamī* platform, as elsewhere in Hampi, foreigners are shown parading horses. Khaṇḍobā's horses in Jejuri (Maharashtra) are traditionally kept by a Muslim family. The importance of foreigners, the Portuguese, but, more pervasively, Muslim horse traders, appears already in legends about the Tamilian Maṇikkavācakar, the famous Nāyaṉār saint: Śiva appeared to him as a Muslim horse trader. Khaṇḍobā was extremely liberal with respect to caste and creed so that even Mlecchas, i.e. Muslims, could be *bhaktas*. The god even assumed a Muslim name: Mallu Khān or Ajmat Khān. See Sontheimer, 'The Mallāri/Khaṇḍobā myth . . .', op. cit., *passim*. This catholicity was shared by the Vijayanagara king, who could hardly have fully realized the orthodox-śāstric principles of purity (for which already Manu V. 93-4 obligingly excused him). See G.-D. Sontheimer, 'Die Ethik im Hinduismus', in: C.H. Ratschow, *Ethik der Religionen. Ein Handbuch* (Stuttgart: 1980), pp. 349ff., at pp. 359f. Nor could the king have established the full rigour of the *varṇāśrama* system, which appears to have been more a visionary *leitmotif* than an established institution. It is in line with this that Muslims formed an important element in the Vijayanagara city and that Hindu kings, including Śivājī, were known to have made donations to mosques. It was loyalty, devotion and bravery which mattered not necessarily birth in a particular caste or in a *varṇa*.
56. See Sontheimer, 'Dasarā at Devaraguḍḍa. . .', op. cit., *passim*.
57. *Mārtaṇḍa Vijaya* (ed. R.C. Dhere, Puṇeṃ, 1975), 18.27.

58. The legendary (?) event referred to is rather drastically described by the Maharashtrian Rāmdas (1608-81). Anantadāsa Rāmdāsi (ed.), *Śrīsamarthāṃca Gāthā* (Puṇeṃ: Śake 1850 [AD 1928]), 1169, p. 353, where the *turuks* (Muslims) are mentioned and Khaṇḍobā is called Mallu Khān.
59. See Sontheimer, 'The Mallāri/Khaṇḍobā myth . . .', op. cit., p. 159 [cp. EK, p. 40]. The 'acquisition' of a defeated demon by the god generally becomes elaborated in a written text like the *Mallāri-Mahātmya.*
60. Sontheimer, *Birobā, Mhaskobā und Khaṇḍobā*, op. cit., pp. 84f., on the assimilation of Kolis, and ibid., pp. 85ff. on the assimilation of the Rāmośīs/ Beraḍs as watchmen [= *Pastoral Deities* . . . , pp. 83f. and 84ff.] Cf. David Shulman, 'On South Indian bandits and kings', in *The Indian Economic and Social History Review*, vol. XVII/3 (1980), pp. 283-306.

Plate I, Fig. 1: Sculpture at the temple of Upper Ahobilam, said to be Ceñcū-Lakṣmī with Narasiṃha extracting a thorn (Photo: Sontheimer).

Plate I, Fig. 2: Narasiṃha and Lakṣmī statue of the time of Krishnadeva Raya (1509-29) (Photo: Sontheimer).

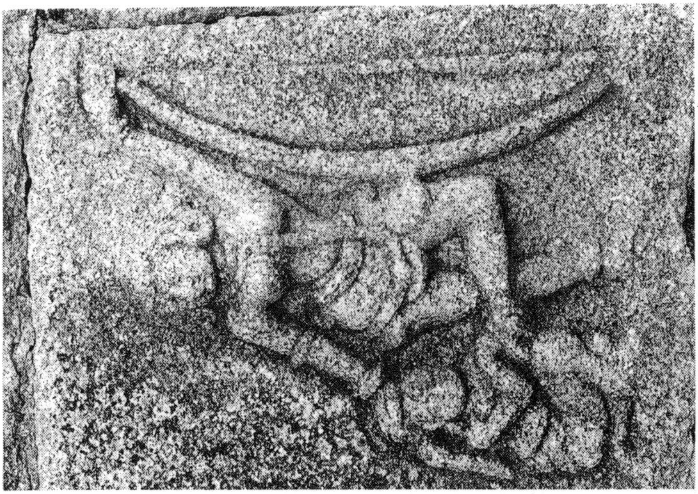

Plate I, Fig. 3a: Ceñcū-Lakṣmī representation on the Mahānavamī platform (Photo: Sontheimer).

Plate I, Fig. 3b: Ceñcū-Lakṣmī representation on the Mahānavamī platform (Photo: Sontheimer).

Plate II, Fig. 1b: Scene on the Mahānavamī platform (Photo: Sontheimer).

Plate II, Fig. 1a: Scene on the Mahānavamī platform (Photo: Sontheimer).

Plate II, Fig. 1c: Scene on the Mahānavamī platform (Photo: Sontheimer).

Plate II, Fig. 1d: Scene on the Mahānavamī platform (Photo: Sontheimer).

Plate III, Fig. 1: Mailār and Malavva, his wife, who holds a lotus bud and embraces Mailār with her right arm. The murti is dated AD 1518 and is in Mailār (Hadagalli Taluka, Bellari District). The heads of three demons are at the base. Height *ca.* 70 cm. I am grateful to S. Settar for help in deciphering the inscription (Photo: Sontheimer).

Plate III, Fig. 2: The god Mailār and Malavva/Mhāḷsā from Mailār. Height *ca.* 70 cm (Photo: Sontheimer).

Plate III, Fig. 3: Mailār or Khaṇḍobā in Mailar. He looks similar to a viran from Tamilnadu except for the four arms. The heads of the demons Maṇi and Malla are at the base. Notice the Kīrtimukha which serves as a kind of belt-buckle. This head is sometimes said to be Dakṣa. Metal masks of the same kind are sewn onto the bags of the Vaggayyas, the special devotees of Mailār. The bags contain turmeric powder, the magic substance of Mailār/Khaṇḍobā (Photo: Sontheimer).

Plate III, Fig. 4: This seems to be a post-Vijayanagara murti of Mailār. The Pānpatra looks like a lotus flower, which may suggest associations with Brahmā's head (Photo: Sontheimer).

The *Vana* and the *Kṣetra*: The Tribal Background of Some Famous Cults

The world of tribals and their religion as well as Indian folk religion in general have become an important subject for the Indologist, who has hitherto emphasized the study of classical languages and literature. The tribal world has ceased to be the exclusive domain of the social anthropologist or ethnologist. Similarly, the ethnologist has to understand the wider context of the tribal community, that is the 'Great Tradition' of India. For example, Lord Jagannāth combines the tribal world, the mythology of the Purāṇas, and the Pañcarātra ritual, and he even admits of the highest philosophical interpretation.[1] In fact, whatever one may discern in the continuum from tribal belief to the highest philosophy is concentrated in the Jagannāth cult. It is a good example to illustrate the speciality of Indian culture: the *unity* of different aspects or levels of Hinduism concentrated in one cult and the nearly uninterrupted continuity from tribal beliefs to the highest philosophy.

It has also long been acknowledged that the tribal world and the villages of India may reveal to us different facets of India's past, leading us to earlier stages of Indian culture right into prehistory. It was D.D. Kosambi, the famous historian, who said long ago that 'history is to be seen displayed in full detail in the villages of India—provided one has the vision and insight required to read that history'.[2] Anncharlott Eschmann always realized this necessity of understanding the *origins* of religion in areas off the beaten track.

The evolution of the cult of a deity is a fascinating study. The deity passes through several stages, but its beginning—for instance, as a mountain spirit or a hunters' patron deity—is still preserved. The emphasis in religious beliefs may shift, but the original core is still preserved. The god may have two shrines: the original one in the forest and one in the village. The forest shrine does not lose its importance, whatever may be added to the cult.

No doubt this unity is a compartmentalized unity. This 'unity in diversity' is achieved not by abolition of the original cult *per force*, but by 'incorporation' and 'subordination' or by what P. Hacker has called

'Inklusivismus'.[3] As is well known, Hinduism is said to have no dogma and no creed. If there had been dogmatic beliefs propagated by an organized church in the Western sense there would probably be no necessity for the Indologist to study folk religion and tribal religion. He could stick to his texts. Though the traditional method of the Brahman author, whether sectarian or non-sectarian, was to distinguish, evaluate and edit the raw material of 'primitive' beliefs and 'unreflected instincts', giving them a new 'prestige-worthy' interpretation, if not a new meaning, the sharp distinction between 'superstition' and 'belief' was absent. The beliefs of others—as, for instance, those of the tribals—may be admitted by the Hindu interpreter to be a way to God, though he may view them as a little less valid than his own. This attitude is as old as the *Bhagavadgītā* (IX.23). It has been argued that there is no traditional word in any Indian language for 'superstition' and new terms had to be created, e.g. *andhā śraddhā*.[4] It was probably only after Western influence had gained wider acceptance that this distinction was introduced and the difference was accentuated. Tribal beliefs today tend to be rejected *a priori* as primitive, immoral and anachronistic, and as *andhā śraddhā*. There are still a few today who respect tribal customs and religious beliefs—as long as they don't interfere with what the Indian Constitution (Art. 26) calls 'public order, morality and health'—as a cherished treasure in the face of the superficiality and conformism of the modern world. We may cite here Sitakant Mahapatra. In an article entitled 'The Tribal World and the Small Community' he wrote *inter alia*: 'It has been the greatness of the Indian nation that it has always thought to create [such] a living and growing community which is in essence a community of communities.' And further he said: 'Technology and tribal cultures are in need of each other today. At the heart of each is an emptiness—a cultural anomie and blankness on the one hand and stark unmitigated poverty and a lack of formal organization, on the other. An exclusive emphasis on the former has led to a loss of the sense of community and a desperate search for alternatives in the West. May be, if we continue to cherish the value of traditional "little" culture as the bond that keeps men together in small communities, we may not be required to trudge the same troubled way of the West as we advance economically.'[5]

What is meant is not 'communalism' or a caste-ridden society, but the preservation of culture in little communities, the 'little traditions' within the regional traditions or the so-called 'Great Tradition' of India. The 'Little Tradition' gives the individual his sense of identity and prevents him from merging into the anonymity of the conformism and superficiality of modern times. I should like to elaborate a little on the important role which the forest as the separate world of the tribals played in the past. I will also consider the relationship between the tribals, the forest, and the world outside the forest, which might be called for the sake of simplicity the world of Hinduism. It is sometimes overlooked how much more India was forested about 100 to 200 years ago, before the great extension of agriculture began. This must have had a considerable and constant influence on the religious attitudes of those living beyond the forest or trying to penetrate it. As a matter of fact, from ancient times a cultural and spatial separatedness between different communities was recognized in India. This is well expressed by the theory of the five landscapes in the Ancient Classical Tamil literature, the Caṅkam literature of *ca.* the second to the fourth century AD. Though this theory is very familiar to scholars working on Tamilnadu, it is not generally known to outsiders. We must, therefore, give a short summary of this theory. These landscapes, called *tiṇai*, were the guiding principles of a theory of poetry which consisted of two components, *puram* and *akam*. *Akam* was concerned with domestic life, with the inner life and with eroticism, the most personal aspect of a human being. *Puram*, on the other hand, represented the sum of outer life, the active life in public, and last but not least warlike occupations. Certain aggressive actions of a tribal chieftain were themes of *puram* and were ascribed to definite physiographical or ecological regions. *Akam*, in short, means love poetry and *puram* war poetry. Certain human situations like separation of lovers, the waiting of a woman for her lover, their meeting, etc., were themes of the *akam* poetry. The term *tiṇai* does not only mean a region characterized by ecological factors, but it also meant an erotic situation. The anxious waiting of the woman for her lover was expressed through the description of the pastoral landscape in the winter season through which she had to pass. The observation of landscapes, seasons, fauna and flora, of the inhabitants of a region and their religious, economic and cultural life was considered an indispensable precondition for the bard composing poetry. The description of the five landscapes became a poetical convention, but basically there was an acute observation which reflects the life and conditions in the five landscapes. It may be that these descriptions developed into poetical conventions and 'petrifications of customs developed in objective reality',[6] but, I suggest that even in very recent times each of these five regions, along with their implications, survived. Each of the regions represented a relatively independent ecological area with its own particular type of people, economy, religion and culture. Each region nevertheless existed in symbiosis or had contacts with the other four regions.[7]

I also think that the concept of the five landscapes even applied *mutatis mutandis* not only to Tamilnadu, but also to other regions in India, especially to the Deccan. I am sure that the application of this concept, particularly to the study of the history of cults, pilgrimage centres and the development of religion in South India in general, can be very fruitful. A very brief outline describing these five landscapes is, therefore, necessary.[8]

The first landscape is the mountainous one called *kuriñci* after a certain flower growing there. Peacocks, parrots, monkeys, elephants, horses and bulls live in it. You find there the jackfruit, bamboo, and the *veṅkai* tree. The impenetrable forests are the home of the mountain tribes called Kānavar and Kuruvar. People live on the produce of the forest, e.g. tubers, wild honey, etc. Bamboo provides 'rice'. Ivory is exchanged for salt from the coast. Some fields are cultivated with millet (*cāmai*). The god of the *kuriñci* is Cēyōṉ.

The second landscape is the pastoral region, called *mullai* after a kind of jasmin-creeper. There are cows, bulls, sheep, and goats. The preponderant crop is millet and the fields subsidiary to pastoral life are cultivated by bullock-drawn ploughs. We find different pastoral communities which keep either cows or buffaloes or sheep. The god of the *mullai* is Māyōn, 'The Dark One'. Cēyōṉ is derived from *cey*, which means either 'red' or 'young'. Cēyōṉ, who is eventually called Murukaṉ, is the 'Lord of the Mountain'—*malaikiḻavōn*. He lives on the hill, but was also worshipped as the *kaṭampa* tree. Very much like the Vedic Rudra as described in the *Śatarudrīya*,[9] he is ubiquitous and lives in forests, groves, bays, rivers, ponds, crossroads and also in the assembly hall. He carries a spear similar to the spear of the tribal chieftains in the *kuriñci*. His priests, who are also soothsayers, are called *vēlaṉ* (carriers of the spear). The *vēlaṉ* perform an ecstatic dance. In these priests we discern the tribal priest, the 'shaman' and exorcist who can be seen as the complementary counterpart of the Brahman. Cēyōṉ/Murukaṉ receives offerings of millet, flowers and the meat of rams. Cēyōṉ/Murukaṉ is not only the famous god of Tamilnadu, but he is also what we might call a manifestation of a proto-Indian god of whom Rudra/Śiva and many other gods, especially in the Deccan, are varying, but basically the identical manifestations. Murukaṉ was eventually associated with Śiva as his son Skanda/Kārttikeya. Whereas the hill tribes, the Kānavars, dedicate their dance to Murukaṉ and his beloved Vaḷḷi, who comes from the Kuruvar tribe, the Āciyar, the pastoral tribe, dance the *kuravai* in honour of Māyōṉ, who is identified with Kṛṣṇa. But one must emphasize here that Vaiṣṇavization happened at a much later stage. There was much symbiosis between the *mullai* and the *kuriñci*, on which I cannot elaborate here. Māyōṉ may have even developed from the corresponding god of the *kuriñci* region, Cēyōṉ. However that may be, two gods of the tribes grown from the beliefs of the tribes were eventually identified with Skanda/Kārttikeya and Kṛṣṇa. What should be stressed here is that regional folk cults and the beliefs of lower castes and the tribes reflect other, if not primordial, aspects of gods like Murukaṉ, Subramanyam, Skanda, Kārttikeya, Māyōṉ/Kṛṣṇa/Vāsudeva, and Tirumāl/Neṭiyōṉ. The identification of these gods with the purāṇic Śiva and Viṣṇu is often rather a tertiary than a secondary development.

The third landscape was the riverine area, the settled 'nuclear agricultural area' (Burton Stein) called *marutam*. It is the riceland inhabited by settled farmers and it is the backbone of the kingdom. It is ruled over by a king (Ventan, according to *Tolkāppiyam* III. 5=Indra) and the subjects do not know the bow of the forester, but only the rainbow, and no other weapon than the ploughshare. We may note here that all land was basically divided between *menpulam*—'paddy land', 'soft and tender land'—and *vanpulam*—'hard and barren land', 'millet land'.[10] According to the *Tamil Index* of the Pre-Pallava period, *vanpulam* consists of 'jungle tracts' and 'pasture lands'.[11]

I will pass over the fourth landscape, that is, the maritime landscape, *neytal*, and come to the fifth area, the *pālai*. It comes into being only in the hot season, namely when parts of the pastoral and mountainous regions dry up. Lakes and water reservoirs are empty and animals suffer. What *pālai* implies one may experience in the hot months from Caitra (March/April) onwards: The trees in forest areas like Bastar are leafless and the red blossoms of the 'Flame of the Forest' (*Butea Monosperma*) and actual forest-fires abound. The *pālai* becomes infested with marauding tribes, especially that of the Maravars, whose descendants still exist and who used to raid caravans of merchants. We shall return to them later. The goddess of the *pālai* region is Koṟṟavai. Even cows are sacrificed to her, and she is the goddess of warring tribes. She also is a huntress and rides a stag. Murukaṉ, 'The Young One', eventually becomes her 'son'. There are many comparable manifestations of this goddess in South India, the Deccan and elsewhere. The goddess lives on in many cults, e.g. in the cult of Aṅkalamman in Tamilnaḍu and Andhra. She seems to come from the *kāṭu*, which may mean 'forest' as well as '*śmaśāna*' (cremation ground), and she is often connected with the *śmaśāna*. Aṅkalamman seems to be derived from *kaṅkal*—an emaciated, dried-out skeleton. Heat, *śmaśāna*, and forest connect her with the ancient goddess of the *pālai*, the forest and pastoral area turned into a desert in the hot season.

Following the distinction in the Old Tamil literature, I would like to distinguish here between the tribals of the forest and the pastoral tribes. Thus the tribals of the forest are, for instance, the Murias and Māḍiyas of Bastar and the Ceñcūs of the Eastern Ghats. But we must also think of the great pastoral tribes, like the Rabāris in Rajasthan, the Gollas in Andhra Pradesh, the Kurubas in Karnatak, and the large Dhangar communities in Maharashtra. All these groups even now have more or less their own ecological niches.

Leaving Old Tamil literature, we may look in the Sanskritic culture for terms and a concept which are used to express a basic religious, economic and spatial separatedness. It is best expressed in the terms *kṣetra* and *vana* or *araṇya*. The terms *vana* and *araṇya* seem to be used more or less as equivalents in the late Vedic and in post-Vedic literature.[12] By *kṣetra* I mean inhabited, well-settled space with regular plough agriculture[13] the village in such space, e.g. the *agrahāra* villages in coastal Karnāṭaka or *śāsana* villages in Orissa and the holy centres connected with them. We are neglecting in this context the question of 'urban' trade centres in ancient and medieval India. By *vana* I mean 'wild space', 'forest' or jungle which harbours the 'hermitage', the tribals, the *saṃnyāsī* and the *āśrama*.[14] I have avoided using the terms *grāma* or *pura* instead of *kṣetra*, though *grāma* or *pura* may well be found in the settled nuclear agricultural area, the heartland of powerful kingdoms. Thus in Maharashtra villages whose names end with *-gaon,-gāv* (Skt. *grāma*), or *-puri* are mostly found in the Godavari basin and the Vidarbha area, which were the bases for the kingdoms of the Sātavāhanas, the Vākātakas, and the Yādavas of Devagirī.[15] Apart from its early connotation of a 'mobile village' or 'migrating cattle-keepers', a 'host of people' or a 'flock of cattle', etc.,[16] *grāma* does not necessarily imply a village inhabited by Brahmans and dominated by their ideology of *varṇa*, *dharma*, and purity, nor does it connote a 'holy centre'.

This dichotomy of *vana* and *kṣetra* is not mutually exclusive, but it is rather complementary, or a continuum like the continuum from tribe to caste. Related to this is the opposition between tribal religion and what has been called 'codified Hinduism' (A. Eschmann) or 'normative Hinduism'.[17] Based on these concepts Hinduism has recently been defined as 'a process, as a *dynamic continuum* operating in both ways between the two theoretical constructs of tribal religion and normative codified Hinduism'.[18] Without losing sight of these concepts and constructs, we emphasize here, however, the spatial separatedness and continuity expressed by the *tiṇais* in Tamil literature and by the terms *vana* and *kṣetra* and their religious, spiritual, economic, and social implications. This dichotomy of nature and culture in Indian terms is now steadily being replaced by an urban–rural dichotomy, city *versus* village.

In the past the *vana* was the realm of the tribals, and at the roots of much of Hinduism is the worship of the spirits of mountains, trees and animals, the *yakṣas*, snakes and their home, termite mounds, but also deified clan ancestors. The more the *kṣetra* spread into the *vana*, the more the tribal cults were integrated by an exceedingly slow but steady process over centuries. As indicated, the assimilation of the tribal cults into the *kṣetra* meant only a transformation, but no abolition. They were reinterpreted in terms of the cults and rituals of the *kṣetra*. The unbound elements of nature became regulated through myths and different rituals which were handled by ritual experts. Such rituals found detailed elaboration in the Vedic rituals or e.g. in the *Pañcarātras*.[19] The *vana* had its ambivalence and ambiguous values as seen from the *kṣetra*: it might be considered deadly, chaotic, primordial, full of *bhūtas*, *daityas*, and *rakṣasas*, but it also had very much its positive values. It was the source of the creation and renewal of life. The burning place, the *śmaśāna*, is sometimes compared with the forest. In Tamil *kāṭu* means forest as well as *śmaśāna*. As from the ash of the slash-and-burn shifting cultivation, once widely practised by tribes, new life and a crop is born, ash not only stands for death in Hinduism, but is also a symbol of fertility.

Brahmanical themes of creation and the forest of the tribals as a source of creation and new life are not necessarily mutually exclusive. There is actually a close identity between the forest and the unmanifest *brahman* and the god Brahmā. Characteristically, fish, tortoise, and boar—*par excellence* animals of the forest and the tribals—are also originally forms of Prajāpati or Brahmā before they become linked with Viṣṇu and incorporated into the *daśāvatāras*. The *daśāvatāras* themselves imply the gradual movement from the *vana* to the *kṣetra*. The reasons and functions of Paraśurāma, Rāma and Kṛṣṇa are more intelligible in the context of the requirements of the *kṣetra*, e.g. saving the Brahmans from the flood of the Kṣatriyas (Paraśurāma), upholding *dharma* (Rāma), protecting or tending cattle and ploughing (Kṛṣṇa and Balarāma). As on a micro-cosmic level the *vana* is a source of renewal of life, and e.g. villagers periodically desert the village and migrate into the forest (see below), the cycle of the *yugas* comes to an end and people will take refuge in a life in the forest (*Viṣṇu Purāṇa* 4.24.25-9).

Already in the Vedic texts and in later Sanskrit literature we find the notion which associates *brahman* or *Brahmā* with the world tree and the origin of heaven and earth.[20] Brahmā is often associated with trees and forests, which also represent unmanifest origin and creation. The connection between forest, Brahmā and the tribals is evident in the origin of the famous cult of Brahmā in Pushkar, Rajasthan. It is told in the *Padma Purāṇa* (*Ādi*. II. 82) that Brahmā was attracted there by a forest near the present Pushkar. He entered the forest and all the trees were pleased about his arrival. They requested him to stay there for ever. He agreed to stay. Three lotus petals fell from his hand and became three sacred lakes. Pushkar is even today a pilgrimage and trade centre for many pastoral tribes, and their influence at the origin of the cult is still preserved in the *Padma Purāṇa*. When Brahmā wanted to perform a *yajña* on the full-moon day of the month of Kārttik (October/November), his wife Sāvitrī was absent, and as he could not perform the sacrifice without his wife, he married a girl of the pastoral Gujara tribe—according to local traditions—or a cowherdess (*gopabālikā*).[21] Her name was Gāyatrī.

The true and ideal Brahman as the human manifestation of *brahman* and Brahmā represents the uncontaminated primordial purity. Purity is thought indispensable in rituals, whether Vedic or non-Vedic. The purity of the Brahman can also be compared with the purity and innocence of a child. Thus human sacrifice often required an unmarried child as a victim. The sacrifice of children at the foundation of forts, etc., was a not so frequent, yet well-known example.

In the *Caritra* of the god Mhaskobā of Maharashtra we come across another example. The five *brahmacārī* grandsons of the founder of the cult were sacrificed on the god's demand to prove the sincerity (*sattva*) of his devotees.[22] When the heads were cut off, they miraculously turned into heads of sheep and the children remained unscathed. This reminds us of the replacement of the human victim by a he-goat in the Vedic *śrauta* ritual.[23] In classical mythology the head of the archetype-Brahman Dakṣa is replaced by the head of a he-goat or, especially in the legends of Karnataka and further South, by the head of a ram.[24] One of the reasons why Dakṣa was beheaded by the furious Śiva or Bhairava was the fact that Śiva was not invited for the *yajña*, or rather Dakṣa's blindness as to the true nature of Śiva. The beheading and replacing of the head by a ram's head amounts to a relapse of the Brahman Dakṣa into the primordial state of a *paśu*, here a ram belonging to the pastoral world. A similar case of relapse in folk religion is that of a certain Brahman who protected his fields with *mantras* which killed any intruder.[25] In this way a shepherd boy who stole some fruits was killed by the evil Brahman. The boy fell down from a tree and was killed. Ever since, the dead boy has been an object of worship. The evil Brahman, however, was metamorphosed into his primordial state of a *pipal* tree (*Ficus religiosa*) and is still worshipped as such in front of the temple of the boy god.[26]

In the *śrāddha* rites for the deceased ancestors, Brahmans officiate. In the *nukto* ancestral rite amongst the Bhils, however, the *vaha* acts as a Brahman or priest. The *vaha* is a male child from the clan of the dead person who gets possessed by the ancestral spirit. For this purpose he is invested like a Brahman with a sacred thread. In other words, because of its innocence the child's status is equivalent to that of a Brahman.[27] The innocence of a child-god is also connected with the primeval forest, and often the child-god is found in a forest or thicket, or in the *śmaśāna*, which is homologous to the forest. The most famous case is, of course, Skanda/ Kārttikeya, who was 'born in a thicket of reeds' (*śara-bhū*) on the bank of the river Gaṅgā. Birobā, the tutelary god of the shepherds (Dhangars) of Maharashtra, was born in the forest and found on a tree by two huntresses, who became his foster mothers.[28] His mother Suravantī was found in a golden casket in a termite mound.[29] The child Birobā or Vīrabhadra is also said to have been found on a *śmaśāna*, according to a Kannaḍa account.[30] The god Dhuḷobā, another Dhangar god, is said to have been found as a child in the ash of the Holī fire.[31] The story of Maturaivīran is very similar to that of Birobā. He was exposed as a child in the forest by a king and was found by an untouchable Cakkili woman who raised him with her husband.[32] The famous god Aiyanār similarly made his first appearance in the forest: the little child was found there by a king on a hunt.[33]

A very good example of the forest and the trees as a source of renewal is Lord Jagannātha, whose *mūrti* and those of Balabhadra and Subhadrā are again and again renewed (in the Navakalevara ritual) after a certain period of years by finding a tree from which the holy wood (*dāru*) is obtained for the new *mūrtis*. Meanwhile, the old deities are believed to be 'sick'. The rites after finding a suitable tree, the so-called 'forest sacrifice' (*vanayāga*), are designed to ward off the evil, which is associated with the forest, and to sanctify the tree. One important incident of the rituals is the conveying of the life-substance, *brahmapadārtha*, from the old *mūrtis* to the new ones.[34]

The tree, which stands for the abounding, exuberant, fertile and divine force of nature, is fashioned into the semi-anthropomorphic *mūrti* of Jagannātha, which still reminds us of its origin from the *vana*. The divine is now renewed, refined, and confined by rituals in the *mūrti* and the precincts of the temple. And though the *daitas* (*daityas*), as the tribals are called in Orissa, play an important role in the rituals, the divine is now primarily served by the expert *pūjā* of the *pujārīs*.

The 'higher', sophisticated, 'Sanskritic' ritual often has an irresistible appeal for those tribals who are in close contact with the world of the *kṣetra*. I recall an incident from Maharashtra. There is a famous temple of Mahādeva at Shingnapur in the Satara District. At the root of the cult were the Koḷīs, who were traditional tribesmen given to hunting and fishing and predatory activities, but were then reduced to ferrymen and water-carriers in the villages. When I asked one Koḷī why the *pūjā* went into the hands of the Brahmans, he answered without resentment: 'They asked us for the *pūjā* of the god. We gave them the *pūjā*. They gave us the cloth ring and said: "You are Koḷīs, take the cloth ring (Mar. *cumbaḷ*) and bring water to the temple".'

For the tribal, the tribal priest, especially the 'shaman', the *mūrti* is less important. He is still in much closer contact with nature than with culture, e.g. with animals of the forest which are identical with deities, or from which gods and ascetics derive their strength.[35] The 'shaman' may be possessed by a god, in fact, himself become the god, and he may also manipulate the forces of nature—which, from the point of view of the settled people of the *kṣetra*, accounts for his reputation as a sorcerer and magician.[36]

On the social level the *kṣetra* is marked by a more rigid, stratified social system. Life, seemingly unbounded and free in the forest prior to the impact of the *kṣetra* is brought into the social fold of the latter. Ideally, the king rules justly with the help of Brahmans and the Dharmaśāstra. Life in the *kṣetra*, in the 'nuclear areas of agriculture' (Burton Stein), in the *marutam* of the classical Tamil literature, was always more strict and hierarchical than in the pastoral area, the *vraja*, or the forest, *vana*. From the point of view of the settled people, who often use clichés and have their preconceived views about the tribal people, the normal rules of social behaviour did not apply in the *vana*. The rules were *anācāra* (or *niśācāra*), rather than *ācāra*. In the notion of the settled people, there was a relative freedom in the *vana*, often associated in poetry and religion with eroticism. Devī cults and tantricism developed in such a context, though we should not identify tribal fertility rites and games with the contents and aims of tantricism.[37]

Fertility rites associated with the tribes also play an important role on the tenth day of the Durgotsava, and the festival is accordingly called *śabarotsava*. The Śabaras were supposed to be a mountain tribe in the Deccan, but by extension the name was applied to any tribe. The ritual involved *inter alia* sexuality, music, dance, auspicious dance and rivalry, and obscene ritual language. All social barriers were to be abandoned on that day.[38] There was also the common dance of the tribal boys and girls in the forest, like the famous marriage dance of the Māḍiyas of Bastar. In the pastoral area (*Vraja* = Braj) we have the *rāsa* dance of the *gopīs* with the *gopas* and with Kṛṣṇa. The dance of the pastoral people and the love-play between Kṛṣṇa and the *gopīs* was gradually absorbed by the settled society in a sublimated way, often turned into philosophy. Many of the Bhakti cults, like the Kṛṣṇa cult itself, sprang up in a pastoral surrounding and atmosphere. Behind this was also the instinctive feeling that the tribals had more readily direct access to the divine, because living in the forest they had retained their innocence, whereas the life and the rituals of the *kṣetra* may apparently turn empty, insipid, and sick.

In the classical Sanskrit texts we find the forest often considered as impure and dangerous or, shall we say, unrefined, and the tribals as cruel and ignorant. But at the same time they are also viewed as innocent and their ignorance gives them more direct access to the divine than the strenuous ritual efforts in the *kṣetra*. There is the famous story of Śabarī, a woman of a tribe of forest-dwellers, who offered berries to Rāma which she had already tasted. Rāma unhesitatingly accepted what was actually from the point of view of the *kṣetra* impure.[39] And there is the other famous story of the king of the Niṣādas—Sundarasenaka—who inadvertently worshipped Śiva by his acts. Śiva abducted the hunter from the army of Yama, taking both the hunter and his dog to Śivaloka.[40] Let me cite an instance from Maharashtra told by a shepherd belonging to the great pastoral Dhangar community of Maharashtra. Traditionally their beliefs and rituals centre around their ancestors and a clan god like Birobā who may have been a deified ancestor. How did the gods come to the Dhangars? How did a god manifest himself among them? These were my questions. And the shepherd told me the following story:

A Brahman went daily to the river to perform his *sandhyā*. He first took a bath, performed his *sandhyā*, and this he did every day. It was in the *satyayuga*. There was also a simple, honest, (*bhoḷā*) Dhangar. He saw the Brahman, who held his nose, dived into the water, came up, dived again and so on. When the Dhangar saw this, he decided to ask the Brahman: 'Uncle, *why* do you *do* so?'—'Well, my boy, I worship the god and when I worship him, the god appears.'—'Is that true?'—'Definitely', the Brahman said and went away. The Dhangar, being simple-minded, *bhoḷā*, told himself: 'Worshipping thus means holding nose and mouth closed and diving into the water.' That was in his opinion the meaning of the words of the Brahman. He jumped into the water, closing his mouth and holding his nose. He sank down and down and was about to get drowned. The god was in a difficulty. 'That Dhangar will kill himself, if I don't show myself.' And when the Dhangar was about to die the god appeared: a real *avatāra* of Viṣṇu, with four arms. 'Leave your nose, you mad fellow, I am the god!' he said. The Dhangar emerged. 'Are you the god?' he asked, 'I am not sure. How can I be sure?'—'Now that I have shown myself to you, you are not sure?'—'No', he said, 'unless the Brahman comes and says, "That is, indeed, the god", I shall not let go of my nose. And thus I shall die. And the blame will be on the god. But I shall go to the Brahman and fetch him.' The god said: 'I have come to show myself to you and not to the Brahman.'—'Well and good. I shall be drowned', answered the Dhangar, 'That is not nice of you', said the god, 'you will die. Better go and fetch the Brahman'.—'You are sending me away to fetch the Brahman', said the Dhangar, 'and when I return, you will be away and off'. It was a simple-minded kind of bhakti. He tied the god to a tree with his turban and ran to fetch the Brahman. 'Uncle', he said, 'the god has come, and whether he is the god or somebody else, you will have to make out for me.' The Brahman said: 'Twelve years have passed, I have closed my mouth and nose and dived into the water and never saw the god anywhere. You have not even touched the water and you mean to say the god has shown himself to you?'—'Yes, indeed', said he, 'I have tied him to a tree.'—'Just don't talk nonsense'.—'No, it is true.' He went along with the Brahman and there it was: the four-armed *mūrti* of Viṣṇu Mahāraja. The Brahman touched his feet in devotion. 'It is the bhakti of the Dhangar which allowed me to see god.' The god said to the Dhangar: 'Because of your bhakti I have shown myself to the Brahman and you. Whatever you wish, I shall grant to you.' But the Dhangar was simple, *bhoḷā*. He said: 'What can you possibly give which I do not already have? I have plenty—four brothers, mother, father, wife, children, 100 sheep—what more could you possibly give to me? I wish that you will daily come to our sheep-pen and have some milk.' The god promised to do that. . . .

Many points of profound meaning are hidden in this seemingly simple story, which comes not from the manuscript of a learned Brahman, but from the vast unwritten oral literature of the pastoral tribes. It is not the complicated, unintelligible ritual of the Brahman, but the simple bhakti of a shepherd from the pastoral area, which makes the god appear.[41] Yet, the more sophisticated Brahman is necessary to identify and interpret the god to the tribal. The simplicity and exigency of the Dhangar is shown in his lack of demands or desires for more and more material wealth. But that characteristic feature the tribal shares with the true and ideal Brahman.

The forest was also the place for the *āśrama* of the Ṛṣis, and Sanskrit *kāvya* literature abounds in descriptions of the *vana* and *upavana*. Here we find a longing for beauty which was echoed in the German *Romantik* and its sympathy for the forest. The forest is also the abode of the ascetic, the renouncer of *saṃsāra*, of worldly life in the *kṣetra*. The dangers and deprivations of *vanavāsa*, of the life in the forest or on mountains, and the direct access to the divine attracted the ascetic to perform *tapas*. The typical example is the ascetic sitting in or on a termite mound. This was not just a self-torturous feat, but also an attempt to deflect something of the unbounded forces of nature, to acquire supernatural powers, *siddhis*, or even enlightenment. The termite mound was an epitome of that unbounded nature of the forest, a very old symbol of the primordial mound and of creation.[42] It is also in a termite mound that often a divinity first appeared to a tribal and was first worshipped by him, to become eventually the object of a famous cult.

In the wilderness the normal rules of *saṃsāra* were not applicable from the point of view of the settled people, and it was thus the natural abode of the ascetic, the renouncer of *saṃsāra*. Even the saint who lived amidst society normally had an often recurring phase in his spiritual development during which he had his *vanavāsa*, if only this meant *vanavāsa* metaphorically speaking.

A typical reaction of a *bhakta* saint and poet to the forest as a place of contemplation is that of the Maharashtrian Tukārām:[43]

Trees, creepers, and the creatures of the forest
Are our kith and kin—
As are birds that sing.
These are the things
That give solitude its wholesome flavour
We are touched by neither good nor evil.
The sky is our canopy
The earth our throne
It is here that our mind enjoys itself alone.
A sack-cloth and a bowl take care of our needs
And the wind
Tells us the time.
It is here that we feast
On the lore of Hari[44]
Course after delicious course.
Says Tukā, the mind
Can converse with itself:
The self is an argument
Unto itself.

In the forest, unity and renewal of life are achieved in many respects on many levels. In Maharashtra the inhabitants of a village periodically move into the forest to have a communal dinner, the *vanabhojana*, or the assembled village used to periodically desert the village and jointly worship the *bhūtas* and deities outside the village (*gāvsaī*).[45] The saint like Tukārām may experience in the forest the unity of all life.

Often the renouncer of *saṃsāra* may join others in an—alas futile—attempt to return to tribal primordiality, communal life and customs. This involves also the return to the simpler life of food gathering and begging.[46] Thus, e.g. the Mahānubhāva sect of Maharashtra, which originated in the thirteenth century, evolved rules in this respect:[47] one should give up one's country, relatives, and village (*Sūtrapāṭha, Ācāra* 1), at the border of one's country one should spend one's life under a tree (*Sūtrapāṭha, Ācāra* 26), one should be in a (tribal) hamlet (*hāḷi* or *pāḷi*), not in a town (*pura*) or city (*pāṭaṇ*. *Sūtrapāṭha, Ācāra Mālīkā* 20), one should sleep outside the village in a dilapidated shrine and so on.

It was in the forest, away from settled society, that the Buddhist monk, the Brahman *vānaprastha*, the *samnyāsin*, the Śaivite *Gosāvī*, and the Liṅgāyat *virakta* could have those spiritual insights and revelations which caused them to formulate principles of universal application. The *daṇḍakāraṇya* or *daṇḍakavana* is said to be the quintessence of the world and the seed of *dharma* and *mukti* in the *Brahmapurāṇa* (129.55; 161.73). It was in the realm of the renouncer living away from the society that consequently *sādhāraṇa dharmas* like *ahiṃsā, dama, dayā, satya, akrodha*, and *ārjavam* could be conceived and from this realm that the *sādhāraṇa dharmas* emanated to make the rigidity of life and caste *dharma* in the settled society in the past tolerable and even worth living. *Ahiṃsā*, for example, was a *sādhāraṇa dharma* born in the forest among ascetics and saints. They were the protectors of animals, living in harmony with them, and they turned against 'ecocide'. The most famous example is that of Vālmīki, the erstwhile robber, who was significantly 'redeemed' and gained his inspiration to compose the *Rāmāyaṇa* by his *tapas* in a termite mound.[48] Later he cursed a Niṣāda hunter who killed a male curlew (*krauñca*) in front of its grief-stricken female partner.[49] Thus the Dharmaśāstras and the bhakti poetry of the saints amalgamated these ethical principles derived from the experience of ascetics and saints and their philosophical insights, which were ultimately related to achieving *mokṣa*, or union with God.[50]

One of the great integrators of the *vana* and the *kṣetra* in mythology and ritual was, of course, Śiva, with his manifold manifestations. These manifestations were ubiquitous, latent and ever-present, not descending from time to time when *dharma* was in danger, as in the case of Viṣṇu. Viṣṇu was always more on the side of the settled people, looking after law and order and often treated as if he were an established, ideal king.[51] His ritual purity made him more acceptable to Brahmans. Kṛṣṇa, the outlandish Gopāla god, was only slowly absorbed by Viṣṇu and Vaiṣṇavism.

Narasiṃha, to whom Anncharlott Eschmann has traced much of what has gone into the Jagannātha cult, is an *avatāra* who has many features which connect him with the world of the *vana*, and perhaps with a Śaivite type of divinity. In Maharashtra, at least, he seems to have been a *yakṣa* or a *bhūta* originally, belonging to a circle of 52 *bhūtas* or *vīras* with whom one would rather associate Śiva than Viṣṇu. Perhaps the very fact that he appears as half a man and half an animal may indicate his belonging to both worlds. In many places in Andhra he is *girija*, hill-born,[52] and, incidentally, he shares similar epithets connected with 'mountain' with Rudra, Śiva, and Murukaṉ. There are beautiful oral legends in Andhra which associate Narasiṃha with the tribe of the Ceñcūs living in the Eastern Ghāts, or e.g. in Madduleti, near Betamcherla in the Kurnool District. It is told there that the king of the Ceñcūs had only one daughter, called Ceñcū Lakṣmī. She used to go hunting with a bow and arrows in the forest. One day she saw a lion and shot him: from the dying lion the beautiful Narasiṃha arose. They fell in love with each other and Narasiṃha wanted to marry her. Ceñcū Lakṣmī wanted to see whether he was a suitable husband and put him to some tests, e.g. climbing trees, jumping over the river, collecting wild honey and finding a golden, life-bringing insect in a termite mound.[53]

If we go to Ahobilam in the Kurnool District we find the same association of Narasiṃha with the tribals. The original cult is in the mountains where there is a rude primitive stone worshipped as Narasiṃha. The temple is built in the Vijayanagara style and has a rather touching sculptural scene: it shows a huge Ceñcū Lakṣmī as a huntress with a bow. She wears a leaf skirt. Before her crouches a miniature Narasiṃha, who removes a thorn from the sole of her foot. Narasiṃha in this temple up in the hills (Eguva Ahobilam), is supposed to be *ugra*. In the much greater and more elaborate temple complex in the plains below (Diguva Ahobilam), where he eventually appeared, he is *saumya*.

The Vedic Rudra or Śiva with his polymorphic manifestations was originally beyond the brahmanical fold and the *kṣetra*. Nor was he originally, strictly speaking, a god of the forest tribals like the Goṇḍs. Perhaps the identification of the 'Highest Being' (Bhagavān, Pharsa Pen, Bārā Deo, Devaru Moi'tto) amongst the Goṇḍs with Śiva/Mahādeva (Śrī Śambhu Mahādeva) has been favoured by their common origin as mountain gods, often connected with the sun.[54] Rudra was thus, so to speak, between the *vana* and the *kṣetra* and was in contact with *all* communities, from the highest to the lowest. It was he who could hold the two different ecological, cultural and religious areas together. Negatively this is expressed in his antagonism to the Brahmans, culminating in the famous myth of the destruction of Dakṣa's sacrifice. On the other hand, one of his manifestations is the *kṣetrapāla*, and he is the protector of Brahmans. He lives on the border between *vana* and *kṣetra*.

It is common to identify, at least partially, the outlandish *rākṣasa*, *asura*, or *daitya* who infests the *vana*, with the god who is victorious over him. The *rākṣasa* and the like thus become a source of protection.[55] Rudra/Śiva is himself of demonic and outlandish origins as seen from the point of view of the people in the brahmanical *kṣetra*. According to the *Śatarudrīya*, he is Lord of all sorts of social groups with a dubious reputation.[56] But nevertheless he becomes a source of protection and a *kṣetrapāla*. The *rākṣasas* may be killed by him, but they may gain *mukti*, continue to live on his name, like Mallāri(see below), become his gate-keepers,[57] support his throne,[58] or continue to exist in an independent, but somewhat inferior cult.[59] On the social level 'criminal tribes' like the Rāmośīs, Beḍars, and Kaḷḷars may—apart from being special devotees of the god and having special privileges in festivals—be turned into watchmen of villages, fields and forts and be assigned police functions.[60]

The *rākṣasas* came from the realm of the *yakṣas* or *bhūtas*. The latter in turn were often identified with outlandish people like hunting tribes or pastoral groups.[61] In the Deccan the tribes are often linked with Mallāri. Mallāri, the enemy of Malla, is an *avatāra* of Śiva who is called Khaṇḍobā in Maharashtra, Mallaṇṇa in Andhra, and Mailār in Karnataka. He is also called Mārtaṇḍa Bhairava. In an inscription of the year AD 1369 in Sanskrit and Telugu from Aiṇavolu near Warangal, it is narrated that god Śiva, in order to protect Arjuna, assumed the form of a hunter (Śabara), fought with the demon Malla and killed him, thus acquiring the name Mallāri.[62] Mallāri is worshipped by pastoral communities with a hunting background, by traditional fishing and hunting tribes like the Koḷīs, by ex-robbers like the Rāmośīs, and also by higher communities like Liṅgāyats, Marāṭhās and even Brahmans. But who is Malla? Already the Roman writer Plinius mentions the Malli tribe, in whose territory the mount Mallus is located. In Tamil, *Mallan* means a wrestler or an important personage. In Karnataka, the *malla*, the chief wrestler in a village, is often from the Kuruba shepherd community. In the *Mārtaṇḍa Vijaya* Malla is depicted as a great king of the *daityas*.[63] 'Malla' is very often an epithet for historical royal personalities in South India who are described as great heroes (*vīras*) and may have been demonized for following the custom of cattle-raids and kidnapping women.[64] But as Śiva/Khaṇḍobā is connatural with practically every-body, the defeated Malla was turned into a *bhakta* and became one with Khaṇḍobā, achieving *sayujyatā*.[65] Thus the outlandish demon was incorporated into the cult.

David Shulman has recently shown the ambivalent position of the South Indian predatory communities like the Kaḷḷars, Maravars, and

Eyinārs, who may in turn function as watchmen of fields, villages and towns.[66] They were given a 'recognized place, both geographically and socially'.[67] The home area of such groups, as we have seen, was the *mullai* or *kuriñci*, the pastoral area and the forested mountainous area which turned into *pālai* in the hot season. That the *tiṇai* concept can be applied to the religious, social, and economic conditions in other corresponding areas of the Deccan and specifically of Maharashtra has been already suggested. Shulman's material offers further possibilities for comparison. A very short summary of these correspondences with Maharashtra may not lead us astray. The South Indian robber communities correspond to those of the Rāmośīs and Koḷīs in Maharashtra. The Rāmośīs were called Beḍars/ Berāḍs and traditionally inhabited an area which is pastoral and prone to famines. The area covers the famine tract with little rainfall eastward of Pune and reaches right into Karnataka into the Rayalaseema.[68] The Koḷīs (Mahādev Koḷīs and Malhār Koḷīs) are found in the same area, but also in the densely forested Western Ghāts. On the other hand both communities had a tendency to become agriculturist Kuṇbīs (Marāṭhās), a fact which corresponds to the closeness of the Kaḷḷars with the agricultural Veḷālars. We may remember that even *mullai* cultivation (of millet) was practised. We also find in Maharashtra the association of Vālmīki with Vālhā, near Jejuri, Pune District, where he is said to have waylaid merchants. There are two etymologies for the term 'Rāmośī'. It is derived from *rānvāsī*, i.e. 'inhabitants of an uncultivable area', forest, which corresponds to the Tamil notion of *marakkuṭi* = 'wild, predatory communities', as contrasted with the *arakkuṭi* or 'settled agriculturists'.[69] 'Rāmośī' has also been etymologically connected with *Rāma+vaṃśi*, i.e. 'descendants of Rāma', whom he created on his way to Laṅkā.[70] Here we recognize the connection of Vālmīki and the Rāmośīs and Beḍars who claim to have descended from the Vālmīki-Gotra.[71] The close association of bandits with kings and the recruitment of kings from the ranks of the bandits in South India may be seen reflected in the fact that Beḍars became *jāgīrdārs* and kings.[72] At least one of the most famous Marāṭhā families is said to have this predatory background. One of the most famous heroes amongst the Rāmośīs was Umājī Nāīk, a 'Sardār' who was hanged by the British in 1832.[73] The 'pastoral area' in Maharashtra was also marked by cattle raids and numerous hero-stones depicting such raids; this corresponds to the Tamil *veṭcittiṇai*, where the distinction between cattle-thief and hero fades.[74] The god of the Rāmośīs is Khaṇḍobā, who has close similarities with Aiyanār and Ka<u>r</u>uppa<u>n</u>, the favourite god of the Kaḷḷars.[75] Ka<u>r</u>uppa<u>n</u> is a violent, non-vegetarian deity who corresponds to Malla, the hill-demon who raids the *āśrama* of the Brahman and is defeated by Śiva/Khaṇḍobā. He subsequently becomes a *bhakta* and doorkeeper—*dvārapāla*—of Khaṇḍobā.[76] The human counterparts of Malla, the Rāmośīs, have a special right to carry the palanquin at the hunting excursion of the God to the river on the Somavatī Amāvasyā day.[77] This may be compared to the Kaḷḷars' special right to pull their god's car. Khaṇḍobā becomes the Lord of 52 *vīras*, all demonic godlings, whom he includes and excels. His most important temple is in Jejuri and is situated on an old route to the South, near the area associated with Vālmīki-Koḷī. The victims of Vālmīki and the Rāmośīs are said to have been caravan merchants travelling on that route. Malla himself is described as the waylayer (*mārgaghna*) who harasses the traveller (*mārgasthā*) in one version of the *Mallāri-Māhātmya*, before being defeated by Khaṇḍobā.[78]

Equally important as the killing of the *daitya* for the integration of the *vana* is the fact that Khaṇḍobā/Mallāri and many similar gods in South India have two wives through whom they combine heterogeneous communities with different spatial and ecological backgrounds. One wife belongs to the settled agricultural/merchant community and has a 'Sanskritic' affiliation. The other wife belongs to a hill/forest/pastoral tribe. Thus the second wife of Murukaṉ is Vaḷḷi from the Kuravar hill tribe. The first wife is Devasena, the Divine Army, or Teyvayānai, the Elephant. Khaṇḍobā's second wife, Bāṇa in Andhra, comes from the Gollas, Mailār in Karnataka has his second wife from the Kuruba shepherd community. In Śrīśailam there is the legend that it was Lord Śiva who once came on a hunting expedition and fell in love with a beautiful Ceñcū woman, whom he married. Even today Śiva is known among the Ceñcūs as Ceñcū Malliah and the members of the tribe have special privileges in the cult. In the case of Khaṇḍobā the first wife is Mhāḷsā, said to be from the Liṅgāyat community, which was once very influential all over the Deccan. Mhāḷsā is still found as an independent goddess.

The second wife thus comes from the forest—the forest being associated with eroticism. The second wife is consequently usually the really beloved of the god. Vaḷḷi stands for *iccai*, passion, love, emotion, and ultimately bhakti. But the second wife also symbolizes unbounded nature, like Gaṅgā, whom Śiva catches and regulates with his matted hair. The first wife, like Teyvayānai and Pārvatī, represents *karma*, action.[79] One may say that the god combines heaven and earth by means of his two wives, one of whom is of fair and one of dark complexion, but at the same time I want to stress that behind these wives there were and still are concrete communities in different stages of development and with different ecological backgrounds which could thus be integrated in one cult.

Very often the god manifests himself for the first time amongst the tribals in the forest and is identified with Śiva or one of his manifestations.[80] There is a very widespread story that a cowherd finds a cow letting milk flow into a termite mound where the god is hidden and eventually manifests himself. When we view Kṛṣṇa Gopāla historically, that is Kṛṣṇa-Govardhana of the Ābhīras, and not the Kṛṣṇa of the Yādavas and the *Bhagavadgitā*,[81] we have the same phenomenon. 'This Govardhana is but an anthill', says one of the antagonists of Kṛṣṇa in the *Harivaṃśa*. The Kṛṣṇa who saved the cattle and the Ābhīra cowherds, was, as Ch. Vaudeville has shown, originally a spirit of the mountain, simultaneously living amongst the cowherds in human form. Thus we read in the famous passage of the *Harivaṃśa*: Upon the summit of Govardhana, Kṛṣṇa presented himself saying: 'I am the manifestation of the mountain (*śailo 'ham iti mūrtimān*)', and he partook of much food presented by the Gopas; whilst in his own form as Kṛṣṇa (*svenaiva Kṛṣṇo rūpeṇa*) he ascended the hill along with the cowherds and worshipped his other self. . . .[82]

Local traditions in Govardhana on which the *vārtās* of the Vaiṣṇavas are based say that Kṛṣṇa lived in the mountain in the form of a snake. The pastoral tribes in Braj are still unaware of much of the later Brahmanical and Vaiṣṇava mythology. And, as the Vaiṣṇava *vārtās* narrate, it was only when Caitanya and the Vaiṣṇava Goswāmīs came from Bengal that Kṛṣṇa manifested himself again in his full form. First only his hand and arm emerged from the mountain top, resembling a five-hooded snake. This is said to have happened on the Nāgapañcamī day—a rather unsanskritic festival—when serpents in termite mounds are worshipped in many parts of India.[83] But for the Vaiṣṇavization of Kṛṣṇa, the central focus of the Vaiṣṇava Bhakti movement, this god or *yakṣa* of the pastoralists might have become another manifestation of Śiva.

The Bhakti movement was itself a kind of protest against empty ritual, the *karmakāṇḍa* of the *Dharmaśāstra*, and the tiresomeness of settled life in the *kṣetra*. At the root was the realization that this god living in an outlying area of hills, woods, and pastures, in the free atmosphere of the tribal world, was a god of immediate access and spontaneous love.[84] Many deities thus have their origin in the wilderness, on a mountain, in an anthill, often as a *svayambhū* manifestation of Śiva or as some mother goddess. Mostly the god passes through a Śaivite phase, turning eventually into a Vaiṣṇava god.

In Tirupati, the famous Veṅkaṭeśvara is Viṣṇu, who had hidden himself in a termite mound and was discovered by cowherds. Afterwards Viṣṇu, having absented himself from Lakṣmī, falls in love with Padmāvatī while on a hunt in a forest and marries her.[85] Padmāvatī is often considered to be a *yakṣī*, who lives in the forest and is worshipped by tribals. It is said that Viṣṇu in Tirupati acquired land from Varāha, and up to this day one has to visit Varāha first before one goes to Veṅkaṭeśvara. Varāha cannot be just an earlier *avatāra* of Viṣṇu, but respect is paid to an earlier deity of the tribals.

Let us consider the famous Pāṇḍuraṅga or Viṭhobā of Pandharpur in Maharashtra. He emerged in a pastoral tribal context in which Gavḷīs (cowherds) and Koḷīs (fishermen, hunters, and eventually ferrymen) dominated. The pastoral communities preserve in their oral traditions the idea that Padubāī/Padmāvatī was Viṭhobā's wife before Padmāvatī became Rukmiṇī. Some would say that Padmāvatī 'has come from the forest', as in Tirupati.[86] It is rather well established that the Viṭhobā cult emerged from a Śaiva cult and that Pandharpur was essentially a Śaivite *kṣetra* before it was 'Vaiṣṇavized'. Besides, a famous goddess called Mhasā/Masādevi (Andhra: Mhaisāmma) = 'Mother Buffalo' was said to be the original goddess. She is identified with Lakhubāī, and the two goddesses have their shrines in the Diṇḍīravana. In fact the original cult spot in Pandharpur is this 'forest of (the Daitya) Diṇḍīra'. It was Śiva, the *nāyaka* of the Kailāsa, who is said to have assumed the form of Mallikārjuna and to have killed the Daitya Diṇḍīra in the forest, thus purifying the ground for Vaiṣṇava bhakti.[87]

It is also said, in the *Līḷācaritra* of Cakradhara (thirteenth century), that originally Viṭhobā was a hero who died defending cattle and that a hero-stone (*bhaḍakhambā*, Skt. *bhaṭaskambhā*) was erected in his honour and people started worshipping it.[88] This reminds us again of the Caṅkam literature, and the traditional pastoral atmosphere surrounding Pandharpur may be compared with the old Tamil *mullai*. The *mullai* is associated with Māyōṉ, corresponding to Kṛṣṇa. But, according to *Puram.* 335, people in the *mullai* region originally worshipped only hero-stones as their gods.[89] In *Puram.* 265 it is said that the cowherds worshipped a hero-stone with garlands made from the flowers of the *veṅkai* tree.[90] In another passage a bard is asked by a nomad (?) to worship a hero-stone, as benefit will accrue from this (*Puram.* 263). Bards passing the hero-stones should sing the favourite songs of the hero (*Malaipaṭukaṭām* 378-91).[91] Ultimately Vaiṣṇava bhakti discovered and transformed hero and god and Pandharpur became famous for its festival of bhakti in honour of Viṭhobā marked by music and dance (*naḍanācu*, Skt. *naṭanṛtya*), according to the *Līḷācaritra* of Cakradhara.[92]

The bhakti poet with his poetry must have been a successor of the bard mentioned in the old Caṅkam literature. He transformed and reinterpreted the earlier cults and the beliefs associated with them. The erotic sentiments, the dance, and the love between Murukan̲ and Vaḷḷi, or Māyōn̲/Kṛṣṇa and the *gopīs*, were transformed into the sacred sentiments of bhakti.[93] In the case of Viṭhobā the memory that there once was a forest at Pandharpur—a forest naturally being infested by ghosts (*bhūtas*) and spirits (*vīras*)—seems to linger on in one of the *abhaṅgas* of Tukārāma on Viṭhobā. It is given a new meaning by him in the context of bhakti:

> There is a powerful ghost (*bhūta*) in Paṇḍharī.
> It seizes the visitors on their way.
> While going into the forest full of imps
> The mind goes mad.
> Nobody should go there.
> Those who have gone, have not come back.
> Tukā went to Paṇḍharī
> And did not come back to the world (*janma*).[94]

Pandharpur was situated not only in a pastoral-tribal area, but also at the periphery of Maharashtra and Karnataka. What Victor Turner would call 'a centre out there', the natural goal of pilgrims, is also a place which had its origin in the *vana*.[95] Twice every year, in the month of Āṣāḍha (July/August) and in the month of Kārttik (October/November), the pilgrims of the Vārkarī tradition, the Vaiṣṇava *bhaktas* of Viṭhobā, go on pilgrimage to this place they call 'city of the saints'. Their traditional route must have already been frequented by prehistoric tribal populations, according to D.D. Kosambi.[96] And, as if basing it on the spirit of an equalitarian tribal life, the pilgrims annually achieve a kind of *communitas*, that is, basically an equalitarian relationship between persons without status or property.

Pandharpur became a holy *kṣetra* with affiliations to the *Padma Purāṇa*.[97] And Śrīdhara, the famous *paṇḍit* and poet, composed a *Sthalamāhātmya* in Marāṭhī, the famous *Pāṇḍuraṅgamāhātmya*.[98] Thus, as in the cult of Jagannātha, we have many layers in the history of the Pandharpur *kṣetra*, all happily co-existing even today: the pastoral-tribal background with its earlier component of a proclivity to cattle-raids, a famous *devī*, Śaivism, the Vaiṣṇava bhakti, and the Māhātmya of a Brahman *paṇḍit* and poet.

The instances could be multiplied to illustrate the dichotomy, or rather 'symbiotic continuity' (Zvelebil), from *vana* to *kṣetra*. With the slow spread of the *kṣetra* and the reduction of the *vana*—whether we take this in the spatial, spiritual, religious, sociological or ecological sense—tribes were reduced to castes and assigned a place in the hierarchical system of the *kṣetra*. The direct access to and experience of the divine in untamed nature became ritualized on a Sanskritic, Hinduized normative pattern. The impure and dangerous became ritually pure and pacified. Local traditions and oral literature gave way to some extent to the literate Sanskritic culture or bhakti poetry. But this was an extremely slow process, stretching over many, many centuries. There was always the natural barrier of the forest.

The forest was certainly not yet an object of commercial exploitation at the cost of the tribals. Today the tribals are much more exposed to middle-class rules and notions than before. We are told by anthropologists that tribal youths exposed to the Western/urban culture are alienated from their society and apologetic about their own culture: 'They are spiritually lost, miserable proletarians.'[99] In other words: the so-called 'Great Tradition' of India, the *kṣetra* with its Sanskrit culture, owed much to the little communities of the tribes with their stupendous oral literature, myths, symbols, arts, religion and worldview. The tribal world of the forest harboured universal values and was in tune with nature, a fact which traditional Indian society, itself not having lost touch with nature, acknowledged, but modern society rapidly forgets.

NOTES

1. See e.g. A. Eschmann, 'Hinduization of Tribal Deities in Orissa, the Śākta and Śaiva Typology', in Anncharlott Eschmann, Hermann Kulke, and Gaya Charan Tripathi (eds.), *The Cult of Jagannāth and the Regional Tradition of Orissa*, Delhi, 1978, pp. 78ff, 85. For a philosophical interpretation see G.C. Tripathi, 'Jagannātha: The Ageless Deity of the Hindus', in: Anncharlott Eschmann etc. (eds.), *The Cult of Jagannāth . . .*, Ch. XXV. Id., 'The Influence of Some Philosophical Systems on the Mode of Worship of Kṛṣṇa-Jagannātha', in *Zeitschrift für Religions-und Geistesgeschichte*, 27 (1975), pp. 206-21.
2. D.D. Kosambi, *History and Civilization of Ancient India in Historical Outline*, London, 1965, p. 22. Cited by Pupul Jayakar in *The Earthen Drum: An Introduction to the Ritual Arts of Rural India*, National Museum, New Delhi, 1981, p. viii.
3. Paul Hacker, 'Religiöse Toleranz und Intoleranz im Hinduismus', in: Lambert Schmithausen (ed.), *Paul Hacker, Kleine Schriften*, Wiesbaden, 1978, pp. 376ff. Cp. R. Burghart, 'Hierarchical Models of the Hindu Social System', in *Man* (N.S.), vol. 13, pp. 519-36.
4. See Agehananda Bharati, 'Hinduism and Modernization', in: Robert F. Spencer (ed.), *Religion and Change in Contemporary Asia*, Minnesota/Bombay, 1971, pp. 94f. 'Superstition' is paraphrased as 'misdirected popular belief' and translated into Marathi as *dharma-bhoḷepaṇā*, in *The Little Modern Dictionary* (English-English-Marathi) by K. Bh. Virkar. *Bhoḷā* has traditionally a rather

positive religious connotation, i.e. 'simple', 'undesigning', and 'unsuspecting'. Molesworth, *Marathi-English Dictionary*, s.v.

5. Sitakant Mahapatra, 'The Tribal World and the Small Community', in *New Quest*, 15 (May-June 1979), pp. 133ff., at p. 139.
6. P.T. Srinivasa Iyengar, *History of the Tamils from the Earliest Times to 600 AD*, Madras, 1960, p. 60.
7. It often happened in the Deccan that a group of intruders in an area took up the occupations and the religious beliefs of their predecessors, adjusting themselves to the social, religious and economic conditions of their new environment. See D.D. Kosambi, *Myth and Reality*, Bombay, 1961, p. 110; Günther-Dietz Sontheimer, *Birobā, Mhaskobā und Khaṇḍobā. Ursprung, Geschichte und Umwelt von pastoralen Gottheiten in Mahārāṣṭra*, Wiesbaden, 1976, pp. 103ff. [Editor's note: English version: *Pastoral Deities in Western India*, New York, 1989, pp. 104ff. (trans. Anne Feldhaus).]
8. The outline is based on Sontheimer, op. cit., pp. 16ff [= *Pastoral Deities* . . ., pp. 11ff.] For further details one may refer to Kamil Zvelebil, *The Smile of Murugan: On Tamil Literature of South India*, Leiden, 1973, pp. 85ff. Idem, 'The Beginnings of Bhakti in South India', in *Temenos*, vol. 13 (1977), pp. 223-57. George L. Hart III, *The Poems of Ancient Tamil: Their Milieu and Their Sanskrit Counterparts*, Univ. of California Press, Berkeley, 1975, pp. 211ff.
9. *Śatarudrīya*, *Taittirīya-saṃhitā*, 4.5.
10. See George L. Hart III, op. cit., p. 19. Such distinctions are ubiquitous in the Deccan. Cp. the Marathi term *jivāyat* for land that may be used for rainfed crops, in distinction from *bāgāyat* for gardenland.
11. N. Subrahmanian, *Pre-Pallavan Tamil Index*, Madras, 1966, s.v.
12. J.F. Sprockhoff, 'Āraṇyaka und Vānaprastha in der vedischen Literatur', in *WZKS*, XXV (1981), pp. 19ff, pp. 43, 84.
13. Sometimes there may be plough cultivation instead of shifting cultivation in the *vana*. Thus the Gonds of Andhra Pradesh raise millet crops by plough cultivation with bullocks, but their magical harvest rituals and their legends do not refer to the plough. Christoph von Fürer-Haimendorf, *The Gonds of Andhra Pradesh*, New Delhi, 1979, pp. 444ff.
14. See Louis Dumont, *Homo Hierarchicus*, London, 1970, p. 195 and fn. 96c.
15. See Irawati Karve, *Maharashtra—Land and Its People, Maharashtra State Gazetteer*, Bombay, 1968, pp. 64ff., 67.
16. See W. Rau, *Staat und Gesellschaft im alten Indien nach den Brāhmaṇa-Texten dargestellt*, Wiesbaden, 1957, pp. 51ff.
17. See the discussion in A. Eschmann, 'Hinduization of Tribal Deities in Orissa. . .', pp. 79ff. see also S. Gupta, 'Modes of Worship and Meditation', in *Hindu Tantrism*, Leiden, Köln, 1979, pp. 127ff., on normative (*smārta*) Hindu rituals, cited by K.V. Zvelebil, *The Irula (Erla) Language*, pt. III, *Irula Lore, Texts and Translations*, Wiesbaden, 1982, p. 131.
18. Zvelebil, ibid.
19. For the ritualization of nature in Tamil temples see e.g. David Dean Shulman, *Tamil Temple Myths, Sacrifice and Divine Marriage in South Indian Śaiva*

Tradition, Princeton, 1980, pp. 26f. For the elimination of Death as a rival in the classical *śrauta yajña*, see J.C. Heesterman, 'Brahman, Ritual and Renouncer', in *WZKSO*, VIII (1964), pp. 1-31.

20. See J. Deppert, *Rudras Geburt. Systematische Untersuchungen zum Inzest in der Mythologie der Brāhmaṇas*, Wiesbaden, 1977, p. 88. *Taittirīya Brāhmaṇa* II.8.9.6 (ASS, Poona, 1898). According to the *Brahmāṇḍapurāṇa* IX.110, Brahmā lived in the forest and was born as a tree. See also K.R. van Kooij, *Worship of the Goddess according to the Kālikāpurāṇa*, Leiden, 1972, p. 9, as regards Kāmarūpa and the cave of Mt. Nīla, the residence of the goddess Kāmākhyā. See Ch. 64.43-6 of the *Kālikāp.*, where Mt. Nīla is held to be the central piece of the first stone made by Brahmā in order to be a support for Viṣṇu in his fights with the demons Madhu and Kaiṭabha. In the Deccan the origin of a cult is often associated with a tree or a termite mound. In Tirupati it was a termite mound raised beside a tamarind tree planted by Brahmā in which Viṣṇu resided and which was the origin of the cult. The termite mound is identified with Ādiśeṣa and also with a local *devī*, Cf. *The Glories and Mysteries of Lord Venkateswara*. English translation of Sri N. Subrahmanyam, *Sri Venkateswara Leela Mahathmyamu*, Tirumalai Hills P.O., 1962, pp. 25ff. The tamarind tree or the tamarind forest (Tamil *tiṇḍivanam*, Marāṭhī *diṇḍīravan*, Skt. *tintiṇī*, *tintriṇīvanam*, etc., and *ciñcā* = tamarind tree) at the origin links Citambaram, Tirupati and Pandharpur. See the important article by Rāmacandra Ciṃtāmaṇ Ḍhere, '*Diṃḍīravanāce rahasya*', in *Navabhārat,* June 1982, pp. 1-10. The origin of the famous Mallikārjuna on Śrīśailam is also said to be a *liṅgam* hidden in a termite mound.
21. *Census of India*, vol. XIV, *Rajasthan*, pt. VII-B, Fairs & Festivals, 1966, p. 78.
22. Sontheimer, op. cit., pp. 205f. [= *Pastoral Deities* . . . , pp. 214ff.]
23. J.C. Heesterman, 'The Case of the Severed Head', in *WZKSO*, XI (1967), pp. 22-43, at p. 32, fn. 41, citing the *Vādhūlasūtra* (extracts ed. and tr. W. Caland in *Acta Orientalia*, VI (1928), pp. 229-33) fragm. 110: 'Previously they used to immolate a man for Prajāpati', but when the gods retired from the sacrifice the human victim was replaced by a he-goat.
24. Dakṣa is depicted in Karnataka in innumerable votive plaques with the head of a ram. He and Satī/Mahākālī stand on the sides of Vīrabhadra.
25. Sontheimer, op. cit., pp. 187f. [= *Pastoral Deities* . . . , pp. 193.]
26. The Gonds believe that Brahmā Dev resides in a Fig tree. For them it is a very uncommon spirit: 'Sometimes he leaps on a man passing beneath his tree, and then for the period of his possession that man goes crazy in his wits.' Shamrao Hivale and Verrier Elwin, *Songs of the Forest*, London, 1935, p. 36. Cited in: Shyam Parmar, *Folklore of Madhya Pradesh*, New Delhi, 1972, p. 25. In Maharashtra a young Brahman who dies before the ungirding of the *munja* thread and the investiture of the sacred thread becomes a spirit in the Munjyā tree (a name of the Pipal tree) and is called Munjābā. The trunk of the tree may be wrapped with white threads by women and worshipped for a son.
27. See Stella Kramrisch, 'Indian Varieties of Art Ritual', in: J. Kitagawa and

Ch. L. Long (eds.), *Myths and Symbols: Studies in Honor of Mircea Eliade*. The Univ. of Chicago Press, Chicago, 1969, pp. 23ff., 26-8.

28. Sontheimer, op. cit., p. 187. [Cp. *Pastoral Deities* . . . , p. 193.] See also idem, 'Some Notes on Birobā, the Dhangar God of Maharashtra', in *Prof. D.D. Kosambi Commemoration Volume. Science and Human Progress*, Bombay, pp. 169ff. [Editor's note: Also in the present volume, pp. 70ff.] The full myth of Birobā is told in *Indische Märchen*, to appear in the Diederichs Verlag, Köln. [Editor's note: manuscript still unpublished.]
29. Sontheimer, 'Some Notes on Birobā . . .', p. 171 [cp. p. 72 in the present volume.]
30. Sontheimer, ibid., pp. 173f. [cp. pp. 74f. in the present volume.] Yallangavḍa Ph. Āṭṭikolla, *Hālumatada Caritra*, Dhārvāḍ, 1949, pp. 53-5.
31. See G.-D. Sontheimer, 'King Vikram and Kamalū Śinde, the Shepherd, *Bhakti* Episodes from an Oral Epic of the Dhangars of Maharashtra', in *South Asian Digest of Regional Writing*, vol. 6 (1977), pp. 97ff., 121, 123. [Editor's note: Also in the present volume, pp. 183ff., 205, 207.]
32. See David Shulman, 'On South Indian Bandits and Kings', in *The Indian Economic and Social History Review*, vol. XVIII, no. 3 (offprint), pp. 284ff., 294ff.
33. Stella Kramrisch, op. cit., pp. 32f.
34. G.C. Tripathi, 'Navakalevara: 'The Unique Ceremony of "Birth" and "Death" of the "Lord of the World",' in: Anncharlott Eschmann, Hermann Kulke, Gaya Charan Tripathi (eds.), *The Cult of Jagannāth* . . . , pp. 223ff. and A. Eschmann, ibid., 'Prototypes of the Navakalevara Ritual and their Relations to the Jagannātha Cult', pp. 265ff.
35. See Alf Hiltebeitel, 'The Indus Valley "Proto-Śiva", Re-examined through Reflections on the Goddess, the Buffalo, and the Symbolism of *vāhanas*', in *Anthropos*, vol. 73 (1978), pp. 767ff., 775, 784ff.
36. W. Ruben, *Eisenschmiede und Dämonen in Indien*, Leiden, 1939—The same author's *Waldabenteuer des indischen epischen Helden*, Berlin, 1962, contains further interesting material on the topic of *vana*.
37. Cp. R.S. Sharma, 'Material Milieu of Tantricism', in: R.S. Sharma (ed.), in collaboration with Vivekanand Jha, *Indian Society: Historical Probings in Memory of D.D. Kosambi*, New Delhi, 1974, pp. 175-89. There are many erotic, 'tantric' sculptures in and around the temples of Barsur in Bastar (now collected in one temple used as a godown and protected by the Archaeological Survey of India). Bastar was ruled by an old Nāga dynasty in the twelfth century and e.g. by the Kākatiyās (thirteenth century). Barsur was again taken over by jungle. The sculptures hardly reflect tribal customs as such, but rather tantric practices and beliefs. Tantric practices may have grown around the cult of the goddess Danteśvarī at Dantevada, about 20 miles from Barsur, where human sacrifices were formerly offered (*E.I.*, IX, p. 160f.).
38. See Kane, *History of Dharmaśāstra*, vol. V, 1, pp. 176f. *Kālikāpurāṇa* 62. 31-2; 63.17-18, 19-22. R.R. van Kooij, *Worship of the Goddess according to the Kālikāpurāṇa*, Leiden, 1972, pp. 109, 121.

39. *Rāmāyaṇa, Araṇyakāṇḍa*, 73. Vettam Mani, *Purāṇic Encyclopaedia*, p. 634b, 659b.
40. See P.V. Kane, *History of Dharmaśāstra*, vol. V, pt. 1, Poona, p. 225f. *Garuḍa Purāṇa* 1.124.
41. Cp. e.g. Sontheimer, 'King Vikram and Kamaḷū' Śinde . . .', op. cit., pp. 113ff. [cp. pp. 198ff. in the present volume]. The Mahākāla of Ujjain goes, thirsty for *bhakti*, in search of a true *bhakta* and literally 'goes out of his way' and finds him finally in a far-away shepherd settlement. The god shows himself first to playing *children*: see ibidem, p. 109 [cp. p. 194 in the present volume]. Sontheimer, *Birobā, Mhaskobā und Khaṇḍobā* . . . , pp. 207f. [= *Pastoral Deities* . . . , pp. 216ff.]. For Khaṇḍobā riding on his horse and joining cattleherd boys on the mountain at Jejuri, see G.H. Khare, *Mahārāṣṭrācīṃ cār daivateṃ*, Pune, 1958, p. 90. As to the oral transmission as compared to the written word of a manuscript: The Dhangars believe that the myth of Birobā should not be laid down in a *pothī* or manuscript because Birobā's power vanishes. His deeds have to be *sung* und are accompanied by music and dance. Sontheimer, *Birobā, Mhaskobā and Khaṇḍobā* . . . , p. 198 [= *Pastoral Deities* . . . , p. 204.] But we should remember that in Brahmanical tradition the *correct recitation of the Vedas* is the true authoritative source of the Veda, and not the manuscript as such. Moreover, song, dance, and the sound of musical instruments, especially the drum, are detrimental to the study of the Veda (cp. Manu IV.113: *vāṇa* = lute) and are eliminated in the classical *śrauta* ritual. See J.C. Heesterman, 'Brahman, Ritual and Renouncer', in *WZKSO*, vol. VIII, 1964, pp. 1ff., 12-14.
42. John C. Irwin, 'The Sacred Anthill and the Cult of the Primordial Mound', in *History of Religions*, 22 (1982), pp. 339-60.
43. *Śrīsaṃta Tukārām Mahārāj yāṃcī Abhaṃgāṃcī Gāthā*, 2138, [ed.] Mā. Kṛ. Deśmukh [and] Śaṃkar Vāman Dāṃḍekar, Puṇe, 1965 (repr.). The translation is by Dilip Chitre.
44. Hari = the reliever.
45. D.D. Kosambi, *Myth and Reality*, Bombay, 1961, p. 195. Groups of villagers dressed in sackcloth can still be seen on a joint pilgrimage which takes them to Pandharpur. They call themselves *vanavāsīs*.
46. Cp. Albrecht Wezler, *Die wahren 'Speiseresteesser' (Skt. vighasāśin)*, Akademie der Wissenschaften und der Literatur, Mainz, 1978, pp. 86ff and fn. 252.
47. H.N. Nene (ed.), *Sūtrapāṭha*, Nagpur, 3rd edn., 1942.
48. Sontheimer, *Birobā, Mhaskobā und Khaṇḍobā*, . . . , op. cit., pp. 169ff. [= *Pastoral Deities* . . . , pp. 174ff.] *Adhyātmarāmāyaṇa, Ayodhyākāṇḍa*, 6, 64ff., Gītāpres [*sic*], Gorakhpūr (n.d.).
49. *Rāmāyaṇa*, I.2.1ff. Erich Hofstetter, *Der Herr der Tiere im alten Indien*, Wiesbaden, 1980, pp. 98f.
50. See G.-D. Sontheimer, 'Die Ethik im Hinduismus', in: Carl Heinz Ratschow (ed.), *Ethik in den Weltreligionen*, Stuttgart etc., 1980, pp. 349ff., at p. 416f.
51. On Viṣṇu treated as king see Friedhelm Hardy, 'Ideology and Cultural Context of the Śrīvaiṣṇava Temple', in *The Indian Economic and Social History Review*

XIV (1977), pp. 149-51, at pp. 132-5. Cp. also Veena Das, *Structure and Cognition, Aspects of Hindu Caste and Ritual*, Delhi, 1977, pp. 26ff., at pp. 81, 70, who cites the legend of king Āma, in which it is said, '... without a part of Vishnu in him, none can become a king'. This sets the king into relation to the Brahman, who asks him to give in charity, perform austerities, worship Brahmans and be steadfast in his devotion to Vishnu.

52. See A. Eschmann, 'The Vaiṣṇava Typology of Hinduization and the Origin of Jagannātha', in: Anncharlott Eschmann, Hermann Kulke, and Gaya Charan Tripathi (eds.), *The Cult of Jagannāth* . . . , Ch. V, pp. 99ff., at pp. 108ff.
53. The author wishes to thank Mr. B.S. Murlidhar Reddy and E.V. Rajendra Sarma, Betamcherla, for their kind help while he was studying the Narasiṃha cult at Madduleti together with Dr. M.L.K. Murty, Deccan College, Pune.
54. See Christoph von Fürer-Haimendorf, *The Gonds of Andhra Pradesh. Tradition and Change in an Indian Tribe*, New Delhi etc., 1979, p. 182: Shri Shambhu Mahadeo [Śrī Śambhu Mahādev], who lives on the mountain Meru; p. 180: Originally three hundred gods were born on the mountain Meru. See also Wolfgang K. Knabe, *Untersuchungen über die Grundlagen der Maria-Religion*, Ph.D. thesis, Köln, 1978, p. 82: 'Geburtsorte der Clangottheiten sind Bergkuppen.' Birobā, the Dhangar god of Maharashtra, similarly lives on the Kailās, and takes birth in the human world on the request of Śaṃkara, who acts as a somewhat otiose God, occasionally visiting the earth with Pārvatī. See Sontheimer, 'Some Notes on Birobā . . .', pp. 171f [cp. pp. 72f. in the present volume]. For close parallels of the Dhangar myth to the Gond mythology, see v. Fürer-Haimendorf, op. cit., pp. 180ff. The movement down from often still spirit-like (*yakṣa*) hill gods to (anthropomorphical in conception, if not iconic) clan gods or village deities and possibly a 'classical' deity of the *kṣetra* is common. See the case of Narasiṃha, Murukaṉ (originally the Cēyōṉ of the *kuriñci*), etc., and also Sontheimer, *Birobā, Mhaskobā und Khaṇḍobā* . . . , p. 182 *and passim* [= *Pastoral Deities* . . . , p. 187.] On the 'folk' and 'tribal' worship of the sun, see John C. Irwin, op. cit., pp. 342f., 353, and Sontheimer, 'Some Incidents in the History of the God Khaṇḍobā', in Marc Gaborieau and Alice Thorner [eds.], *Asie du Sud. Traditions et changements. VIth European Conference on Modern South Asian Studies*, Paris, 1978, pp. 111ff. [cp. pp. 20ff. in EK]; pp. 112f. [cp. pp. 23f. in EK]. Śiva/ Mahādeva, the hill-god, the worship of the sun and worship of the termite mound merge in the Khaṇḍobā/Mārtaṇḍa Bhairava cult. The worship of a termite mound as the origin of Mārtaṇḍa Bhairava or Maṇ-Mailār (Ka. *maṇṇu* [*clay*]+*malla*+*ari*) in Ādimailār in Karnataka has been made clear by R.C. Dhere, Khaṇḍobā, Pune, 1961, pp. 37ff.
55. Thus the demon defeated by Māruti/Hanuman depicted in his *mūrtis* may be painted red, 'because he may come up again', as a Maharashtrian villager explained. Māruti himself, the Mahāvīra, and one of the 52 outlandish *vīras*/ ghosts in Maharashtra, becomes a devotee of Rāma.
56. *Śatarudrīya* 4.5.1ff.
57. See Māṇikkavācakar's *Tiruvācakam* 14.4; 15.9, and see below the case of Malla.

Also discussed in G.-D. Sontheimer, 'The Mallāri/Khaṇḍobā Myth as Reflected in Folk Art and Ritual', in: *Anthropos* 79, 1-3 (1984), pp. 159ff. [cp. EK, pp. 40ff.]

58. Sontheimer, 'The Mallāri/Khaṇḍobā Myth . . .', *passim* and plates.
59. See e.g. Sontheimer, *Birobā, Mhaskobā und Khaṇḍobā*, op. cit., pp. 36, 84f. [= *Pastoral Deities* . . . , pp. 32, 83f.]
60. Sontheimer, ibid., pp. 84f. (Koḷīs), pp. 86f. (Rāmośīs) [= *Pastoral Deities* . . . , pp. 83f., 85f.]
61. Viewed from the point of view of settled people, nomadic tribes may be called *bhūtas*. S. Westphal-Hellbusch, 'Changes in the Meaning of Ethnic Names as Exemplified by the Jat, Rabari, Bharvad and Charan in North Western India', in: L.S. Leshnik and G.-D. Sontheimer (eds.), *Pastoralists and Nomads in South Asia*, p. 123.
62. D.C. Sircar (ed.), in *Annual Report on Indian Epigraphy for 1957-58*, Delhi: Govt. of India Press, 1967, pp. 8-9, 21.
63. See e.g. *Mārtaṇḍa Vijaya* 11.26 (ed. R.C. Dhere, Puṇe, 1974).
64. Sontheimer, 'The Mallāri/Khaṇḍobā Myth . . .', ibid.
65. E.g. *Mārtaṇḍa Vijaya* 20.90.
66. David Shulman, 'On South Indian Bandits and Kings', in *The Indian Economic and Social History Review*, vol. XVII, No. 3, p. 285ff.
67. Shulman, ibid., p. 304.
68. See Sontheimer, *Birobā, Mhaskobā und Khaṇḍobā*, pp. 8ff. [= *Pastoral Deities* . . . , p. 3ff.]
69. Shulman, op. cit., p. 289.
70. Sontheimer, op. cit., pp. 85f. [= *Pastoral Deities* . . . , pp. 84f.] Alexander Mackintosh, *An Account of the Origin and Present Condition of the Tribe of Ramoossies, including the Life of the Chief Oomiah Naik*, Bombay, 1833, p. 3.
71. B.A. Saletore, *The Wild Tribes in Indian History*, Lahore, 1935, p. 170.
72. Sontheimer, *Birobā, Mhaskobā und Khaṇḍobā*, p. 85 [= *Pastoral Deities* . . . , p. 84].
73. Sontheimer, ibid., p. 86 [= *Pastoral Deities* . . . , p. 85.]
74. Shulman, op. cit., p. 290.
75. See L. Dumont, 'A Structural Definition of a Folk Deity of Tamil Nad: Aiyanar, the Lord', in L. Dumont, *Religion/Politics and History in India*, Paris, 1970, pp. 20-32.
76. *Mallāri Māhātmya* of Śrīdhara, 2.115.
77. Sontheimer, *Birobā, Mhaskobā und Khaṇḍobā*, p. 86 [= *Pastoral Deities* . . . , p. 85].
78. *Mallāri Māhātmya* of Śrīdhara 2.28.
79. Kamil V. Zvelebil, 'A Guide to Murukan', in *Journal of Tamil Studies*, pp. 1-22, at p. 10.
80. See e.g. Sontheimer, 'Some Incidents . . . ', p. 112 [= EK, pp. 23f.]. The hunter (Koḷī) and the cowherd (Gavlī) at the origin of a Śaivite cult in the forest and the cow shedding milk over an anthill in which a *svayambhū-liṅga* is found are so

widespread in the Deccan and South India (e.g. Śrīśailam) that instances could be multiplied *ad infinitum*.

81. See the discussion in: R.N. Dandekar, 'Vaiṣṇavism and Śaivism', in: R.N. Dandekar (ed.), *Ramkrishna Gopal Bhandarkar as an Indologist*, Poona, 1974, pp. 26ff.
82. Charlotte Vaudeville, 'The Govardhan Myth in Northern India', in *Indo-Iranian Journal*, 22 (1980), pp. 1-45, at p. 5.
83. See Vaudeville, ibid., p. 19.
84. For the personal devotion, inner religion, and unmediated vision of god through bhakti between the established 'public' religions of the 'Great Tradition' and 'Little Tradition' one may refer to A.K. Ramanujan, *Speaking of Śiva*, Penguin Books, 1973, Introduction, pp. 19ff. There is a spatial aspect of *bhakti*: Bhakti cults often originate in the 'wilderness', e.g. in the early Pandharpur. But the ritual of pilgrimage and the worship developing in the eventual *kṣetra* and *tīrtha* may again provoke the saint to revert to inner religion, which can be practised beyond *vana* and *kṣetra*, or, as Tulasīdāsa expresses it: If one protects or leaves [in order to go to the forest] the house, it will go. Tulasīdāsa says: one should dwell in between the forest and the house, in the city of God. Cited by R.D. Ranade, *Paramārtha Sopāna (A Source-Book of Pathway to God in Hindi Literature)*, Allahabad, 1958, p. 232.
85. *Sri Venkateswara Leela Mahathmyamu*, Ch. XVI.
86. Sontheimer, *Birobā, Mhaskobā und Khaṇḍobā*, op. cit., p. 51 [= *Pastoral Deities* . . . , p. 47].
87. G.-D. Sontheimer, 'Gopajanāṃcā dev: Śrīviṭhṭhala', in: Go. Ma. Kulakarṇī [and] Vi. Tryaṃ. Śeṭe [eds.], *Rā. Ciṃ. Ḍhere Ābhinaṃdangrantha* [Festschrift for R.C. Dhere] *Mahārāṣṭrācī Sattvadhārā*, Puṇeṃ, 1983, pp. 103-10.
88. Vi. Bhi. Kolate, *saṃpādak* [ed.], *Līḷācaritra*, Mumbaī, 1978, *Uttarārdha*, *līḷā* 508, pp. 656f. See the discussions by S.G. Tulpule, 'The Origin of Viṭṭhala: A New Interpretation', in *ABORI*, *Diamond Jubilee Volume*, Poona, 1977-8, pp. 1009-15, and G.-D. Sontheimer, 'Hero-and Satī-Stones of Maharashtra', in: S. Settar and Günther D. Sontheimer [eds.], *Memorial Stones*, Dharwad/Delhi, 1982, pp. 261ff. [Editor's note: Also in the present volume, pp. 245ff.]
89. See V. Mahadevan, 'Naṭukal Valipāṭu [The Worship of Hero-Stones]', in: R. Nagaswamy, *Seminar on Hero-Stones*, State Dept. of Archaeology, Govt. of Tamilnadu, 1974, pp. 5ff., at pp. 6ff. I am thankful to Dr. A. Dhamotharan for reading with me the Tamil texts of this publication.
90. Mahadevan, op. cit., p. 6.
91. T. Nānacuntaram, 'Naṭukallum ilakkiyamum [The Literature on Hero-Stones]', in *Seminar on Hero-Stones*, pp. 88ff.
92. *Līḷācaritra*, ibidem.
93. See Zvelebil, 'The Beginning of Bhakti . . .', pp. 253ff.
94. '*Paṃḍharīceṃ bhūt moṭheṃ*. . . .' *Abhaṃgācī Gāthā* 2606. See note 43.
95. Victor Turner, 'The Center Out There: Pilgrim's Goal', in *History of Religions*, vol. 12 (1972), pp. 192ff.

96. *Myth and Reality*, pp. 130-2.
97. I.M.P. Raeside, 'The Pāṇḍuranga-Māhātmya of Śrīdhar', in *BSOAS*, vol. XXVIII, pt. 1 (1965), p. 6.
98. Ibid., p. 85. See also Māṇik Dhanapalavār, *Puṃḍalīka Caritra*, Haidarābād, 1972, p. 14, who refers to the *Padma Purāṇa*, in which the story of Puṇḍalīka is mentioned, but not Pandharpur.
99. 'Progress turns bitter for tribals', *Free Press* (Bombay), 7-9, 83.

The *Rāmāyaṇa* in Contemporary Folk Traditions of Maharashtra

Neither the classical *Rāmāyaṇa* of Vālmīki nor the Marāṭhī versions of the Rāma story have become the nucleus of a dominant religious movement in Maharashtra.* A crucial reason for this is the basically Śaiva orientation of Maharashtrian folk religion. Folk religion is a very self-conscious element in Maharashtrian religion. It centres on cults such as that of the eight Gaṇpatis, who became very prominent in Peśvā times, or Khaṇḍobā, or Dattātreya, or some of the Nine Nāths, or *devīs*. These deities are primarily worshipped as autochthonous and are not located in any purāṇic heaven. Many Maharashtrian families worship one of these folk deities as their family god. The majority of these deities are essentially Śaivite. In the past, 'sectarian' movements like the Nāths or the Liṅgāyats were also part of these Śaivite traditions. Vaiṣṇava traditions were often superimposed on Śaivite cults or Śaivite sectarian movements. Eventually the Mahānubhāva sect with its 'Five Kṛṣṇas' began to be eclipsed by the Vaiṣṇava Vārkarī movement with its famous Bhakti saints and the worship of Viṭhobā of Pandharpur. But somehow the Śaivite background always remained coexistent; this made Charlotte Vaudeville call the phenomenon 'nominal Vaiṣṇavism' (Vaudeville 1987: 32). Because of the Vaiṣṇava Bhakti movement of the saints and the Vārkarīs, the scriptural authority of the *Bhāgavata-Purāṇa* became responsible for the spread of Vaiṣṇavism rather than that of the Rāmāyaṇa. In modern times, the personal belief of the Maharashtrian middle class more and more transcends the belief in local and family deities and turns to saints and gurus of varied provenance. This also strengthens the worship of Viṭhobā, the belief in the saints, and the pilgrimage of the Vārkarīs to Pandharpur.

But within this Maharashtrian complex we do find Rāmāyaṇa traditions interwoven, as it were. It is perhaps from the time of the Yādavas of Devgirī that we can notice a slow but continuous rise of the Rāma cult. Especially the combination of the worship of the Devī or Durgā and Rāma came into prominence in the late middle ages. This was a phenomenon which seems to have occurred in many parts of India and was supported by many royal courts. Dasarā, with the worship of the Devī and Rāmacandra, was an important feature of the Vijayanagara Empire, especially under Kṛṣṇadevarāyā (1509-29), and it was duplicated, if not taken over directly, by the Marathas (cp. Stein 1985: 388f.). In Maharashtra Bhavānī or Tukāī emerged from her prehistoric roots as the famous protective deity of the Marathas and Śivājī. It is said in the oral traditions of Tuḷjāpūr that at a place to the south-west of the town, where there is a temple known as Ghāṭ Śilā, Śrī Rāmacandra decided to proceed to Laṅkā in search of Sītā. It is also told that the goddess Tukāī escorted Rāma and Lakṣmaṇa up to this point on their way to the Dakṣiṇāpatha and waited there for their return. The Bhavānī of Tuḷjāpūr is also connected with the famous saint Rāmdās, who composed a hymn about her, the *Rāmvardāyinī* ('She who gives a boon to Rāma') (Pāṃgārkar 1978: 387-9). Thus Rāmdās, the Bhavānī of Tuḷjāpūr, King Śivājī and the Dasarā festival are all linked together and constitute a complex religious and political ideology.

Though this tradition is still alive, the *Bhāvārth-Rāmāyaṇ* of Eknāth (b. 1533) and even more so the *Rāmvijay* of Śrīdhar (completed in 1703) enjoy widespread popularity. And such regional versions of the Rāmāyaṇa are today matched by the general growth of a new all-India Rāmāyaṇa tradition. On every Sunday morning people are glued to their television sets when a new episode of a seemingly unending series on the *Rāmcaritra* is shown. The series is based on a medley of all-India and regional versions.[1] Such Rāmāyaṇa and Mahābhārata traditions, in my view, are steadily replacing local myths and legends. Today there is a noticeable shift towards uniform regional and all-Indian traditions which perhaps affect rather the group and the village than the individual. Let me cite just one instance, which to me seems to be an illustration of this change: One of my best Dhangar informants was a famous singer of *ovīs*, and the best legends of my story collection about Birobā, the special god of the Dhangars, were sung by him. Yet he was sensitive to modern change. He was 'illiterate' and had a friend, also a Dhangar, who could not *write*, but could *read*. He asked him to read the *Rāmvijay* for him, so that he could render it in *ovī* form. When he showed less and less interest in the *ovīs* about Birobā and the other pastoral gods of the Dhangars, I enquired about the reason. He expressed it in his own way, saying: 'Oh, you see, the old gods are no longer that strong. That is why I make *ovīs* out of the *Rāmvijay*.'

However, what I want to sketch here is how folk traditions in Maharashtra borrowed elements from the classical *Rāmāyaṇa* and subordinated them to their own local beliefs, needs, and conditions. By doing so the folk tradition retained its own identity in the past. There are numerous examples, but I confine myself to two. I must stress again that here, though I speak of *local contemporary living traditions*, the making of such traditions, in my view, is occurring less and less, because of modern trends which increasingly replace local traditions by regional or all-India traditions. I will give a third example which shows how from a folk custom a new tradition evolves with the help of a regional scripture, the *Bhāvārth-Rāmāyaṇ* of Eknāth.

Before I present the three examples, we must take a brief look at how Vālmīki's *Rāmāyaṇa* is localized in Maharashtra as a region. According to Vālmīki, the sage Agastya was followed by several other sages who established their *āśramas* on the bank of the Godāvarī river. The cluster of hermitages was called Janasthāna to distinguish it from the surrounding forest country. The region to the south was inhabited by the aboriginals, who are called Rākṣasas in the *Rāmāyaṇa*. The sages living in the Janasthāna were constantly harassed by these Rākṣasas: 'These shapeless and ill-looking monsters testify to their abominable character by various cruel and terrific displays. They implicate the hermits in impure practices and perform great outrages. Changing their shapes and hiding in thickets adjoining the hermitage, these frightful beings delight in terrifying the devotees; they cast away their sacrificial ladles and vessels; they pollute cooked oblations, and utterly defile the offerings with blood. These faithless creatures inject frightful sounds into the ears of the faithful and austere hermits. At the time of the sacrifices they snatch away the jars, and the sacred grass of these sober-minded men.'[2] We are told in the *Rāmāyaṇa* (III. 11-30) that Rāma, accompanied by his brother Lakṣmaṇa and Sītā, met Agastya on the bank of the Godāvarī. The sage presented him with a bow and two quivers and advised him to settle down at a place called Pañcavaṭī named after the five great banyan trees which grew there. Today the old part of Nasik is called Pañcavaṭī. There are caves near Pañcavaṭī on the Godāvarī one of which goes by the name of 'Sītā's cave'. Here Rāma is said to have lived for some time and to have killed many Rākṣasas who were harassing the sages. It was also from here that Sītā was abducted by Rāvaṇa. Janasthāna and Pañcavaṭī were situated on the fringe of the great forest called the Daṇḍakāraṇya, which covered the Deccan and was known in Marathi literature as the proverbial home of the hosts of demons. In many village histories and stories of the origin of temples of Maharashtra we hear without reference to Rāma that there was a Daṇḍakāraṇya until the god came and defeated the demon and turned the place into a hospitable area or even a holy *kṣetra* (Sontheimer 1976: 27). But, unlike in the classical *Rāmāyaṇa*, the defeated demon was not killed, but became the devotee of the god, a *dvārapāla*, and a faithful follower. I would suggest that this is analogous to the policy of the medieval king in the Deccan. Tribal groups were not eradicated by the king, but subordinated and incorporated, leaving them some degree of the autonomy in this area. Some of the forest inhabitants became auxiliaries in the armies of the kings; some of them, like the Māvaḷīs of the Western Ghats, became the most faithful followers of the king, in this case Śivājī. In this connection we should mention the well-known story of Śambūkā, the Śūdra sage who was beheaded by Rāma because it was an irreligious act for Śūdras to practice *tapas* (Uttarakāṇḍa 75). This is supposed to have happened on the hill of Rāmṭek, 45 km to the north of Nagpur. In Maharashtra the gruesome story has a somewhat conciliatory end. Whereas the beheading is the end of the matter for Śambūkā in the classical *Rāmāyaṇa* episode, the oral traditions of Rāmṭek give a typical folk twist. The dying Śambūkā asks three boons from Rāma: first, that Rāma should forever stay on the hill; secondly, that his, Śambūkā's, body should turn into a *śivaliṅga*; thirdly, that pilgrims who arrive at Rāmṭek must first have his, Śambūkā's, *darśana* before having the *darśana* of Rāma. Rāma granted these boons, and pilgrims there first have *darśana* of Śambūkā in the form of a *śivaliṅga* up to this day (*Bhāratīy Saṃskṛtikoś* 1974: 106). Thus we ought to conclude that, according to the folk traditions of Maharashtra, Rāma never returned to Ayodhya—this might help to alleviate some of the tribulations of modern Oudh.

Occasionally Śaivite temples are traced back to Rāma and his worship of Mahādeva during a halt in the forest. For instance, the oldest temple in Vīr, in the Purandar Taluka of the Pune District, is dedicated to Vīreśvar. Rāma is said to have made a *liṅg* out of sand on the bank of the little stream there. The temple faces east, and such temples are said to have been founded by Rāma, whereas the usual Śiva temples face north. In spite of the hoary past attributed to Vīreśvar, the far more important temple is that of Mhaskobā. He was brought to Vīr by Dhangar shepherds and is of much greater importance. Mhaskobā, a typical folk deity, has acquired supra-local importance.

VĀLMĪKI, THE KOḶĪS AND OTHER ROBBERS

The first of the three instances I am going to relate brings me back to the tribes, especially the Koḷīs. In the past they were one of the notoriously unruly tribal elements of Maharashtra: the Koḷīs who did not merge with the Kuṇbī population or become ferrymen and water carriers in the villages tended to be classified as 'criminal tribes' by the British. Already in the beginning of their rule in Maharashtra (in 1823), they noted that the Koḷīs claimed Vālmīki as their ancestor (Sontheimer 1976: 169f.) Vālmīki, the Koḷī, was a robber before he performed *tapas* and eventually composed the epic. The story of Vālmīki has its localized version in the village history of two places in the Purandar Taluka of the Pune District: Valha and Koḷvihire. Śekh Mahaṃmad (1560-1650) already mentions Vālhā, alias Vālmīki, who is a robber belonging to the Koḷī community (*Yogsaṃgrām* 18.13; Śekh Mahaṃad [Ḍhere] 1981: 171). The story of Vālmīki as a robber according to the *Adhyātmarāmāyaṇa* (2.6. 65ff.) was transposed to many places in India, and it would be a mistake simply to take it as having an historical core. It could be told about any place and enter into local traditions whenever conditions were present which matched with those in the legend: a forest or wasteland, a trade or pilgrimage road passing through it, and robbers who threaten this route. All of these conditions were found in the case of Koḷvihire, which, in addition, is located near the temple of Khaṇḍobā, a tutelary god of the Rāmośī robbers as well as the Koḷīs. Further south the Rāmośīs, or rather Beḍars or Beraḍs of Karnataka, also claim Vālmīki as their tutelary ancestor (Sontheimer 1976: 169). It is said that Vālmīki, who is called Vālhyā Koḷī in our case, used to rob the caravans passing by on the old Satara road in the times when there was only jungle in this region. For every person he killed he would throw a small stone into a jar. He had stone jars and filled seven of them in this way. After his robberies, Vālhyā Koḷī was naturally thirsty. He would come to Koḷvihire and drink water from the well there, whence the village received its name, that is, Koḷvihire—'the well of the Koḷī'. Vālmīki would also stay where the village Vālhā is situated today. For twelve years Vālhyā Koḷī performed *tapas* in the termite mound, murmuring *marā-marā* ('kill! kill!'), which turned into *Rāma-Rāma*. Then leaves sprang forth from the stick which he had formerly used for killing. It grew to become the big tree under which today the wrestling bouts take place during the annual village festival (*jatrā*).

THE CASE OF NIṂBĀ, THE DAITYA

The second example is the case of Niṃbādaitya of Nāndūr in the Pathardi Taluka of the Ahmednagar District. Every year a *jatrā* or, more respectfully, *yātrā*, takes place on Guḍī Pāḍvā in the month of Caitra.[3] On the day of the festival, which is of supra-local importance, many worshippers follow the widespread Maharashtrian practice of bringing *kāvaḍs* (vessels) filled with water from the rivers to bathe their god. The real folk custom is to bring water from the river, in the present case from the river Godāvarī. In more classical temples the water would be fetched from a temple well or temple tank. Whereas the river represents a direct contact with unbounded nature, the water from the temple tank or well indicates a ritualized ordering of domesticated nature. A folk song (*ovī*) which women sing in the village while grinding millet describes the ritual. Each line is of the length of the time it takes to turn a grindstone once. There are still many such songs, though grinding is increasingly done with the help of electrical mills. The songs are extremely simple, but melodious and haunting, especially as the end of a line may be drawn out while singing in order to complete the turn of the grindstone.

At the crossroads of Nāndūr
there is an exciting show.
The rhythm of bells [tied to the ankles],
in the rear the waterpot dances,[4]
O Lady! L(= N)iṃbā Daitya—he is the King,
the juggler from the Bengal Land,[5]
In front the musicians play,
behind [them follows] the pot [with water] from the Gaṅgā.
On the day of Pāḍvā, Liṃbā Daityā
[looks like] a bridegroom god.
The whole village fetches water from the Gaṅgā
[and] bathes the God.
On the day of Paḍvā, Liṃbā Daityā
is finely dressed.

Dressed in a fine *dhotar*,
he wears silken slippers.
In Nāndūr, the village,
things go on happily.
To the right of the Daitya,
there is the shrine of Lakṣmī.
In Nāndūr, the village,
things go on happily.
Around the Daitya,
there are wells with water.
A place called Nāndūri,
a little, graceful village.
In front of the temple,
there is a huge Piṃpal tree.

Niṃbādaitya also was a part of unbounded wilderness and derives his name from the numerous Neem trees (*Azadirachta Indica*), which are said to have originated from a formidable forest in the past. In recognition of the close connection between Niṃbādaitya and the Neem tree, one family has inherited the custom of not using the Neem tree as firewood. So here there is a forest *rākṣasa* or forest deity (*vanadevatā*) who has become a popular village deity. Behind the rather recent temple of Rāmbhakt Niṃbādaitya on the outskirts of the little village, there are the ruins of a classical temple in the so-called Hemāḍpantī style of the Yādava period, that is, the thirteenth century. There is no *mūrti* in the temple, but a medallion of Hanumān—or rather Māruti, as he is called in Maharashtra—is carved on the doorjamb at the entrance to the temple.

The oral myth of the village about Niṃbādaitya runs as follows:

> Niṃbādaitya was one of seven brothers who belonged to the circle of friends of Vibhīṣaṇa. When Rāma left Pañcavaṭī and was on his way towards Laṅkā, Niṃbādaitya was of great help to Rāma. Rāma was greatly pleased. But Māruti entirely disliked the superb and dashing style of Niṃbādaitya. Maruti became jealous.
>
> Both went to Rām,
> Niṃbādaitya put a troublesome question:
> Am I the true *bhagat* or is it this monkey?
> Tell us!
> With the left eye he looked at Hanumān,
> with the right eye at Niṃbādaitya.
> See the play of Lord Rām!
> Niṃbā flew into a rage.
> I don't want in my Nāndūrī
> the pranks of this redfaced monkey.
> Take him to Ayodhyā,
> along with you.[6]
>
> Rāma dislike the jealously of Māruti and gave a boon to Niṃbādaitya. Niṃbā asked for the village of Nāndūr as a *jāgīr*. Rāma ousted Māruti and thus Nāndūr, it is said, is the only village in Maharashtra in which there is no temple of Māruti and in which he is not worshipped in a house shrine.

So far the village myth is about Niṃbādaitya. Such village myths do not fall out of the blue sky, but often have some original stimulus to which they react. To explore this phenomenon we have to refer to the *Līḷācaritra*, the biography of Cakradhara by Mhāiṃbhaṭ which was composed in about 1378. Cakradhara was the famous founder and one of the five Kṛṣṇas of the Mahānubhāva sect. During his wanderings Cakradhara also came to Nāndūr. The *Līḷācaritra* say (Mhāiṃbhaṭ [Kolte] 1978: 'Pūrvārdh' 516):

> *mag gosāvī nāndaurāsi bījeṃ keleṃ. āditī pākhū dīseṃ avasthān jāleṃ.*
>
> 'Then the Gosāvī proceeded to Nāndūr. Fourteen days he spent in the Āditī temple.'

Possibly the present Nāndūr is the village which Cakradhara visited. It was also Cakradhara who prophesied in the thirteenth century that the Śiva and Viṣṇu temples would disappear in the Kaliyuga, and that village deities or *kṣetrapālas* would rise and get their temples established ('Uttarārdh' 436). This is astonishingly true of the historical development in Maharashtra after the thirteenth century. At that time the classical Hemāḍpantī temples dedicated to Śiva and Viṣṇu disappeared, and folk deities, or *kṣetrapālas*, became popular and even superseded the classical, purāṇic deities in importance. Thus it may be suspected that the Āditya temple in Nāndūr was ruined and the popular Niṃbādaitya rose to importance. Folk etymology may even have contributed to this development. Playing on phonetic similarities is a very frequent means of identification in folk religion. I suspect that from 'Āditya' eventually the name 'Daitya' developed. The connection with 'Āditya/Sūrya' may have been forgotten in the course of time.[7]

Thus we may recognize here, following McKim Marriott (1955: 171-222), a process of parochialization of a classical deity, namely 'Āditya/Sūrya', or perhaps a combination of Sūrya and Śiva, who became Niṃbādaitya, the folk deity. At the same time one notes a process of universalization connecting with another element of the Great Tradition, namely Rāma. The *Rāmāyaṇa* connection lends Niṃbādaitya a certain dignity and legitimation or *mahimā*, but beneath this veneer he remains a folk deity, fondly loved by his *bhaktas*, and especially remembered in the songs of women. He protects the village as the *koṭvāl*, *pāṭīl*, *karbhāri*, and fulfils requests for jobs and children. His *mūrti* is said to be *ugra*, that is, covered with red lead (Ma. *śendur*, Skt. *sindūra*), the unmistakable sign of a folk deity. Niṃbādaitya has the size of a dwarf. He is armed with shield and sword and wears a moustache reminiscent of martial, outlandish deities. Only recently has he become a vegetarian, under the influence of a certain modern Vaiṣṇava saint.

THE FOREST OF RENEWAL

I have referred to the importance of the forest, the *vana*, the Daṇḍakāraṇya, in the religious traditions of Maharashtra. In fact, the forests of Maharashtra only began to shrink significantly in the nineteenth century, when the plough started conquering the soil on a large and systematic scale. The forest was not only terrifying, haunted by *rākṣasas* and *bhūtas*, and inhabited by cruel, but occasionally faithful and loyal tribals. It was also the source of the renewal of life, of unmitigated, direct access to the divine, less hampered by rituals and social divisions, the home of ascetics who sometimes performed *tapas* on or in a termite mound and then deflected onto themselves something of its primordial power. 'The source or *bīja* of *dharma* and *mukti* is in the forest', says the *Brahmapurāṇa* (129.55; 161.73). This importance of the forest is expressed in many rituals of folk religion. In Maharashtra, e.g., the custom of *gāṃvsāī* has by now been nearly forgotten: the main point used to be the propitiation of all local deities, spirits, and goblins. Its most impressive feature was that every human being had to go to live beyond the village (residential) limits for three, seven or nine days, during which the place would be completely deserted. After living in the *rān* (Skt. *araṇya*), i.e. the fields or forest, for the period and performing the required worship and blood-sacrifices, the inhabitants would return with the assurance of more plentiful crops, less illness, and, in general, greater well-being.[8] The ceremony of return is conceived as a resettlement. Another custom which is widely practised is the *vanbhojan*, during which the whole village populace assembles outside the village to have a common meal and thereby renews its solidarity, at least for the time being. In the region of Marathvada, villagers observe a particular vow if there is no rain: for fourteen days they wear sackcloth, stay in the forest and sleep on the bare ground. This is supposed to cause rain (Māṇḍe 1975: 170). This folk custom is the basis for the more recent re-enactment of the *vanvās* (forest-dwelling) of Rāma. Rāma, of course, did not go to the forest to ask for rain, but, as we can put it, had to cross the wilderness and experience the deprivations of living in the forest in order to gain the maturity needed to rule Ayodhya (cp. Shulman 1981: *passim*).

THE FOREST SOJOURN OF THE RĀM-VANVĀSĪS

The *vanvās* of Rāma is re-enacted by the inhabitants of numerous villages in the Ahmednagar, Bid, Usmanabad, and Sholapur Districts. It is probably no coincidence that the Rām-Vanvāsīs come from areas in Maharashtra where there is insecure rainfall: the background of the dramatization of Rāma's stay in the forest seems to be the folk custom of going into the forest to ask for rain. Whereas the folk custom appears to be very ancient, the Vaiṣṇava version seems to be fairly recent.[9] Our present short account is mainly based on information given by prominent Rām-Vanvāsīs.[10]

Fourteen years and fourteen days—the Vanvāsīs say—Rāmcandra stayed in the forest. They, however, limit their own stay to fourteen days, and traverse the forest mostly on metalled and tarred roads. Some of the groups do the pilgrimage on three consecutive years. The forest, of course, now hardly exists and because of its disappearance the object of the sojourn tends to shift. The destination is Pañcavaṭī, that is, Nasik, and Tryambakeśvar. At least, when one makes the pilgrimage for the first time, one has to go to these places. But, as Rāma went to many other *tīrthas* as well, one can also go to other places, e.g. to Pandharpur and Alandi, two main centres of the Vārkarī *panth*, or to Tuḷjāpūr, the capital of Bhavānī, or Gāṇgāpūr, the centre of Dattātreya worship. Nevertheless, Vanvāsīs do not go to the extremes of Saint Rāmdās, who identified every god, e.g. Viṭhobā or Khaṇḍobā, with Rāma.[11]

Thus, more and more the object of the pilgrimage is not just a stay in the forest; rather, it tends to become a *tīrtha yātrā*, that is, a pilgrimage to holy centres, not to the forest as such—or, as a Vanvāsī put it: 'In order to spread the example of Rām, who kept his life clean, one does not have to go to the forest.' The basic motivation for most of the Vanvāsīs is, however, to experience the life led by Rāma in the forest, to experience his suffering and happiness (*sukhduḥkhācyā anubhāvācī jān*). Of course, the pilgrimage is also a kind of worship of the Lord from which one derives deep satisfaction (*bhagavantācyā śevāce samādhān miḷāve*), but joining the group of pilgrims, and playing, walking, conversing with each other, bring diversion to the mind. Otherwise the worship of the Lord can never be fully realized, because one does not become free from one's preoccupation with worldly affairs (*prapañcātun suṭkā hot nāhī*). On leaving the village the pilgrims formally bid farewell to their family deity (*kulsvāmī*), a very suggestive sign of their temporary separation from settled, routine life.

Their life in the wilderness is reflected in the outfit of the pilgrims. They have to walk without *cappals* and they have to wear sackcloth. Their headgear, which has the shape of a pointed cone, is also made of sackcloth. The jute clothes are a substitute for the garments which Rāma wore and which were actually made of bark. Here, as during the whole pilgrimage, the re-enactment of Rāma's fate is always present to the mind of the pilgrims: did not Kaikeyī take away even the ornate clothes from Rāma (cp. *Vālmīki-Rāmāyaṇa* 2.18.37)? Like Rāma, who possessed nothing when he left for the forest, Vanvāsīs do not carry any belongings (*barobar kāhī net nāhī*). Some of them, however, change over to ochre clothes, because 'sackcloth is too hot', as one of them observed. They carry a polychrome picture of Rāma, Sītā, Lakṣmaṇa and Hanumān. While on pilgrimage they remember and shout the name of Rāma, for example:

Śrī Rām, jay Rām, jay jay Rām,
Rāmācā sevak jay Hanumān!

But they also sing verses composed 'spontaneously' (*āpo-āp*) on the model of 'old' verses. For instance:

jibale [SM *jibhali*] *kāy dhandā.*
ghaḍoghaḍī smarave Govindā.

O tongue, what is your task?
To remember Govinda continuously.

Both lines end with *-dā*. On the model of this verse we might hear the following verse about Rāma in which the two lines rhyme to *-sā*:

Rāma jāu nako vanavāsā.
parata yeśila' re kiti divasā.

Rāma, don't go to live in the forest.
After how many days will you return!

Some of the verses refer to the Sants rather than to Rāma.

dārī tuḷasa hirvīgāre
ha santāncā saṅsāre.

In front of the door there is the green Tuḷsī plant.
That is the world of the Sants.

The songs are not composed by any particular poet, though there is always a singer and poet more gifted than others who composes them spontaneously (*śīghra kavi*). The songs have not been collected and published in book form so far. Instead of the *Haripāṭh*, the sacred collection of *abhaṅgas*, which is carried by the Vārkarīs on their pilgrimage to Pandharpur, the Vanvāsīs carry a copy of the *Bhāvārth-Rāmāyaṇ* of Eknāth. Chapters of the *Bhāvārth-Rāmāyaṇ* are read before the pilgrimage and during the halts. The *vinā* [SM *vīṇā*], a four-stringed instrument, plays an important part during the pilgrimage. It should never touch the ground, and each of the participants in the pilgrimage has to alternately hold and protect it, even in the night. The *vinā* is considered to be a pure instrument. It keeps the *pitch* (*sūr*). It brings order into the singing of *bhajans*, which would otherwise be like the braying of a female donkey in the open field (*moklyā rānī gaḍhvī savāśīn* [SM *suvāsinī* = a married woman] . . . *kasāhī varḍāyce* [SM *orḍāyceṃ*]). Only after the return to the village, at the end of the nocturnal ceremony terminating the pilgrimage, may the *vinā* be put down on the ground.[12]

The walk through the 'forest' is an affair which involves not only a particular group of pilgrims, but the whole village community. It is decidedly 'non-communal', that is, there is no distinction of caste (*jātībhed*, *jātībhāv*), and Marāṭhās, Rāmośīs, Māṅgs (i.e. Harijans), Cāṃbhārs (Harijans), Māḷīs, and even Muslims participate. This is expressed by commensality: during the pilgrimage everyone sits in one row (*ekā pangtāt*), and not in different rows according to caste. 'Thigh touches thigh while eating' (*jevtānā te māṇḍilā māṇḍī lāvun jevtāt*), which means that there is equality between the pilgrims, who are also joined by a few women. One has to 'keep fast', which means to eat the uncooked food allowed during a fast, e.g. groundnuts, sweet potatoes, fruit or any poor man's grain (*bhagar*), like *vari*, a kind of sago. The distinction between pure and impure is suspended as regards food and commensality, and we are reminded of Rāma eating the berries which Śabarī offered after tasting them herself (Araṇyakāṇḍa 73).

Food is provided by villagers wherever the Vanvāsīs halt. They are received with great respect. The idea that 'It is Rām who has come to our village' leads to a kind of communion between the Rām-Vanvasīs and villagers (*śirlelī maṇḍalī āṇi gāvātīl hi donhī antaḥkaraṇāni ek hotāt*). The Vanvāsīs first circumambulate the village, and then stay outside the village in some temple. One should not stay as a guest in a house. The Vanvāsīs will not proceed before they have sung the praise of the deity of the village. After fourteen days the pilgrims return to their own village. Those who have remained at home anxiously wait for them. The houses are decorated. Especially the women folk of the Vanvāsīs have been experiencing a kind of *viraha* and have been singing songs which subtly suggest that their lot may be compared to that of Sītā, who suffered from separation in the Aśoka *vana*.

sod[SM: ḍ]*ūna gele Rāma*,
kase malā sodūna gele Rāma?

Rāma has left me,
how is it that Rāma has left me?

After circumambulating the village the Vanvāsīs are conducted into the village with the accompaniment of music and drums. It is as if Rāma were returning from the forest to jubilant Ayodhya. As one of the Vanvāsīs put it: 'Those who come back return successfully and victoriously like Rāma. The evil ones have been defeated, and the good ones on earth have been reinstated.'

But this is not yet the conclusion of the pilgrimage. It ends with the so-called festival of Lakṣmaṇa *śakti* (*Lakṣmaṇ śaktīcā sohaḷā*). The rite is based on seven chapters of Eknāth's *Bhāvārth-Rāmāyaṇ*.[13] In these chapters we are told that Lakṣmaṇa saves Vibhīṣaṇa, who has sought refuge with him. Lakṣmaṇa deflects the *śakti* missile (a lance) which Rāvaṇa throws at Vibhīṣaṇa; it hits Lakṣmaṇa on the chest. The personified *śakti* is freed from the hands of the villain Rāvaṇa and comes to take shelter with Lakṣmaṇa. Lakṣmaṇa faints and remains unconscious the whole night. The whole night the Vanvāsīs have to stand on their feet and are watched by a large audience which consists of more women than men. Meanwhile the last seven chapters are being read by notable reciters and expounders who are invited from outside the village on that occasion. The recitation is interspersed with *bhajan* songs. The seven chapters have to be finished on time, and the *ovī* which tells of Lakṣmaṇa's regaining consciousness has to be recited just before sunrise, otherwise the ceremony remains fruitless (*niṣphal*). At the point when the last *ovī* is recited, everybody breaks a coconut. The noise of the crushing is tremendous: [and the observer feels] no wonder Lakṣmaṇa regains his consciousness. This completes the *vanvās* and the desired result is obtained (*lābh*).

CONCLUSION

The interaction of all-India and regional and scriptural versions of the Rāmāyaṇa with local or regional folk traditions has been a neglected field in Maharashtra studies. There is some urgency for this research, because local myths, ancient customary rituals, and old oral literature tend to become erased or modified beyond recognition by the imposing, modern all-India Great Tradition.

Three cases of the reception of scriptural Rāmāyaṇa versions in a local or regional context have been described here. The first case shows how a once rather desolate 'forest' area with a caravan; reputed to be infested by robbers, attracted the legend of Vālmīki, 'the Robber'. The legend has raised the village out of anonymity. Certain well-known features of the 'classical' legend are identified and localized in the village tradition and form a part of the annual village festival (*jatrā*). In addition, the legend of Vālmīki, the erstwhile robber, helped a traditional robber caste, the Rāmośīs (or Berads), to associate themselves with Vālmīki. He became their mythic ancestor. By a folk etymology they derive their name from Rāma: Rāmośī is said to be derived from *Rāma-vaṃśa*. Others say it is derived from *rān-vāsī*: he who lives in the wilderness (Sontheimer 1976: 85f.).

The second case demonstrate how a typical folk deity, Niṃbādaitya, attracts respectability and publicity because of his association with Rāma and his legend. The 'concession' made to this development is the abandonment of non-vegetarian offerings. Yet Niṃbādaitya retains typical features of a folk deity: the red colour, the ability to answer vows (*navas*) by granting children and jobs, and the role of protector of the village.

The third case shows how an old custom of folk religion is being transformed towards a 'panthic' Vaiṣṇava bhakti movement. No longer does the desire for rain tend to motivate the Rām-Vanvāsīs to go for a pilgrimage—this would be *sakām* in their eyes—but more general, spiritual (*niṣkām*) aims are professed: worship of Rāma by enacting his *vanvās* on the scriptural basis of the *Bhāvārth-Rāmāyaṇ* of Eknāth, singing Rāma's name, and reading the scripture; the sheer joy of absenting oneself from settled life for some time and joining a group of pilgrims amongst whom caste distinctions are suspended, paired with the feeling of performing *tapas* (or *kaṣṭ*, i.e. 'toil') by exposing oneself to the 'dangers' of the pilgrimage; and the attainment of more vaguely expressed aims such as *lābh* (spiritual merit) and *mān* (prestige). Remarkable is the high moral tone of the informants, who are prominent Vanvāsīs and are considered to be 'gurus'. Here the Rāmāyaṇa as a source informing the ethical behaviour, perhaps rather of the group and the village than of the individual, becomes more and more evident. Moreover, we may say that the gurus of the modern Vanvāsīs are initiators of a 'new' tradition using elements of older traditions.

In the folk-religious ritual the need to reinvigorate nature and to procure rain is pre-eminent. The modern Rām-Vanvāsīs—influenced by scripture and saints—emphasize spiritual gains. In both cases we observe the important role of the forest as a source of renewal of life. Amongst the Vanvāsīs we may notice the tendency to locate the 'centre out there' (V. Turner) no longer in the forest, but in a *kṣetra* or *tīrtha*. Such a centre itself often originally emerged out of a *vana*: e.g. Pañcavaṭī, which is situated in the mythical Daṇḍakāraṇya, or Pandharpur. In Pandharpur the memory of the primordial forest is still preserved by the existence of the Diṇḍīra grove (cp. Sontheimer 1987: *passim*). Generally we can notice the important role the forest has played in myth and ritual, and in this respect the Rāmāyaṇa also had much inspiration to offer.

NOTES

* This paper includes material which was collected during a stay in Maharashtra from August 1984 to April 1985. I am grateful to the German Research Association (DFG) for financial support. Subsequent visits were financed privately. I have to thank Rajaram B. Zagade and Ramdas S. Atkar, who helped me in collecting and transcribing material some of which has been used here. Dr. C. Kiehnle and Dr. James Laine have made helpful remarks on the paper.

Abbreviations: Ma. = Marathi, Skt. = Sanskrit, SM = Standard written Marathi.

1. This is what the director (Ma. *digdarśak*), Rāmānand Sāgar, had to say in an interview about the sources of the series: 'The main works are Vālmīki's *Rāmāyaṇa* and Tulsīdās' *Rāmcaritmānas*. Besides I have seen and read all *Rāmāyaṇas* available in Indian languages [*sic*]. I have read Rajgopalachari's English version, in Telugu there is Raṅganāth's *Rāmāyaṇa* [*c*. AD 1240], there is Sant Eknāth's *Bhāvārth-Rāmāyaṇ*, and I have considered versions in Bengalī, Kannaḍa, and Hindī.'

   Sakāḷ, Friday, 2 October 1987, p. 20.

   The effect of the series has frequently been experienced in public: A Langur monkey which had lost one of its hands in an accident had become unusually tame and attached to humans in Jejuri (Pune District). Ever since Hanumān appeared in the series for the first time, the long-tailed, black-faced monkey was and still is pampered with offerings of up to twelve bananas. Or: in Goa the burning of Laṅkā by Hanumān was enacted by children a little bit too realistically, with the result that a number of hutments were set ablaze.
2. Ayodhyakāṇḍa 116. Cited from Muir's *Original Sanskrit Texts* (vol. V) by Mahāmahopadhyāya V.V. Mirashi in *Maharashtra State Gazetteers*, *Nagpur District*, Bombay, 1975, pp. 44f.
3. Preliminary information about Niṃbā Daitya was obtained from an interview given by Suresh Joshi in the newspaper *Kesarī*, dated 30 March 1984. The short article is entitled 'Rāmbhakt Niṃbādaityācī pāḍavyās yātrā'.
4. This is a typical expression in folk religion and folk literature: It is not the person carrying the pot who is said to be dancing but the *pot* is seen as dancing. Similarly the flagstaffs (Ma. *kaṭhyā*, Skt. *dhvaja*) of folk deities dance, or we should perhaps say that their human carriers cause them to dance. In any case it looks this way from a distance. In folk festivals of the Dhangar shepherds, the

bhūts (the ancestral spirits), are brought to life by the dance of the shepherds.

5. Folk deities are often considered to be jugglers and magicians while performing their miracles, e.g. taking all sorts of forms at will. Magic knowledge (the fourteen *vidyās*) is believed to come from Bengal. See Sontheimer (1976: 39, 54f.) and cp. ibid., p. 183 [cp. *Pastoral Deities of Western India*, pp. 35, 51f. and 188] for the meaning of *māyā* (Ma. *māv*) in this context.
6. The text is quoted in translation from the article in *Kesarī* (see above n. 3).
7. But we may be wrong. Shri Suresh Joshi mentions that the *Sthānapothī* of the Mahānubhāva sect refers to a temple of Niṃbādaitya in Paithan. The temple does not exist today and the reference to Niṃbādaitya could not be traced in the *Sthānapothī*. According to Joshi, Niṃbādaitya is a name of the sun and Niṃbādaitya must have been a worshipper of the sun. The animosity between Hanumān and Niṃbādaitya may thus be traced to the myth which says that when Hanumān was born he ran after Sūrya to swallow him, thinking that he was food.
8. Kosambi (1962: 95), Cāphekar (1923: 320f). During the exile from the village no lamp was to be lit in the village. The re-entry into the village had to take place from the village gate and from nowhere else. Two stalks of the *sāvarī* tree were buried between which one had to enter the village. The sequence of the participants in the procession entering the village suggests the sequence of the original settlement: the Mahārs (significantly, often considered to be the original settlers of villages) would go ahead, followed by the Pāṭīl. Then the Brāhmaṇs would follow, along with the rest of the people. In some places a young married couple would go ahead.
9. Some Vanvāsīs say that the new custom is 30-40 years old, others say it is about 60 years. One Vanvāsī said that the custom gathered momentum after 1972.
10. Information has been obtained amongst others from Śrī Rāmcandra Nāmdev Cākṇe (Cāṇḍgāv, Taluka Śrīgonde, District Ahmednagar, about 47 years old, of the Māḷī caste), Śrī Bhosle Gurujī (Pāprī, Taluka Mohol, District Sholapur, about 60 years old, a Marāṭhā), and Śrī Mārtaṇḍ Rāmu Kacre (Mūrti Moḍhve, Taluka Bārāmati, District Pune, about 90 years old, a Kolhaṭī by caste).
11. *Rāma toci Viṭhṭhala jālā. Rāmadāsāsī bheṭalā.* Rāmadāsi Anantādās, ed., *Śrīsamarthāṃcā Gāthā*, Vāī. Vyaṃkaṭrāv Śrīnivāsrāv Solāpūrkar, Loksaṃgrah Chāpkhānā [Press], Puṇeṃ, Śake 1850 [AD 1928], abhaṃg 52, p. 26. Pāṃgārkar (1978: 633).
12. The great emphasis on the purity of the *vinā* is intriguing. Dance and music, in particular the sound of a lute, were considered impure in the *śrauta* texts (Heesterman 1985: 32f.). According to the *Manusmṛti*, the recitation of Vedic texts had to be avoided on hearing the sound of a lute (10.113). Similarly, the study of Vedic texts had to be suspended at the braying of a donkey (10.115). In the view of the Vanvāsīs, the *vanvās* is not without danger, e.g. because of stray dogs. Thus the sojourn also means challenging and playing with death. *Vanvās* as well as the lute are both associated with death (Heesterman 1985:

ibid.), so that the whole ritual may imply that life is won out of death. Death and chaos have to be controlled and ordered by the rhythm of the *vinā*, which is, in the Vanvāsīs' view, a weapon of Life rather than of Death. It is the rhythm which regulates and channels the singing towards auspicious ends.

13. The 'seven chapters' are chs. 43-9 in the 'Yuddhakāṇḍ' of the *Śribhāvārth-rāmāyaṇ*, ed. Narhari Viṣṇuśāstrī Paṇsikar, Yaśvant Prakāśan, Puṇe 2, 1968.

REFERENCES

Bhāratīy Saṃskṛtikoś, 1974, Aṭhvā khaṃd [vol. 8], ed. by Paṃ[dit] Mahādev-śāstrī Jośī [and] Tarktīrth Sau[mati] Padmajā Hoḍākar. Puṇe: Bhāratīy Saṃskṛtikoś Maṃḍaḷ.

Cāphekar, Nārāyaṇ Govind, 1923, *Badlāpūr*. Puṇe: Āryasaṃskṛti Mudraṇālay, Śake 1855.

Heestermann, J.C., 1985, *The Inner Conflict of Tradition: Essays in Indian Ritual, Kingship, and Society*. Chicago: University of Chicago Press.

Kosambi, D.D., 1962, *Myth and Reality: Studies in the Formation of Indian Culture*. Bombay: Popular Prakashan.

Māṇḍe, Prabhākar, 1975, *Lokasāhityāce antaḥpravāh*. Puṇe: Kāntinenṭal Prakāśan.

Marriott, McKim, 1955, 'Little Communities in an Indigenous Civilization', in McKim Marriott (ed.), *Village India*. Chicago: University of Chicago Press, 171-222.

Mhāiṃbhaṭ [Kolte], 1978, *Līḷācaritra*, ed. by V.B. Kolte. Muṃbaī: Mahārāṣṭra Rājya Sāhitya Saṃskṛti Maṇḍal.

Pāṃgārkar, Lakṣmaṇ Rāmcandra (ed.), 1978, *Śrīsamarth-granth-bhāṃḍār*. 2nd edn. Bombay.

Śekh Mahaṃmad [Ḍhere], 1981, *Śekh Mahaṃmad viracit* Yogsaṃgrām, [ed. by Rāmcandra Cintāmaṇ Ḍhere]. Puṇe: 'Vardā', Senāpati Bāpaṭ Mārg.

Shulman, D.D., 1981, 'The Crossing of the Wilderness: Landscape and Myth in the Tamil story of Rāma', *Acta Orientalia* 42: 21-54.

Sontheimer, Günther-Dietz, 1976, *Birobā, Mhaskobā und Khaṇḍobā: Ursprung, Entwicklung und Umwelt von pastoralen Gottheiten in Māhārāṣṭra*. Wiesbaden: Harrassowitz. [Editor's note: English version: *Pastoral Deities of Western India*, New York, 1989.]

———1987, 'The *Vana* and the *Kṣetra*: the Tribal Background of Some Famous Cults', in G.C. Tripathi and Hermann Kulke (eds.), *Eschmann Memorial Lectures*, vol. 1 (1978-86), Eschmann Memorial Fund, c/o Dept. of History, Utkal, Bhubaneswar-4: 117-64. [Editor's note: Also in the present volume, pp. 353-82.]

Stein, Burton, 1985, *Peasant, State and Society in Medieval South India*. 1st. pb. edn. Delhi: Oxford University Press.

Vaudeville, Charlotte, 1987, 'The Śaivite Background of Santism in Maharashtra', in Milton Israel and N.K. Wagle (eds.), *Religion and Society in Maharashtra*. South Asian Studies. University of Toronto: 32-50.

Hinduism: The Five Components and Their Interaction

HINDUISM AND THE STUDY OF HINDUISM

The approach to Hinduism here is not to work out another monolithic conceptualization, but first to distinguish the different layers, levels, strands, currents, or, as I shall call them, *components*, and to treat each of them in its own right. They will then, however, not be viewed as watertight compartments, but rather as presenting a continuum and as interacting among themselves in a fluctuating process over thousands of years.

There is no comparable theology or religious conceptual framework or even terminology in Western religions which completely fits what we call 'Hinduism'; this has made comparative religion hazardous. There may be an underlying unity of Hinduism, expressing itself in a statement such as 'India is one'. But this unity is often postulated more or less on the basis of partial and selective evidence. Modern scholars have made many important and stimulating contributions towards understanding Hinduism, but their methodological approaches and key concepts are open to criticism and rarely stand the test of time. The study and understanding of Hinduism are handicapped not only by the vastness of divergent material and sources, but also by the compartmentalisations of academic specializations such as philology, anthropology, sociology, religion, philosophy, psychology and so on. But Hinduism necessarily partakes of all these fields. In the past Hinduism was comprehended by the term *dharma*, but *dharma* did not mean the same thing at all times in all contexts for all people. It had to be defined again and again, not only from case to case, but also at several levels. It has been suggested that Hinduism is *sanātana dharma*: this may mean the conformity to old customs and the preservation of the solidarity of society not only at any given time, but also through time. The stress was on maintaining eternal *dharma*, deviation from which spelled personal and social ruin (Creel 1977: 20f.). Nowadays it is stressed that it is ultimate reality which is eternal and changeless, but that there is no ultimacy about socio-religious institutions and customs (Creel 1977: 46 citing T.M.P. Mahadevan).

Ultimately the nature of Hinduism as a comprehensive religion is characterized by features which would make some say it is no religion (in the Western sense), namely the absence of dogmatic tenets or an overarching authority, however influential a particular belief may be, e.g. the belief in the authority of the Veda. But, as has been pointed out, one can be a good Hindu without believing in the Veda. Marglin formulates this aptly: '. . . to conceptualize the Hindu life-world from a single consistent point of view is to ignore the fact that there is not one privileged point of view from which to look at things. The 'objective', non-situated viewpoint is a myth dear to the Western scientific life-world but I would suggest not to the Hindu life-world.' (Marglin 1985: 289).

We have tried to distinguish five components which appear whenever one investigates Indian religious phenomena (cp. Kelkar 1977: 23f., who speaks of three elements). Our approach is motivated by a desire to teach Hinduism to students systematically and by an uneasiness which comes to us from seeing that some components are often ignored or misunderstood for various reasons. Such 'endocentric' perceptions of the multiple elements or strata of Hinduism as *mārga* ('classical') and *deśi* ('folk'), *dharma* and *deśadharma* (cp. Wezler 1985: 1ff.), Sanskrit and Prakrit, *saumya* = 'peaceful', 'auspicious', etc., and *ugra* are extremely useful and have hardly been systematically explored, but we have to be cautious whose 'endocentric' view we take. Thus, for example, a 'lower' deity would be called by some *ugra* = 'fierce', 'ferocious', 'ogre-like', 'appalling', 'shocking', etc. (Molesworth 1857: 86). But this might not be acceptable to the actual adherent of such a deity, for whom *ugra* (if he knows the term) would imply 'powerful', 'mighty', 'strong', 'high', 'noble' (cp. Monier-Williams 1956: 172). And we may take a contextual view, as did, e.g. the Maharashtrian saint Rāmdās (1608-81): in one place he lists the famous folk deity Khaṇḍobā amongst the ghosts (*Dāsbodh* 3.2.29), but nevertheless sees him elsewhere as powerful enough to grant children (ibid. 3.3.47), and in yet another context even identifies him with Rāma (Sontheimer 1986a: 19). Khaṇḍobā, God as king, and Rāma, the ideal king, thus share an essential element of successful kingship, i.e. both are *ugra*.

Indian religious phenomena may partake of some or all of these components, but the important point is *which component is emphasized* and *which may be just secondary, subordinated, peripheral, or amounting to lip service in a particular case or at a particular time*. Once the components are distinguished we can use 'endocentric' perceptions and also test and apply the theories developed by modern scholars as far as they are relevant to the interaction of the different components. I shall list some of the most important theories below. I shall not try to be exhaustive, because this is not the main concern of this paper. It may seem superfluous to summarize the contents of some well known theories, but that has to be, because they may not be so well known to followers of other disciplines. It may also be unnecessary to reiterate that these theories are often based on the approach and object of *one* discipline and cannot explain the *whole* phenomenon of Hinduism. In this context it is tempting, though admittedly arrogant in view of the path-breaking but restricted contributions which scholars in various disciplines have made, to recall the famous parable of the 'Elephant and the Blind Men' (*Udāna* 6, 4 and elsewhere).

We may start with the well known concept of *Sanskritization* developed by M.N. Srinivas (1952; Staal 1963: 261ff.). According to him Sanskritization is a process by which a lower caste tries to raise its status and to achieve a higher position in the caste hierarchy. Sanskritization can happen by adoption of vegetarianism, teetotalism, worship of Sanskritic deities, or employment of Brahmans for ritual purposes. It can refer to ritual and custom, ideas and beliefs, as well as to the pantheon. The material to which Sanskritization applies consists of non-Sanskritic gods, beliefs, and rituals, e.g. the worship of village deities, ancestors, trees, rivers, mountains, and generally local cults. Sanskritization happens *at the expense* of non-Sanskritic elements.

Following Robert Redfield and Srinivas, Milton Singer introduced the distinction between 'Little Tradition' and 'Great Tradition'. The 'Great Tradition' was identified with Srinivas' Sanskritic Hinduism, i.e. the generalized practice and beliefs which have an All-India spread. The local forms of Hinduism can be seen as the 'Little Tradition', and Sanskritization becomes the process by which the 'Great Tradition' spreads to the 'Little Tradition' and absorbs it (see summary in Staal 1963: 263f.).

McKim Marriott (1965: 171-222) pointed out that Sanskritization does not necessarily take place *at the expense of* the little tradition, and that the identification of a local deity with a universal deity is one of the main techniques of Sanskritization. He introduced instead the concepts of universalization and parochialization. One finds in an Indian village a transmutation and transformation of great and little traditions resulting from upward universalization (the carrying forward of religious contents which are already present in the little traditions to the levels of the literate Sanskritic great traditions of Hinduism under the influence of the latter) and parochialization (downward evolution of great traditional elements and their integration with the little traditional elements). But it is difficult to know whether the present religious tradition of a community is the result of one, and not also the result of the other, of these two processes. After all, as Staal reminded us (1963: 269), Sanskrit culture itself originated from the little tradition and these origins are generally visible in a later stage.

Another concept relevant in our context is 'Inklusivismus'. This is a term which Paul Hacker uses to describe data

> aus demjenigen Bereich, den wir indische Religionen und speziell indische Religionsphilosophie nennen. Inklusivismus bedeutet, dass man erklärt, eine zentrale Vorstellung einer fremden religiösen oder weltanschaulichen Gruppe sei identisch mit dieser oder jener zentralen Vorstellung einer Gruppe, zu der man selber gehört. Meistens gehört zum Inklusivismus ausgesprochen oder unausgesprochen die Behauptung, dass das Fremde, das mit dem Eigenen als identisch erklärt wird, in irgendeiner Weise ihm untergeordnet oder unterlegen sei. Ferner wird ein Beweis dafür, dass das Fremde mit dem Eigenen identisch sei, meist nicht unternommen. (Hacker 1983: 12)

Hacker uses the term 'Inklusivismus' mainly in textual criticism of Sanskrit literature and in the field of theology and philosophical ideas expressed in texts. Hacker's views have been reviewed by Halbfass, Oberhammer and Wezler (Oberhammer: 1983). According to Wezler, *Inklusivismus* mainly implies a relationship of tension between the *old* and the *new*, *tradition* and *change*. He extends the theory to psychological, social and similar conditions which he considers responsible for the *practice* of inclusivism. For example, the strict tradition of family values handed down in the joint family might psychologically generate the attitude of Inklusivismus, which leads to taking over the new without radically abandoning the old. We are reminded here of the suggestion of McKim Marriott, who proposes the term 'dividuality' of the person 'in the flow of social relationships' (1976: 196)—for example, a member of a joint family may belong at the same time to a sect which may transcend family, caste and religion (cp. Derrett 1976: 60f.).

Modifying Dumont's theory of the dichotomy of pure and impure based on one model of hierarchical Hindu society, i.e. the *varṇa* model (Dumont 1966), Burghart (1978) has suggested that there are three hierarchical models, which are incongruent: (a) the Brahmanical organic model of the sacrificial body of Brahmā as the cosmic-based social organism composed of four *varṇas*, (b) the continuum of the incorporated *jīvas* which are separate from the ascetic, who ranks highest in this hierarchy, and (c) the king who rules over the earth (*bhūpati*) and men irrespective of caste, tribe or sect, differentiated by their respective rights and duties towards him.

Brahman, ascetic and king each claim their highest rank and godhood within the respective hierarchies. But the hierarchies do not face each other as rigid structures, but rather interact (in a typically Indian way?). Elements of the codices of another hierarchy were incorporated into each one's own hierarchical model, and the highest ranking person of the other hierarchy was assigned an honourable but subordinate rank within the enlarged model (Burghart 1978).

Recently A.K. Ramanujan has presented the important theory of 'reflexivity' for the interactions between different Indian literatures, oral and written. Unfortunately the paper is as yet unpublished (Ramanujan 1985a). Ramanujan says that similar observations can be made about other aspects of the culture, such as ritual, philosophy, eating, or socio-linguistic patterns. He states: 'Reflexive elements may occur in various sizes: one part of a text may reflect on another part; a whole tradition may invert, negate, rework and revalue another. Where cultures (like the 'Indian') are stratified yet interconnected, where different communities communicate but do not commune, the texts of one strata tend to reflect on those of another: encompassment, mimicry, criticism and conflict, and other power relations are expressed by such reflexivities. Self-conscious contrasts and reversals also mark off and individuate the groups.... Stereotypes, foreign views, and native self-images on the part of some groups, all tend to think of one part (say, the Brahmanical) as original, and the rest as variations, aberrations: so we tend to get monolithic conceptions. But the civilization, if it can be described at all, has to be described in terms of all these dynamic interrelations. . . .' It follows that a view of what Hinduism is cannot be exclusively derived from the attitudes, written and/or oral texts, or statements of members of *one* group, however articulate they may be. Admittedly, modern middle class notions favour certain aspects of Hinduism; these may be summarily circumscribed by the preference for 'Rāmrājya', Kṛṣṇa, the *Bhagavadgītā* (now nearly a 'scripture' like the Bible), bhakti, sectarian guru worship, and emphasis on the spiritual and philosophical contents of Hinduism, especially the Vedānta of 'Neohinduism' (cp. Derrett 1968: 560). In this process, much of the ritual world (the *karmakāṇḍa*) of the Smṛtis or the culture of the 'Little Traditions', for example, gets out of focus or even disappears, along with its enormous oral literature, whereas middle class notions become more and more assertive and dominant, if not monolithic. All the more does the past of Hinduism have to be studied and recorded taking *all* components and their interaction into account, so that we can isolate modern trends towards reductionism, and detect change or persistence.

These theories and concepts, as well as the five components—which I shall outline below—must also be reviewed in the context of time and space. Mythological, astrological, sacred and historical/secular time have to be taken into account. The element of time plays a role, e.g. in the fixing of festivals: for example, tribal festivals especially are seasonal, and every year the exact dates for the *madhais* in Bastar in the month of Māgh are fixed *ad hoc* by a secular body at the end of the harvest season. All-India festivals are determined by astrological considerations. Equally important is the dimension of space. The old Tamil theory of the landscapes (*tiṇai*) may be referred to here. The *tiṇai* theory may have become just a literary convention, but I would still maintain that it was based originally on direct observations of facts which persisted in later times. Each of the five landscapes (*kuṟiñci* = the densely forested, hilly region, *mullai* = the pastoral region, *marutam* = the riverine agricultural region, and *pālai* = the 'desert', are especially relevant here) is inhabited by its own deities, roughly typical of the environment, and by people following occupations adapted to the landscape. It can be shown that the theory has at least a great heuristic value in explaining the basic pattern of religious forms (Sontheimer 1985a: 131ff.) and can be applied to other parts of India at least until the '*pax britannica*' and the subsequent deforestation and systematic extension of agriculture on a scale never before experienced in Indian history. The contents of the *tiṇai* theory and of Caṅkam poetry reflect a rather 'secular', though not irreligious, outlook on life.

The spatial dimension also plays a great role in Sanskrit culture and literature. I have called this Indian version of the 'dichotomy' of 'nature' and 'culture' summarily and for the sake of simplicity *vana* and *kṣetra*, or 'wilderness' and 'settled space' (Sontheimer: 1994 [1987]). I have avoided the terms 'nature' and 'culture' since *vana* and *kṣetra* may be partially co-extensive. As A.K. Ramanujan has said with reference to the classical Tamil poems (1985b: 286), nature and culture are in these poems not opposed but co-substantial. Between the two poles of *vana* and *kṣetra* there is a reversible, fluctuating continuity. A Brahmanical *kṣetra* with a purāṇic deity may relapse again into a locality where pastoral people and 'predatory' people dominate. The deity is forgotten and is superseded by a folk deity attended by Guravs, a non-brahminical caste (Sontheimer 1976: 23ff.). The forest with all its implications, e.g. social, mythological, ritual, philosophical and so on, was also, as we have said, very much a physical reality until the extension of agriculture in modern times. 150 years or so ago Rāma still would not have had to go very far from Ayodhyā to be in the midst of a forest. *Kṣetra* I would describe, in brief, as well-ordered space, the riverine agricultural nuclear area which is ideally ordered by the King, and by the Brahmans with their *dharmaśāstra*. If we speak in terms of settlement patterns, the two poles are demarcated by the 'movable' tribal hamlet, the *halli* or *palli* (Sontheimer 1985a: 134), on the one hand and the ideal but static city of Ayodhyā as described in the *Rāmāyaṇa* (cp. Ramanujan 1970: 234).

THE FIVE COMPONENTS OF HINDUISM

(1) THE WORK AND THE TEACHING OF THE BRAHMANS

The Brahmans were the authors of authoritative scriptures which formed the elements of what is sometimes called codified Hinduism (Eschmann 1978: 82) or its normative ideology (Hardy 1984: 13ff.), though we must remember that this normative Hinduism rather had only persuasive power and was no law in the western sense. The basis of the Brahmans' belief and of their prestige was the eternal imperishable Veda (*śruti*), that is, texts which are not derived from God or Man (*apauruṣeya*). The Brahmans were the compilers of the *Dharmaśāstras* (*smṛti*), in which they ordered life, teaching what was righteousness in their view. Dharma was strictly speaking to be interpreted according to the *mīmāṃsā* rules of the Vedic sacrifice. Accordingly all customs conflicting with *śruti* and *smṛti* were to be treated as void. The king was not obliged to follow *mīmāṃsā* rules: the Brahmans who advised him had no power to require him to follow their advice. In practice the public followed customs, even when repugnant to the *śāstra* (Derrett et al. 1976: 17ff., 57, 111). The Brahmanical world view in the *Dharmaśāstras* may be seen as a ritual model of the universe expressed in social categories. The universe is a manifestation of Brahmā or a totality of ordered time and space. According to the organic model, society was founded by Brahmā at the beginning of time and from him emerged the four *varṇas* (Burghart 1983: 637). Within this framework the Brahmans searched out and formulated the hidden values of human behaviour. They reflected on what were only human instincts. They were the great ritual experts, and they are still indispensable today, at least in the most important rites de passage (i.e. the *saṃskāras*), or, for example, in the *vastu-śānti-pūjā* for a new factory.

In the epics and the Purāṇas Brahmans gathered and reworked a part of the immense oral literature. They responded to the human inclination to assign the miraculous deeds of heroes and gods to the Golden Age of truth (*satyayuga*) and divided time into four cyclical ages. According to the Purāṇas, the gods normally resided in heaven; only from time to time when *dharma* was in danger Viṣṇu descended as an *avatār* to restore *dharma*. The kings were not so much deities as in folk belief but rather had the *functions* of deities. What was alien to the epics and the Purāṇas, which are also a part of *smṛti*, was a deity immediately accessible to man, 'here and now'. The gods who were part of the universe created by Brahmā became secondary in importance in the Vedic *yajña* of the *śrauta* ritual, and they were subordinated to the ritual act as such. When *mūrtis* became common the deity in the *mūrti* was not a visible, tangible manifestation of god as in folk religion, but, as Śabara, the commentator on the *Pūrvamīmāṃsāsūtras*, argued: *na lokavad iha bhavitavyam, iha pūjyamānaṃ pūjā pradhānam* (IX, 1, 9; Sontheimer 1964: 50f.) 'The *worshipping* of the worshipped is the main factor in the ritual.' This corresponds with the notion that the Brahmans are highest gods (Manu IX. 317-19: *daivataṃ paramam*) on earth and that strictly speaking they should not serve as *devalakas*, i.e. as temple priests (Manu IX. 152).

(2) ASCETICISM AND RENUNCIATION

Asceticism (*tapas*) and renunciation (*saṃnyās*) and resulting 'sectarian movements' constitute another component. Asceticism and abstinence may have various aims, e.g. the achievement of the heightening of life-potentiality by the *tapasvin* (Piatigorsky 1985: 229-31), like the demon who performs *tapas* to obtain a boon of immortality from Brahmā. This kind of *tapas* brings the 'yogī' close to the 'warrior'. Often juxtaposed in folk religion, both achieve superhuman feats (Sontheimer 1981: 15). Whereas in folk religion the aim of *tapas* is to acquire supernormal powers, side by side we find the effort to ethicize and spiritualize *tapas* (cp. Rüping 1977: 81-98).

The aim of asceticism may also be to renounce the life of the householder and caste. According to the *Dharmaśāstras*, the ascetic renounces family and property, though not the world emanating from Brahmā; this he internalizes (Burghart 1983: 639). Standing apart from ordinary society, the ascetic lives a wandering life in the wilderness, at least during the initial phase of his career; he is beyond the plurality of phenomena and sees the unity of man, though he may visualize the *jīvas* caught in the cycle of rebirth bound by their *karman*. He discerns the unity of *ātman* and *brahman*. His discipline (*tapas*) may involve a wandering life in the forest (*vanavāsa*). This normally lasts twelve years, just as Cakradhara—to cite one example—wandered twelve years in the forest before he re-emerged and attracted followers who eventually formed the Mahānubhāv 'sect' (Sontheimer 1982: 334). The preconditions of the ascetics' insights are not the performance of the *karmakāṇḍa* of the *Dharmaśāstra* but self-discipline and the pursuit of such ethical principles as *dama*, *satya*, *akrodha*, and *dayā*. *Ahiṃsā* was another principle which was born in the realm of the ascetic renouncer who lives in harmony with the animals of the forest. The ascetic's *dharmas* also found a place as the *sādhāraṇa dharmas* in the *Dharmaśāstra*. Although they were subordinated to *varṇa* and caste *dharmas*, they made life in the *kṣetra* tolerable and acceptable, and made the *varṇa* ideology a viable proposition.

(3) TRIBAL RELIGION

As the third component I would like to consider tribal religion. One may object that postulating 'tribal religion' means unnecessarily introducing an 'etic' or 'exocentric' category as a component which is not found in Hinduism. But the tribals are mentioned from the earliest times in texts and they stand in relationship to the social and ritual order of the plains, if only with an antithetical function as the necessary evil. As such they are referred to as robbers and even as demons (*piśācas* or *bhūtas*). At the same time we find seemingly paradoxical references to their honesty, gratitude and innocence (Deliege 1985: 11f.). This is reflected, e.g. in the famous episode when Śabarī, a woman of the tribal forest-dwellers, offered Rāma berries which she had already tasted (*Rāmāyaṇa, Āraṇyakāṇḍa 73*). This notion of the tribals accords well with the image of their habitat amongst the people of the plains. The forest is as ambivalent as the tribal: fearsome and at the same time the source of renewal and 'the seed of dharma'. By tribal religion I mean not only the religion of the forest tribes, e.g. of the Murias and Marias of Bastar, but also the great, often nomadizing pastoral groups who live in Rajasthan and in the Deccan. Mountains, the termite mound, trees, animals of the forest, rivers, all characteristic of untamed, dangerous nature, are close to them and intrinsically divine. Religion reflects human life and the relation to deities is marked by intimate familiarity. Anthropomorphic *mūrtis* of deities are rare (Elwin 1955: 577; Eschmann 1978: 81f.), because 'shamans' get possessed by and deal with ancestors of the family, clan gods, or the earth-goddess, the *devī* of the village. For example, the shrine of the goddess Dantesvarī at Chota Dongar in Bastar has no *image*, and the 'seat' of the *devī* is empty. There are now often bell-metal *mūrtis* in temples, but the art of casting *mūrtis* is a relatively recent import to Bastar.

Drumming and dancing activate the spirits and divinities. Dance and music are also the expression of the deities (the marriage god) which grant fertility, as in the marriage dances of the Marias of Bastar. Part of the marriage dances may also be the enactment of encounters with bison. Similarly, the bull-grappling of pastoralists preceding marriages is mentioned in early Tamil literature and bull-baiting is common in some parts of contemporary Tamilnadu (Hardy 1983: 616ff.).

In the view of people adhering to other components, tribal customs are reputed to be marked by sexual licentiousness and freedom. Misunderstood as these customs are by the people in the *kṣetra*, they contributed to the inversion in such tantric practices as the *śabarotsava* (*Kālikāpurāṇa* 63.17ff.), in which the normal rules of hierarchy and sexual propriety are abandoned. Similarly, the love of the *gopīs* for Kṛṣṇa is interpreted as erotic or it is interpreted as a pure example of emotional bhakti, or it is interpreted philosophically in terms of *yoga* or *advaita* (Hardy 1983: 494ff.). Thus we must keep in mind that there was not only a process of 'Hinduization' of tribes but also the influence of tribes on Hinduism (see Kulke 1979: 17ff.).

(4) FOLK RELIGION

A crucial ingredient in folk religion is the immediate presence and access to a god or a goddess in the form of a *mūrti* or *mūrtis* which may be aniconic or iconic. The god exists 'here and now', is earthbound, and does not live in some purāṇic *svarga*.

The folk deity is well-described in the view of the *pūrvapakśin* in the *devatādhikaraṇa* (IX. 1.6-8) of the *Pūrvamīmāṃsāsūtras*. Of course, this view is unacceptable to the *siddhāntin*, who presents the 'orthodox' interpretation of the Veda. The *pūrvapakśin* suggests:

(a) *vigrahatva devatā*: the deity possesses corporality.
(b) *devatā bhuṅkte*: the deity actually eats food in the form of offerings.
(c) *prasīdati devatā*: the deity is actually pleased by the offering.
(d) *pritā satī phalaṃ prayacchati*: the deity rewards the worshipper with the desired fruit.
(e) *arthapati devatā*: the deity can be an owner of property.

The *mūrti* has as it were a living personality and is treated as a living person: institutions like *prasād*, *darśan*, etc., indicate this. But there are many more terms in regional languages which form an unwritten inventory of folk cults. They point to a pervasive, coherent and conservative system of folk religion which is spread all over South Asia and which can never be expected to have been reproduced in its original form in Brahmanical texts. In practice the Brahman would nevertheless often participate in folk religion, and it would form the raw material for textual interpretation. Thus, the primordial cult of the mother goddess reappears in Māhātmyas and śaktic-tantric texts and ritual. We may cite *some* terms which are ubiquitous in the practice of Maharashtrian folk cults and which also have their equivalents in other regions and languages (cp. e.g. Höfer and Shrestha 1973: *passim*).

aṅgāt yeṇeṃ—possession by a deity or a *bhūt*. This normally does not happen in a Śiva or Viṣṇu temple with a purāṇic (*saumya*) emphasis.

devruṣi (Sanskrit *deva+ṛṣi*)—the medium who can get possessed by ancestors and god(s) and deal with them.

jāgṛt dev—the deity is alive, attentive, heedful and responsive, that is

dev pāvto—the deity responds to the offerings and wishes of his devotees. Therefore one can make a vow

navas—and the deity grants children, cattle, etc., and healing in return for the gift.

kaul lāvṇeṃ—the deity when approached decides cases. This aspect is known even on the level of inscriptions, which even tell us that the deity's signature may be forged at times (cp. Derrett 1968: 484f., Sontheimer 1964: *passim*). A nineteenth-century Maratha document informs us that in villages where there is a *jāgṛt daivat*, disputes have been settled with the help of the deity 'since the beginning'. (Pune Archives, Deccan Commissioner 1825, Rumal Nr. 151; I owe the reference to N.K. Wagle).

kheḷ—participation in the divine play of the deity. People get possessed by ancestral spirits or deities during a dance. Cp. kheḷ-Khaṇḍobā.

jatrā—participation in the god's divine play, e.g. in his hunting excursion or his marriage. In the Khaṇḍobā cult, for example, devotees act like horses and dogs of the god.

svayaṃbhū liṅg or *piṇḍ*—Unlike an image or a *liṅgam* and *yoni* installed in a ceremony (*prāṇapratiṣṭhā*), the god shows himself (*svarūpa*) for the first time spontaneously, to his devotee or to a cow, in the form of a stone, in an anthill, etc.

But the deity can be also a 'walking and speaking god' like Cakradhara (*Līḷācaritra*, Uttarārdha 564). The deity may be like Rudra, the folk god (Sontheimer 1986a; 1985b), as reflected in the *Śatarudrīya* hymn. He is omnipresent and transcendent, but at the same time very much earthbound and very close to and similar to the folk; he has personal characteristics which distinguish him from other Vedic gods. Though incorporated into the Vedic ritual as Agni, Rudra was basically antagonistic to the Brahmanical outlook and ritual. Rudra was emulated by his followers. For example, the Ekavrātya or *sthāpati* of the Vrātyas became Rudra, Īśāna, Mahādeva, etc., in his cosmogonic ritual, just as even today the very similar *kāraṇikadevarus*, the chief Vaggayyas and devotees of Mailāra/ Khaṇḍobā, are possessed by the god and make their prophesies at the annual *jatrā* at Devaraguḍḍa and Mailār in Karnataka. Rudra appears as the leader of groups, just as Khaṇḍobā appears as the leader of particular groups on their terms, e.g. to the hunter he is a hunter, to the thief a lord of thieves, to the merchant he is the merchant *par excellence*. Similarly, Kṛṣṇa Gopāla lives among the *gopas* as a *gopa*, ascending Govardhana with them to worship his *alter ego*, which was originally probably a mountain spirit (Vaudeville 1980: 1ff.). In Caṅkam literature the *vēlaṉ* is described. He dances the *veriyāṭu*, is a reflection of Murukaṉ, and in fact becomes *Vēlaṉ* with a capital 'V' in his frenzied dance (Ramanujan 1981: 115).

Charismatic persons endowed with *tejas* and considered divine were and are frequently found. After their death the surviving power of such persons or of those who had a premature or accidental death are still worshipped. In fact, after a premature or unnatural death, as well as a warrior's or *satī's* death, a person can be deified. But it is a formality or a means of glorification rather than a necessary condition that the deified person should first be associated with a purāṇic heaven and deity (cp. Blackburn 1985: 259ff.). For example, a person may be famous as an animal doctor in his life, and after his death continue to be worshipped as a famous god without the need of ascending Kailās and returning as an *avatār* (Sontheimer 1976: 177).

In folk belief the king also tends to be identified as a god, with all the associations of fertility, heroship, and secular and divine powers. Especially the robber, or a hero rising from 'obscure' origins, is such a king. His followers are heroes, for whom 'the king is god' or 'the god is king'. Here the ethical considerations, the *dharmas* of the *kṣetra*, do not necessarily apply. The reaction in the Purāṇas or Māhātmyas would be to demonize these rulers for assuming the position of gods and for allowing themselves to be worshipped: e.g. the demons Maṇi and Malla called themselves *īśvara* and had to be killed by Khaṇḍobā (*Mallāri-Māhātmya* by Cintāmaṇi, 1.97), only to live on as devotees of Khaṇḍobā. In the *dharmaśāstra* the king tends to be subordinated to the śāstric order of the world. He may be allowed to be considered a god in some contexts, but essentially he is given only the *position* of a god: here *kṣatra* may tend to be subordinated to *brahman*.

(5) BHAKTI

The emphasis of the fifth component is on devotion to a personal, single god (*iṣṭadevatā*) who on his part yearns (Marāṭhī: *bhūkelā* = is hungry) for a true *bhakta* and supports him throughout his life. Pure love is emphasized, even if the god tends to be transcendent, as in the more philosophical or 'intellectual' bhakti of the *Bhagavadgītā*. Bhakti, though heavily influenced by the sexual love-relationship, as illustrated by the tribal Kṛṣṇa Gopāla and the *gopīs* or the love between Murukaṉ and Vaḷḷi in the early *akam* poetry, transcends both 'tribal' and 'folk' religion. Bhakti poetry borrows from folk religion its metres and genres and the belief in the immediate presence of the deity, but rejects its 'primitive' (*ugra*) features. The spontaneous, emotional bhakti movements of the Āḷvārs, Nāyaṉārs, Vīraśaivas and Maharashtrian saints also reject and transcend caste barriers and the scriptural *karmakāṇḍa*, at least initially. It is sincerity of devotion expressed through song-poetry, dance (as in *kīrtans* and *bhajans*), and the community of saints which matter, not the ritual as such. The saint or guru who has realized God may become the mediator between the *bhakta* and God, though in the monistic Śaivite bhakti the human guru tends to be obliterated. His only role is to make manifest the true nature of guruhood. This expresses itself in the divine *śabda* which participates in the transcendent nature of the *satguru* (Vaudeville 1974: 116f., 137).

THE KHAṆḌOBĀ CULT AS A MIRROR OF HINDUISM

In order to illustrate our arguments we may again refer briefly to the cult of Khaṇḍobā. This is one of the most complex and widespread cults of Maharashtra and has equivalents in Karnataka and Andhra Pradesh. Basically Khaṇḍobā is a *folk deity*. He closely resembles the Vedic deity Rudra as reflected in texts of the Vedic period: the *Atharvaveda*, the *Brāhmaṇas* and the *Śrautasūtras*. There we find Rudra portrayed as an ambivalent *folk deity* who had to be integrated into the brahmanical *śrauta* ritual. It seems clear, however, that he belonged primarily to the Vrātyas and to the groups mentioned in the *Śatarudrīya* rather than to the Brahmanical sacrificial priests. In these early texts we also get a picture of a god who has not yet been dynamically interpreted by later epic and purāṇic authors nor by Śaivite 'sectarians' with their own peculiar ritual and philosophy. The references to Rudra and his followers provide us with as it were a detailed checklist for describing the continuity of Rudra in the

Khaṇḍobā cult (Sontheimer 1986a: *passim*). Rather than postulating a unilinear development from the Vedic Rudra to a purāṇic Śiva and eventually a parochialized Khaṇḍobā we are led to see a persistent continuity of *folk religion*. The least we may find is a structural identity between Rudra and Khaṇḍobā. For instance, the wandering Vrātya, Māgadha or Sūta (bard) who is joined by the *puṃscalī* ('harlot') has his counterparts in the Vāghyās (Ma.) or Vaggayyas (Ka.), the special devotees of Khaṇḍobā. The Vāghyās are joined by the Muraḷīs, the female devotees (*devadāsīs*) of Khaṇḍobā, on their alms rounds (*vāri*). The Vāghyās are the poets and bards of Khaṇḍobā, who is considered to be a king. They sing his deeds during vigils (*jāgraṇ*) while the Muraḷīs sing and accompany them with their dance. Like the Vrātyas, the Vāghyās are the 'dogs' of the God. Whereas the *Mallāri-Māhātmya* (in Sanskrit and with Marāṭhī versions) is much more 'universalized', the contents of their songs refer to historical events and specific locations and rituals. Unlike the written Sanskrit text, the contents and form of their songs are subjected to simplification and effacement on account of the general modernization which nowadays is occurring in Maharashtra on an unprecedented scale (Sontheimer 1986b: *passim*).

Tribal groups equivalent to those mentioned in the *Śatarudrīya* are also represented. Not only were outlandish groups like thieves and robbers devotees of Khaṇḍobā but traditional tribal groups also form an important element in the cult (Koḷīs, Gavḷīs, and Dhangars in Maharashtra; Gollas, Kurumas, and Ceñcūs in Andhra Pradesh; Kurubas in Karnataka). In accordance with this we also have, especially among the Dhangars, the 'shaman' or *devruṣi* who gets possessed by Khaṇḍobā. The ritual hunt of the god on Somvatī Amāvāsyā, accompanied by hosts of Dhangars equipped with ceremonial spears, also reflects the tribal component.

Khaṇḍobā, the family god (*kulasvāmī*) of many different groups, is also the object of fervent devotion of individual devotees exceeding the normal loyalty shown by family members towards their *kulasvāmī*. Devotion expresses itself in the irresistible desire to be near and one with the god, even by imitating his dress and outfit (as Vrātyas did and the Vāghyās still do). This kind of bhakti could result in the self-sacrifice of the devotee. Self-mortification could elicit a boon from the deity. But 'standard' bhakti would reject these rituals and attitudes as *ugra*, or reinterpret them. Tukārām e.g. interprets Khaṇḍobā and the ritual objects of the cult as metaphors for his 'inner' religion.

Like Rudra, Khaṇḍobā is the god of heroes (*vīras*) who are on that level not yet ethicized as rescuers of women, cows and Brahmans. Since the sixteenth century the *Mallāri-Māhātmya* gained importance as the Brahmanical-textual component. It would, however, be misleading to present the cult exclusively on the basis of this Brahmanical text: it is so far little known to those devotees who represent other components. If it is known, it tends to be subordinated to the folk religious point of view. On the whole the 'ethicisation' of the cult by Liṅgāyats, Jains and Brahmans (though Khaṇḍobā is the *kulasvāmī* of many Deśastha Brahmans) remains incomplete and partial. Nevertheless the *Māhātmya* (said to be a part of the *Brahmāṇḍapurāṇa*) set the trend of purifying the cult and making it purāṇic: the demon is killed by Śiva, who becomes (quite unusual for Śiva) a full *avatār* and not a partial manifestation called Khaṇḍobā or Mārtaṇḍa Bhairava. Śiva thus restores the *yajña* of the Brahmans and the dharmic order. He remains on earth as Khaṇḍobā for the sake of his *bhaktas*. While doing all this he assumes many of the attributes, weapons and *vāhanas* (horse, elephants, chariots) of his opponent, the demon king Malla or the two royal demon brothers Maṇi and Malla. Malla actually resembles the demonic Rudra much more than the epic or purāṇic Śiva. The folk deity, so to say, splits into two halves, the classical Śiva and the demon. Or we can say, the *Māhātmya* implies that the god should transcend his own asuric form. But in Jejurī people still ardently worship the *mūrti* of the demon king who on his death became Khaṇḍobā's *bhakta*, before they proceed to worship Khaṇḍobā in the main temple.

The component of renunciation and asceticism is inherent in certain features already mentioned. The wandering habits of the Vāghyās (and also the Vaggayyas), the merit of doing *tapas* by going to the '*old*' temple far away on the distant mountain plateau rather than to the '*new*' temple (the 'hill fort') just above the city, Khaṇḍobā's wife turning into Yogeśvarī, the *yogī* Śiva turning into a warrior, the influence of the Nāth sect—all this points to the fact that the component of *saṃnyās* and *tapas* is also present. Even the Muslims are reflected in a typical Hindu manner: Khaṇḍobā, the god on earth masquerading as a pragmatic king, welcomes them as *bhaktas* or loyal followers. On the other hand, according to a legend, the aggressive Aurangzeb and his army were driven away by 900,000 hornets sent by the god (Sontheimer 1986a).

Thus we would suggest that a study of the Khaṇḍobā cult would yield a reflection of Hinduism as a whole if we keep in mind the different components and their dynamic interrelationship. We cannot generalize on the basis of one component; this would be to assume *pars pro toto*.

SUMMARY

This view of Hinduism emerged from an occupation with Indian texts of various periods and provenance, from field research, and only secondarily from modern theories and conceptualizations. In the course of this procedure five components have time and again suggested themselves: (1) The work and the teaching of the Brahmans; (2) Asceticism and renunciation; (3) Tribal religion; (4) Folk religion; (5) Bhakti.

Though the emphasis here is on religion, these components may be seen to entail other aspects of culture, e.g. social, physical, linguistic, philosophical and ideological aspects. Each of these components—before it is compounded with others—has to be viewed in its own right in order to avoid monolithic conceptualizations or the indigenous self-images of a *single* group (e.g. the Brahmans). Once we have admitted the 'simultaneous order' (A.K. Ramanujan *re* texts) of the components we can proceed to investigate a particular institution of Hinduism or Hinduism as a whole in terms of dynamic interrelations among the components. We can test, apply, and, if necessary, modify modern theories on interrelations (e.g. Srinivas, Dumont, Marriott, Staal, Hacker, Ramanujan, Burghart—to mention only a few) as well as indigenous concepts.

It may be that one or the other component received more or less emphasis and elaboration at a particular historical period, but all of them are present from Vedic times, even if they survive only as (possibly distorted) reflections in available written texts.

In this approach it seems unnecessary to split Hinduism into distinct though related religions. This splitting may serve the purposes of the comparative religionist, but ignores the fact that a particular religion or more appropriately a 'sect' (in itself a problematic term in the Indian context) was never immutable, but would develop and revert to structures which it initially rejected (Ramanujan 1973: 34-6). The process of mutual interaction between the components is best described as 'reflexivity', which takes many forms (Ramanujan), e.g. 'Inklusivismus' (Hacker), or complete inversion, as in Tantrism. If phenomena of these components have reflected on each other for many centuries and oscillated between 'divergence and convolution' (Derrett 1968: 437), we can expect a civilization which formed a close network of religious interaction and interdependence. This religious network cannot be refused the label Hinduism, even if it does not fit the definitions of religion deriving from the West. We would also not seem to be justified in foregoing the term, just because modern self-interpretations, called 'Syndicated Hinduism' by Thapar, eclectically utilize, emphasize, and choose components or elements of components and neglect or even reject others, sometimes in order to create a dogmatic or fundamentalist Hinduism. One would think that this 'Syndicated Hinduism' contradicts the essential character of Hinduism.

REFERENCES

Blackburn, S.H., 1985, 'Death and Deification. Folk Cults in Hinduism'. *History of Religions* 24/3, 225-74.

Burghart, R., 1978, 'Hierarchical Models of the Hindu Social System'. *Man* (N.S.) 13, 519-36.

——— 1983a, 'Renunciation in the Religious Traditions of South Asia'. *Man* (N.S.) 18, 635-53.

——— 1983b, 'For a Sociology of India: an Intracultural Approach to the Study of "Hindu Society"'. *Contributions to Indian Sociology* (N.S.) 17/2, 275-94.

Burghart, R. and A. Cantlie (eds.), 1985, *Indian Religion*. London.

Creel, A.B., 1977, *Dharma in Hindu Ethics*. Calcutta.

Deliege, R., 1985, *The Bhils of Western India*. New Delhi.

Derrett, J.D.M., 1968, *Religion, Law and the State in India*. London.

——— 1976, 'Rājadharma'. *Journal of Asian Studies* 25/4, 597-609.

Derrett, J.D.M., G.-D. Sontheimer, Graham Smith, 1979, *Beiträge zu indischem Rechtsdenken*. Wiesbaden.

Elwin, Verrier, 1955, *The Religion of an Indian Tribe*. OUP.

Eschmann, A., H. Kulke, G.C. Tripathi (eds.), 1978, *The Cult of Jagannath and the Regional Tradition of Orissa*. Delhi.

Eschmann, A., 1978, 'Hinduization of Tribal Deities in Orissa: The Śakta and Śaiva Typology'. In: Eschmann/Kulke/Tripathi (eds.), 79-97.

Hacker, Paul, 1983, 'Inklusivismus'. In: Oberhammer (ed.), 11-28.

Hardy, F., 1983, *Viraha-Bhakti. The Early History of Kṛṣṇa Devotion in South India*. Delhi: OUP.

Höfer, Andras and B.P. Shrestha, 1973, 'Ghost Exorcism among the Brahmans of Central Nepal'. *Central Asiatic Journal* 17/1, 51-77.

Kelkar, A.R., 1977, 'Bhakti in Modern Marathi Poetry: An Essay (by Sadashiv S. Bhave)'. A Response to Sadashiv S. Bhave's Essay. *South Asian Digest of Regional Writing* 7, 18ff., 24.

Kulke, H., 1979, *Jagannātha-Kult und Gajapati-Königtum. Ein Beitrag zur Geschichte religiöser Legitimation hinduistischer Herrscher*. Wiesbaden.

Kulke, H. and D. Rothermund (eds.), 1985, *Regionale Tradition in Südasien*. Wiesbaden.

Marglin, F. Apffel, 1985, *Wives of the God-king*. OUP

Marriott, McKim, 1965, 'Little Communities in an Indigenous Civilization'. In *Village India*, ed. McKim Marriott, 171-222. Chicago.

——— 1976, 'Interpreting Indian Society: A Monistic Alternative to Dumont's

Dualism'. *Journal of Asian Studies*, XXVI/1, November, 189-95.

Molesworth, J.T., 1857, *A Dictionary, Marāṭhī and English*. Bombay.

Monier-Williams, Monier, 1899, *A Sanskrit-English Dictionary*. Oxford.

Oberhammer, G. (ed.), 1983, *Inklusivismus: Eine indische Denkform*. Wien.

Piatigorsky, A., 1985, 'Some Phenomenological Observations on the Study of Indian Religion'. In Burghart and Cantlie (eds.), 208-58.

Ramanujan, A.K., 1970, 'Towards an Anthology of City Images'. In *Urban India: Society, Space and Image*. Monograph Series, ed. Richard G. Fox. Durham, N.C.: Duke University.

——— 1973, *Speaking of Śiva*. Penguin Books.

——— 1981, *Hymns for the Drowning*. Princeton.

——— 1985a, 'Where Mirrors are Windows. Towards an Anthology of Reflections'. (unpubl. ms.). [Editor's note: The paper appeared in *History of Religion* 28. 3 (1989), 187-246. It has been reprinted in: V. Dharwadker (ed.), *The Collected Essays of A.K. Ramanujan*. Delhi: OUP, 1999, 6-33.]

——— 1985b, *Poems of Love and War*. New York.

Rüping, Klaus, 1977, 'Zur Askese in indischen Religionen'. *Zeitschrift für Missionswissenschaft und Religionswissenschaft* 2, 81-98.

Sontheimer, G.-D., 1964, 'Religious Endowments in India: The Juristic Personality of Hindu Deities'. *Zeitschrift für vergleichende Rechtswissenschaft*, 69/1, 45-100. [Editor's note: Also in the present volume].

——— 1976, *Birobā, Mhaskobā und Khaṇḍobā: Ursprung, Geschichte und Umwelt von pastoralen Gottheiten in Mahārāṣṭra*. Wiesbaden. [Editor's note: English version: *Pastoral Deities of Western India*, New York, 1989.]

——— 1981, 'Dasarā at Devaraguḍḍa. Ritual and Play in the Cult of Mailār/Khaṇḍobā'. *South Asian Digest of Regional Writing*, 10, 1-28. [Editor's note: Also in EK].

——— 1982, 'God, Dharma and Society in the Yādava Kingdom of Devagiri according to the *Līḷācaritra* of Cakradhar'. In *Indology and Law. Studies in Honour of Professor J. Duncan M. Derrett*, Günther-Dietz Sontheimer and Paramesvara Kota Aithal (eds.), 329-58. Wiesbaden. [Editor's note: Also in the present volume.]

——— 1985a, 'Cāturvarṇya, Bhakti und der Aufstieg von Volkskulten in Maharashtra: Religionsgeschichtliche Skizze einer Region'. In Kulke and Rothermund (eds.), 129-48.

——— 1985b, 'Folk Deities in the Vijayangara Empire: Narasiṃha and Mallanna/Mailār'. In *Vijayanagara—City and Empire. New Currents of Research*, (ed.) A. Dallapiccola in collaboration with S. Zingel-Avé Lallement, 144-58. Wiesbaden. [Editor's note: Also in present volume.]

——— 1985c, 'Bhakti in the Khaṇḍobā Cult'. Paper read at the Third Conference on Early Literature in New Indo-Aryan Languages. Leiden. [Editor's note: Also in EK.]

——— 1986, 'Rudra and Khaṇḍobā: Continuity in Folk Religion'. In *Religion and Society in Mahārashtra*, (eds.) Milton Israel and N.K. Wagle. Univ. of Toronto, Centre for South Asian Studies, 1-31. [Editor's note: Also in EK.]

——— 1994 [1987], 'The *Vana* and the *Kṣetra*: The Tribal Background of Some Famous Cults'. In *Religion and Society in Eastern India*, Eschmann Memorial Lectures, (eds.) G.C. Tripathi and H. Kulke, Delhi: Manohar 1994, 117-64. [Editor's note: Also in the present volume.]

——— 1990, 'Between Ghost and God: A Folk Deity of the Deccan'. In *Gods and Demon Devotees*, (ed.) Alf Hiltebeitel. Albany. [Editor's note: Also in EK.]

Srinivas, M.N., 1952, *Religion and Society among the Coorgs of South India*, Oxford.

Staal, J.F., 1963, 'Sanskrit and Sanskritization'. In *Journal of Asian Studies*, 12/3, 261-75.

Weber, Max, 1920, *Gesammelte Aufsätze zur Religionssoziologie*, vol. II. *Hinduismus und Buddhismus*. Tübingen.

Wezler, Albrecht, 1983, Bemerkungen zum Inklusivismus-Begriff Paul Hackers. In *Oberhammer*, 61-91.

Vaudeville, Ch., 1974, *Kabīr*, Oxford.

——— 1980, Govardhana Myth in Northern India. In *Indo-Iranian Journal* 22. 1-45.

Günther-D. Sontheimer, List of Publications

BOOKS

The Concept of Dāya: A Comparative Study (Academic Postgraduate Diploma Dissertation, unpublished), London, 1962.

The Joint Hindu Family: Its Evolution as a Legal Institution. Delhi: Munshiram Manoharlal, 1977 (South Asian Studies, VII).

Birobā, Mhaskobā und Khaṇḍobā: Ursprung, Geschichte und Umwelt von pastoralen Gottheiten in Maharashtra. Wiesbaden: Franz Steiner, 1976 (Schriftenreihe des Südasien-Instituts der Universität Heidelberg, vol. 21).

Pastoral Deities in Western India. Translated by Anne Feldhaus. New York: Oxford University Press, 1989.

King of Hunters, Warriors, and Shepherds. Essays on Khaṇḍobā by Günther-Dietz Sontheimer, ed. by Anne Feldhaus, Aditya Malik and Heidrun Brückner. Delhi: Indira Gandhi National Centre for the Arts/Manohar, 1997.

(with H. von Stietencron) *German Indology—Past and Present*. Bombay: Shakuntala Publishing House, 1969. Translated into Hindi (1970), Bengali (1970), Malayalam (1970), Tamil (1970), Marathi (1971).

(with J.D.M. Derrett and G. Smith) *Beiträge zu indischem Rechtsdenken*. Wiesbaden: Steiner 1979 (Studien zu nichteuropäischen Rechtstheorien, 1).

EDITED VOLUMES

(with L. Leshnik) *Pastoralists and Nomads in South Asia*. Wiesbaden: Otto Harrassowitz, 1975 (Schriftenreihe des Südasien-Instituts der Universität Heidelberg, vol.15).

(with S. Settar) *Memorial Stones, a Study of their Origin, Significance and Variety*. Dharwad and New Delhi: Institute of Indian Art History, Karnatak University, Dharwad and South Asia Institute, University of Heidelberg, Germany, 1982. (Indian Art History Series: No. 2 and South Asian Studies: No. XI/11).

(with P.K. Aithal) *Indology and Law. Studies in Honour of J. Duncan M. Derrett*. Wiesbaden: Steiner, 1982 (Beiträge zur Südasienforschung, 77).

(with H. Kulke) *Hinduism Reconsidered*. New Delhi: Manohar, 1989 (rpt. 1991, 1994); revised edn. 1997 (South Asian Studies, XXIV).

(in collaboration with Helma Werny) *Südasien-Anthologie. 44 Übersetzungen aus südasiatischen Literaturen*. Stuttgart: Steiner, 1993 (Beiträge zur Südasienforschung, 140).

(with D. Chitre, A. Feldhaus, R. Kimmig and H. Brückner) *Tender Ironies. A Tribute to Lothar Lutze*. Delhi: Manohar, 1994.

Folk Culture, Folk Religion and Oral Traditions as a Component in Maharashtrian Culture. Delhi: Manohar, 1995 (South Asian Studies, XXVIII).

The Concept of Hero(-ine) in Indian Culture. Papers of a Seminar Conducted by Günther-Dietz Sontheimer. Ed. by Heidrun Brückner, Hugh van Skyhawk and Claus Peter Zoller. Delhi, Manohar (in press).

(with M.L.K. Murty) *Durgā and the Buffalo* (under preparation by M.L.K. Murty).

ARTICLES

'Die große Reform'. In *Indo-Asia*, April 1959, vol. 1/2, 139-43.

'Das indische Lichterfest'. In *Indo-Asia*, Oct. 1959, vol. 1/3, 336-8.

'Brief aus Mysore'. In *Indo-Asia*, Jan. 1960, vol. 2/1, 10-12.

'Die Teilung Bombays'. In *Indo-Asia*, April 1960, vol. 2/2, 107-9.

'Die "Unberührbaren" Indiens'. In *Indo-Asia*, Oct. 1960, vol. 2/4, 323-9.

'Der indische Familienverband'. In *Indo-Asia*, April 1961, vol. 3/2, 150-4.

'Recent Developments in Hindu Law'. In *Some Aspects of International Law Today*. Published as a supplement to: *The International and Comparative Law Quarterly* 13, 1964, 32-45.

'Religious Endowments in India: The Juristic Personality of Hindu Deities'. In *Zeitschrift für Vergleichende Rechtswissenschaft* 67, 1965, 45-100.

'XVI. Deutscher Orientalistentag in Heidelberg'. In *Kairos* VII, 1965, 4, 319-21.

'Religion und Recht in Indien. Eine Würdigung des Buches von J. Duncan M. Derrett'. In *Zeitschrift für vergleichende Rechtswissenschaft* 71, 1970, 141-55 (Review article).

'Kontinuität und Wandel von Religion, Recht und Staat in Indien. Bemerkungen zu einigen Untersuchungen über die Probleme des 'säkularen' indischen Staates' In *Internationales Asienforum* II, 1971, 146-58 (Review article).

'Features of Localization in Contemporary Indian Fiction: Marāṭhī'. In: *South Asian Digest of Regional Writing* 1, 1972, 32-46.

'The Making of a Poem: Marāṭhī'. In *South Asian Digest of Regional Writing* 2 (1973), 1974, 125-53.

'Some Notes on Biroba, the Dhangar God of Maharashtra'. In: Prof. D.D. Kosambi Commemoration Committee (ed.), *Science and Human Progress. Essays in Honour of Late Prof. D.D. Kosambi, Scientist, Indologist and Humanist*, Bombay: Popular Prakashan, 1974, 167-74.

'Field Research in Maharashtra and Karnatak: The History of Some Pastoral Communities and Their Cults'. In: M.S. Mate and G.T. Kulkarni (eds.), *Studies in Indology and Medieval History* (*Prof. G.H. Khare Felicitation Volume*), Poona: Joshi and Lokhande Prakashan, 1974, 246-61.

'The Dhangars: A Nomadic Pastoral Community in a Developing Agricultural Environment'. In: L.S. Leshnik and G.-D. Sontheimer (eds.), *Pastoralists and Nomads in South Asia*, Wiesbaden: Otto Harrassowitz, 1975, 139-70. (Schriftenreihe des Südasien-Instituts der Universität Heidelberg, 15).

'Eine Tempellegende der Dhangars von Maharashtra'. In: H. Berger (ed.), *Mündliche Überlieferungen in Südasien. Fünf Beiträge*. Wiesbaden: Otto Harrassowitz, 1975, 82-110 (Schriftenreihe des Südasien-Instituts der Universität Heidelberg, 17).

'Some Memorial Monuments of Western India'. In: Cultural Department of the Embassy of the Federal Republic of Germany, New Delhi (ed.), *German Scholars on India. Contributions to Indian Studies*, Bombay: Nachiketa Publications Limited, 1976, 264-75, XI plates, between pp. 268 and 269.

'Religion in Modern Marathi Literature. Some Trends and Voices'. In *South Asian Digest of Regional Writing* 3 (1974), 1976, 53-78.

'Dharma- and Arthaśāstra Studies in Germany'. In: V. Raghavan (ed.), *International Sanskrit Conference*, 26-31 March 1972, vol. I, 2, Delhi, 1979, 664-72.

(With J. Duncan M. Derrett and Graham Smith) 'Gerichtsverfahren und Richter im traditionellen indischen Recht'. In: J.D.M. Derrett, G.-D. Sontheimer, G. Smith, *Beiträge zu indischem Rechtsdenken*. Wiesbaden: Franz Steiner Verlag, 1979, 59-85 (Studien zu nicht-europäischen Rechtstheorien, 1).

(With J. Duncan M. Derrett) 'Der Begriff des Eigentums im Hindurecht'. In: J.D.M. Derrett, G.-D. Sontheimer, G. Smith, *Beiträge zu indischem Rechtsdenken*. Wiesbaden: Franz Steiner Verlag, 1979, 87-106 (Studien zu nichteuropäischen Rechtstheorien, 1).

'Ein Dorf in der Dürrezone Maharashtras'. In *Indo-Asia*, 21 April 1979, 2, 158-66.

'Some Incidents in the History of the God Khaṇḍobā'. In: M. Gaborieau and A. Thorner (eds.), *Asie du Sud. Traditions et Changements*. VIth European Conference on Modern South Asian Studies, Sèvres, 9-13 July 1978. Paris: Centre National de la Recherche Scientifique, 1979, 111-17 (Colloques Internationaux du Centre National de la Recherche Scientifique, no. 582).

(With M.L.K. Murty) 'The Prehistoric Background to Pastoralism in the Southern Deccan in the Light of the Oral Traditions and the Cults of Some Pastoral Communities'. In *Anthropos* 75, 1980, 163-84.

'Die Ethik im Hinduismus'. In: C.H. Ratschow (ed.), *Ethik der Religionen. Ein Handbuch. Primitive, Hinduismus, Buddhismus, Islam.* Stuttgart, etc.: Kohlhammer, 1980, 349-436.

'King Vikram and Kamaḷū Śinde, the Shepherd. Bhakti Episodes from an Oral Epic of the Dhangars of Maharashtra'. In: G.-D. Sontheimer (ed.), *Bhakti in South Asian Regional Literatures*, Heidelberg, 1981, 97-128 (South Asian Digest of Regional Writing, vol. 6, 1977).

'Gopāḷāñcā Deva Śrī Viṭṭhala' (in Marāṭhī). In: G.M. Kulkarni and V.T. Shete, *Mahārāṣṭrācī Satvadhārā.* R.C. Dhere Felicitation Volume. Poona, 1981, 103-12.

'Ursprung und Entwicklung der Bhakti-Bewegung in Maharashtra'. In: *Indo-Asia* 1981, 3/4, 97-107.

'On the Memorials of the Dead in the Tribal Area of Central India'. In: S. Settar and G.-D. Sontheimer (eds.), *Memorial Stones, a Study of their Origin, Significance and Variety.* Institute of Indian Art History, Karnatak University, Dharwad and South Asia Institute, University of Heidelberg, Germany, 1982, 87-99 (Indian Art History Series, 2 and South Asian Studies, 11).

'The Hero- and Satī-Stones of Maharashtra'. In: S. Settar and G.-D. Sontheimer (eds.), *Memorial Stones, a Study of Their Origin, Significance and Variety.* Institute of Indian Art History, Karnatak University, Dharwad and South Asia Institute, University of Heidelberg, Germany, 1982, 261-81 (Indian Art History Series, 2 and South Asian Studies, 11).

'God, Dharma and Society in the Yādava Kingdom of Devagirī according to the *Līḷācaritra* of Cakradhar'. In: G.-D. Sontheimer and P.K. Aithal (eds.), *Indology and Law, Studies in Honour of J. Duncan M. Derrett.* Wiesbaden: Franz Steiner Verlag, 1982, 329-58 (Beiträge zur Südasienforschung 77).

'The Mallāri/Khaṇḍobā Myth as Reflected in Folk Art and Ritual'. In: J. Deppert (ed.), *India and the West. Proceedings of a Seminar Dedicated to the Memory of Hermann Goetz.* New Delhi: Manohar, 1983, 237-51 (10 figures between pages 240 and 241) (South Asian Studies, 15).

'The Mallāri/Khaṇḍobā Myth as Reflected in Folk Art and Ritual'. In *Anthropos* 79, 1984, 155-70 [substantially enlarged and revised version of the previous article].

'Das Tier im Hinduismus'. In *Tropisch-Asien.* Heidelberg: Zoologisches Institut der Universität, 1983, 35-45.

'Scriptural Religion and Folk Religion in India—The Case of Rudra, Śiva and Khaṇḍobā'. In: Sitakanta Mohapatra (ed.), *Folk Culture-Pt. 2: Folk Ways in Religion:*

Gods, Spirits and Men. Cuttack, Orissa: The Council of Cultural Growth and Cultural Relations, Institute of Oriental and Orissan Studies [ca. 1983]. Reprinted in: Sitakant Mahapatra [*sic*] (ed.), *The Realm of the Sacred. Verbal Symbolism and Ritual Structures*. Calcutta: OUP, 1992, 201-16.

'The Dasarā Festival at Devaraguḍḍa (Karnāṭaka): Ritual and Dramatic Performance in the Cult of Mailār'. In: K. Ballhatchet and D. Taylor (eds.), *Changing South Asia: Papers Presented to the Seventh European Conference on Modern South Asian Studies [London 7 to 11 July 1981], Vol. 3. City and Culture*. Hong Kong: Asian Research Service, 1984, 111-22.

'Dasarā at Devaraguḍḍa. Ritual and Play in the Cult of Mailār/Khaṇḍobā'. In *South Asian Digest of Regional Writing* 10 (1981), 1984, 1-28. [Largely identical with the previous title.]

'Folk Deities in the Vijayanagara Empire: Narasiṃha and Mallaṇṇa/Mailār'. In A.L. Dallapiccola in collaboration with S. Zingel-Avé Lallemant (eds.), *Vijayanagara—City and Empire. New Currents of Research*, vol. 1 Texts, vol. 2, References and Documentation. Stuttgart: Steiner-Verlag-Wiesbaden-GmbH 1985, vol. 1, 144-58; vol. 2, 139 (list of photographs), 157-9 (plates). (Beiträge zur Südasienforschung, 100).

'The Power of Valour and Sacrifice. Memorials of Heroes, Satis, and Ancestors in Maharashtra'. Prepared for: *Marg* (unpublished; manuscript has not been located so far).

'Cāturvarṇya, Bhakti und der Aufstieg von Volkskulten in Maharashtra: Religionsgeschichtliche Skizze einer Region'. In: H. Kulke and D. Rothermund (eds.), *Regionale Tradition in Südasien*. Stuttgart: Steiner-Verlag-Wiesbaden-GmbH, 1985, 129-48 (Beiträge zur Südasienforschung, 104).

'Keshav Meshram's *Hakikat āṇi Jaṭāyū:* An Example from the Dalit Literature of Maharashtra'. In *South Asian Digest of Regional Writing* 11 (1982), 1985, 105-16.

'Das Zeitalter der Indo-Arier und Draviden'. In *Börsenblatt* 68/26.8.1986, 2198-2204.

'Rudra and Khaṇḍobā: Continuity in Folk Religion'. In: M. Israel and N.K. Wagle (eds.), *Religion and Society in Maharashtra*. Toronto: University of Toronto, Centre for South Asian Studies, 1987, 1-31 (South Asian Studies Papers, no.1).

'The *Vana* and the *Kṣetra*: The Tribal Background of Some Famous Cults'. In: G.C. Tripathi and Hermann Kulke (eds.), *Eschmann Memorial Lectures*, vol. I (1978-86). Bhubaneswar [*sic*]: The Eschmann Memorial Fund, 1987, 117-64; rpt. in: G.C. Tripathi and Hermann Kulke (eds.), *Religion and Society in Eastern India. Eschmann Memorial Lectures*. Bhubaneswar [*sic*]: The Eschmann Memorial Fund, 1994, 117-64 (distributed by Manohar, New Delhi).

'The Religion of the Dhangar Nomads'. In: E. Zelliot and M. Berntsen (eds.), *The*

Experience of Hinduism. Essays on Religion in Maharashtra. New York: SUNY Press, 1988, 109-30.

'Hinduism: The Five Components and their Interaction'. In: G.-D. Sontheimer and H. Kulke (eds.), *Hinduism Reconsidered*. New Delhi: Manohar, 1989, 195-210 (rept. 1991, 1994); revised edn. 1997, 305-24 (South Asian Studies, 24).

'Der Khaṇḍobā-Kult von Maharashtra als Spiegel des Hinduismus'. In: E. Weber (ed.), *Indien in Deutschland*. Darmstädter Beiträge zum Diskurs über indische Politik, Kultur und Gesellschaft. Frankfurt am Main, etc.: Peter Lang, 1989, 97-121.

'Between Ghost and God: A Folk Deity of the Deccan'. In: A. Hiltebeitel (ed.), *Criminal Gods and Demon Devotees: Essays on the Guardians of Popular Hinduism*. Albany: SUNY Press, 1989, 299-337.

'The Myth of the God and his Two Wives: Two Pastoral Versions from Maharashtra'. In: R. Barz and M. Thiel-Horstmann (eds.), *Living Texts from India*. Wiesbaden, 1989, 7-40 (Khoj—A Series of Modern South Asian Studies, 2).

'"Natur" und "Kultur" in der Weltsicht des Hinduismus'. In: B. Mensen (ed.), *Die Schöpfung in den Religionen*. Nettetal: Steyler Verlag, 1990, 33-46 (Vortragsreihe/ Akademie Völker und Kulturen St. Augustin, 1989/90, vol. 13).

'God as King for All: The Sanskrit *Mallāri Māhātmya* and its Context'. In: Hans Bakker (ed.), *The History of Sacred Places in India as Reflected in Traditional Literature*. Leiden etc.: Brill, 1990, 103-30 (Panels of the VIIth World Sanskrit Conference [Kern Institute, Leiden: 23-9 August 1987]).

'The *Rāmāyaṇa* in Contemporary Folk Traditions of Maharashtra'. In: M. Thiel-Horstmann (ed.), *Rāmāyaṇa and Rāmāyaṇas*. Wiesbaden: Otto Harrassowitz, 1991, 115-37 (Khoj — A Series of Modern South Asian Studies, 3).

'Das Fest in Indien: Jagdausflug des königlichen Gottes Khaṇḍobā'. In: J. Assmann (ed.), *Das Fest und das Heilige*. Gütersloh: Gütersloher Verlagshaus Gerd Mohn, 1991, 54-68 (Studien zum Verstehen fremder Religionen, 1).

'Bhakti in the Khaṇḍobā Cult'. In: D. Eck and F. Mallison (eds.), *Devotion Divine. Bhakti Traditions from the Regions of India*. Studies in Honour of Charlotte Vaudeville (Groningen Oriental Studies, 8). Groningen and Paris, 1991, 231-53.

'King Khaṇḍobā's Hunt and His Encounter with Bāṇāī, the Shepherdess'. In: H. Brückner, L. Lutze and A. Malik (eds.), *Flags of Fame. Studies in South Asian Folk Culture*. Delhi: Manohar, 1993, 19-80 (South Asian Studies, 27).

'The Folk Festival (Jatrā) in the Religious Traditions of Maharashtra: The Case of Khaṇḍobā'. In: G.-D. Sontheimer (ed.), *Maharashtra: Culture and Society. Folk Culture, Folk Religion and Oral Traditions as a Component in Maharashtrian Culture*. Delhi: Manohar, 1995, 129-45 (South Asian Studies, 28).

'The Erosion of Folk Religion in Modern India: Some Points for Deliberation'. In: V. Dalmia and H. von Stietencron (eds.), *Representing Hinduism. The Construction of Religious Traditions and National Identity*. New Delhi, etc.: Sage, 1995, 389-98.

'All the God's Wives'. In: A. Feldhaus (ed.), *Images of Women in Maharashtrian Literature and Religion*. Albany: SUNY, 1996, 115-34.

REVIEWS

S V. Gupte, *Hindu Law of Succession*, Bombay, 1963. In *The International and Comparative Law Quarterly 13*, 2 (1964), 751-2.

S.V. Gupte, *Hindu Law of Marriage*, Bombay, 1961. In *Rabels Zeitschrift für ausländisches und internationales Privatrecht* 28, 4 (1964), 772-4.

R.L. Choudhari, *Hindu Woman's Right to Property* (*Past and Present*), Calcutta, 1961. In *Rabels Zeitschrift für ausländisches und internationales Privatrecht* 28, 4 (1964), 772-4.

J.D.M. Derrett, *History of Indian Law* (*Dharmaśāstra*). *Handbuch der Orientalistik*, 2. Abt.: *Indien*. Hrsg. von J. Gonda, vol.3: Geschichte. 1. Abschnitt. In *Orientalische Literaturzeitung* (*OLZ*) 5 (1978), 490-1.

J.D.M. Derrett, *Dharmaśāstra and Juridical Literature*. In *A History of Indian Literature*. Hrsg. von J. Gonda, vol. 5, part 1, Wiesbaden, 1973. In *Orientalische Literaturzeitung* (*OLZ*) 5 (1978), 490-2.

M. Thiel-Horstmann (ed.), *Bhakti in Current Research, 1979-1982*, Berlin, 1983. In *Anthropos* 80 (1985), 749-51.

Dalmia, Yashodhara, *The Painted World of Warlis. Art and Ritual of the Warlis Tribes of Maharashtra*. New Delhi: Lalit Kala Akademi, 1988. In *Anthropos* 85 (1990), 584-6.

Preston, Laurence W., *The Devs of Cincwad. A Lineage and the State in Maharashtra*. Cambridge, 1989. In *Anthropos* 85 (1990), 636-8.

LEXICON ARTICLES

'Kabura', 'Kalingai', 'Kalliena', 'Kalliga', 'Kathaioi', 'Kolchoi', 'Kophen', 'Märchen (indische)'. In *Der Kleine Pauly. Lexikon der Antike*, vol. 3. Stuttgart, 1968.

'Ethik im Hinduismus', 'Das Böse / Leid im Hinduismus', 'Die Sikhs', 'Ehe, Familie im Hinduismus', 'Der Mensch im Hinduismus'. In H. Waldenfels (ed.), *Lexikon der Religionen*. Freiburg: Herder, 1987.

TRANSLATIONS

Prem Chand, 'Die Prüfung'. (translated from Hindī). In: H. von Glasenapp, *Indische Geisteswelt*, vol. 2, 1959, 144-7.

Vyankatesh Madgulkar, 'The Pilgrimage' (translated from Marāṭhī). In *South Asian Digest of Regional Writing* 3 (1974), 1976, 105-11.

Durga Bhagawat, 'The Viṭhobā of Paṇḍharī'. In *South Asian Digest of Regional Writing* 3 (1974), 1976, 112-20.

Vyankatesh Madgulkar, *Das Dorf hieß Bangarvadi*' (novel translated from Marāṭhī), Freiburg, 1986.

UNPUBLISHED GERMAN TRANSLATIONS (MANUSCRIPTS)

Keshav Meshram, *Jaṭāyū* (German translation of a Marāṭhī novel).

Indische Volksmärchen [Oral folktales recorded in various parts of India] (annotated German translations).

ENGLISH TRANSLATIONS IN PROGRESS (AT THE TIME OF SONTHEIMER'S DEATH, 1992)

The *Līḷācaritra*. The biography of the 13th century saint Cakradhara (translation and analysis).

The Songs of the Bards and Courtesans of King Khaṇḍobā. Texts, translations (in collaboration with Dilip Chitre) and Introduction.

EDITORSHIPS

I. *Neuindische Studien*

(with H. Berger and L. Lutze), started 1970. Published by Harrassowitz Verlag, Wiesbaden. Twelve volumes, mostly linguistic studies of oral languages, under the co-editorship of G.-D. Sontheimer. Continued by H. Berger, L. Lutze and H. Brückner, vol. 13 (1998), vol. 14 (1998).

Vol. 1 (1970): N. Ucida, *Der Bengali Dialekt von Chittagong*. Grammatik, Texte, Wörterbuch.
Vol. 2 (1973): K.V. Zvelebil, *The Irula Language*.
Vol. 3 (1974): H. Berger, *Das Yasin-Burushaski* (*Werchikwar*). Grammatik, Texte, Wörterbuch.

Vol. 4 (1975): A. Weidert, *I Tkong Amwi*. Deskriptive Analyse eines War-Dialekts des Khasi.
Vol. 5 (1978): M. Thiel-Horstmann, *Sadani-Lieder*. Studien zu einer nordindischen Volksliedliteratur. Mit einem Anhang 'Musiktranskriptionen' von R. Schlenker-Sonnenschmidt.
Vol. 6 (1979): K.V. Zvelebil, *The Irula Language*. Part II.
Vol. 7 (1982): D.B. Kapp, *Ālu-Kurumbaru Nāyan*. Die Sprache der Ālu-Kurumbas.
Vol. 8 (1983): C.P. Zoller, *Die Sprache der Rang pas von Garhwal* (*Raṅ po bhāsa*). Grammatik, Texte, Wörterbuch.
Vol. 9 (1983): K.V. Zvelebil, *The Irula Language*. Part III.
Vol. 10 (1986): K. Meissner, *Māluśāhī and Rājulā*. A Song from Kumaun, as sung and told by Gopī Dās.
Vol. 11 (1990): N. Ucida, *A Saurashtra-English Dictionary*.
Vol. 12 (1995): H. Brückner, *Fürstliche Feste*. Texte und Rituale der Tuḷu-Volksreligion an der Westküste Südindiens.
Vol. 13 (1998): H. Berger, *Die Burushaski-Sprache von Hunza und Nager*. Teil I Grammatik, Teil II Texte mit Übersetzungen, Teil III Wörterbuch Burushaski-Deutsch, Deutsch-Burushaski.
Vol. 14 (1998): A. Degener, *Die Sprache von Nisheygram im afghanischen Hindukusch*.

II. *South Asian Digest of Regional Writing*

Vol. 1 (1972): *Features of Localization in Contemporary Indian Fiction* (ed. by L. Lutze).
Vol. 2 (1973), 1974: *The Making of a Poem: Towards a Theory of Creativity in Contemporary Indian Poetry* (ed. by A. Dasgupta and L. Lutze).
Vol. 3 (1974), 1976: *Religion in Modern Indian Literature* (ed. by A. Eschmann).
Vol. 4 (1975), 1978: *Word-Borrowing and Word-Making in Modern South Asian Languages* (ed. by A. Dhamotharan).
Vol. 5 (1976), 1979: *Biography and Autobiography in Modern South Asian Regional Languages* (ed. by M.H. Zaidi).
Vol. 6 (1977), 1981: *Bhakti in South Asian Regional Literatures* (ed. by G.-D. Sontheimer).
Vol. 7 (1978), 1983: *Problems of Translation from South Asian Languages* (ed. by A. Dasgupta).
Vol. 8 (1979), 1983: *Sources of Illness and Healing in South Asian Regional Literature* (ed. by B. Pfleiderer and G.-D. Sontheimer).
Vol. 9 (1980), 1988: *Essays on Folktales, Satire and Women* (ed. by G. Bandini) [Papers of three different Interregional Seminars].
Vol. 10 (1981), 1984: *Drama in Contemporary South Asia: Varieties and Settings* (ed. by L. Lutze).
Vol. 11 (1982), 1985: *'Minorities' on Themselves* (ed. by H. van Skyhawk).

Vol. 12 (1987), 1992: *Mythology in Modern Indian Literature* (ed. by H. Berger).

The series was discontinued after vol. 12. Papers of some of the subsequent 'Interregional seminars' were published in the South Asian Studies series.

FILMS

Gott Birobā gab uns die Schafe. (In German, 45 minutes, 1987; in collaboration with Marie-José van de Loo and Henning Stegmüller).

The Journey of the Hatkar Dhangars (45 minutes/colour/U-matic). A film by Henning Stegmüller and Marie-José van de Loo, based on the research of Günther-D. Sontheimer [English version of the above].

(With G. Unbescheid), *König Khaṇḍobā. Szenen aus dem Leben eines indischen Volksgottes* (36 minutes, no year).

(With G. Unbescheid), *King Khaṇḍobā. Scenes from the Life of an Indian Folk God* (36 minutes/colour/16 mm/U-matic) [English version of the above].

(With Henning Stegmüller), *Vārī—Eine indische Wallfahrt*. 90 minutes (German TV version 60 minutes). München: Adanos-Film, 1990.

(With Henning Stegmüller), *Vārī—An Indian Pilgrimage* (90 minutes/colour/16mm or U-matic) (English version of the above].

(With Henning Stegmüller), *König Khaṇḍobās Jagdausflug*. München: Adanos-Film 1992 (81 minutes, colour, 16mm).

(With Henning Stegmüller), *King Khaṇḍoba's Hunting Expedition* (81 minutes/colour/U-matic) [English version of the above].

UNPUBLISHED/UNEDITED FILMS

Thirty hours of three-minute super-8 films taken between the early 1960's and the late 1980's mainly in Maharashtra and on the Deccan. Digitalised copies of the material prepared by Henning Stegmüller are kept in the archives of the Tübingen Seminar of Indology and of the Würzburg Chair of Indology (H. Brückner).

UNPUBLISHED AND UNEDITED MATERIALS IN THE SONTHEIMER ESTATE

These comprise unpublished lectures, files with materials used for teaching and, most importantly, field-materials such as the following:

1200 hours (rough estimate) of audio-recordings of oral Marāṭhī literature, part of it transcribed in more than 200 notebooks. The material has been copied in Heidelberg and the copies transferred to Pune. The transcriptions have been continued in Pune by Sontheimer's former assistants, organised by Anne Feldhaus and with financial assistance of the South Asia Institute (1993-8) and (1998-2001) by a grant to Arizona State University from the National Endowment for the Humanities (USA).

About 40,000 slides (kept at the South Asia Institute, University of Heidelberg as yet uncopied), uncatalogued, mostly unlabeled, taken mainly in Maharashtra and on the Deccan, of folk religious places of worship, festivals, hero-stones, landscapes, etc., since the 1960's and up to the early 1990's. Some of the hero-stone slides have been indexed by Dr. Ajay Dandekar.

A collection of folk bronzes, with Sontheimer's family at Stuttgart, Germany, documented (photographs) by Dr. Cornelia Mallebrein.

Sontheimer's library (also containing rare Marāṭhī books) is kept at the South Asia Institute library, Heidelberg.

PUBLISHED PH.D. THESES SUPERVISED BY G.-D. SONTHEIMER

Unbescheid, Günter, 1980. *Kānphaṭā: Untersuchungen zu Kult, Mythologie und Geschichte śivaitischer Tantriker in Nepal.*

König, Ditte, 1984. *Das Tor zur Unterwelt: Mythologie und Kult des Termitenhügels in der schriftlichen und mündlichen Tradition Indiens.*

Meyer, Eveline, 1986. *Ankāḷaparamēcuvari. A Goddess of Tamilnadu, Her Myths and Cult.*

Steinmann, Ralph Mark, 1986. *Guru-Śiṣya-Sambandha: Das Meister-Schüler-Verhältnis im traditionellen und modernen Hinduismus.*

Skyhawk, Hugh van, 1990. *Bhakti und Bhakta: Religionsgeschichtliche Untersuchungen zum Heilsbegriff und zur religiösen Umwelt des Śrī Sant Ekanāth.*

Müller, Klaus-Werner, 1992. *Das brahmanische Totenritual nach der Antyeṣṭipaddhati des Nārāyaṇabhaṭṭa.*

Ungemach, Anton, 1992. *Śaṃkara-mandāra-saurabha: Eine Legende über das Leben des Philosophen Śaṃkara* [von Nīlakaṇṭha]. Text, Übersetzung, Einleitung.

Malik, Aditya, 1993. *Das Puṣkara-Māhātmya. Ein religionswissenschaftlicher Beitrag zum Wallfahrtsbegriff in Indien.* Erörterung, Text, Übersetzung.

Jansen, Roland, 1995. *Die Bhavānī von Tuljāpūr. Religionsgeschichtliche Studie des Kultes einer Göttin der indischen Volksreligion.*

Stark-Wild, Sonja (under preparation). *Die Göttin Reṇukā in Mythos und Kultus. Eine Analyse ihrer sakralen Präsenz unter besonderer Berücksichtigung ihrer Verbreitung in Maharashtra* (thesis Heidelberg, 1997). Ph.D. completed under the supervision of Anne Feldhaus, 1997.

Index